# Wiley AP*
# U.S. History

by Greg Velm

**WILEY**

John Wiley & Sons, Inc.

**Wiley AP* U.S. History**

Published by
**John Wiley & Sons, Inc.**
111 River St.
Hoboken, NJ 07030-5774
www.wiley.com

For general information on our other products and services, please contact our Business Development Department in the U.S. at 317-572-3205.

Library of Congress Control Number: 2012952201

ISBN 978-1-118-49026-6 (pbk); ISBN 978-1-118-49027-3 (ebk); ISBN 978-1-118-49025-9 (ebk); ISBN 978-1-118-49029-7 (ebk)

Manufactured in the United States of America

10 9 8 7 6 5 4 3 2 1

**Publisher's Acknowledgments**

**Project Editor:** Tracy L. Barr

**Executive Editor:** Lindsay Sandman Lefevere

**Copy Editor:** Megan Knoll

**Technical Reviewer:** Albert Lowey-Ball

**Project Coordinator:** Katie Crocker

**Cover Photo:** © aleksandar velasevic / iStockphoto.com

**About the Author**

**Greg Velm** is the author of the best-selling book *True Gold: History and Adventure* in Northern California. He's been in *The New York Times, Time, Youth,* and *Via Magazine.* Greg has lectured at Berkeley, the University of San Francisco, and the University of California, Davis, on social history. He lives with his family near the American River in California. When he's not living in the past, Greg rides mountain bikes through the Sierra foothills and tries to outsurvive other old dudes in the shortest triathlons he can find.

**Author's Acknowledgments**

Nobody ever writes a book by himself; I get by with a little help from my friends and fellow thinkers Bob Strickler, Mike Tucker, Patricia Rose, Albert Lowey-Ball, Bob Greeley, P. K. Agarwal, Rayne Dawson, Wayne Fiske, Terry Taylor, Mary Ann McDonnell, John Azzaro, Irick Collins, Bodhi Garrett, Jean Caspers, Stuart Bair, Craig Lovell, Dan Egerter, Rick Kraus, and Terry and Mo Burton. Thanks to the dedicated teachers who create beautiful history sites and to the thousands of anonymous contributors to the ever-expanding and improving world of Wikipedia. Thanks to Matt Wagner of Fresh Books and to my talented editors at Wiley: Tracy Barr and Lindsay Lefevere.

WILEY

# Contents

## Part IV: Practice Tests and Answer Sheets ..................... 311

# About the
# AP U.S.
# History Exam

# 1

# An Introduction to the Exam and General Study Strategies

## KEY CONCEPTS

- Important themes and topics in U.S. history
- AP grading policies
- How to discover the AP credit policies at your college of choice
- Test day preparation

Of course, you want to pass the AP U.S. History exam. To do that, you need to know how the test is structured and what kind of information you're expected to know. After you understand how the test makers think, you can begin to prepare for success on test day. To set yourself up for success, you also have to get a clear understanding of what a good grade on the AP U.S. History exam looks like.

# WHAT'S ON THE TEST

The AP U.S. History exam is a comprehensive ordeal composed of 80 multiple-choice questions and 3 essay questions. You have to face one big *Document-Based Question* (DBQ), where the College Board (CB) shows you a bunch of original documents and you formulate a thesis and support it, using these sources plus the knowledge you (hopefully) possess about the events behind the sources. The other two essay questions come in two groups of two questions each; you get to choose one question from each group to answer. Fifty percent of the exam score comes from the multiple-choice portion of the test; the other 50 percent comes from the essays.

If I knew *exactly* what questions would be on your AP U.S. History test, I would have to be one of the six teachers on the AP U.S. History Development Committee — and even those teachers don't know until the last minute. But it is possible to look at past tests to see what subjects tend to come up again and again. It is possible to judge the trends by seeing the direction the big test is moving. You can also look at the announced subject material and time-period proportions to help choose which baskets to put most of your studying eggs in. In the following sections, you get a look at AP U.S. History teaching priorities as outlined by the very folks who make up the test. In Chapter 3, you learn how to study the way the Test Masters recommend. You even discover how to find previous tests to help you prepare for this year's AP challenge.

 **TIP**

Don't mess with AP test security. Forbidden actions include discussing multiple-choice questions from the exam with anybody — even your AP teacher. You can talk about essay questions a day after the test (to make sure that test takers in all the time zones around the world are done writing). The CB doesn't let you talk about multiple-choice questions, ever, because it may use the questions again.

## Advanced placement in the year 0

Standardized testing for advancement in China started with the Han Dynasty, around the year 0. And, like an ancient College Board, Chinese placement exams kept cranking out the grades for almost 2,000 years. Over the years, the tests included military strategy, civil law, revenue and taxation, agriculture and geography, and plenty of confusing Confucian religious classics. If you think the AP U.S. History test is hard, try taking it in Chinese characters!

Students studied for a year in tiny cells that contained boards that they moved around to make either a bed or a desk. The actual tests took two days, but the 5 percent who passed got great government jobs. Later, the Chinese standardized tests inspired Western nations, including the United States, to have civil service exams. One day in the 1900s, an education guy said, "Hey, we could invent the College Board and head whip students with Advance Placement tests!" Just be glad you don't have to fold up your desk to make a bed.

# Key facts

You can get a good grade — even a 5 (the top AP score) — without having to correctly answer all the multiple-choice questions presented to you. In fact, if you get only half the multiple-choice points and score big on the essays, you can walk away with the top grade. That said, you really need to stock up on knowledge about social trends and movements, which is particularly useful for tying together essay responses. The good news is that this information also helps you answer multiple-choice questions.

The AP U.S. History exam is center-loaded, with a bias toward post-colonial history between 1800 and 1950. That doesn't mean you should neglect the way-back and only-just-recently events; you have plenty of points to gain from these time periods as well. But as you review, put a special polish on the time periods with the most credit attached.

> **TIP**
>
> Historians have a natural aversion to recent events; when happenings are still news, many don't consider them history yet. Sorting out the importance of recent events is difficult. For instance, Lady Gaga gets a lot of media coverage, but does that mean she belongs in the history books? Also, the AP test occurs in early May, and school often runs into June. The College Board is kind enough to not test you on material you haven't covered yet. So don't spend much time on last year's hot topics; the AP test probably doesn't know they exist yet.

Why do the 300 years of early American history get less coverage than the 200 plus years after the birth of the United States as a nation? Well, this is U.S. History, and the U.S. didn't exist before 1776. More important, history is what humans choose to save to tell the later generations about themselves. Historians believe people can learn more about their present selves from studying, for example, the rise of democratic ideas in the 1800s than from analyzing cod-fishing stories from the 1600s. But you don't have to give up on that 20 percent of credit from before the Constitution; it's not just fishing stories.

# Important themes and topics

Balance has been a big issue in the history field since the end of the days of boring names-dates-and-places history. The test writers stress the social and cultural trends that underlie political events, but it's important to know how trends and events fit into time. Dates are the buckets that hold social trends and political events together. You don't have to remember specific years, but you should have an idea of the decade in which trends and events unfolded. For instance, it's good to know that the Republican Party started after the Compromise of 1850 but before the Civil War.

The 80 multiple-choice questions that make up 50 percent of your score on the AP exam are a natural place for questions about hard-and-fast political events to appear. While fitting the nuances of schools of painting into five-choice questions is hard, it's relatively easy to ask multiple-choice questions about elections and wars. Even so, 4 out of 10 multiple-choice questions will be about cultural trends rather than political events. (You can find more about multiple-choice questions in Chapter 3.)

The Document-Based Question (DBQ), worth 22.5 percent of your total score, is all about the social and economic trends illustrated by political events. You'll analyze actual letters, pictures, and reports from a historic period and use the information you remember from your own knowledge stores to explain the era of the documents given to you. (More about answering the Document-Based Question is in Chapter 4.)

Two regular essay questions are each worth 13.75 percent of your overall score on the AP exam. These questions each require about a five-paragraph essay. If your essays make a good argument by referencing social, political, and economic events, you're on your way to a high score. (You can discover more about creating teacher-friendly essays in Chapter 5.)

## Themes

*Themes* run through U.S. history. In the form of social or cultural history, these themes show up in 40 percent of the multiple-choice questions on the AP exam. Additionally, themes are the life-blood of the essays. You can improve your score on that section of the exam by referencing at least two themes in every essay answer. Here, in alphabetical order, is a list of what the AP U.S. History Development Committee considers to be important themes in American history:

- **American Diversity:** The roles of class, ethnicity, race, and gender in the history of America. Discuss different groups in the United States and the relationships between them; this theme is about how groups in the United States are different.

- **American Identity:** What it means to be an American, as seen in different parts of the United States and during different periods in history. Just what is the American national character, and how are Americans different from other people in the world? This is what teachers call *American exceptionalism.* You may think of American Identity as how various groups in the United States have certain similar characteristics.

- **Culture:** What was popular and earth-shaking in different periods of U.S. history. This category includes literature, art, philosophy, music, theater, television, and film. Culture — what people eat, watch, read, and sing, for example — reveals a country's real beliefs.

- **Demographic Changes:** The political, economic, and social effects of immigration and movements within the United States. It also covers the way marriage, birth, and death rates have changed. How many kids were in the average family? How long did people live? What was the overall population size and density? Counting people helps in understanding trends.

- **Economic Transformations:** The effects of business and personal financial incentives on the United States, including buying and selling, and the changes in business structure (from small store owners to big corporations). You can discuss the effects of labor unions and consumer movements. Basically, if you want to get a handle on why people do things, check out their bank accounts.

- **Environment:** How the expansion of the United States has affected the environment in different periods of history. What's the impact of more people, the expansion of cities and suburbs, pollution, and industrialization? Mother Nature has limits that affect human history.

- **Globalization:** The relation of the United States to the rest of the world, from the first colonies in the 1500s to the present. This topic includes global leadership and dominance, colonialism, mercantilism, imperialism, development of international markets, and cultural exchange. The United States isn't an island, however much isolationists want to make it one.

- **Politics and Citizenship:** What Americans believe about their revolutionary past, the importance of democracy, and the development of the U.S. nation. What do citizenship and civil rights mean? Just what is the United States, and who really is an American?

- **Reform:** The movement for social change. U.S. history has seen reform in areas like women's rights, civil rights, the existence of slavery, education, labor, public health, temperance, gay rights, war, and government.

- **Religion:** The variety of religious experiences and practices in the United States, covering the time period from the American Indians to the Internet. What's the influence of religion on economics, politics, and society? What you see as your purpose in life influences everything you do.

- **Slavery and Its Legacies in North America:** The meaning of slavery and other forms of forced labor (such as indentured servitude) in different periods of the nation's development. Subthemes include the money behind slavery and its racial dimensions, movements of resistance, and the long-term political, economic, and social consequences of slavery. After all, many of the leaders who founded the United States had the time to talk about freedom because slaves were doing their work for them.

- **War and Diplomacy:** How armed fights changed the United States, from the time before Columbus to the early-21st century war on terrorism. Perhaps the United States is a peace-loving nation, but the fact remains that the nation has been involved in a war about once every 20 years.

> **TIP**
>
> You need a rough idea of the way trends developed, at least in ten-year periods. Abolition, for instance, was minor in the 1820s but huge in the 1850s. Also, it helps to tie trend answers to the approximate year of key developments. For example, *The Liberator* was an important abolitionist newspaper founded by William Lloyd Garrison in 1831. The founding of this newspaper marks the beginning of the growth of abolition in the northern United States. (Because knowing the general timeframe of trends is so important, in this book, you'll find major events and the names of important people italicized and followed by dates in parentheses.)

## Topics

Although knowing historical themes can give you a more nuanced understanding, historical events and topics still pay the rent when it comes to your overall AP exam score. Here are the important event topics specified by the College Board in its U.S. History Course Description, arranged in roughly chronological order:

- **Pre-Columbian Societies:** The first people who lived in the Americas. American Indian polities in the Southwest, the Pacific Northwest, the Northeast, and the Mississippi Valley. The civilizations of Mesoamerica. All Indian cultures of North America before the explorers arrived.

- **Transatlantic Encounters and Colonial Beginnings (1492–1690):** Spain's empire in North America. The English settle New England and most of the Mid-Atlantic and South regions, and the French set up in Canada. Settlers arrive, sometimes with hope and sometimes in chains, in the Chesapeake region. Religious diversity leads to different American colonies. Early revolts against colonial authority: the Glorious Revolution, Bacon's Rebellion, and the Pueblo Revolt.

- **Colonial North America (1690–1754):** How the population expanded with more immigration. Trade made the port cities like Boston and New York grow, while farming expanded in the country. The impact of the Enlightenment and the First Great Awakening. How British and other colonial governments affected North America.

- **The American Revolutionary Era (1754–1789):** The French and Indian War leads to the Imperial Crisis and fighting back against British rule. Next come the U.S. Revolution, state constitutions and the Articles of Confederation, and the federal Constitution.

- **The Early Republic (1789–1815):** Washington, Hamilton, and the building of a national government. Political parties begin with the Federalists and Republicans. The meaning of Republican Motherhood and education for women. Effects of Jefferson's presidency. The Second Great Awakening. Settlers move into the Appalachian West. The growth of slavery and free black communities. American Indians fight back. The causes and outcomes of the War of 1812.

- **Transformation of the Economy and Society in Antebellum America:** The start of industrialization and changes in social and class structures. How steamboats, trains, and canals created a national market economy. Immigration and reactions against it from nativists. Planters, independent farmers, frontiersmen, and slaves in the South growing cotton.

- **Transformation of Politics in Antebellum America:** The development of the second party system. Federal authority and the people who fought against it: judicial federalism, tariff controversy, the Bank of the U.S., and states' rights debates. Jacksonian democracy increases popular government but has limitations.

- **Religion, Reform, and Renaissance in Antebellum America:** Evangelical Protestant revivals, ideals of home life, and social reforms. Transcendentalism and utopian communities. American growth in literature and art.

- **Territorial Expansion and Manifest Destiny:** Americans push American Indians across the Mississippi river to the West. The United States adds new territory. Western migration and cultural changes, and the beginning of U.S. imperialism and the Mexican War.

- **The Crisis of the Union:** Slaveholder-versus-antislavery arguments and conflicts, the Compromise of 1850 and popular sovereignty, and the Kansas-Nebraska Act. The emergence of the Republican Party, the election of 1860, Abraham Lincoln, and the South leaves the Union.

- **Civil War:** North and South societies are at war. Resources, mobilization, and internal disagreement. Military strategies and foreign diplomacy. The role of blacks in the war. Emancipation. The social, political, and economic effects of war in the North, South, and West.

- **Reconstruction:** The reconstruction plans of Lincoln and Andrew Johnson versus Radical Reconstruction. Southern state governments: goals, achievements, and shortcomings. The role of blacks in politics, education, and the economy. The outcome of Reconstruction. The end in the Compromise of 1877.

- **The Origins of the New South:** Retooling Southern agriculture: sharecropping and crop-lien systems replace slavery. The expansion of manufacturing plants and business. The politics of segregation: race separation, Jim Crow, and disenfranchisement.

- **Development of the West in the Late-19th Century:** Rivals for the West: miners, homesteaders, ranchers, and American Indians. Building the Western railroads. Government policy toward American Indians. Men and women, race, and ethnicity in the far West. What Western settlement did to the environment.

- **Industrial America in the Late-19th Century:** How corporations took over industry. The effects of technology on the worker and workplace. National politics and the growing influence of corporate power. Labor and unions. Migration and immigration; the changing demographics of the nation. Fans and foes of the new order, including Social Darwinism and the Social Gospel.

- **Urban Society in the Late-19th Century:** City growth and machine politics. Urbanization and the lure of the city. Intellectual and popular entertainment, and cultural movements.

- **Populism and Progressivism:** Farmer revolts and issues in the late 19th century. Roosevelt, Taft, and Wilson as Progressive presidents. The beginnings of municipal, state, and national Progressive reform. Women's roles in the family, politics, the workplace, education, and reform. Black America: city migration and civil-rights initiatives.

- **The Emergence of America as a World Power:** U.S. imperialism grows with political and economic expansion. The beginning of WWI in Europe and American neutrality, WWI at home and abroad, and the Treaty of Versailles. Society and economy in the postwar years. The first American troops in Europe.

- **The New Era (1920s):** The consumer economy and the business of America. Republican presidents Harding, Coolidge, and Hoover. Modernism: the culture of science, the arts, and entertainment. Responses to modernism: nativism, religious fundamentalism, and Prohibition. The ongoing struggle for equality for blacks and women.

- **The Great Depression and the New Deal:** What created the Great Depression? The Hoover administration tries to do something. American society during the Great Depression. FDR and the New Deal. The New Deal coalition and its critics. Labor and union recognition.

- **World War II:** The rapid growth of fascism and militarism in Italy, Japan, and Germany. America's policy of neutrality. The attack on Pearl Harbor and the U.S.'s declaration of war. Diplomacy, war aims, and wartime conferences. Fighting a multifront war. The United States as a global power in the Atomic Age.

- **The Home Front during the War:** The mobilization of the economy for World War II. Women, work, and family during the war. City migration and demographic changes. Reduced liberties and civil rights during wartime. War and regional development. The expansion of government power.

- **The United States and the Early Cold War:** The beginning of the Cold War. Truman's policy of containment. Strategies and policies of the Eisenhower and Kennedy administrations. The Cold War in Asia: China, Korea, Vietnam, and Japan. The Red Scare and McCarthyism. The impact of the Cold War on American society. Establishment of NATO and the Berlin Airlift, both of which tie the U.S. to Europe.

- **The 1950s:** The beginning of the modern civil rights movement. The affluent society and "the other America." Agreement and conformity in the suburbs and middle-class America. Nonconformists, cultural rebels, and critics. The impact of changes in technology, science, and medicine.

- **The Turbulent 1960s:** Moving from the New Frontier to the Great Society. Developing movements for civil rights. Cold War confrontations in Latin America, Asia, and Europe. The beginning of *détente*. Hippies, the antiwar movement, and the counterculture.

- **Politics and Economics at the End of the 20th Century:** America moves right. Nixon wins in 1968 with the Silent Majority. Nixon's challenges: China, Vietnam, and Watergate. Changes in the American economy: deindustrialization, the energy crisis, and the service economy. The New Right and the Reagan revolution. The end of the Cold War.

■ **Society and Culture at the End of the 20th Century:** America sees the social realities of being a rich nation. The changing face of America: surge of immigration after 1965, Sunbelt migration, and the graying and tanning of America. New developments in biotechnology, mass communication, and computers. A multicultural society faces the future.

■ **The United States in the Post-Cold War World:** The American economy faces globalization. Unilateralism versus multilateralism in foreign policy. Home-grown and foreign terrorism. Environmental issues that affect the whole world. Short term power versus long term idealism.

# POLITICAL, ECONOMIC, AND SOCIAL (PES) QUESTIONS

History isn't just facts; even more important is the meaning behind the facts. These meanings are called *trends* or *themes*. When you've got the themes, you have a framework on which to remember the facts. Plus, the AP is really big on themes. The main themes fall into these three categories: political events and decisions, economic realities and incentives, and social trends and conditions. Connect these themes (use the acronym *PES* to help you remember what the themes are), and you'll connect to success on exam day.

The multiple-choice section on the AP History exam will include questions that fall into these three categories:

■ 35 percent on political institutions and policy

■ 40 percent on social history, including cultural developments

■ 25 percent on economic and international relationships

Half the credit on the AP U.S. History test comes from 80 multiple-choice questions. Your score on this section depends on preparation and reasoning skill which will be held together by your understanding of political, economic, and social (PES) trends. The other half of the credit on the big test comes from just three essay questions. Anybody can memorize facts; leaders are the people who can use those facts successfully. Political, economic, and social trends let you show how the facts come together.

**TIP**

Throughout this book, the political, economic, and social topics are presented *in italics* with a date, like *Progressives* (1910). If the important topic is a law, the date is when it was passed, like the *Seventeenth Amendment* (1913). If the topic is an institution like *Hull House* (1889) or a person like *John D. Rockefeller* (1885), the date is a key year in what could be a long career. The AP test doesn't care much about exact dates, but you do need to be able to keep key events in chronological order.

## Politics trends

In this context, *political events* include presidents and other important leaders, laws, legal decisions of the Supreme Court, civil conflicts, international relations, and wars. As you're studying your way through U.S. history, be armed with a reasonable idea of how political events fit together and have a general sense of the order in which leaders and laws happened.

> **TIP**
>
> The past has always been influenced by the beliefs and actions of ordinary people, not just by leaders. In addition to knowing laws and presidents, you also need to know economic and social factors to have a real understanding of history.

## Economy trends

Economics includes prosperity, recessions, depressions (sometimes called *panics* in the past), taxes, tariffs on imported goods, inflation, corporate expansion, and profit incentives.

Thinking about economics helps explain human behavior. Economics led to the settlement of most of the United States. Many of the early settlers left Europe for America because they were starving, and settlers moved inland from the Atlantic coast because they needed land to farm so that they could make money and support their families. Britain's economic taxes pushed the colonists toward revolution, and in the decades before the Civil War, the South hung on to slaves because each slave was worth as much as $50,000 in modern money, and slaves picked cotton, which was the biggest profit maker in the United States. In the 1930s, the Great Depression made people so poor that they were ready to change the politics of the country.

## Trends in social history

*Social history* includes beliefs about religion, race, national origin, and the roles of men, women, and families. Social developments also include the influence of literature, science, art, and philosophy on events. Here are a few examples of the strong social currents in American life:

- The first permanent settlements in Massachusetts consisted of Pilgrims and Puritans, groups who made the dangerous voyage to the unknown New World for religious, not economic, reasons. In fact, the Pilgrims' original decision to leave Europe was social: They had religious freedom in Holland, but they couldn't stand the idea that their children were growing up Dutch. (See Chapter 7.)

- Perhaps the greatest example of the power of literature and social thought was the best-selling novel of the 1800s: *Uncle Tom's Cabin*. The depictions of the evils of slavery in this book helped send hundreds of thousands of men off to fight and die in the Civil War. (See Chapter 12.)

- Sensationalized newspaper stories and pictures helped launch the U.S. into war with Spain in 1898. (See Chapter 14.)

- The Democratic Party's increasing support of civil rights helped lead to both the loss of its traditional political hold on the South and the fact that the Democrats managed to elect only one two-term president in the last half of the 1900s. (See Chapter 19.)

> **TIP**
>
> Understanding social trends has been an increasingly important part of history, and the AP U.S. History exam allots 40 percent of the multiple-choice questions to social history and cultural developments, making social history a major focus of the exam.

# WHAT THE AP GRADES MEAN

If the College Board got a grade on how well it runs its Advanced Placement (AP) tests, it would probably get an A–. The big exams are well-organized and contain interesting original thought, and you certainly have to admire the College Board for grading 1 million U.S. history essays by hand in six weeks. But if you said A–, the College Board wouldn't know what you were talking about, because the AP deals in numbers rather than letters. The following sections explain what this scoring means, how it affects your college credit, and what impact certain scores have.

## Converting letters to numbers

The College Board talks in numbers. Most people know the famous range from flunky 200 to perfect 800 on the College Board's SAT tests. For the AP U.S. History exam, you can count the important numbers on one hand: You will receive a score from 1 to 5.

How do those numbers relate to the working alphabet world of most students: A, B, C, D, and F? By checking the grades past AP U.S. History exam takers actually get in college, the College Board sets AP exam grade boundaries so that exams earning an AP grade of 5 are roughly equivalent to the average AP exam score of students who go on to earn college As. They then make sure the exam receiving an AP grade of 4 equals the average scores of those college students receiving Bs, and the lowest score corresponding to an AP grade of 3 equates to the average score of college students receiving Cs. About half of the students who take AP U.S. History exam get a grade of 3 or better. So there you have it:

| AP Exam Score | College Grade Equivalent |
|---|---|
| 5 | A |
| 4 | B |
| 3 | C |
| 2 | D |
| 1 | F |

In most institutions, you can get college credit simply by doing as well on the AP exam as college students who get Cs in Intro U.S. History. And you won't have a C on your college record; just a nice, satisfying notation that college credit is in the bank. Besides possibly earning you an actual college credit, an AP U.S. History score of 5 also looks great on your college application.

## College credit policies

Colleges are big institutions with impressive buildings and really smart people. You may be surprised, therefore, to hear that these colleges have widely differing Advanced Placement credit policies. The College Board can help you get it straight.

Go to collegesearch.collegeboard.com/apcreditpolicy/index.jsp to search for your school(s) of choice. You can also google *College Board* and *AP credit policy*. When you're on an AP Credit Policy search page, search by the names of the colleges you may attend. If the Internet doesn't work for you, call the admissions office of the schools you're interested in and ask where you can find the school's AP policy in writing. You can get the phone numbers of your prospective colleges from your school advisor.

When you've got the information, make a copy. Beware the colleges that have no clear AP policy. If you're in the final strokes of choosing between two colleges, double-check to make sure each college's AP policy covers U.S. History.

# TEST PREPARATION

As test day gets closer, make the most of the time you have. Although you'd ideally be reading this on a calm day months before the test, chances are you're getting close to crunch time. Here's how to profitably spend the precious time you have.

Say you have only a month to go before the exam. Now more than ever, paying attention to your schedule and timing determines your success. Here are a few basic tips to get you started:

- Stick with the AP History review your teacher has planned for you. Ask your teachers for copies of previous AP test questions.

- Work your way through this book like you do your school review — a little each day.

- Plan a time to study that you can stick to. A lot of brainy people spend a little time studying at night before bed and a little time reviewing first thing in the morning. This study technique lets you sleep on the information and double-check it in the morning with a clear mind.

 **TIP**

At some time during this month, the age-old dilemma of "Study or a movie?" will arise. Before you jump in the car, remember that you're on a mission for college credit. You can save a whole college course by getting a good score on the AP — a college course that would otherwise have cost you and your dear parents a few hundred (or possibly thousands of) dollars. And just think about how much better it'll be to party later with advanced credit (and money) under your belt. Meanwhile, do something you like that goes well with studying. Perhaps you can take a refreshing run in the park and/or treat yourself with some double-good premium ice cream. Then get back to work.

The following sections show you how to prepare for the AP exam so completely that the actual exam will come as naturally as opening a candy bar in the dark.

## A study strategy

You can make preparing for the AP exam as fun and easy as possible by turbocharging your study time with the best techniques.

How much should you study? That depends; how smart are you? Despite what you've heard, *smart* doesn't mean good, brave, or even successful in the world. Henry Ford was weak on facts and no good at theory, but he built an industrial empire. You have some facts to remember to get through the big test, but they should be facts that you know how to use — not just rote memory pop-ups.

The following list presents some tips to help you set up your studying schedule and strategies you can use to maximize your strengths (and your grade):

- There are different kinds of smart. Some people (call them Copy Machines) can photo-copy facts in their head. Some folks don't remember facts as well, but they can write essays like Shakespeare could write sonnets. You have the kind of intelligence that you were born with, but you also can build up performance through exercise — just like muscles at the gym. On the AP exam, you'll need to be both a Copy Machine and a Shakespeare, so you need to study based on your strengths. If you're good on multiple-choice, your Copy Machine is running strong. If you're shaky on essays, you want to work on your inner Shakespeare.

- Study enough to know the themes and topics (outlined in the earlier section "Impor-tant themes and topics on the test"). An hour a day is reasonable for the AP U.S. History exam — more if you have a thick head for facts and less if you can already ace through the tests in Part IV of this book.

- Studying should never be just reading; it should be work with a marker in your hand. Take notes in this book. If you can't write in your school textbooks, mark key passages with sticky notes. *Remember:* Highlight only the most important parts; if you use the highlighter to turn the whole book yellow, you're just coloring, not studying.

- Make lists of key events and themes and write out their definitions and years (perhaps on notecards). Always quiz yourself. What was the first state to permanently allow women to vote? (Wyoming in 1869.) Who was the guy who took over after Lincoln? (An-drew Johnson in 1865.) What year did the Constitution take effect? (1789.) What was the big deal about the Second Great Awakening? (It renewed personal salvation and linked churches to social reform — 1800 to 1830s.)

- Use the best programs and apps to practice for the test.

Another way to prepare for the AP exam is to figure out what historical periods or facts tend to stump you. To do that, take one of the tests in Part IV of this book. Time yourself and stick to the schedule you'll have to follow on test day. How many multiple-choice questions did you get right? Were you a little foggy about a certain time period? How did the essays come out? Ask somebody you trust who's wise in the ways of history to score them, using the criteria in Chap-ters 4 and 5. Need more experience writing these short but loaded factual stories? Practice until writing them becomes easier.

Don't get too stressed if you didn't do well the first time through a practice test. That's why you call them practice. Use the knowledge you just gained to focus your study efforts on the areas you had the most difficulty with.

## Time limits

The AP U.S. History exam isn't like a surprise pop quiz; you have a good idea of what the big test looks like and how it's run. You'll devote a chilling three hours and five minutes of your life to searching frantically but calmly through the history hard drive of your mind. You'll be under the control of the test proctor, who will give you the usual warnings about food, time, copying, and reading answers off your history tattoos. And you'll have to shift gears at least once in order to complete the two sections of the test.

## Time limit for Section I

You'll have 55 minutes to answer the multiple-choice questions. You'll receive a Scantron form to fill in (with pencil, of course). With the form comes a booklet that contains the 80 multiple-choice questions — each of which has five possible answers, labeled from A to E. The questions are arranged from easy to hard, with chronological years and themes sprinkled in all levels of difficulty. The changes in difficulty come gradually; don't expect to find yourself lost in genius-land all of a sudden. And remember, what's hard for somebody else may be easy for you, especially if you've studied.

Even though the multiple-choice questions in Section I take less than a third of your test time, they're worth half your test score. Because wrong answers aren't penalized, you should take a shot at every question. Do the easy ones first and mark the hard ones to go back to after you have picked all the low hanging fruit.

On the Scantron form, fill in the oval completely and erase thoroughly when you want to change your answer.

## Time limit for Section II

In Section II, you get a question book containing one DBQ, or Document-Based Question (Section A), and four regular essay questions arranged in two groups of two questions each (Sections B and C). You answer one question from Section B and one from Section C.

Starting with the DBQ, you have a total of 1 hour and 55 minutes to write the three essays. You get 15 minutes during which you can only review the questions. During this time, you can't start an essay, but you can read and take notes in the question booklet.

The DBQ is challenging. You are given anywhere from 7 to 10 documents, which could be diaries, letters, speeches, charts, graphs, political cartoons — almost anything you can read. Use the first 15 minutes to read those documents and think about how you can bring them together with some relevant outside knowledge to write a stunning DBQ essay. You can discover everything you ever wanted to know about the DBQ in Chapter 4. (For information on the regular essay questions, go to Chapter 5.)

> **TIP**
>
> You may be tempted during your 15 minutes of calm before the writing storm to peak ahead at the questions that come after the DBQ. Don't. Just concentrate on the DBQ during the reading period. The other essay questions will take care of themselves when you get to them. Don't cloud your brain — you have plenty of documents and outside facts to marshal for the DBQ.

The suggested time for the DBQ essay is 45 minutes. The suggested time for the two regular essays is 35 minutes each.

> **TIP**
>
> Don't get caught out of time on the big exam. Nothing is worse than having important, grade-winning points to make in an essay and no time left to write them. Before the exam, practice writing five-paragraph essays in 30 minutes. Get used to timing yourself as you write. Better to write short and smart than long and pointless.

## Making up your own exam questions: Challenge Questions

Taking practice tests helps you get ready for the AP exam. Part IV of this book contains two tough exams. But better than any printed test are the exam questions you make up yourself while you study. Creating Challenge Questions means turning the history that you read into questions that challenge you to find the answers as you study.

To create Challenge Questions, make every major heading you see into a question. For example, if the heading in the history text says "Jacksonian Democracy transforms the United States," you say to yourself, "Name the ways Jacksonian Democracy transformed the United States." Find the answers about Jacksonian Democracy as you're reading the section and write them down. Close your eyes and repeat the question and the answers.

To get good at making your own Challenge Questions while you study, though, you need to actually take a sample AP U.S. History Test. Study the AP U.S. History Released Exams to find out what actual past tests looked like. These exams may be available at your school; you can also look at them on the College Board website: http://apcentral.collegeboard.com/apc/members/exam/exam_information/2089.html.

If you take the practice tests in this book, you may discover some areas of weakness. If so, be sure to create Challenge Questions that focus on these areas. Doing so enables you to focus on areas where it will do the most good for you.

# Avoiding test-induced panic

As the big day approaches, no matter how hard you study, you'll feel a bit scared. So much history, so little time. What was that XYZ Affair? (Diplomatic incident with France, 1797.) How many Great Awakenings were there? (Two — one before the Revolution and one after.) The more you know, the more you know you don't know.

Pre-show jitters are normal, but relax: The AP exam isn't like the tests you took in school, where you were supposed to know everything. It's impossible to know everything about U.S. History. The AP exam is more like an endurance race; even if you limp over the finish line, you deserve applause. Nobody is supposed to get all the questions right. The test has a theoretical perfect score of 180, but you can get the highest grade of 5 with a raw score as low as 117. It's as if an A grade on AP U.S. History starts at 65 percent.

The AP U.S. History test is curved to ensure a certain proportion of high grades every year. You just have to finish ahead of enough other people taking the exam to get ahead of the curve. Think of the story of two guys running away from a grizzly bear. The first guy stops, takes out a pair of running shoes, and starts to put them on. The second guy says, "Don't be stupid! You can't outrun a bear." Replies the first guy, "I don't have to outrun a bear; I just have to outrun you."

# 2

# Getting Mentally Prepared for the Big Test

CONFIDENCE IN WHAT YOU LEARN

## KEY CONCEPTS

- ■ How to use your learning style to maximize retention of information
- ■ Relaxation methods to concentrate your mind
- ■ A rundown of test day

The first chapter of this guide shows you how to use Challenge Questions, history review, and political, economic, and social (PES) information to squirrel away some key information that you can access on the big day. The next three chapters show you how to approach each of the three question types you'll encounter on the AP U.S. History exam. Success comes from more than just what you know, however; it also comes from how you use what you know. You'll succeed on the day of the big test because you're going to have an unstoppable combination of knowledge and attitude. This chapter gives you pointers on how to prepare yourself for exam day so you stay calm, cool, and collected. Don't worry if you're a little anxious; that's good. You can use that nervous energy to slay the test dragon. This chapter gives you pointers on how to do it.

# IDENTIFYING THE WAY YOU LEARN

As I outline in Chapter 1, your goal is to arm yourself with information by studying U.S. history and the AP exam for an hour a day. There are three basic ways of learning — lean naturally on the way that works best for you.

- **Visual learner:** Visual learners prefer to learn things through what they see. That's why we invented writing instead of just singing or tap-dancing history to one another. Research says that 65 percent of humans are visual learners.

- **Auditory learner:** Auditory learners prefer to learn things through sound. That makes them good at learning from lectures and songs, but not as good at grabbing facts through reading. Auditory folks need to say the words out loud to themselves as they read. (Thirty percent of humans are auditory learners.)

- **Kinesthetic learners:** Kinesthetic learners learn best through body movement. (Five percent of us fit in this category.)

Just because you have a preference for one kind of learning doesn't mean you can't remember facts in the other ways as well. Using more than one learning style helps break up your intellectual traffic jam.

## Studying by sight

Visual learners remember colorful emotional images best. Make a picture of a bright, loud religious revival in your mind when you read about the First Great Awakening. You may people the scene with Jonathan Edwards holding a sign that says "1730 — Revolution's Coming." That's visual learning.

---

### Be a poet, and you won't blow it

The secret to remembering a varied assortment of facts, dates, ideas, and so on is *mnemonics*, the art and science of memory. (Naturally, just to mess with your head, the big brains over in the Word Design Department picked a word for memory that's both hard to remember and tricky to say. Just pronounce it without the first letter, and you'll be close enough.) Mnemonics is the psychological system you can use to get ready to score on the big exam.

For example, most people have heard this mnemonic: "In 1492, Columbus sailed the ocean blue." Sadly, basing an entire essay response around this fact is hard. But it's a hint: You can make facts as stick-to-your-brain as a song in your head you just can't stop singing. How about this one? "Thirty days hath September, April, June, and November. When short February's done, all the rest have thirty-one. . ." When is the last time you used *hath* in daily conversation? But there it is, stuck in your brain.

In addition to bad poetry, you can make up first-letter lists. Did you ever wonder *Will A Jolly Man Make A Jolly Visitor*? Bet not, but the first letters of those silly words help you remember the first eight presidents: Washington, J. Adams, Jefferson, Madison, Monroe, J.Q. Adams, Jackson and Van Buren. In the same way, *HOMES* can help you remember the Great Lakes: Huron, Ontario, Michigan, Erie, and Superior. This technique may sound stupid, but what's *not* stupid is being able to remember an impressive list when AP time rolls around.

Writing key events into your own notes helps fix facts in your mind. This technique can be especially useful for timelines. History is, at its core, the study of change over time. Write out a timeline for major topics so that you can see the big picture of how the changes in one field developed. You could make a timeline of women's rights, U.S. expansion, the 50-year run up to the Civil War, and other key themes.

Flash cards don't work for everybody, but they have saved more than one determined student on the AP exam. At the very least, you get to write down terms and their meaning one more time. The more you write stuff down, the better you'll remember it. You may want to color-code your flash cards by era. Just don't go overboard and spend more time decorating beautiful flash cards than using them. (Although the web has lots of useful flash card and multiple-choice apps you can download, it helps to actually write the words to remember them.)

**TIP**

> Studying is a great example of instant karma. Research shows that students who put 50 percent more time into preparation do 50 percent better on big tests.

## Studying by sound

If you're having trouble remembering the facts you read, you may be much better as an auditory learner, someone who needs to hear something to remember it. If you're a passive learner, hunched over your desk watching the textbook pages of history facts flip slowly by, you'll be lucky to remember 10 percent of what you see. Even people who aren't auditory learners remember 20 percent of what they hear. So close your eyes, visualize the facts with their dates, and say them to yourself.

As an auditory fan, while studying, make sure to say things like "First Great Awakening, Jonathan Edwards, 1730 — Revolution's Coming" out loud repeatedly to yourself with your eyes closed. (Don't do this in a crowded coffeehouse; people may think you're crazy instead of brilliant.)

Even if you do prefer sound to sight, in addition to saying the words, try forming them into a vivid picture in your mind; most folks can remember at least 30 percent of what they see.

**TIP**

> A high-tech solution is available for auditory learners: You can actually scan text and have the facts read to you by a friendly computer voice. Text-to-speech is built into the operating systems of both Windows and Apple.

## Studying through movement

Kinesthetic learners are hands-on people who concentrate better and learn more easily when movement is involved. Although you can't dance your way through the AP exam, you can learn to use movement sense to help your memory.

Kinesthetic people can make a scene into a movie in their heads. As you study, stand up and imagine yourself as Jonathan Edwards, pounding the pulpit and waving a "1730 — Revolution's Coming" banner. It doesn't matter how silly the connection is; in fact, the sillier the better.

Humor is an easy emotion to remember, and anything out of the ordinary is better than trying to remember gray words on paper. Then, during the test, remember your standing up as John Edwards. Chances are you'll remember the pulpit and the banner, too — key bits of info that can help you answer questions about him on the exam.

If you have to see the facts spatially because you are a kinesthetic learner, try putting color-coded sticky notes containing key facts in date order along a route that you take through your house. Walk that route several times, stopping to associate each fact with where you are standing. That way, you can associate facts with known locations. Don't leave the sticky notes up too long, though; your mother may come along and vacuum a hole in the 1800s.

# WAYS TO MAXIMIZE YOUR STUDY TIME

The topic of study skills sounds about as interesting as lint collecting, but there are some moves that can help you get more miles to the gallon out of your learning time:

- Tap into study resources at your school. If your school offers after-class review sessions for AP U.S. History, be there. Your teacher can't slip and tell you exactly what is going to be on the test, because he doesn't know. He *does* know what has been on the test in the past, however.

  Also, review sessions are great places to practice that short essay writing. You weren't very good at riding a bike until you had the chance to try again and again. You won't be really good at writing short history essays until you have written at least ten. Just as you wouldn't want your first time on a bike to be at the bike races, you don't want your first experience with a DBQ to be on the big test. If your school offers feedback on practice essays, make sure you are first in line.

- Have a regular study place and time, and stick to them every day.

- When you study outside class, break up your 1-hour study time into two 30-minute chunks, with a 5-minute walk-around break between chunks.

- Review during the day, when you are really awake. An hour during daylight can be worth two hours at night.

- As New Agey as this sounds, tell yourself that you strongly intend to remember what you are studying. At the beginning of your study session, for example, say, "I am going to remember the presidents from Abe Lincoln to Teddy Roosevelt tonight." Research shows that the act of seriously committing to remember improves retention as much as 50 percent. Trying and not quite making it is okay; you can always do better tomorrow. What is not okay is just waiting to see what you just happen to remember. You have to set a clear goal and push hard to make it. Dreams come true because people make them come true.

- Always associate a new fact with an old one, as in "Oh, I see. John Charles Fremont becomes the Great Pathfinder for the Republican Party as its first presidential candidate (1856) after he was the Great Pathfinder of the West on the trails to California (1836–1853)."

- Study the difficult stuff first. Set some reward milestones. After you make it through the Civil War, it's time for a small party!

- Get emotional about the events you are studying: Women's rights were awesome and long overdue; slavery sucked. You remember facts that mean something to your heart, not just your fine mind.

- Although your friends and family may not seem to be begging for the latest in history insights, teach them about some of the important events you are learning. Teaching a concept to someone else more than doubles your memory of that concept.

# STRATEGIES TO REDUCE PRETEST ANXIETY

If you're a worrier, be honest with yourself. Are you worried because you really haven't prepared for the test? Here's the reality check: If you've gotten decent grades in your high school AP U.S. History course and are following your hour-a-day test-prep schedule, you need to deal with your real problem: chronic anxiety. This condition is nothing to be ashamed of; the United States itself once suffered from overwhelming anxiety. In the inaugural words of longest-serving president, Franklin Delano Roosevelt, "We have nothing to fear but fear itself — nameless, unreasoning, unjustified terror which paralyzes needed efforts." If you have done the study basics but are restless, check out the relaxation techniques in the following sections. Relaxation doesn't just keep you comfortable; staying loose also helps you perform better on the test.

If your worry is justified because you really haven't done the preparation you need, consider the words of Death Valley Scotty. In the early 1900s, Scotty was a prospector in the hottest place in the United States: Death Valley, California. Scotty never found gold, but he did find a beautiful oasis and many adventures, laughs, and friends. Scotty said, "There's just two things ain't worth worrying about: things you can change and things you can't." If you still have a few days to get a study program together, start working right now. Doing something takes your mind off your anxiety.

## Progressive relaxation

Lots of people, auditory learners or not, feel better hearing progressive-relaxation steps read out loud to them. You can get a spoken recording of relaxation instructions on the web. Many slightly different versions of this technique are available; all of them work if you let them.

---

### What students overseas are studying

While Americans are sweating the APs and SATs, students in Japan are attending *juku*, or private cram schools. Japanese students sometimes go to juku every day after school and up to 16 hours a day on weekends to prepare for "examination hell" in January, which will decide their university future. Row upon row of quiet students stare at the blackboard. Kids in the back even look through binoculars to grasp every word.

Meanwhile, in jolly old England, students are obsessing about the *A levels*. A levels come in a variety of subjects, just like the APs, and you need to pass at least three to get into a good university. U.K. schools have grades like those in the United States, except that the land of Harry Potter has not forgotten about *E*. Average grade distribution is 10 percent *A*, 15 percent *B*, 10 percent *C*, 15 percent *D*, and 20 percent *E*. A further 20 percent are allowed an O-level pass, which is sort of like saying, "Thanks for showing up." The real flunkies get a *U* and have to play in rock-and-roll bands.

Relaxation is a natural state: it's what you do when you are asleep. You can learn to do progressive relaxation while you're awake and use it to clear your mind. First, get into comfortable clothing and choose a quiet space. Then follow these steps:

1. Lie flat on your back, with your eyes closed.

2. Feel your feet getting heavy. Consciously relax them and let them sink down. Start with your toes and move up your foot to your ankles.

3. Feel your knees getting heavy. Consciously relax them and let them sink down.

4. Feel your upper legs and thighs getting heavy. Consciously relax them and feel them sink down.

5. Feel your abdomen and chest while you breathe. Consciously let them relax. Let your breathing be deep and regular. Let your abdomen and chest sink down.

6. Feel your back down to your upper legs. Consciously relax and let your back sink down.

7. Feel your hands getting heavy. Consciously relax them and feel them sink down.

8. Feel your arms getting heavy. Consciously relax them and feel them sink down.

9. Feel your shoulders getting heavy. Consciously relax them and feel them sink down.

10. Feel your head and neck getting heavy. Consciously relax your neck and feel your head sink down.

11. Feel your mouth and jaw. Pay attention to your jaw muscles and unclench them if they are tight. Feel your mouth and jaw relax.

12. Feel your eyes. Are you forcibly closing your eyelids? Consciously relax your eyelids and feel the tension slide off your eyes.

13. Mentally scan down your body. If you find any place that's still tense, consciously relax that place and let it sink down.

14. Lie still for 5 minutes.

## Deep breathing

As simple as it seems, deep breathing is a great way to relax your body and concentrate energy, which is why it's an important part of spiritual, meditation, and martial-arts traditions around the world.

1. **Sit comfortably, straight up, with a loose waist and your stomach relaxed.** Sitting in a chair is fine; you don't have to sit cross-legged on the floor. Just check that your back is comfortably straight and your middle is loose and relaxed (don't worry about looking fat; no one is watching).

2. **Let your whole self relax.** You can work your way from bottom to top, as in the progressive-relaxation technique in the preceding section.

3. **Begin to inhale slowly through your nose. Count to 4 as you fill your lungs in four parts from bottom to top. Breathe in slowly, taking about 5 seconds for a full breath.**

4. **Hold your breath for a couple of seconds.**

5. **Quietly relax and let the air flow all the way out through your mouth.**

6. **Wait a few seconds and inhale, hold, and release your breath slowly again.** Breathe in through your nose in four sections; let the air out completely through your mouth in a long, peaceful "Ahh" or "Ohm," the dial tone of the universe. If you get dizzy, you're going too fast. Slow down.

7. **Imagine that you're floating, and pretty soon you will be.** Practice deep breathing for 15 minutes at a time.

## Quiet Ears

This technique works like listening to a seashell at the beach. Because it stills the world around you, Quiet Ears helps you connect to your own inner strength. This technique works for everybody, but especially if you are easily distracted by outside sounds:

1. **Close your eyes.**

2. **Place your hands loosely on top of your head.**

3. **Cup your hands and cover both your ears.** You hear the slow, rushing sound of your own blood circulating. This is a good thing.

4. **Listen to this sound while you count to 10, ten times.**

5. **Relax your arms, and repeat Steps 3 and 4.** You may find yourself breathing peacefully.

If outside sounds are very distracting to you and Quiet Ears doesn't help you filter them out, wearing ear plugs when you study can also help.

# TWO DAYS BEFORE THE EXAM

Just because a lot of people stay up late cramming the night before the test doesn't mean it works. Because the AP U.S. History test involves heavy writing as well as remembering facts, you're way better off with a rested body and fresh mind the day of the test than you are trying to tip just one more woozy date into your tired cerebellum the night before.

You'll want to benefit from maximum sleep the two nights before the test. If you usually sleep for seven hours on vacation, give yourself room for eight both nights. You need two nights of good sleep, because sleep deprivation can skip a day. People can have a low-rest night, skate through the next 24 hours on fumes, and run out of gas on the second day. You don't want to get stuck in AP Land.

Triathletes and marathon racers knock off training two days before their event to build up an energy reserve. You can study your regular amount up to the last day, but you should knock off anything that distracts your mind or body two days before the big test. Replace coffee, junk food, and media with exercise and relaxation techniques. Kick up your exercise routine by 50 percent; more exercise keeps you calm and helps you think.

# EXAM DAY

On the day of the test, eat a medium breakfast. You're on your way to a performance, and you don't need heavy food to slow you down. Give yourself more time than you think you need to get to the test site; no last-minute parking problems or traffic tickets should spoil your mood. If you get to the site early, walk around. You'll be sitting for a long time, and you want to get your blood circulating. Don't drink a lot of liquid. You'll get a break in the middle, but you don't want to be going to the bathroom while the test clock is running. If you run into friends, be nice, but don't listen very hard to what they say. Watch the pros before a race. They acknowledge one another with a nod, but they're already in their own space.

Bring three No. 2 pencils and a good separate eraser for the multiple-choice questions. If you change a scan-marked multiple-choice answer, you want to make sure that the mark in the scan oval you rejected is erased completely. Bring a couple of your favorite ink pens for the essay section. Wear a watch. You won't be allowed to look at your cell phone, and time control is important.

Pick a spot in the test room with good light and a minimum of possibly distracting people. You'll get an exam packet with the Section I multiple-choice questions and the Section II essay questions. Section I has a Scantron answer form with more than enough spaces. You mark your answers to the 80 multiple-choice questions by filling in the correct ovals carefully with a pencil. Section II essay prompts are in a question booklet, and you write your compositions in a separate essay book. For both Section I and Section II, you can make notes in the question books but not on the answer pages.

You have 55 minutes to answer as many of the 80 multiple-choice questions as you can. After a 10-minute break, you have 2 hours and 10 minutes to study and write three essays. The Section II essay time begins with a mandatory 15-minute reading period, during which time you should make notes in the question book. During the reading period, you study the questions but are not allowed to begin writing the essays in the answer book.

## Section I: Multiple choice

With the proctor's word "Begin," you open the Section I multiple-choice book and dive in (Chapter 3 covers the strategy for handling multiple-choice questions). For now, just realize that the 80 questions each have 5 alternatives for a total of 400 possible answers. You are going to be reading 400 possible answers, 320 of which are wrong and designed, at least minimally, to trick you into picking them. You have 55 minutes to answer the multiple-choice questions, which means you have 41 seconds per question and only 8 seconds per possible answer. Don't panic; the time is longer than it seems. Try holding your breath for 41 seconds; you'll feel how long that is.

> **TIP**
>
> You don't have to be right about everything to score a perfect 5 on the AP exam. The test grade is curved; test writers realize that few people are going to burn through all 80 multiple-choice questions at 41 seconds each and come up with a perfect score. You can skate by on Section I by getting fewer than 50 questions right and still pull it out with a perfect 5 score just by getting two-thirds of the possible credits for essay writing in Section II.

Panicking is something to avoid at all times during the test, but especially during the multiple-choice section. If you panic on multiple-choice questions, you'll lose concentration and stop reading carefully. The situation only gets worse; the reality is that the questions get harder as you move through the 80 mini-challenges.

If you aren't sure about a question, cross off the answer choices that you know are wrong in the question book. If you can cross out only one, do it and move on. Keep going, moving along, harvesting all the good answers that you know (most people don't even get through all the questions). After you've got all the easy answers, go back and work on the tougher questions. Use every minute to complete multiple-choice questions that you skipped earlier and to double-check the answers you've already marked. You need to put an answer on every question because there's no penalty for guessing, and you just may be right.

 **TIP**

Don't outsmart yourself on the multiple-choice section. Save double-checking for last, because you don't want to trap yourself by overthinking. Usually, your first hunch is your best shot; you don't get any smarter by squinching up your eyebrows. Obsessing over every question as you go only slows you down. If you have time for a recheck, don't change any answers unless you're sure those answers are wrong.

## Break time

When 55 minutes are up, the proctor will say, "Stop working. Close your booklet, and put your answer sheet on your desk." You've got a 10-minute break before the Section II essay section calls upon you to create great history fast. Use those 10 minutes to get up and walk as far as you can from the crowd. Practice deep breathing lightly as you walk: four-count deep inhalation through your nose and a long, peaceful exhale through your mouth. Shake your arms; roll your shoulders and neck. Now's not the time to impress people or gossip; you are in the middle of a race. Make sure to hit the bathroom on your way back, if there's any chance you'll need to go in the next 2 hours.

As you walk, think about what was good about how you did on Section I. Congratulate yourself for the answers that you knew and leave the other ones behind. Professional athletes are champions partly because they shake off the past and concentrate on what's coming up.

## Section II: The DBQ and essays

Section II of the exam covers short essay writing, and it's divided into three sections: Parts A through C. Part A is the Document-Based Question (DBQ). Chapter 4 is devoted to nothing but this single topic. The DBQ is perhaps the greatest moment of high art in any history exam. For now, you don't have to appreciate its beauty. Just remember: Make notes and collect your thoughts before you write. Part B and Part C each contain two regular essay questions. Here, you get to pick the one question from each of the two parts that seems the least scary.

Before you can set pen to paper for the DBQ, Section II wants you to spend 15 minutes alone with it, just reading. Your proctor will recommend that you take the entire 15 minutes to read the documents and to scan the pictures and charts in the DBQ. This time, the grownup is right.

The proctor can't do anything to stop you from sailing right past the documents in Part A and having a peek at what questions await you in Parts B and C. Don't do it. Whatever is in Parts B and C will wait for you to get there. You don't need it hanging over your head while you do the DBQ.

Plan before you write, making notes on the question insert and not in the answer booklet, which is *only* for your essays. Look at the essays this way: It's like 2 hours and 10 minutes to use what you have learned to make points. You can only gain credit by weaving the themes and topics you know into a well-argued essay.

> **TIP**
>
> As you work through the three essays, keep this positive thought in mind: Each of your compositions will be scored by a completely different reader who doesn't know who you are, what you've done on the other parts of the test, or even who graded your other essays. It's a new chance every time.

# 3

# Strategies for the Multiple-Choice Section

## KEY CONCEPTS

- How to avoid traps in multiple-choice questions
- How to use details in illustrations
- Tactics to enhance test-taking time management

Fifty-five minutes seems really long when you have to get through a whole period in school. But in the AP U.S. History exam, when you're faced with 80 multiple-choice questions, each with 5 possible answers lettered from A to E, those same 55 minutes don't even seem to be enough time to say hello. Yet 55 minutes is plenty of time for 80 multiple-choice questions, when you follow the test-proven strategy provided in this chapter for digging up the winning answers.

## THINKING LIKE THE TEST WRITERS

If you look at the AP test as payday for all the studying you've done, Section I of the test is where you can score some fast bucks. In only a third of the test time, you can earn half of the test credits. The trick is to avoid turning multiple choice into multiple guess.

You're going to be getting a great grade on multiple-choice Section I because you'll be working like the pros do. Don't waste your time on hard questions. You get the same credit for answering hard questions as easy ones. Get all the easy answers before you bang your head on the hard ones.

Think of each multiple-choice question as a puzzle holding one point worth of credit toward a great score on the AP. To get to that point, you have to avoid four false moves per question. Read carefully, because you can't choose the right answer for sure until you have carefully rejected the four wrong answers.

>  **TIP**
>
> If you get stressed during your run through the multiple-choice warehouse, do a couple of the deep-breathing exercises outlined in Chapter 2. Breathe in deeply through your nose for a count of four. Breathe out completely through your mouth. Don't overdo it, and keep your eyes on the test.

## Points hidden in plain sight

To be fair, the test writers try to hide the points in the most important spots. The AP folks want you to know the key trends in U.S. history, not a bunch of board game trivia. You don't have to remember all the battles or the name of every explorer who ever leaned on a tree. The right answer is often the broadest, most important concept.

Take a look at this example:

1. What was the most important impact of the Great Depression of the 1930s on the United States?

   (A)  It led to Prohibition.

   (B)  Lots of Americans were depressed.

   (C)  Businesses did better with less competition.

   (D)  It led to an expansion of the role of government and social programs to protect people from poverty.

   (E)  The United States got off the gold standard to make more money.

The question on the Great Depression almost gave you the answer: It asked for "most important" impact. Even though some of the other answers contain a little bit of truth, the only one that can be the key concept is expansion of the role of government and social programs, choice (D). Some answer choices are attractive bait to lure you into a quick wrong decision. For the question about the Great Depression, some students might guess (B), that lots of Americans were depressed, because that answer could sound like a fit. Watch out for answers that sound a little too simplistic; they're traps.

The key concepts to study for the AP are in this book in italic type: The really big concepts are section headings in this book *and* your textbook.

## Educated guessing

Up to a few years ago, the College Board took away a quarter of a point for every wrong answer on the multiple-choice. Because you got penalized for guessing wrong, occasionally it was better not to guess at all. Those dangerous days are gone. Today, wrong answers aren't penalized. Therefore, you need to take a shot at every question. To make it your best shot, think like the people who wrote the test. You may not know everything about U.S. history, but at least you know that you can guess when you need to.

## Leveraging what you know

Test takers' minds often go blank when they are confronted with alphabet soup. Suppose that you're confronted by this mind-numbing question:

1. Which treaty did away with most of the trade restrictions among the United States, Canada, and Mexico?

   (A) SALT

   (B) NBA

   (C) The Gulf of Tonkin resolution

   (D) SDI

   (E) NAFTA

In a question like this, take a deep breath and start eliminating answers you know aren't correct: The NBA is that league with hoops, tall guys, and 3-point plays. Because you don't play basketball with trade restrictions, choice (B) is wrong. If you can eliminate only that one wrong answer, you've improved the odds: You have one chance in four of guessing correctly on the remaining four choices, just by pure chance. Guess this way 80 times, and you'll pick up 20 points on average just by eliminating one bad response.

The odds get better if you can eliminate three bad multiple-choice answers. With random chance, you would pick up an average of 40 points on 80 questions if you can narrow each question down to two choices. Suppose that, in addition to eliminating the NBA answer, you have a strong suspicion that the Gulf of Tonkin is a long way from the United States, Canada, or Mexico, so you eliminate answer (C). And don't these three nations make up North America? With that information to go on, you may conjure up the North American Free Trade Agreement — also known as NAFTA — from the misty outlands of your mind.

## Avoiding word traps

Make sure that you read each question carefully, *twice*, before you grab one of the five answer choices. In sports, *juking* is when you fake out an opponent by dodging in the opposite direction from where he thinks you're going. Juking is a favorite strategy of test writers. If you don't study their moves carefully from a safe distance *before* you move in to grab an answer choice, you may well find yourself headed in the wrong direction.

Questions meant to juke you typically contain the words EXCEPT, NOT, or LEAST. Notice that these words are in capital letters. They're printed this way to give you a fighting chance to see them even if you're in a hurry. Juking words change the direction of the question.

## EXCEPT questions

Take a close look at the following sample question:

1. All these important foods came to Europe from discoveries in the New World EXCEPT

    (A) chocolate
    (B) corn
    (C) tomatoes
    (D) coffee
    (E) potatoes

So you're blowing by at the rate of a question every 40 seconds; you see the terms *foods*, *Europe*, and *New World*, and you think, "Oh, boy. I know — it's got to be tomatoes, because how did the Italians make pizza without tomatoes before they discovered the New World?" Or you think, "It's chocolate for sure, because I remember wondering how Europeans even bothered to keep living in a pre-New World era without chocolate."

This question has too many good answers — and that's the tip-off that you're the target of an attempted juke. Perhaps you were going so fast that you didn't see the word EXCEPT, even though it's in brazen capital letters. Even if you miss EXCEPT, all is not lost. If you read all the choices and don't just swallow the first bit of bait set out to trap you, you'll begin to notice that a lot of the answers seem to fit a little too well. Suspiciously, all but one of the answers look like they could work. Look back at the question, and you find the juke in all caps.

**TIP**

Read the whole question and all the answers. Twice. Repeat the capitalized word to yourself as you read the possible answers.

## NOT questions

In addition to the EXCEPT trick, you need to watch out for questions with NOT in them. You can save yourself from disaster by reading carefully. Read the question twice, so you definitely see the giant NOT. Say "NOT" to yourself as you read the possible answers twice. Consider this example:

1. Which of the following was NOT included in the Northwest Ordinance of 1787?

    (A) procedures for organizing territory and state governments
    (B) a ban on slavery
    (C) guaranteed religious freedom
    (D) the right to a jury trial
    (E) specific reservations for American Indians

Like *EXCEPT*, *NOT* is hoping you're reading too fast to notice it lurking there in capital letters. *NOT* is banking on your seeing just the phrase "Northwest Ordinance of 1787," glancing down at the answers, seeing one of the attractive first four answers (A) through (D), and patting yourself on the back as you rush your wrong answer to the Scantron sheet.

But how do you know which of the five answers is the right one? Here are some things to consider:

- You know the Northwest Ordinance of 1787 was written by the same guys who brought you the American Revolution. Therefore, it should contain Declaration of Independence issues such as jury trials, answer (D) and religious freedom, answer (C).

- Setting up state governments, answer (A), is a noncontroversial housekeeping matter; it had to be there.

- Slavery, answer (B), certainly was controversial, but — clue — you know the Northwest ended up without slaves, so that had to be included.

- Perhaps the least-noble reason for the Revolution was to let the new Americans settle on American Indian lands the British government had declared off limits. It wouldn't make sense to set aside specific reservations when the American Indians were still fighting to have no settlers at all. So the most "NOT" answer is (E). This is it.

> **TIP**
>
> When you scan a list of possible answers, especially in EXCEPT, NOT, and LEAST questions, look for the most extreme outlier to be the answer you want. The most extreme choices tend to be right when it comes to answering negatively phrased juke questions. They go beyond the list presented and just don't quite fit in.

## LEAST questions

The final juke word to look out for is *LEAST*. You're sailing along normally, looking for the best match between the key word in the question and those tricky multiple choices when you come upon a *LEAST*. Take a big pause. *LEAST* switches up the meaning, so now you're looking for the worst match. Check out this example.

1. Which of the following was the LEAST important reason Andrew Jackson was popular with American voters in the 1820s and 1830s?

   (A) opposed the Bank of the United States

   (B) stood up to nullification

   (C) dressed like a frontiersman

   (D) supported more democracy for the common man

   (E) won the Battle of New Orleans

You don't have to worry about one of these answers being false. Because this is a *LEAST* question, they're all at least partly true. Dressing like a frontiersman seems to be pretty trivial, even in a symbolic field like politics. The 1820s and 1830s had no TV and few pictures anyway, so not many people could have seen Jackson. Choice (C), dressed like a frontiersman, is the *LEAST* reason and your best answer.

## Strong words (absolutes)

In addition to EXCEPT, NOT, and LEAST, watch out for strong words like *complete*, *always*, *never*, *only*, *all*, *every*, and *none*. Because history almost always has exceptions, strong words that seem to cover the whole story are often the sign of a wrong answer. Take a look at the following example:

**1.** Abraham Lincoln freed the slaves with the Emancipation Proclamation of 1863 because

(A) the only reason he wanted to win the Civil War was to abolish slavery

(B) Lincoln always sided with the abolitionists

(C) the Emancipation Proclamation completely freed the slaves

(D) emancipation made political and moral sense in 1863

(E) Lincoln never made a political decision when he could make a moral one

The strong words in (A), (B), (C), and (E) mark them for extinction from your answer choices. Lincoln said he wanted to preserve the Union, whether it meant freeing all the slaves or freeing none of the slaves. Although Lincoln certainly was personally opposed to slavery, he put being president of a united America before the cause of abolition. The Emancipation Proclamation freed only slaves in rebel states. Lincoln was a great and honest person, but he wouldn't have won the presidential election if he weren't also an experienced politician. Answer (D) is correct.

Strong words don't always indicate an answer should be eliminated. They are your friends when the test writers try to juke you with one of those tricky EXCEPT, NOT, or LEAST questions. Here's a different take on the Emancipation Proclamation question:

**1.** Which of the following causes is NOT a part of the reason Abraham Lincoln freed the slaves in the Emancipation Proclamation?

(A) The North had better news from the battlefield.

(B) Lincoln always sided with the abolitionists.

(C) Freeing the slaves had popular support in the North.

(D) Lincoln was personally opposed to slavery.

(E) Fleeing slaves may weaken Southern war efforts.

In this version, the very word *always* that made choice (B) wrong in the first question makes it right in the tricky NOT question.

# Going with what you know

You're smarter than you think. You can usually come up with more than one way to figure out a question. When you hit a blank wall, try thinking around the wall. Eliminating even one bad answer choice puts the odds in your favor. Sometimes, you can rule out answers by looking at them closely. Here's an example:

1. Upton Sinclair's book *The Jungle* led to the passage of which law?

   (A) the Clayton Antitrust Law
   (B) the Northwest Ordinance
   (C) the Pure Food and Drug Act
   (D) the Stark Amendment
   (E) the Hepburn Act

How would you know? If all those complicated acts look like a foreign language to you, stop and think back for a moment. On a slow Friday in literature class, the teacher was talking about *The Jungle* not being about a tropical forest at all, but about filthy food factories. That would lead you to (C), the Pure Food and Drug Act. Or you may just have been wrestling with the question about the Northwest Ordinance covered earlier in this chapter, and you picked up something about the Ordinance from answering that question and now know it can't have anything to do with *The Jungle*.

On a history test, time is on your side. Knowing about when events happened helps you to see when a possible answer is way out of its chronological period. If you know the key terms, their approximate dates, and why they're important, you have a great chance of scoring well. You may make this note: "Northwest Ordinance (1787 — at the beginning of U.S. government) = rules for setting up new states from the Ohio River to the Mississippi River; no slavery; freedom of religion; jury trials." Knowing the general time period related to the Northwest Ordinance eliminates it from the Sinclair/Jungle answer possibilities. Upton's *grandfather* wasn't even born when Congress passed the Northwest Ordinance.

## Making a little knowledge go a long way

You don't really need to know everything by heart to choose the correct answer. You can make a little knowledge go a long way. Suppose you faced a question like this:

1. American artists painting around 1900 in what was called the Realist school tended to paint which subject?

   (A) American frontier life
   (B) urban scenes
   (C) rural family life
   (D) wild natural landscapes
   (E) pastoral scenes

A little time with art can go a long way. You may have a vague feeling that the late Victorians painted some pretty sentimental scenes, certainly not what people would call Realism. That would mean that common subjects like (A), (C), (D), and (E) probably wouldn't earn a special name like Realist school; they all blend together and make (B), the right answer, stand out.

## Using common sense

Sometimes, common sense alone can help you solve a problem, as it does with this question:

1. When a U.S. reporter coined the phrase *Manifest Destiny*, he meant that

    (A) the struggle for racial equality should be the purpose of America

    (B) the United States should set all of South America free from colonialism

    (C) America must become either all slaveholding or all free

    (D) it's the fate of the United States to cover the whole continent from ocean to ocean

    (E) all Americans should pursue happiness until they're happy all the time

Your best bet is to know that Manifest Destiny means (D). But what if you just knew that Manifest Destiny sounded like something you'd heard a lot? That would probably eliminate events that didn't happen, such as (B) and (C). You can eliminate (E) because it sounds like a smart-aleck answer. You may know that Manifest Destiny started way before the Civil War and that, even 100 years after the outbreak of the Civil War, racial equality still didn't have full support, which pretty much leaves (A) out. Knowing a little and taking the time to use your common sense can be a lifesaver.

## Using historic eras to gain points

As pointed out previously, knowing the approximate year of a key term can give you the power to answer a multiple-choice question correctly. Here's an example question that you can answer if you have an idea about what happened during particular eras:

1. All the following were results of the First Great Awakening EXCEPT

    (A) more and stronger churches

    (B) the founding of new colleges and universities

    (C) nationwide religious enthusiasm

    (D) a return to the persecution of witches

    (E) ministers with followings of thousands

You could score on this question from several directions. First, the minute you see the word *EXCEPT, LEAST,* or *NOT,* you know you need to be careful. You're looking for an extreme that just doesn't fit with the rest of the answers.

Even if you are not clear about the First Great Awakening (covered in Part II), you can work with whatever you have in your brain. You may know that the witch hunting died out in the 1690s and that the First Great Awakening didn't occur until 40 years later. You may realize that history is written by the winners and that they'd be unlikely to give the name Awakening to something as ugly as burning women. You could also figure out that persecution of witches is a standout in a list with unifying words like *churches, colleges, enthusiasm,* and *ministers.* Therefore, you know that the First Great Awakening *was not* about a return to the persecution of witches. The answer is (D).

If you have to, guess. Before you do, eliminate what you can. For example, because (A), (C), and (E) all sound like they are in the same theme, you can eliminate them from being the extreme. You'd be statistically way ahead even if you had to guess between (B) and (D).

## Questioning illustrations

The test writers usually throw in few multiple-choice questions illustrated with pictures or charts. These illustrated questions can actually be easier than regular multiple-choice challenges. The illustration contains most of the answer; you just need to know what it's telling you.

**1.** What does the following chart, which conveys the median personal income by educational attainment, illustrate about income and education?

| Measure | | | | | | | | |
|---|---|---|---|---|---|---|---|---|
| Some High School | High School Graduate | Some College | Associate Degree | Bachelor's Degree | Bachelor's Degree or Higher | Master's Degree | Professional Degree | Doctorate |
| Persons age 25+ w/earnings | | | | | | | | |
| $20,321 | $26,505 | $31,054 | $35,009 | $43,143 | $49,303 | $52,390 | $82,473 | $70,853 |

(A)  It's always better to stay in school.

(B)  Many people older than 25 are rich.

(C)  Everybody with a bachelor's degree makes at least $43,143.

(D)  Income tends to rise with education.

(E)  These figures are the minimum salaries for each education level.

The right answer is (D), income tends to rise with education. The important point with illustrated questions is to look hard at the picture and stick to what the illustration shows. Don't think too hard and outsmart yourself by overinterpreting. The chart shows *median* personal income, not a guarantee. The correct answer on illustration questions is often the most moderate one with words like *tends* instead of the words *better*, *rich* or *everybody*, which appear in the wrong answers.

Sometimes, the test asks you to identify a picture's background information; as in this example:

*Provided courtesy of HarpWeek, LLC*

1. What are the era and social orientation of this cartoon?

   (A) Southern Confederates

   (B) Northern Democrats

   (C) Slave owners, before the Civil War

   (D) Northern abolitionists

   (E) Reconstruction education, post–Civil War

The illustration indicates that the orientation is Northern, with strong abolitionist sentiments, making (D) the correct answer. (A) and (C) are incorrect because Confederates and slave owners would not have supported "Emancipation" written at the top of the picture. There is no image of education in the illustration, so (E) can't be it. And (B) is wrong because Northern Democrats before the war were almost never abolitionists.

# TIME MANAGEMENT DURING THE TEST

Time management is a key to winning on the multiple-choice section of the test. Even though you have only 55 minutes, you have all the time you need to pull out the easy questions and have a good shot at the harder ones. The key is to get through the multiple-choice section quickly and accurately.

> **TIP**
>
> Because the minutes make a difference, bring your own watch to the exam. You won't be allowed to check your cell phone, and the clock in the exam room just may be wrong. Having a watch lets you be your own time manager.

## Target easy questions first

The multiple-choice section is like a free shopping trip in which you get to keep everything you can find in 55 minutes. Trouble is, if you take too much time trying to reach things on the top shelf, you may not have time to load up on items that are easily within your grasp. In general, the multiple-choice section of the AP exam moves from easier to harder questions, but toward the difficult end, you may find questions that you know by heart. That's why you need to swing past all the questions quickly.

You have, on average, 40 seconds for each question. But relax. Forty seconds is longer than you think. To prove it, try looking at a clock with a second hand. Watch that second hand slowly glide around the dial for 40 seconds. That's the seemingly interminable time you'll have for each question.

Don't get hung up agonizing over an answer. Try to scan and answer all the easy questions, and then go back and work on the questions that need a little more thinking. If 10 more seconds of thinking doesn't solve the problem, move on. Hitting the side of your head with your palm won't loosen up any secret knowledge. Give quick insights a chance to arrive, but spread your attention over as many questions as possible.

## Pace yourself

As you know, the AP exam has 80 multiple-choice questions and gives you 55 minutes to complete them. To gauge whether you're on track to finish the multiple-choice portion of the test within the allotted time, pace yourself.

When you get your question book, make a mark right after question 20 and another mark next to question 40. The first mark puts you one quarter of the way through the multiple-choice section. If you're running on time, you should be at question 20 about 14 minutes after you begin. When the testing starts, add 14 minutes to the time on your watch. When you get to question 20, check to see whether you're on pace. Check once more when you get to question 40. If you've used more than half an hour of your 55 precious minutes, you need to pick up the pace. If you've used only about 20 minutes when you hit question 40, you can afford to take a little more time.

## Mark in the question book

When grades are on the line, smart people write and mark while they read. You should mark *in the question book* as you roll rapidly (but in a controlled fashion) through the multiple-choice questions in Section I of the AP exam. Here are some pointers to follow to make the process faster and easier for you:

- If you're sure that you've locked into the right answer after reading both the question and all the answers twice, just circle that for-sure answer in the question book and carefully blacken its oval on the Scantron answer form.

- If you can eliminate some but not all of the choices, cross out the answers you know are wrong in the question book.

- If you have one or more wrong answers crossed out, mark your best guess for the answer in the question book.

- If you don't have a clue and can't eliminate any of the choices, put a zero next to the question and don't fill in the Scantron sheet for that question. Then put a light mark opposite the Scantron number of the question you're not answering so that you don't accidentally put the answer to a known question in the wrong place, which can screw up every answer that comes after it. (Make sure you completely erase any light marks on the answer sheet before you hand in the answers.)

When you've made it through all the questions, you should still have time to go back to the beginning and take another look at the questions you skipped. First focus on the questions with the most eliminated wrong answers; these are the questions you're closest to being sure about. When you're through with the easier ones, go back and do the tougher ones. If you have time, give a last once-over to all the questions.

**TIP**

Don't linger on any question after you've marked it. Instead, pause just long enough to make sure the mark is in the right place. Also, go with your first hunch unless you actually have a reason to change. Research shows that if you can't come up with any additional information, your first hunch is usually the best bet.

Getting all the way to the end quickly, after marking off the trouble spots, gives you an advantage in terms of both time sequence and answer elimination. You'll actually pick up some history just from the juxtaposition of topics on the exam. You may be able to eliminate some wrong answers from early questions based on what you've noticed on questions closer to the end of the test. Also, answering later questions helps jog your memory.

# 4

# Scoring Well on Document-Based Questions (DBQs)

**KEY CONCEPTS**

- How to read documents accurately
- The proof, analysis, and thesis (PAT) method
- The use of outside information
- How to write a grader-friendly DBQ

To score high on the Document-Based Question (DBQ, for short) that appears on every AP U.S. History exam, you must create a thesis, analyze the documents as they relate to your thesis, and bring in outside evidence (proof) that supports your thesis. Depending on your level of preparation, the DBQ can be either an interesting chance for self-expression or a confusing and desperate search for words. Most people who take the AP test don't do as well as they could on the DBQ because they get overwhelmed by the detail. Using the proof, analysis, and thesis (PAT) method introduced in this chapter, you can be prepared for Document-Based Question. PAT is the essay-writing system that has what teachers look for: You use historical proof with analysis to support a clear thesis or idea.

# USING DOCUMENTS LIKE A HISTORIAN

After working through the 80 multiple-choice questions in Section I, you will return from your well-deserved 10-minute break to take on Section II, the free-response questions. For these questions, you write essays on topics the AP selects. The Document-Based Question essay comes first. On the DBQ, you combine what you know about history with what you can pull from a supplied set of documents to answer an assigned question. After you finish the DBQ, you choose two additional regular essays from four available topics. (Regular essays are covered in detail in Chapter 5.)

If you've ever wondered what being a historian would feel like, the Document-Based Question is your chance. For the DBQ, you write history from primary sources, just like college students and professors do.

A people's history is what they choose to remember to explain who they are. The historian's job is to make sure that these collective memories are facts interpreted in as honest a manner as the historian's current understanding of the world allows. History doesn't come from wizards with long white beards; it comes from scholars working patiently with primary source material to provide accurate facts plus reasonable analysis and interpretation. That's what your task is on the DBQ.

On the test, you'll confront one interesting analysis question from an important period in U.S. history. To help build your essay on that question, you'll receive a set of 8 to 10 primary source documents. These documents could be letters, news reports, political cartoons, financial reports, pictures, diary entries, charts, graphs, love notes — almost anything that can be printed on paper. Your essay for the DBQ needs to combine your interpretation of the supplied documents with outside history facts you remember about the period and topic in question.

> **TIP**
>
> You may not feel like you're ready to interpret everything that happened in U.S. history, but the DBQ is a good place to be as smart as you can. This is the most important essay on the AP exam; your score on the DBQ makes up 22.5 percent of your final grade. Since the AP U.S. History exam is graded on the curve, to get a final grade of 4 or 5, you don't have to have a perfect score — just one that's better than the scores of most other AP test takers. You have a chance to get ahead of the pack on the DBQ because people tend to do poorly on this question due to a lack of organization.

# DBQ SCORES

All essays on the AP are scored by test graders on a scale from 0 (awful) to 9 (perfect). The average score on the DBQ in recent years has been a pathetic 3. With practice you can do better than that, and when you do, your final score improves dramatically.

The teachers behind the AP want you to think, not just memorize. For that reason, the highest scores on the DBQ go to students who have developed a clear thesis or way of understanding the era of their assigned documents. Here are the guidelines the test graders use for scoring the DBQ.

# The 8-to-9 essay

Only a few hundred students — about a tenth of 1 percent — get a 9. A few thousand — still less than 1 percent — get an 8. An essay that earns an 8 or 9 has these characteristics:

- Contains a well-developed thesis that may explain most of the changes within the DBQ era

- Supports the thesis with an effective analysis of economic, social, and political trends

- Effectively uses a substantial number of documents

- Supports or proves the thesis with substantial (ideally, at least 50 percent) and relevant outside information

- May contain minor errors

- Is clearly organized and well-written

# The 5-to-7 essay

Fewer than 2 percent of test takers get a score of 7; around 4 percent get a score of 6; and 10 percent score a 5. An essay that scores in the range of 5 to 7 has these characteristics:

- Contains a thesis that explains many of the changes within the era

- Has a limited analysis of the information supporting the thesis

- Effectively uses some documents

- Supports the thesis with some outside information for proof

- May have some errors that don't seriously get in the way of main essay points

- Shows acceptable organization and writing; language errors don't stop understanding

# The 2-to-4 essay

Unfortunately, scores in the 2 to 4 range are the most common. About 18 percent of test takers get a 4; around 30 percent get a 3 (3.16 is the average DBQ score); and 27 percent get only a 2. An essay within this scoring range has these characteristics:

- Contains a limited or undeveloped thesis

- Lacks analysis and deals with questions in a simplistic way

- Just parrots back a laundry list of documents

- Contains little outside information or includes information that's wrong

- May contain substantial factual errors

- Is poorly organized and/or poorly written

## The 0-to-1 essay

Seven percent of test takers get a 1; about half a percent get a 0 (and another half a percent get nothing because they apparently drifted off before they got to the DBQ). An essay earning a 0 or 1 has these characteristics:

- Lacks a thesis or just restates the question
- Shows the test taker doesn't really understand the question
- Shows the test taker has little understanding of the documents or just ignores them
- Contains no outside information
- Contains wrong information
- Is badly written

# PAT: A STRATEGY FOR ANSWERING DOCUMENT-BASED QUESTIONS

To do well on the DBQ, you need a strategy to follow. One such strategy is the PAT system. PAT stands for proof, analysis, and thesis. This system begins with framing your essay. The best way to learn how to do that is through practice. Your practice starts with a sample question based on Reconstruction in the South (see Chapter 13 for more information). In this section, I share tips on answering the sample question and how to apply the PAT method when writing your answer.

To write a winning answer for *any* DBQ, you first have to understand the question. Unfortunately, understanding the question is where a large number of DBQ answers begin to go wrong. To avoid this scenario in your own essay, follow these steps to prepare yourself before writing your answer.

1. **Read the question and sweep your brain for *proof by proofreading*, which is the beginning of the PAT system.** Don't even read the documents until you have taken a sober inventory of what you know about the question. Don't worry — you'll remember more as you go. Just note on the question book every related event and theme you can think of off the top of your head related to the question — before you read the documents.

2. **Read the documents twice; on the second round, circle words within the documents that you may want to refer to in your essay.**

3. **Do a little *analysis* — the second component in the PAT method.** What are some points you want to make about the question, and how does the information you have support these points? Jot quick notes in the question book.

> **TIP**
>
> When you're looking for space to write in the question book, don't skip ahead to read the other regular essays. Deal with the regular essays when you get to them; you have no reason to get distracted now. Chapter 5 explains how to write the regular essays.

4. **At *thesis* time — the final step and solid foundation in the PAT approach — you argue your idea with analysis, focusing on one major point in each body paragraph.** State your thesis in the first paragraph and restate it (with proof) in the last paragraph. Remember to take a stand! It doesn't matter whether you're wrong; historians love to argue. Most of the topics presented in the DBQ do not have a single accepted interpretation; in other words, there is no one right answer.

The benefit of structuring your DBQ argument under the PAT system is that you don't have to be perfect to win; *you* are the judge of history. The fact that you can corral evidence and use proof and analysis to support a clear thesis makes you a contender for a high score. And you don't have to be very high to get above the average score of 3; just keep citing proof.

## Writing a good thesis

A clear thesis stops a bored reader dead in her tracks and makes her pay attention to your analysis and proof. Make sure your thesis provides a philosophy or road map for everything in your essay. In the Reconstruction example shown in the next section, the thesis could be "The South's resistance was too strong for Reconstruction to work" or "The North succeeded in changing a primitive slave society in the South into the beginnings of a modern, if racist, culture." Remember, don't just rewrite the question. Take a stand.

## Using appropriate proof

A good paper successfully uses three pieces of proof in each body paragraph, taken from a mix of outside information and document analysis. Most DBQs are presented in chronological order. Because you'll arrange your essay by analysis points, you probably won't cite the documents in letter order, and your essay won't look like a laundry list. Just remember to use every document that fits into your analysis; it's okay if you don't use them all. It's better to use four or five documents well than to use all of them poorly.

Defend your point, but don't get *too* creative. Remember, your reader, who has only about two minutes to read each essay, may be getting a little blurry from reading hundreds of versions of the same essay. Your test scorer is looking for analysis and proof, and he doesn't have much time to find it, so don't confuse him. State your thesis clearly and simply. Cite the documents (with document letters bracketed) and underline your outside evidence. Stick to one major thesis; don't try to snow the reader with a bunch of mini-concepts. Even if they are not perfect, make sure the facts you use support your analysis and thesis points.

# SAMPLE DOCUMENT-BASED QUESTION: THE RECONSTRUCTION

Here's a DBQ like the one that a third of a million students will be answering on the upcoming AP U.S. History exam. As you read it, remember that, during the actual AP exam, you'll have 15 minutes to read the material and 45 minutes to write your answer. The documents are original source material, so they contain some misspelling and bad grammar.

# The question and source documents

**Directions:** The following question requires you to construct a coherent essay that integrates your interpretation of Documents A through F *and* your knowledge of the period referred to in the question. Only essays that both cite key pieces of evidence from the documents and draw on outside knowledge of the period will earn high scores.

1. Discuss the experience of Reconstruction in the South following the Civil War. What factors influenced the lives of the people affected by Reconstruction in both the South and the North? How did Reconstruction change over time, and what motivated these changes?

## Document A

Source: Letter from black Union soldiers

June 1865

Genl We the soldiers of the 36 U.S.Col Reg[t] Humbly petition to you to alter the Affairs at Roanoke Island. We have served in the US Army faithfully and don our duty to our Country, for which we thank God (that we had the opportunity) but at the same time our family's are suffering at Roanoke Island N.C.

1 When we were enlisted in the service we were prommised that our wifes and family's should receive rations from goverment. The rations for our wifes and family's have been (and are now cut down) to one half the regular ration. Consequently three or four days out of every ten days, thee have nothing to eat. at the same time our ration's are stolen from the ration house by Mr Streeter the Ass[t] Sup[t] at the Island (and others) and sold while our family's are suffering for some thing to eat.

2nd Mr Steeter the Ass[t] Sup[t] of Negro aff's at Roanoke Island is a througher Cooper head a man who says that he is no part of a Abolitionist. takes no care of the colored people and has no Simpathy with the colored people. A man who kicks our wives and children out of the ration house or commissary, he takes no notice of their actual suffering and sells the rations and allows it to be sold, and our family's suffer for something to eat.

## Document B

Source: Andrew Johnson vetoing the Reconstruction Act of 1867

It is plain that the authority here given to the military officer amounts to absolute despotism. But to make it still more unendurable, the bill provides that it may be delegated to as many subordinates as he chooses to appoint, for it declares that he shall "punish or cause to be punished."

Such a power has not been wielded by any monarch in England for more than five hundred years. In all that time no people who speak the English language have borne such servitude. It reduces the whole population of the ten States — all persons, of every color, sex, and condition, and every stranger within their limits — to the most abject and degrading slavery. No master ever had a control so absolute over the slaves as this bill gives to the military officers over both white and colored persons.

## Document C

Source: Charles Sumner on the Impeachment Trial of Andrew Johnson, 1868

I would not in this judgment depart from that moderation which belongs to the occasion; but God forbid that, when called to deal with so great an offender, I should affect a coldness which I cannot feel. Slavery has been our worst enemy, assailing all, murdering our children, filling our homes with mourning, and darkening the land with tragedy; and now it rears its crest anew, with Andrew Johnson as its representative. Through him it assumes once more to rule the Republic and to impose its cruel law. The enormity of his conduct is aggravated by his bare faced treachery. He once declared himself the Moses of the colored race. Behold him now the Pharaoh. With such treachery in such a cause there can be no parley. Every sentiment, every conviction, every vow against slavery must now be directed against him. Pharaoh is at the bar of the Senate for judgment.

## Document D

Source: Ulysses S. Grant's first inaugural address, 1869

The country having just emerged from a great rebellion, many questions will come before it for settlement in the next four years which preceding Administrations have never had to deal with. In meeting these it is desirable that they should be approached calmly, without prejudice, hate, or sectional pride, remembering that the greatest good to the greatest number is the object to be attained.

This requires security of person, property, and free religious and political opinion in every part of our common country, without regard to local prejudice. All laws to secure these ends will receive my best efforts for their enforcement.

## Document E

Source: Blanche K. Bruce, Black Senator Temporarily Elected under Reconstruction, Speech in the Senate, 1876

The evidence in hand and accessible will show beyond peradventure that in many parts of the State corrupt and violent influences were brought to bear upon the registrars of voters, thus materially affecting the character of the voting or poll lists; upon the inspectors of election, prejudicially and unfairly thereby changing the number of votes cast; and, finally, threats and violence were practiced directly upon the masses of voters in such measures and strength as to produce grave apprehensions for their personal safety and as to deter them from the exercise of their political franchises.

It will not accord with the laws of nature or history to brand colored people a race of cowards. On more than one historic field, beginning in 1776 and coming down to this centennial year of the Republic, they have attested in blood their courage as well as a love of liberty — I ask Senators to believe that no consideration of fear or personal danger has kept us quiet and forbearing under the provocations and wrongs that have so sorely tried our souls. But feeling kindly toward our white fellow-citizens, appreciating the good purposes and politics of the better classes, and, above all, abhorring a war of races. we determined to wait until such time as an appeal to the good sense and justice of the American people could be made.

**Document F**

Source: Nat Crippens, black historian after Reconstruction, 1880-1965

> Until the civil rights movement overturned systematic segregation, thousands of African Americans and other minorities were brutally maimed or killed by white vigilantes taking the law into their hands. Established law, which codified white supremacy, failed to protect the civil rights of black citizens. In the end, white segregation rested on open violence.
>
> At the turn of the century, lynchings occurred every week, and most of the victims, denied the due process of courts, were innocent of the charges held against them. Some were not even accused of having committed a crime.

# Answering the Reconstruction DBQ

The secret to successful DBQ essays is using both the documents presented *and* relevant outside information from the period covered by the documents. To do this successfully, you need to have a plan. That plan is based on the PAT method for scoring high on essay questions (refer to the earlier section "PAT: A Strategy for Answering Document-Based Questions").

## Taking notes in the question book

First, the proof. The question book that contains your essay challenges and documents is also the place for you to make notes during the AP exam. Use the essay-writing booklet only for your essays; make notes in the question book.

Read the DBQ question twice. The second time through, carefully circle the key words in the assignment:

> 1. Discuss the experience of Reconstruction in the South following the Civil War. What factors influenced the lives of the people affected by Reconstruction in both the South and the North? How did Reconstruction change over time, and what motivated these changes?

*Before you even read the documents,* list proof by making notes in the question book about themes and events you remember from this period. You're going to use these events as proof to support the thesis that forms the backbone of your DBQ essay. You're wise to record your outside history knowledge before the documents distract you from what you already know.

Now read the documents. Circle the most important points in each primary source. You'll weave references to each of several documents in your essay. To make your writing more than a list of the documents, show how each reference supports your central point. For maximum impact, base your essay on a thesis, analyzed in at least three main points and defended with proof from both your outside history knowledge and the documents.

## Using analysis

After you have your outside history knowledge written down and your document proof circled in the question book, you're ready to proceed to an analysis of the question which will produce your thesis. Read the question one last time, paying careful attention to the words you circled.

## Winning points with the test grader

Historians like to argue about events and trends that are old enough to have developed some proof. Can't decide who should win the next election? That's nothing to historians, who are still arguing about the causes of World War I. You need to remember two things about the person who grades your DBQ: She'll be overwhelmed by piles of tests, and she'll be a historian. When historians don't agree about causes (which is usually), they love to argue about trends and documents. For extra credit with your historian-grader, join in the professional discussion by doing these things:

■ **Defining your terms clearly:** In the sample question cited, an essay might start with "The term 'Reconstruction' has been used to signify the formal programs enacted by the United States government from the period following the end of the Civil War and including the period up until 1877 during which the national government maintained troops in the South. It can also mean the social and political changes including but not limited to government programs during that period. In this essay, I am using the term 'Reconstruction' in the second sense to include all social and political changes." Defining terms is the first step in most professional writing.

■ **Admitting that the other side may have a point counter to your thesis and then attacking that point with analysis:** This method is called the *straw-man argument*. Don't think that you need to neglect documents that seem to run counter to your thesis. You can deal with seemingly contrary proof through analysis and gain extra test grader credit. If you have the time, analyze the documents by date and author to show how the author's social bias fits into an ongoing cultural trend; this strategy always impresses historians.

■ **Not reaching for facts of which you are unsure:** When a teacher is grading lots of papers fast, he naturally notices a fact that is clearly wrong. This could be something as small as saying Federal troops were withdrawn under Reconstruction in 1879 instead of the correct date of 1877. Unfortunately for the test taker, teachers often note finding even a minor factual error by marking down a major decrease in score. If you're not sure of a name or year, use a generality such as *the president* or *around this time*. Never quote directly from a document; summarize.

For the Reconstruction question, your thesis might be

> The North's initially tough Reconstruction rules provided some protection for blacks in the South but caused a violent reaction from white Southerners threatened by change. Northerners with their own political agendas were unwilling to maintain strict Reconstruction enforcement. In 1877, 12 years after the end of the Civil War, the last Northern troops were withdrawn from the South, leaving Southern blacks free but segregated, with little political or economic opportunity.

This thesis becomes the first paragraph of your five- or six-paragraph DBQ essay. The second paragraph could talk about the angry retribution with which the North applied Reconstruction immediately after the Civil War. It could show that the North came within one vote of impeaching its own Union President after Andrew Johnson opposed tough measures by the Radical Republicans.

You should cite documents clearly in brackets, like this:

> After the war, even black Union soldiers who had fought bravely were treated badly in the South by their own white officers [Document A]. This demonstrates the ongoing racism after the war of even Northern officers.

> **TIP**
>
> Bracket all references to documents, but don't waste time copying the titles of the documents. The reader who grades your essay is an expert on this specific DBQ question; she has seen hundreds of essays on this year's DBQ, and she knows the document letters by heart.

Don't just refer to the documents as if you were trying to prove you can list them all. Show how they support your thesis. Weave documentary evidence throughout your essay on Reconstruction as proof of your thesis. Some documents require explanation to show that you understand them. For the DBQ, you're trying to show that you can analyze an era by using primary source documents; you're not just proving that you can read by spouting back what the documents say. It can even be good to cite documents that do not seem to support your thesis if you can show that they are biased by their source.

Here are some examples from the supplied documents:

> Grant's speech [Document D] suggests that the first elected President after the Civil War was sincere but even-handed in enforcing the law.

> Union Soldiers [Document A] and Crippens [Document F] record the level of violence against blacks (even from the North) which often went unreported in the contemporary press.

> Sumner [Document C] shows the strong feeling for strict enforcement of civil justice in the South coming from Northern Republicans immediately after the war.

## Grading the AP U.S. History exam

During one week in June of each year, more than 1,000 determined history teachers and professors gather at a college, usually in Texas, to grade more than 1 million AP U.S. History essays. About 400,000 students take this test — traditionally the largest single-subject College Board test in the world. Each student writes three essays, and all of these 1.2 million essays must be graded by hand.

If the teachers grade 1,000 essays each and spend 2 minutes reading and scoring each essay, the job will take them 33 hours of solid work. With training, consultation, and occasional breaks, that's a very full week. Some of the most experienced graders arrive early to serve as coordinators. These super-specialists develop specific criteria for each of the five exam questions. Coordinators and regular graders specialize in only one question; they learn the grading criteria for their question and stick to it.

The upside to this specialization is that each of your essays will be read by a different, custom-trained person who is guaranteed to completely understand the question. The downside is that if your answer is trying to hide the fact that you do not understand, your grader has seen it all a hundred times before. Leaders double-check a random sample of each grader's work to keep the grading consistent and fair.

Even as hard as they try, graders can make mistakes. If you're sure you've been given a much lower score than you deserve, you can pay the College Board a few extra dollars to have an independent reader rescore your test. No one has yet complained about getting too high a score.

# Bringing in outside proof

To get the highest grade on the DBQ essay, you need to bring in as much as half the evidence from outside the supplied documents. Any outside evidence is good, so highlight what you have. For this Reconstruction DBQ, you want to mention as outside proof items like the following:

- The Thirteenth, Fourteenth, and Fifteenth Amendments to the Constitution ended slavery and intended to give equal protection of the law and the vote to all males.

- In economics, Reconstruction saw the end of the Southern plantation economy and the beginning of sharecropping. You might mention how that changed the South. The North's industrial base continued to grow, and its own economy drew Northern attention away from trouble in the South.

- The Civil Rights Bill of 1866 didn't actually overturn Black Code laws in the South; the Supreme Court limited the application of this early civil-rights legislation to only national laws. Southern states later adopted Jim Crow laws to further limit the rights of blacks.

- Under early Reconstruction rules, former slaves — but not Confederate leaders — could vote in Southern state elections. Southern blacks helped pass important social legislation, including the establishment of public schools for all citizens. After the Southern states officially rejoined the Union, local white officials made their own laws and quickly found ways to keep blacks from voting.

- President Hayes agreed to withdraw all troops from the South in 1877 as part of a deal to win a disputed election.

- The Ku Klux Klan and other groups orchestrated repressive violence against blacks in the South.

- In reaction to what it viewed as harsh Reconstruction pushed by Republicans, the Solid South voted Democratic for 75 years until the early 1960s. When the Democratic Party sided with the civil rights movement in the 1960s, it did so knowing that Democratic politicians would lose the votes of what had been called the "Solid South." Reconstruction and its aftermath affect U.S. politics to this day.

The length of a DBQ response should be five or six paragraphs. The first paragraph states the thesis; the last paragraph reiterates the thesis and proof. The middle paragraphs provide point-by-point analysis, supported by document citations and outside information.

> **TIP**
>
> Underline the names of all outside information and dates, like this: Solid South, Civil Rights Bill of 1866, Jim Crow. This method helps make sure that test graders clearly see the outside information you're submitting. Test readers score so many essays so quickly that they have only a minute to see information you've spent months absorbing.

# 5

# Writing AP-Quality Essays

- How to manage the time allotted for the regular essay portion of the AP History test
- How to apply the proof, analysis, and thesis (PAT) method of response
- Strategies for improving your regular essay scores

During the last part of the AP U.S. History exam, right after you complete the Document-Based Question (DBQ — covered in Chapter 4), you have a little more than one hour to write answers to two regular essay questions. At this point, the test is about time- and fact-management — careful but direct selection of one of the two questions in Part B and then one of the two questions in Part C. This chapter gives you some tips on how fast writers select and write their essay answers for a winning score.

## HOW TO HANDLE TIMING

Without a break, you need to go from an insightful discussion of the Document-Based Question to carefully writing two regular essays in about an hour. These regular essays are officially known as

Section II, Part B and Part C of the test. They're "regular" only compared with the DBQ; in these last two essays, you don't have any documents to worry about (or lean on). You *do* have thought-provoking history problems that require a combination of analysis and appropriate facts.

When you get started on these last two essays is suggested on the test, but it's not mandatory. After the 15-minute required reading time that begins your Section II period, you have a grand total of 1 hour and 55 minutes to write the DBQ and the Part B and Part C essays. The test proctor will pop up like a human alarm clock to remind you when the recommended time to move on to the next section has arrived. After the 45 minutes recommended for writing the DBQ, your test monitor will say, "You should now move on to Part B." Although you don't have to, you are wise to pretty closely follow this advice and move to the regular essays if you have not done so already.

You have a recommended 70 minutes to devote to both regular essays. The College Board suggests you spend 5 minutes planning and 30 minutes writing each one. There is no rule that you have to work exactly 35 minutes on each of the essays in Part B and Part C. Just don't move too much time from one part to the other; both parts are worth the same number of points, and a great score on one won't make up for a 0 on the other. Do not forget to leave time to check your work.

As on the DBQ, you have a chance to get ahead against a slow field on these essay questions. The AP U.S. History exam is graded on a curve. To win a 4 or 5 as your final grade, your test score doesn't have to be perfect; it just has to be better than that of most other AP test takers.

> **TIP**
>
> Although the DBQ section has the most credit (22.5 percent of the total test) and the most writing time assigned to it (45 minutes), Parts B and C are definitely worth the effort. Each of these regular essays represents almost 14 percent of the exam — a total of 27.5 percent for both.
>
> The average student performance on the regular essay questions is even slightly worse than the low scores on the DBQ, because people are running out of gas by the time they get to them. When *you* get there, remember that you're almost to the finish line; you just need one last burst of careful writing to take advantage of the situation. The essays on the AP are scored on a scale from 0 (for no intelligence detected) to 9 (for Shakespeare reborn). The average score on the regular essay questions in recent years has been less than 3 on the 9-point scale. You can do better than that even if you're a bit spotty on some facts. If Woody Allen was right that 80 percent of success is showing up, then the other 20 percent depends on careful communication.

# SELECTING THE BEST QUESTIONS

Although they are often referred to as "regular essays" to distinguish them from the DBQ, the free response topics require a high level of information and presentation. The AP is, after all, a college test you take before you've had any college classes. The featured topics give you an opportunity to write about a limited period of history.

You will choose your best *prompts* (essay questions), one from Part B and one from Part C. In general, each topic covers a 20- to 50-year history range from different time periods. For example, recent exams have asked about differences in colonial policy, responses to the French and Indian War, the North and South before the Civil War, and cultural changes in the 1920s.

You will have a choice of four time periods, with the topic limiting the scope of your answer to a particular issue during that period. You need to pick topics that you can come up with the greatest number of related events for. Getting the best score on these essays takes a combination of knowledge and reasoning. (If you want to know how common that combined skill-set is in the AP U.S. History test-taking population, just look at the average score: 2.86 on a scale of 9. Don't worry; you can do better.)

> **TIP**
>
> You don't have to answer the two regular essay questions in order. The specialist essay readers will find the essay they grade by its number in your answer book. You can read all four essay prompts and pick the one that seems easiest for you so you can get a running start. Just remember to do one essay from Part B and one from Part C. To leave time for both, switch to the next essay within a few minutes of the 35-minute advisory you get from the test proctor. Even better, bring a watch and keep your own time.

## Writing like a professor

You know that your essay will be graded by a slightly bleary-eyed history teacher. One thing that professors insist on in their professional journals is that writers define their terms. If your essay question asks for the impact of changes on the common man, state the way you define "common man." If you're writing about the Progressive movement, use a sentence in the first paragraph to say what that word means. You can signal your high-level understanding of academic protocol by using this well-loved professional prelude: "It is important to define terms. By the Progressive movement, I mean newly organized initiatives in the early 1900s that had a goal of efficiency and fairness in U.S. society, economy, and government." Defining a term takes only a sentence and can impress a test grader.

If you're asked to assess the validity of a statement, you've just been given an invitation to jump into the middle of an argument. You may see something like this: "Assess the validity of this statement: The New Deal brought an end to the Great Depression." You need to say what *you* think. Take a position and make it your thesis statement. Here are two example theses:

> Although economic problems remained that were not settled until after the U.S. entry into World War II, New Deal programs were effective in blunting the worst problems of the Great Depression.

> Although New Deal programs created a public perception of progress, they were largely ineffective in dealing with the economic roots of the Great Depression.

Take note that both thesis statements begin with the effective word *although*. The use of this gentle, reasonable word signals that you're being intellectually fair in your thesis position by acknowledging from the start the limits of your argument. Professors know that modest arguments provide a safety shield from academic attack.

Later in each thesis statement, you can use more qualifying words to make the thesis argument easier to defend. The first example says "effective in *blunting* the *worst* problems." That way, you have to defend only *blunting* (not actually solving) and *worst* (but not all) problems. In the second version, the thesis reads "*largely* ineffective in dealing with the economic *roots*," so that the essay can admit that the New Deal was effective sometimes on the little issues but not the answer for solving problems at the economic *roots*, or causes, of the Great Depression. Then writers of these two essays can go on to define *worst* problems or economic *roots* in a way that makes their thesis arguments seem like the only reasonable interpretation.

# Using proof, analysis, and thesis (PAT)

Writing regular essays that score well involves applying the proof, analysis, and thesis (PAT) approach (see Chapter 4) to the political, economic, and social trends that win points with test graders (see Chapter 1). With the PAT formula, you select everything you know about the topic as proof and then analyze that proof to support your own theory about the question. The proof you use can be trends, people, or events. In the DBQ (Chapter 4), the documents themselves supply some of these proof points; with regular essays, it's just you and your history knowledge bank.

The regular essay questions are an interesting combination of political, economic, and social trends. Here are some basic strategies:

- You need to be able to combine developments in different areas, such as the political outcomes of social issues or the economic influence on policy decisions. For example, you may have a chance to discuss changes in the U.S. government brought on by urbanization or the role of cotton and money in the Civil War.

- You have to analyze common themes that run through an extended period — how women's rights changed society from 1830 to 1930, for example.

- You should show how the same events had a different effect on specific groups in the population. An example could be the impact of the Great Depression of the 1930s on women, men, and minority groups in the United States.

On the regular essay questions, the grader judges you on the thesis you develop, the quality of your analysis, and the historic proof you use to support your thesis. When you're figuring out your essay, plan what you're going to write in PAT order:

1. **Proof:** List in the question booklet all the political, economic, and social facts you can remember about the essay topic.

2. **Analysis:** Figure out how these facts can go together to explain the essay topic.

3. **Thesis:** Develop an opinion to tie the facts together with the essay topic.

When you actually write the essay, PAT turns into TAP: First, you state your thesis, and then you provide analysis supported by proof. Make an outline in the question book before your begin.

> **TIP**
>
> Make sure your answer has at least a vague relationship to the question. It doesn't have to be perfect; you want to show off any knowledge you have in the general area. Just don't try writing about 1800s shipping if the question is about the Mayflower.

The official AP position is that your supported argument is more important than the amount of factual information you produce. In other words, they want students who think, not just people who remember words. You can't write down only a laundry list of names, trends, and events; you have to show how they fit together. This idea fits the great humanistic tradition of scholarship. In the rest of this chapter, you can see how supporting an argument works in practice.

# GRADING CRITERIA FOR ESSAY QUESTIONS

The following list of grading criteria may look daunting, but remember, the average score on AP essay questions only reaches the second to lowest rung. Do better and you are on your way to a high score.

Because the AP values connections even more than reciting historic facts, you want to make your essays on any topic show how trends interact. Your essays should stay positive. Slavery and the Trail of Tears, for example, are blots on the U.S. record of freedom (see Chapter 11), but they're also part of trends that need to be viewed within the context of their times. Save political speeches for political meetings; when you're taking a test with your grade hanging in the balance, emphasize unity and progress.

By starting and concluding with a clear thesis, you help your overworked, weary grader find what he's looking for: a sense of meaning. Make sure the hurried test grader sees the proof you're using by underlining two or three key phrases in your essay. Highlighting facts about trends and dealing with them in paragraphs separated into political, economic, and social themes that all connect to your thesis makes for an essay that clearly deserves a good score. Regular essays follow the same grading scale as the DBQ, with a high score of 9 and a low score of 0. The average grade for essays is in the 2 to 4 range.

**The 8-to-9 essay:**

- Contains a clear, well-developed thesis that deals with the question at hand
- Supports the thesis with a large amount of relevant information
- Analyzes the main categories completely (somewhat uneven treatment of the categories is okay)
- May contain minor errors

**The 5-to-7 essay:**

- Contains a thesis that deals only partially with the question
- Supports the thesis with a modest amount of relevant information
- Analyzes all categories at least somewhat; treatment of categories may be very uneven
- May contain errors that don't detract completely from the essay

**The 2-to-4 essay:**

- Restates the question without providing a clear thesis
- Provides either minimal facts or minimal application of the facts
- Doesn't analyze all the categories, but may get one or two in a general way
- Contains lots of errors

**The 0-to-1 essay:**

- Omits a thesis

- Doesn't make sense

- Displays little or no understanding of the question

- Contains major false statements

# CONVERTING QUESTIONS TO PAT ANSWERS

AP U.S. History essay-grading week is a busy time for the College Board. More than 1,000 teachers grade around 1.2 million essays in the course of a few days, sitting around tables with only one 20-minute break in the morning and afternoon — an example of hard work and dedication if ever there was one. The average reader could be covering as many as 1,000 essays, with only around 2 minutes to read each contribution.

The graders look quickly for proof and analysis supporting an overall thesis (PAT). Grading leaders develop clear criteria that the graders use for each essay, and each grader spends the whole time scoring only one question, over and over again.

The College Board makes grading a million plus essays as fair as it can, but no one has time to ponder garbled proof, vague analysis, or a thesis that's not clearly stated. For that reason, you want to make your PAT answers simple and direct.

Some football teams use a five-yards-and-glory strategy. They're not looking to score a touchdown on every play; they just want to gain five yards on each down with short passes and runs because, if they keep doing that, they'll move on down the field and eventually win. AP U.S. History essays are like that. You write approximately five paragraphs with a goal of showing that you know and can analyze historic information. You're not trying to list everything that went on during the era you're writing about. The official College Board policy is that carefully selected facts connected by a reasonable thesis is better than a long list that doesn't have a common theme.

Follow these suggestions to make sure your essay dodges the test hazards and emphasizes your strongest points:

- **Make sure you address all the parts of the free-response essay questions.** Missing a subtopic can affect your grade. Get all three PES parts: political, economic, and social.

- **If you can't remember a name or date, don't guess.** A wrong specific is worse than a possibly incorrect general. If you can't remember Seneca Falls in 1848, for example, say "an important women's-rights meeting before the Civil War." Don't let your grader see a clear error that she can use to slap you down.

- **Don't worry if the only essay questions available look hard.** If the questions are tough for you, they're tough for everyone. The test is scored on a curve, so grading is survival of the fittest. You could even get lucky. If you did well on the multiple-choice part of the exam and score very low on an essay, the grading coordinator may automatically ask that your essay be reread to make sure you're not being underscored. You could have two chances to make an impression.

■ **Don't get anxious and start to write before you really understand the question.** You may be missing the main point of the prompt while you're rattling off random facts. Carpenters have a saying: "Measure twice, cut once." You won't have a chance for a second cut at your essay, so read the question prompt twice.

■ **Jot down important things in the question book.** Circle the key words and make notes before you write.

■ **Follow standard essay organization for a five-paragraph essay.** The first paragraph is the introduction and includes your thesis statement. Each of the body paragraphs has a different theme that supports the thesis. A good goal is to have three proof facts in each of the body paragraphs. (Deemphasize your weakest point by putting it in the middle.) The final paragraph of your essay restates the thesis in slightly different words and provides a summary that mentions the themes of the middle paragraphs.

■ **If the prompt decides the themes for you, address those themes in the order given.** If a question asks how post–Civil War government policies affected American Indians, Western settlement, and economic development, for example, the middle paragraphs of your essay need to deal one-by-one with American Indians, settlement, and development. If no clear division is obvious from the prompt, write a paragraph each on *political* events, *economic* conditions, and *social* trends.

■ **Stay on-topic.** Don't let your essay wander around the subject like some drunk in a bar. Check back during the writing of each paragraph to make sure what you're saying supports the thesis in the introduction.

■ **Tie each trend or event you mention to the theme of your essay.** You don't want to introduce historic facts just to prove you know something. Fortunately, you shouldn't have to exclude too many facts; you can usually find a way to logically tie almost any trend or event to the theme you're supporting.

■ **Make sure you tie your proof together with analysis to support your thesis.** You get no penalty for having a wrong thesis, but you sink fast if you don't use proof and analysis to support your theme.

## Analyzing an essay question

Here is an example of how to handle the kind of questions you'll find in Parts B and C. Suppose you get question like this in Part B:

**Directions:** Choose ONE question from this part. You are advised to spend 5 minutes planning and 30 minutes writing your answer. Cite relevant historical evidence in support of your generalizations, and present your arguments clearly and logically.

1. How did the New Deal (1932–1944) change U.S. society? Consider TWO of the following factors in your response:

   Social movements, economic development, political change

2. The period from 1824 to 1848 is often called the era of Jacksonian democracy. What social and political changes characterized this era?

For the sake of this example, assume that you choose Question 2, because you think you can recall more about this era and have a thesis point you want to make. (Check out Chapter 11 to familiarize yourself with the important things to know from this era.)

First, read the prompt twice. Circle the terms that are key parts of the prompt:

> **2.** The period from ⟨1824⟩ to ⟨1848⟩ is often called the era of ⟨Jacksonian democracy.⟩ What social and political ⟨changes⟩ characterized this era?

Make a list of what you know about this era. You could list a number of topics, but the following points would more than get you started:

- Election of 1824 (the Corrupt Bargain)
- Andrew Jackson elected in 1828 and 1832
- Trail of Tears
- Nullification
- Spoils system
- Increased voter turnout
- 1848 women's rights meeting at Seneca Falls
- Universal white male suffrage
- Defeat of the Bank of the U.S.

Now that you have your proof facts, you're ready to apply the PAT formula. Your analysis will support your thesis.

## Settling on your thesis

Forming a thesis isn't something you can get wrong. Historians love to argue, and one of the topics they argue about is the era of Andrew Jackson. History changes: Jackson has gone from American hero to dangerous redneck to rough but effective champion of the common man. The only position you can take that is wrong on an AP essay question is to fail to have a clear point of view. You know what you've been taught, but what do you *believe* about Jacksonian democracy? Imagine what you would teach to someone else.

A thesis — your point of view — unifies your essay and makes it worthy of a higher score. Just think about your grading audience as one tired teacher who has endured hundreds of unfocused fluff-a-thons loosely connected to the Jackson era. Give him something clear and decisive, and he'll thank you with a better grade.

For most history questions, you can go in either of two broad directions with a thesis: mainstream history or revisionist argument. Following are examples of both in the case of the Jackson era:

> **Mainstream:** The 1820s to 1840s was a time when the United States began to move toward being true to its democratic ideals.

> **Revisionist:** From the 1820s through the 1840s, the United States made some surface changes toward greater representation for the common man, but these changes were largely symbolic. The real economic and social conditions of slavery and sectionalism changed little during this period.

As much as you may hate to agree with mass opinion, you should go with the mainstream view on this one. The Jackson era really did involve a move toward democratic ideals. Think for yourself, but when you can see both sides of an argument, it is better to go with the most accepted position on which you have the most proof.

## Planning the essay

Now you're ready to plan the essay. You want to have a five-paragraph essay, structured as follows:

- The thesis anchors the first paragraph.

- The three body paragraphs support your central point (ideally with three pieces of analysis each).

- The final paragraph reiterates and amplifies the thesis.

Look for the subjects of the three body paragraphs. Sifting through the history topics in your notes, you see that they can be arranged in political, economic, and social categories. Political events include elections, increased voter turnout, universal white-male suffrage, and the spoils system. Economic trends include nullification and the defeat of the Bank of the U.S. Social happenings include the Trail of Tears, the Second Great Awakening, and women's rights.

## Writing the essay

Following about five minutes of planning, you're ready to write the essay. Keep the terms that form the proof for your thesis in capital letters to make them easier for the grader to see when she's reading quickly. Let the English teachers complain about unnecessary capitalization and underlining; this exam is about history, and you're in a high-traffic situation. Capitalizing provides a road marker to help direct your reader to the destination.

In another high-traffic detour from the refined world of English composition, you may want to start your essay with the thesis sentence, not keep it waiting demurely for the end of the first paragraph. You may also want to actually label it "Thesis" so that it's difficult to miss. Make sure the thesis doesn't just repeat the question; after reading hundreds of essays, the grading teacher knows what the question is. Your thesis should restate the prompt with your own thoughts to show that you understand it.

Consider beginning your thesis with the magic word *although,* which (as explained in Chapter 4) is how to acknowledge that the other side may have a point counter to your thesis. This approach makes you look fair and allows you to counter possible objections to your argument on your own terms. In full debate, developing your opponent's argument and then destroying it is called the *straw-man argument.* The use of the word *although* is a quickie version of the straw-man move.

TIP

Give your essay a title. A title doesn't cost anything and makes the essay look official.

# Checking out a sample essay

Here's a sample essay that contains a clear thesis, reasonable analysis, and enough historical proof to ring the test grader's bell.

### Democracy Comes to the United States in the Jackson Era

Thesis: Although important issues like slavery and states' rights remained unresolved, the period from the 1820s to the 1840s, known as the Jackson era, was a time when the United States began to move toward being true to its democratic ideals. This era saw the increase in the power of ordinary people in political, economic and social areas. These power changes were brought home to people through Religious and Moral Reform movements and through Political Campaigns that were conducted on a large public scale for the first time. Citizens began to see themselves as having real freedom to change their own lives and the course of the nation in which they lived.

The most important political event was the introduction of white Universal Male Suffrage in most states in the early 1820s. Although it was a far cry from the voting rights we enjoy now, it was an unimagined freedom in earlier days, when voting was limited by property, class, and race. The newly enfranchised citizens responded by increasing Voter Turnout by large numbers. People began to see themselves as more powerful, not just as the pawns of destiny. Greater democracy spelled the end of leaders selected by small elites and the beginning of the election of popular national leaders like Andrew Jackson in 1848 and 1832. Even the Spoils System can be seen as a democratization of public employment.

The Second Great Awakening increased social as well as spiritual growth by getting people together away from the farm in newly organized religious congregations. These congregations in turn provided a religious base for small but growing Temperance, Abolitionist, and Women's Suffrage movements. The era ended with a symbolically important women's meeting at Seneca Falls, New York, in 1848. Even an event that we now view as negative, such as the Trail of Tears removal of American Indians from the South, had its beginning in increased public social pressure for land.

Economics are never far from any social or political change. The birth of the Industrial Revolution with factory jobs offered urban alternatives to rural isolation. The rising price of Cotton and Slaves brought prosperity to Southerners and their Northern financiers. Rapidly improving transportation by Canal, Railroad, and Steamship made the sale of crops and manufactured goods into the beginning of a National Economy. Transportation allowed ordinary people to move where they wanted to go to seek a new fortune. Even the Nullification Crisis, with its argument about tariffs, was a sign of the economic strain on sectionalism brought by an increasingly powerful National Interest.

When Thomas Jefferson wrote "Life, Liberty, and the Pursuit of Happiness," most of his upper-class congressional colleagues could recognize the theory of freedom only as it applied to them and people of their class. Most common people could not vote and had no time for economic and social betterment. That's why the Founding Fathers created the Electoral College and chose senators and presidents in private meetings. But with the new nation, the theory of freedom had become an ideal. As reform improved the power of ordinary people, those people were more likely to use their power to improve social, political, and economic life. The era of Jacksonian Democracy, with its emphasis on personal beliefs and more universal suffrage, brought the idea of freedom that had begun in the American Revolution to reality: the beginnings of real democracy in the United States.

## Unintentionally humorous answers

Apparently, some people studied even less for their history exams than your slacker friends. Here are some essay responses gone terribly wrong:

"It was an age of great inventions and discoveries. Gutenberg invented removable type and the Bible. Another important invention was the circulation of blood. Sir Walter Raleigh is a historical figure because he invented cigarettes and started smoking. And Sir Francis Drake circumcised the world with a 100 foot clipper.

Later, the Pilgrims crossed the ocean, and this was called Pilgrim's Progress. The winter of 1620 was a hard one for the settlers. Many people died and many babies were born. Captain John Smith was responsible for all this.

One of the causes of the Revolutionary War was the English put tacks in their tea. Also, the colonists would send their parcels through the post without stamps. Finally the colonists won the War and no longer had to pay for taxis. Delegates from the original 13 states formed the Contented Congress. Thomas Jefferson, a Virgin, and Benjamin Franklin were two singers of the Declaration of Independence. Franklin discovered electricity by rubbing two cats backwards and declared, "A horse divided against itself cannot stand." Franklin died in 1790 and is still dead.

Soon the Constitution of the United States was adopted to secure domestic hostility. Under the constitution the people enjoyed the right to keep bare arms.

Abraham Lincoln became America's greatest Precedent. His mother died in infancy, and he was born in a log cabin which he built with his own hands. Abraham Lincoln freed the slaves by signing the Emasculation Proclamation.

The nineteenth century was a time of a great many thoughts and inventions. People stopped reproducing by hand and started reproducing by machine. The invention of the steamboat caused a network of rivers to spring up.

World War I broke out around 1912–1914. Germany was on one side of France and Russia was on the other. At war people get killed, and then they aren't people any more, but friends. Peace was proclaimed at Versigh, which was attended by George Loid, Primal Minister of England. President Wilson arrived with 14 pointers."

# Wrapping up the essay plan

Following are some final pointers to help you improve your essay and your score:

- **Use simple, short sentences.** Your audience, the test grader, has seen a lot of convoluted essays and may well be tired from a long day of grading. Make it easy for her to follow your theme.

- **Throw in a big history term, if you know one.** Here are some terms beloved to teachers: expansionism, utopia, ratification, peculiar institution (slavery), oligarchy, nativism, mercantilism, jingoism, imperialism, egalitarian, capitalism, and the all-time American favorite, Manifest Destiny. But don't try to force in terms you don't understand; you'll get caught and lose points.

■ **Take the time to write clearly and neatly.** Graders hate chicken-scratch writing and love clear printing. Your grader may be nearly blind from reading others' illegible writing by the time she gets to your essay, so make it easy for her. Compose each whole sentence in your mind *before* you put it down on paper. If you absolutely have to cross something out, do it neatly. But don't bother crossing out bad spelling; this test isn't English class. If the grader can recognize the word, she won't count off for bad spelling. By making too many corrections, you only call attention to your mistakes. If you really have to insert a line or even a paragraph, do it neatly. Write the words to be inserted clearly away from the main body of the essay; circle them; and draw a neat arrow to where they go in the essay. Don't use carets to crowd text on top of what you have already written. Keep your essay readable by thinking before you write.

■ **Smooth out the flow of your writing by using transition phrases.** Such phrases include "in addition," "furthermore," "also," and "in another example." When you're changing directions, use "however," "yet," and "although."

■ **Number your points.** Numbering lists of arguments makes it look like you have a plan. For example, "First, the New Deal never claimed to solve all the problems. Second, the Great Depression was caused by world as well as national problems. Third, even the best programs often took time to work."

■ **Use examples to back up your idea.** Nothing gets wooly faster than academic papers that are all about concepts without real-life examples. You start with this: "Third, even the best programs sometimes worked slowly." Then you add this: "Two examples of programs that had delayed effects were the WPA and CCC. In these programs, government-supported jobs eventually helped lift the economic fortunes of certain communities, but these examples took time to work."

■ **Make sure your last paragraph directly addresses the question.** This paragraph is the applause section, when you set yourself up for your well-earned high essay score. Tie up the loose ends by answering the original question clearly as you restate your thesis.

# II

# U.S. History from America's Beginning to Now

# 6

# American Indians from 20,000 BCE to 1491 CE

- Background of the American Indian
- Empires to the South
- Disease and change before European settlement

The AP U.S. History exam doesn't ask too many questions on American Indian history before Christopher Columbus, partly because high-school AP courses vary too much on pre-Columbian American history for the test makers to be sure what students have learned.

Although the AP may not have many questions on pre-Columbian America, you'll want to scan this chapter anyway as insurance, should an early-times question arise. Knowing as much as you can about the long years of this nation's American Indian forebears is important. After all, if the room you're sitting in were the history of human beings in North America, the amount of time European settlers and their descendants have lived here would be only one little corner.

# THE FIRST AMERICANS

Christopher Columbus wasn't looking for a new world in 1492; he was just trying to get to China without having to walk through Asia, as his Italian predecessor Marco Polo had done more than 200 years before. Polo had reported in his book *The Million* that China was full of untold riches. Columbus had a well-thumbed copy of Polo's story by his side as he dreamed of sailing to the riches of the East. He also saw a map based on one that Polo had brought back with him years before. On this map, you can still make out Europe, Asia, and Africa in rough form, right where they are supposed to be. What's missing is the entire New World.

Not surprisingly, when Columbus landed, he called the people he met *Indians*. They didn't look Chinese, so they must be Indians from the East Indies, related somehow to the India that Polo had talked about and where Alexander the Great had actually fought in the days of the ancient Greeks. It took six years of return voyages before Columbus confronted this inconvenient fact in a message to his royal sponsors: "I have come to believe that this is a mighty continent which was hitherto unknown . . . .Your Highnesses have an Other World here."

Of course, the people Columbus called Indians didn't think they were in a strange new world; they were home in the land that their legends told them had been theirs since the beginning of time. They knew every rock and tree and had a name for every valley and river. These first people had well-practiced ways of surviving with the thousands of plants and animals around them.

## 20,000 years before Columbus to Columbus's time

Even the first American Indians were relative newcomers to their lands when compared to those who had settled the Old World; human beings have lived in the New World for less than a fifth of the time they have been settled in Asia, Europe, and Africa. Human beings have lived in Africa, Europe, and Asia for at least 200,000 years. Then, about 20,000 years ago, an ice age froze over the water between what is now Siberia and Alaska. Hunters and their families, probably following migrating herds of game, walked across this convenient ice bridge to Alaska. Because it was cold, most kept heading south.

When the ice age ended about 10,000 years ago, the Bering Straits went back to being water, and the New World was cut off from the Old. This was okay for the American Indians; the same big thaw opened passes through the mountains to the south. Roaming gradually through the wilderness that still covers much of North America, the first people reached the tip of South America by 9,000 BCE, some 15,000 miles from the land bridge they had crossed from Siberia. That means they averaged about 1 mile of migration every 2 years.

In the year before Columbus landed, 100 million Indians probably inhabited the New World. More people lived in North and South America than in Europe. Only some of these first people whom Columbus called Indians were hunter-gatherers; most were farmers. The New World had cities before the Egyptians built the pyramids.

At the time of Columbus, the Aztec capital city Tenochtitlan (later Mexico City) was larger than any city in Europe. Unlike the dirty European cities of the 1400s, the Aztec capital had running water, clean streets, and botanical gardens. This beauty didn't lead to mellow living; as many as 5,000 human beings were sacrificed every year to please the Aztec king and his gods.

## The focus on Mesoamerican cultures

Whereas kingdoms like the Aztec and Incas were able to control large areas of land for a time, most American Indians were split into small tribes that spoke at least 2,000 different languages — ten times the number of languages spoken in Europe. American Indians spoke a lot of languages because they had little reason to conquer and consolidate with neighboring groups. Hunter-gatherers aren't very interested in dominating their neighbors. Only with the beginning of agriculture did property become worth seizing, and people were vulnerable to domination because they couldn't move away from valuable growing crops to avoid being conquered.

Agriculture also fed the large population centers. The Aztecs in Mexico, Mayans in Central America, and Incas in Peru built networks of roads and amazing cities with incredible buildings and artwork. They were experts at raising more than 100 varieties of corn — one kind for every taste and climate. One modern scientific journal calls the American Indians' development of many corn types from a barely edible wild plant the greatest feat of genetic engineering in history.

 **TIP**

> If the AP test has a question on pre-Columbian American Indians, it may well contain that favorite buzzword of people who write early-history tests: *Meso-america. Meso* means *middle* of the New World, as in south Mexico and Central America. This term throws a lot of people because it refers to an area that's not part of the current United States that you thought you were studying.

Questions about advanced southern American Indians may appear on the AP U.S. History test because historians know more about them than they know about the hunter-gatherers and early agriculturalists who peopled what's now the United States. The Mesoamerican culture area included some of the most complex and organized people of the Americas, including the Olmecs, the Mayans, and the Aztecs. These cultures developed advanced political systems; discovered technological, scientific, and mathematical concepts; and participated in long-distance road networks that covered hundreds of miles and resulted in the transmission of ideas and products.

# EARLY AMERICAN INDIAN EMPIRES

For the AP U.S. History exam, you need to know about the three great American Indian empires that existed hundreds of miles south of the current U.S. border: the Mayan empire, the Incan empire, and Aztec empire. The reason they're important is because these southern American Indian superstates influenced the development of the United States, both directly and indirectly.

The riches that the American Indian empires amassed with the gold and silver they discovered attracted the Spanish conquistadores. Easy conquests of large civilizations emboldened Europeans armed with guns and swords. Spanish riches sped the development of the New World and provided rich plunder for the buccaneers of other European nations.

The American Indian empires funded the Spanish empire. After the defeat of the Spanish Armada by England in 1588, other nations started colonies in the New World in hopes of finding similar riches. Many of these colonies were financed by private investors — undertakings that wouldn't have found support were it not for the Spanish experience with rich American Indian empires. There is more information on the colonial period in Chapter 7.

Tales of cities of gold eventually led explorers overland into what's now the American Southwest. Accounts of distant civilizations and hopefully rich new worlds to discover stirred European adventurers into action.

**Note:** The Maya, Inca, and Aztec empires were the three large American Indian empires encountered by Spanish explorers. In Mesoamerica, predecessor civilizations dated back as far as 2,000 years before the Spanish arrived but started some of the traditions common to later American Indian empires.

> **TIP**
>
> Don't confuse the Big Three American Indian empires. Just remember this:
>
> - "I'm not confused, AM I?" From north to south, the first letter of each of the three empires, in order from north to south, spell AM I. The Aztecs are in Mexico, the Mayans are in Central America, and the Inca are in South America.
> - In terms of age of the empires, they run MIA, as in "missing in action." Mayans are the oldest, followed by the Incas, and then the Aztecs. Both the Incas and the Aztecs got to rule for only a short time before the Spanish arrived. The Mayans had thousands of years to enjoy the limelight and were in serious decline when the Spanish arrived to end Mayan rule.

> **EXAMPLE**
>
> **Question:** What were the major American Indian empires encountered by Spanish explorers in Mesoamerica?
>
> **Answer:** The Mayan, Incan, and Aztec empires.

## The Mayan empire

North of present-day Panama and extending into what's now southern Mexico, the *Mayas* (800 CE) built temple cities with tall pyramids surrounding wide plazas in the mountains and rain forests. About 700 miles south of what's now Mexico City, the Mayan were a Mesoamerican civilization noted for having the only fully developed written language of the pre-Columbian Americas. They were also known for their intricate art, building techniques, and mathematical and astronomical developments. Mayan civilization continued until the arrival of the Spanish.

Mayan writing used a system similar to that of the early Egyptians and Chinese. Mayan scribes had picture words, called *glyphs,* that could stand for a noun or a syllable sound. The Mayan were productive farmers who grew early corn variants, called *maize,* in raised fields. The Mayan people never disappeared, neither with the rise of other powerful American Indian kingdoms nor with the arrival of the Spanish conquistadores.

Today, the Mayan and their descendants form sizable populations throughout the Mayan area and maintain a distinctive set of traditions and beliefs that are the result of the merger of pre-Columbian and post-conquest ideas. The Mayan may seem to worship in Christian churches, but many of their beliefs are thousands of years old.

# The Incan empire

The *Incas* (1400) are the latest pre-Columbian civilization based in the Andes of South America. Their empire began about 1,200 CE. At its height, the Incan empire stretched for 2,500 miles, a distance almost as long as the distance across the continental United States. From 1438 to 1533, the Incas used both conquest and peaceful assimilation to influence a large portion of western South America. The center of their empire was in the Andean mountain ranges, including modern Ecuador, Peru, western and south-central Bolivia, northwest Argentina, north and north-central Chile, and southern Colombia.

Incan palaces were surrounded by high walls made of huge, closely fitted stones. Like their Aztec empire neighbors to the north, the Incan people connected their vast holdings with paved roads. Their mountain towns include the stunning Machu Picchu. To allow farming in the mountains, the Incas developed a system of terraced agriculture fed by canals and aqueducts; they gave the world the tomato and the potato. Incan government and agriculture were well developed by the time the conquistador *Francisco Pizarro* (1532) managed to defeat them.

With just 180 men, 27 horses, and 1 cannon, Pizzaro often had to talk his way out of potential fights that could have easily wiped out his little band. The main type of battle in the Andes consisted of siege warfare, in which large numbers of drafted men were sent to overwhelm opponents.

Along with material superiority in the form of armor, weapons, and horses, the Spaniards acquired tens of thousands of native allies only too glad to end the Incan control of their territories. Combined, a few weapons and lots of Indian allies allowed the Spanish to capture the Incan emperor and subsequently throw the Incan ruling classes into a political struggle. The Spanish kept increasing their native allies until they had enough people and resources to launch a successful attack on the Incan capital city.

# The Aztec empire

The *Aztecs* (1300) were the youngest of the Big Three American Indian empires. As the northernmost empire in Mesoamerica, the Aztec developed around modern-day Mexico City in about 1,300 CE, ruling for about 200 years before Hernan Cortez and his Spanish army arrived to take over their empire. Mexico City was a city in the middle of a lake, with beautiful temples built along canals and a system of floating island gardens that fed much of the population.

Mexico City was connected with its provinces and tributary states by a system of roads usually maintained through tribute from local rulers. Because the people had no horses or any kind of wheeled vehicles, the roads were intended to facilitate fast foot travel. By order of the Aztecs, travelers had places to rest, eat, and even use a latrine at regular intervals — roughly every five to seven miles. Couriers with messages constantly traveled along those ways, keeping the Aztecs informed of events and reporting whether the roads needed work. Due to this steady surveillance, even women could travel alone — a fact that amazed the Spaniards because lone women hadn't been safe in Europe since the time of the Romans.

The Aztecs were a warlike people with an emperor, nobles, priests, tax collectors, and a merchant middle class. They captured prisoners in constant conflicts and used them for human sacrifices. American Indian enemies of the Aztecs' helped Cortez and his small band of brave and bloodthirsty soldiers conquer the Aztecs and kill their king. This event led to an uprising in Mexico City, from which Cortez barely escaped with his life. Other American Indians were glad to see the Aztecs removed from the complete power they'd enjoyed for only a comparative few years.

## Corn cultivation and American Indian civilizations

Corn made all the difference to American Indian civilization. The first planted-corn agriculture occurred in the Mexican highlands in about 5,000 BCE — a full 6,000 years after the first European people got to the New World and around the time large-scale crop-raising got going in Egypt and the Middle East. Corn-growing took 4,000 years to reach the American Southwest, where corn supported an advancing culture 1,000 years before the birth of Christ.

The Anazazis in what's now New Mexico managed to build an apartment house with more than 600 interconnecting rooms. When the Spanish explorers reached the Southwest, they found villages of terraced multistory buildings. (*Pueblo,* the Spanish word now used for these American Indian settlements and the people who lived in them, means *village.*)

Two thousand years later, the American Indians in what's now the Eastern United States finally learned to plant corn. In about 1,000 CE, corn helped support a settlement of 25,000 people near modern-day St. Louis, a city twice as big as London at the time. By the time that agriculture got to the eastern section of what's now the United States, the American Indians had only a few hundred years to enjoy cultivation in peace before the arrival of the Europeans.

# AMERICAN INDIANS IN NORTH AMERICA

The American Indians living in North America before Columbus's arrival are divided into Northeast, Southeast, Great Plains, Southeast, Great Basin, Plateau, California, and Northwest Coast cultural areas. They consisted of thousands of small groups of loosely connected tribes. Western American Indians were mostly hunter-gatherers. The Eastern American Indians devised a clever system of what they called *three sisters* agriculture: corn, beans, and squash. Beans grew on the stalks of corn, and squash covered the planting mound to hold moisture in the soil. This agriculture method supported some of the largest tribes, including the Cherokee, Creek, and Choctaw in the Southeast.

In the northern woodlands of what are now New York and New England was a remarkable alliance called the *Iroquois Confederacy* (also known as the *League of Peace and Power,* the *Five Nations,* the *Six Nations,* and the *People of the Longhouse*). This group of First Nations/American Indians originally consisted of five tribes: the Mohawk, the Oneida, the Onondaga, the Cayuga, and the Seneca. A sixth tribe, the Tuscarora, joined after European settlers came. The Iroquois Confederacy constitution, called the *Great Law of Peace,* was handed down from the time of the Middle Ages, when Europe was just a collection of feuding local rulers. The Iroquois Confederation actually served as one model for the development of the U.S. Constitution.

Although what's now the United States had some centers of development, the American Indian population of this area before Columbus probably never exceeded 4 million. Agriculture simply arrived too late to support large urban areas. In some areas, planting never arrived at all. The California American Indians spoke more than 200 languages and lived in small, stable communities near rich seashore and mountain food sources. These early Californians had the chance to develop agriculture but never bothered.

# NATIVE AMERICANS AND THE SPREAD OF INFECTIOUS DISEASES

Explorers are biological weapons in that they carry diseases for which native populations have no immunities. Europeans brought smallpox, measles, bubonic plague, influenza, typhus, diphtheria, and scarlet fever to the New World, and close American Indian communities spread these diseases, which killed most of the American Indians in the New World before they had ever seen a European.

Good roads in the Mesoamerican empires and nomadic migration by the North American Indians allowed diseases to spread quickly. In addition, American Indians had no tradition of quarantine, which Europe had learned to use for epidemics, and so they stayed close to their sick friends, unknowingly facilitating the transmission of infectious diseases.

When explorers spread out to settle new lands, their diseases went with them. Friendly Taino natives met Columbus when he landed on Hispaniola, the island the Spanish named for themselves. Within 50 years, the population of the local people on Hispaniola — estimated at 1 million — had fallen to only 200 survivors. The conquistadores managed to defeat big American Indian empires largely because these empires were already collapsing from within. With friends and allies dying all around them, the American Indians fought desperate wars among themselves for the few resources left. Fighting and illness left them relatively easy conquests for the Europeans.

Europeans had fished in southern New England waters for more than 100 years before the Pilgrims landed in 1620. They met the American Indians and, without meaning to, passed on diseases. The native inhabitants had no resistance to the illnesses brought by the Europeans, and within a few years, a plague wiped out 90 percent of the inhabitants of coastal New England. This death rate was unknown in all previous human experience. Even the Black Plague in the 1300s left 70 percent of Europe's population alive.

In the face of the horrible losses caused by the epidemics attacking their communities, many American Indians felt that their Supreme Being had abandoned them. Some survivors of the Cherokee lost all confidence in their religion and destroyed the sacred objects of their tribe. American Indians were so reduced in numbers that they offered little real opposition to European invaders; some even looked upon the settlers for possible salvation.

In 1491, before the arrival of European explorers, the native population of North and South America may have been 100 million, while the entire population of Europe at the time was 70 million. By 1900, the American Indian population of the New World was less than 1 million — a drop of 99 percent from Columbus's day. By that time, the United States had only 250,000 American Indians. If colonists hadn't been able to take over lands that the American Indians had already cleared and cultivated, and if the American Indian population hadn't suffered devastating epidemics, the settlers would have had a far more difficult time of taking over the New World for themselves.

> **EXAMPLE**
>
> **Question:** What was the largest cause of death for American Indians during the European conquest?
>
> **Answer:** The largest cause of death were diseases unintentionally spread by explorers.

Today, people are proud of their American Indian blood. In the 2010 U.S. census, more than 5 million Americans listed themselves as all or part American Indian.

# UNEVEN GIFT EXCHANGE

What settlers brought to the New World versus what they took home leaves the American Indians way ahead on the gift exchange. The Old World brought death and domination to the people who lived in North and South America; the New World gave the Old World a new life. Eventually, European ideas of individual freedom would bring more options to American Indian survivors, but in the short run, the settlers profited far more than the American Indians. Here are two examples of how exploration into the New World changed Europe:

- Spain was poor and barely united when Columbus sailed. Through New World gold and silver, Spain became the richest country in Europe within a few decades.

- After the importation of corn, potatoes, pineapples, tomatoes, beans, vanilla, and chocolate from the New World, Europe had a chance to expand both its power and its appetite. The population of Europe more than doubled and the European standard of living improved steadily.

Tobacco and syphilis also came from the Americas, but getting involved with either was generally a personal choice. Europe got tomato sauce for spaghetti and pizza, potatoes to go with meat, plus vanilla and chocolate for ice cream.

# 7

# The New World: 1492–1690

**KEY CONCEPTS**

- The initial forays of Europeans into the New World
- The development of the Colonies in North America
- Challenges the early colonists faced
- Political and social changes during America's early years

When European nations established colonies in America, the Spanish went to Central and South America, where they found gold and silver. The British had to deal with Spanish power, including the Armada, but eventually they went north, where they found mostly rocks and swamps and some farm land. Clearing their way through some lean years, British settlers built homes and livings in ways that differed in significant ways among the different colonies. These colonies forged a new path toward religious and political freedom, even while the institution of slavery became more entrenched. These trends helped make the New World a major influence on the Old World. In this chapter, you discover history from Columbus through the establishment of the early colonies and on to the Salem witch trials on the eve of the 1700s.

>
> **TIP**
>
> Don't miss the forest for the trees. The AP exam concentrates on overall political, economic, and social trends, not so much on individual personal or state history. You need to understand the whole story to have the right background for writing essays. Don't try so hard to memorize everything that you lose the big picture. Pay special attention to early U.S. colonial trends; questions about this period are bound to show up on the AP test.

# EUROPEANS SETTLE INTO THE NEW WORLD

Explorer *Christopher Columbus* (1492) originally intended to land in the East Indies, but after six weeks at sea, the East Indies were still really 10,000 miles away, and his sailors were beginning to get a little testy. Just when Columbus looked as though he may end up on the sharp end of a pike, over the horizon loomed history's greatest consolation prize, the New World of North and South America.

## The far-reaching impact of Columbus's discovery

The settlement that began with Columbus eventually changed nearly all the world's continents in the following ways:

- North and South America through conquest and new communities
- Europe through gold and food from the Americas
- Africa through slavery and trade
- Asia, Australia, and the South Seas through commerce encouraged by New World discoveries

Settling the New World was actually more of a team effort: Europe provided the money and the markets; Africa furnished some of the labor; and North and South America produced gold and land for growing high-profit crops like sugar cane and tobacco. (More than half of all the kinds of food grown around the globe today originated in the New World.) Fed by potatoes, tomatoes, corn, and beans first grown in the Americas, the population of Europe doubled. Although Africa suffered from slavery, it also benefited from new foods like cassava and sweet potatoes. For better or worse, the Old World changed through the influence of the New World.

In addition to colonization, the biggest impact that the European colonists had on the New World was the introduction of diseases against which American Indians had no defense. Within a few hundred years of the October morning when Columbus's ship sighted land, as much as 90 percent of the Indian population in North and South America was dead. This situation made the conquest of America much easier for the Europeans, leaving room for settlement and not just military victory. Many of the American Indians whom the Europeans did meet were dazed and confused survivors of ancient cultures that had been lost forever. Tribes moved and intermingled, but they had limited resources for taking united action against the European invaders.

> **TIP**
>
> The AP U.S. History exam isn't going to dwell much on Columbus. He gets competition from Leif Eriksson and his voyaging Vikings of 1,000 CE for first-discoverer naming rights. In addition, we now realize that American Indians discovered the Americas thousands of years before. The AP likes to concentrate instead on what Columbus's discovery meant. Columbus in 1492 was important because he represented the beginning of permanent European settlement in the New World.

# The Spanish and Portuguese settlement of the New World

Before colonizing America, Europeans had been fighting one another for hundreds of years. Due to some smooth-sailing explorers, Spain and Portugal were in the lead for international conquest moving into the 1500s. So that these two countries wouldn't step on each others' toes, the pope issued a decree in the year after Columbus's first voyage, dividing the New World between Spain and Portugal. Because the pope's line managed to miss pretty much all the land, leaving Portugal holding nothing but waves, the two countries got together and amicably signed the *Treaty of Tordesillas* (1494). This agreement moved the dividing line a few hundred miles west so that Portugal got Brazil, plus some land in Africa and Asia. Spain got the rest of the "heathen" world and immediately sent in the conquistadors.

Spanish explorers spent the first half of the 1500s in heavy armor looking for gold. Some looked in the wrong places in North America, but they all managed to make some interesting discoveries:

- *Vasco Balboa (1513)* made it across the Isthmus of Panama to become the first European to wade into the Pacific Ocean. He found pineapples and pearls.

- *Ferdinand Magellan (1519)* sailed west from Spain with five small boats and an international crew of Portuguese, Spanish, Italian, French, English, and German sailors. After making it around South America (the Strait of Magellan is named for him), he died in the Philippines, but a few members of his crew made it all the way around the world and home again in 1522 with a cargo of cinnamon and cloves.

- *Ponce de Leon (1513)* explored Florida. The Indians he met were so tall and beautiful that he thought he must be near a fountain of youth.

- *Francisco Coronado (1540)* spent years marching around the American Southwest. Coronado found the Grand Canyon and millions of buffalo but no riches that he could easily add to the Spanish treasury.

- *Hernando de Soto (1539),* with 600 men in bright armor, marched through the middle south of what is now the United States. De Soto ended up sunk in the Mississippi River, but after three years, a few of his men made it back to Mexico wearing animal skins.

- *Francisco Pizarro (1532)* persuaded the Incan sovereign to turn over his gold, and then Pizarro turned over the whole empire looking for more. He conquered the Incan Empire covering most of Peru, Bolivia, and Ecuador. The mines in what's now Bolivia produced the largest amount of silver the world has ever seen. (Read more about the Incan and other early American empires in Chapter 6.)

■ *Hernán Cortés* **(1519)** took over the Aztec Empire, centered in Mexico City, trading the lives of his men and thousands of Aztecs and other natives for gold.

Soon, Spain and the rest of Europe were glittering with precious metal. New World treasure made Europe rich. Having money to explore, trade, and conquer made Europe even richer.

## The introduction of Christianity

The *encomienda* (1503) system was a decree from the Spanish rulers assigning groups of American Indians to colonists whose purpose supposedly was to protect and Christianize them. However, rather than Christianizing the American Indians, many colonists actually used them as slaves. Soldiers called *conquistadores* (1510) signed agreements with the Spanish king, raised money from investors, and then marched off looking for plunder. The total number of these mercenaries was about 10,000, but they had guns, horses, and no hesitation about killing anybody who got in their way. To turn a profit for themselves and their investors, the conquistadores were experts at getting American Indians to fight one another. Many sincerely believed they were bringing the gift of true Christianity to a savage world and that any gold they picked up along the way was their just reward.

A Black Legend historical theme popular in the 1900s said that the Spanish killed, raped, and looted for treasure, leaving nothing but suffering behind. Although some Spaniards certainly were cruel and greedy, Spain hardly had a monopoly on those bad habits.

Despite the abuses, Spanish settlers who thought they were spreading the word of God founded missions and settlements in places where the Spanish found no gold, including New Mexico and California. (Ironically, gold was discovered in California in 1848 just nine days before Spain's successor, Mexico, turned the territory over to the United States.)

## Blending cultures and people

The conquerors also married American Indian women. The women converted to Catholicism, couples got married, and the Spanish-American Indian children were called *mestizos*. This mixture of ethnic groups and cultures forms a majority of the population of Mexico, Central America, and South America to this day.

### La Malinche

La Malinche was an Indian woman who accompanied Hernán Cortés and played an active role in the Spanish conquest of Mexico. Acting as interpreter and intermediary, La Malinche smoothed the way for Cortés. She also was the mother of Cortés's son, who's considered one of the first mestizos. In Mexico today, people both love and hate La Malinche. She's remembered alternately as a traitor, a sellout, a heroine who helped save at least some of the native peoples of Mexico, and the symbolic mother of the new Mexican people. The Mexicans also celebrate Columbus Day as *Día de la Raza* — the birthday of what they see as their whole new race of people.

Spaniards' ideas of civilization often backfired on them. The Pueblo Revolt, also known as *Popé's Rebellion* (1680), was an American Indian uprising in New Mexico that killed hundreds of Spanish settlers and priests. The American Indians rebuilt their sacred *kiva* (ceremonial chamber) on the ruins of the Spanish plaza in Santa Fe; it took Spain almost 30 years to regain control. In the New World as a whole, the influence of a Spanish culture having intermarried with the native society is still evident from San Francisco, California, to the tip of South America, 8,000 miles south.

No more than 50 years after Columbus discovered the Bahamas, hundreds of small Spanish and mestizo towns had sprung up, especially near the gold and silver mines in Mexico and Peru. In addition, the Spanish founded the first universities in the New World, 85 years before the English got around to starting Harvard. They also are credited with establishing the first permanent town in what would become the United States — *St. Augustine, Florida* (1565) — before the first English settlers arrived in the New World.

## Caribbean piracy and Spanish wealth

All the treasure Spain amassed from the New World attracted fortune hunters with ships who didn't mind stealing from the Spanish. Privateers (a name they preferred to *pirates*) operated for 200 years, from approximately 1560 to the mid-1760s. These pirates were most successful during the 1640s through the 1680s.

Caribbean piracy arose out of conflicts over trade and colonization among the rival European powers, including England, Spain, Holland, Portugal, and France. Most of the privateers who had permission from their governments to attack foreign ships were from Holland and England.

Because Spain controlled much of the Caribbean and all of the gold, most of the attacked cities and ships belonged to the Spanish Empire. Some of the best-known pirate bases were in the Bahamas (1715 to 1725), Tortuga (established in the 1640s), and Port Royal in Jamaica (after 1655). Among the most famous Caribbean pirates were Edward Teach (also known as Blackbeard) and Henry Morgan.

## The decline of Spanish power

Closer to home, the Spanish were having trouble maintaining their European domination over the mostly Protestant country of Holland and sent their great fleet — the *Spanish Armada* (1588) — to invade and subdue England, Holland's Protestant supporter.

In a battle just north of the English Channel, the English and Dutch attacked the Armada. Even though the attacking ships were outnumbered, they managed to scatter the Spanish fleet and sink some of the Spanish ships. More Armada ships were lost in storms that arrived just in time to help the English and Dutch fleets. When England and Spain finally signed a peace treaty in 1604, the English were free to move to unclaimed North America. Spanish power began a slow decline that lasted for more than 300 years.

# English colonies

Poor and distracted by local conflicts, the best the English could do to get into the exploration game was to send out a stand-in. A captain the English called *John Cabot* (1497) (even though he was really an Italian named Giovanni Caboto) sailed along the coast of what's now Canada. (Such national stand-ins were not unusual: Columbus was an Italian sailing for Spain. Magellan, also representing Spain, was actually Portuguese.) The Cabot exploration received funding from British businessmen eager to make a profit trading with the Spice Islands. When Cabot didn't come back from his second voyage, England decided to delay any further excursions for a while.

Spain and Portugal had a 100-year head start in colonizing Mexico and South America, but in the 1500s, not a lot was happening in the area that would eventually become the U.S. The Spanish sent out major expeditions led by Ponce de Leon, Francisco Coronado, and Hernando de Soto, but did not find gold or silver. Then, at almost the same time and still without finding gold themselves, other European nations joined in. In the end, these three nations had established permanent footholds in three corners of North America:

- The French built a fur-trading post at *Quebec, Canada* (1608).
- The Spanish built a mission at *Santa Fe, New Mexico* (1610).
- The English established their first permanent colony at *Jamestown, Virginia* (1607).

(**Note:** Germany and Italy didn't start colonies in the New World because these nations didn't even exist until the late 1800s.)

Jamestown wasn't England's first experience in New World colonization:

- *Sir Francis Drake* **(1580)** had done so well as a pirate in the Caribbean that Queen Elizabeth I knighted him as a way of saying thanks for all the Spanish gold he brought back.
- *Sir Walter Raleigh* **(1585)** founded a short-lived colony of 100 men and women on Roanoke Island. The colony survived long enough for the birth of Virginia Dare, the first English child born in the New World. When a ship carrying supplies arrived after a three-year absence, the crew found everybody gone, with houses and fortifications neatly removed. The only clue was the word Croatoan carved into a remaining post of the fort and Cro carved into a nearby tree. The survivors of the colony may have gone to live with a nearby friendly tribe of Croatoan Indians and intermarried.

The latter point, if true, represents the last major occurrence of intermarriage between the English colonists and the native population because, unlike the Spanish, the English brought their wives with them to America. In the 50 years leading up to 1600, the population of England increased by one third. At the same time, a change from growing crops to growing sheep displaced a lot of English farmers. People were looking for a place to go, and settling in America seemed like an ideal solution.

## The settlement of Jamestown, Virginia

The English went to Jamestown for the same reasons the Spanish came to the New World a hundred years earlier. Their privately financed joint-stock Virginia Company wanted to find gold or at least a passage to the rich Spice Islands of Asia. The colonists were under pressure to produce riches; if they didn't, they could be abandoned in the wilderness.

**EXAMPLE**

**Question:** Who owned Jamestown?

**Answer:** The colony was owned by a joint-stock company eager for profits.

Jamestown was named after then-ruling English King James I. The territory's name, Virginia, honored the Virgin Queen, Elizabeth I.

The Charter of the Virginia Company guaranteed the colonists basic rights as Englishmen. The colony had about 100 settlers to start, all of them men. In the first years, they were too busy looking for gold to gather much food, so many died from hunger and the diseases that go with it.

In 1608, Captain John Smith took over and whipped the surviving colonists into shape with a simple rule: "He who shall not work shall not eat." Earlier, Smith had been saved by the American Indian princess Pocahontas, who went on to marry another settler, helped protect the colony, and visited England to meet the king.

Still, times were tough: Of the 400 settlers who had gone to Jamestown, only 60 survived the "starving time" winter of 1609. Twelve hundred English people lived in Virginia by 1625, but an additional 6,000 died trying to live on this edge of the New World wilderness.

## Forming and breaking alliances with the American Indians

Pocahontas tried to keep the peace, but after she died during her trip to England, the colonists and American Indians started to fight wars. By 1650, the Chesapeake tribe had been banished from all the land around Jamestown. By 1685, only a few American Indians remained anywhere near the settlements. This pattern was repeated as English colonies came in contact with American Indians across North America: first cooperation, then conflict, and finally removal and severe population decline for the American Indians. As outlined in Chapter 6, disease brought by the explorers often destroyed native people and their cultures before the native people ever saw a European settler.

American Indian tribes moved, made and broke alliances, and fought wars with one another for thousands of years before the Europeans came. The arrival of the settlers made an already complicated system of alliances and land control even more complex. Looking for land to live on, tribes moved hundreds of miles and fought other Indians. For some American Indians, this migration was good; they got guns from settlers and made profits delivering furs and acting as scouts for the Europeans. But competition for shrinking hunting grounds led to increased violence between tribes.

Lots of American Indians moved west toward the Great Plains as English settlements spread out from the East. Tribes like the Sioux, who previously led quiet lives on the edge of the forest, learned to ride escaped Spanish horses and became Great Plains buffalo hunters and raiders. The Iroquois Confederation in the northern colonies benefited from alliances and trades with settlers and actually grew in power for 100 years. But for most American Indians, the arrival of Europeans was an unmitigated disaster. In a world governed by survival of the strongest, the concept of human rights was still a long way off.

## Setting up offshore sugar plantations

As the first wave of settlers left Britain, twice as many English pioneers opted to go to the West Indies rather than come to the rocky, swampy shores of North America. They chose the West Indies because there, they could grow sugar, one of the two big money-makers of the New World. Although English settlers in Virginia could grow tobacco in their backyards, sugar cane required large plantations and thousands of workers.

New World slavery really got its start in the West Indies. While small farmers were working their own land in the mainland colonies during the late 1600s, West Indies plantation owners were busy importing more than 250,000 enslaved people from Africa. Before long, blacks outnumbered their white overseers in the West Indies four to one.

The inhuman *Barbados slave code* (1661) required that slave owners give their slaves clothes to wear (about the only thing it required) and denied slaves even the most basic right guaranteed under English common law: the right to life. The code allowed slaveholders to do whatever they wanted to their slaves, including mutilating and burning them alive for punishment.

The big plantation owners in the West Indies squeezed out most of the small farmers who grew food for the islands. These farmers, in turn, moved to the North American colonies, bringing a few slaves and the slave code with them.

## The different approaches to colonization

The English settlements along the American east coast grew because they had more settlers who came to stay. The French were either happy at home in France or would have left the New World settlements, but as in the case of Protestants, the French king forbade them to go. The Spanish and Portuguese viewed the New World as more of a money-making enterprise than a place to start a new life. While the English began to settle down and build some permanent family homes in the New World, the Spanish colonial administrators just sent money back to the central government in Europe. Whereas English colonies were mostly self-governing in politics and religion, Spanish colonies were ruled centrally from the mother country.

**EXAMPLE**

**Question:** What were some differences between the Spanish and English colonies?

**Answer:** The English operated politics and religion locally (instead of reporting back to the central mother country like Spain) and used their New World settlements to build personal wealth rather than sending all payments back to Europe.

# THE AMERICAN COLONIES

For an Englishman choosing where to settle in the new colonies during the 1600s, the Northern colonies, with their cold climate, did not offer much money-making potential compared with the chances of growing tobacco in the South or sugar in the West Indies. What the North did have was a place to raise a family and own land. As the country grew up, the Northern colonies made up for what they lacked in agricultural riches with smart money from commerce and industry. Meanwhile, they attracted early settlers interested in a search for religious freedom.

Maryland, Virginia, the Carolinas, and Georgia all developed as large plantation colonies focused on growing and exporting agricultural products. Whereas independent North Carolina and reform-born Georgia protected the rights of small farmers, overall, the economic system of the South favored large landowners. With lots of slaves and not many citizens, developing a system of schools or even alternative types of religion was hard. The standard Church of England dominated the South and collected taxes to ensure its support. By growing tobacco, rice, and eventually cotton, the South made a lot of money for a limited number of rich planters. These planters controlled politics because only landowners voted. Because big planters lacked interest in factories and public education, the South had virtually no industry and no public school system until after the Civil War.

The Middle colonies of New Jersey, Pennsylvania, New York, and Delaware fell midway between small-farm New England and the big-plantation South. Pennsylvania, New York, and New Jersey came to be known as the *bread colonies* because they grew grain for the rest of the Eastern Seaboard. But their industry wasn't all agriculture. They had forests of big trees to cut down, and the lumber from these trees built houses, businesses, and ships. All these crops and construction opportunities gave business to the growing ports of New York City, Philadelphia, and Albany. The government system fell midway between the democratic town meetings of New England and the autocratic rich-man's government of the South. The Middle colonies weren't middle in freedom. Especially in Pennsylvania, people enjoyed religious freedom and a cosmopolitan tolerance for minorities.

# The settling of Massachusetts

America was built in the smoke from the great fire of the Protestant Reformation. A German priest named *Martin Luther* (1517) broke with the Roman Catholic Church, which had ruled most of Christianity since the late Roman Empire. Luther said that individuals had to have a personal relationship with God and the Bible; priests and popes couldn't tell them what to think or sell them a ticket to heaven. John Calvin, another reformer, went further. In his *Institutes of the Christian Religion* (1536), Calvin said God had already chosen who would go to heaven and who would burn in hell; this theory was the *predestination of the elect*. God knew everything, and no amount of good works would change his mind.

Conveniently for English religious debaters, *King Henry VIII* (1533) had just kicked the Catholic church out of England over his multiple-marriage issue. As England scrambled to piece together its own church, religious beliefs were up for grabs. This confusion drove both radical Protestants (who didn't think the English church was changing fast enough) and out-of-favor Catholics (who felt it was changing too fast) to the New World for spiritual breathing room.

## The Pilgrims and Plymouth

First out the door were the most radical Protestants, a small group of Separatists who wanted to separate completely from the new Church of England. They first went to Holland, where they stayed for 12 years. Although the Dutch were tolerant of the group's religious rights, the Pilgrims feared that their children were becoming more Dutch than English. After a short stop back in England to gather supplies, 50 Pilgrims and 52 other settlers sailed for Virginia on a small boat called the *Mayflower*.

After two months, the *Mayflower* landed 700 miles north of their intended destination, on a peninsula now called Plymouth in what is now Massachusetts. Before they even got off the ship, the settlers signed the *Mayflower Compact* (1620), agreeing to make decisions by the will of the majority. From this simple agreement and the open town meetings that followed came a feeling for participatory democracy that now has a history of almost 400 years in the United States.

The Pilgrims had great leaders: a non-Separatist soldier named Myles Standish (also called Captain Shrimp because he was short) and William Bradford, an eloquent self-taught scholar who could read five languages. More than half of the Pilgrims died the first winter, so when they brought in a good harvest the next year, they really did have a happy Thanksgiving. The Plymouth colony never had more than a few thousand people; later, it merged with the Massachusetts Bay Colony a few miles to the north.

## The Puritans and the Massachusetts Bay Colony

The *Massachusetts Bay Colony* (1630), which would become Boston, was settled by Puritans who believed they had to purify, but not actually leave, the Church of England. They came to America to escape political repression, a bad economy, and restrictions on their religion. They got off to a strong start with almost 1,000 well-equipped settlers arriving on 11 boats. They also had an excellent leader in John Winthrop, who served for 19 years. Around 20,000 more settlers arrived during the first 12 years of the colony's existence, although twice as many headed south for the warm breezes and easy sugar living of Barbados.

**Question:** Were the Puritans Separatists?

**Answer:** No. They wanted to purify the Church of England from within.

The Bay Colony near Boston offered freedom but not easy living. All men who belonged to the Puritan church could vote, which meant about two out of five people — a much higher percentage of voter participation than any place else at the time — could vote. The catch was that, to be in the church, you had to have had a conversion experience that identified you as one of the *visible saints*, one of those whom God had to picked to go to heaven. Prospective church members had to explain to an interview panel how they knew God had chosen them (without sounding prideful, of course).

**Question:** Why did the Puritans leave England?

**Answer:** They left to escape political repression, recession, and religious restrictions.

In the early days of Puritan orthodoxy, the freethinking *Anne Hutchinson* (1638) challenged the religious authority of the leaders of the Bay Colony. She believed she had a direct revelation from God that, if predestination were true, everybody had a duty to follow his or her own conscience. Leaders banished her from the colony, and she happily left with her whole family.

*Roger Williams* (1635) was another purifying spirit. He said the Congregationalists (a more modern name for the church that started with the Puritans) should make a complete break from the corrupt Church of England, treat the American Indians fairly, and not try to legislate religious behavior. Hounded out of Massachusetts, he helped found the colony of Rhode Island to protect freedom of thought and expression.

**Question:** Why did Anne Hutchinson get in trouble with the leaders of the Bay Colony?

**Answer:** She challenged their religious authority.

# The founding of Rhode Island

After being hounded out of Massachusetts and helped by sympathetic American Indians, Roger Williams fled to what would become the colony of *Rhode Island* (1636) in the midst of a bitterly cold winter. He built his own church and established complete religious freedom of thought, even for Catholics and Jews (an unusual position at the time). Nobody had to believe a fixed creed; no one had to go to church or pay taxes to support a state religion. These freedoms sound normal now, but they were rare at the time.

Rhode Island was also the first to embrace universal male suffrage: Any man could vote. This right was limited later, but from the start, Rhode Island was a progressive beacon in an already freedom-loving country. The colony grew with people who didn't fit in, in other locations, including Anne Hutchinson and her family. Critics from other colonies called it Rogues' Island. Originally highly unofficial, Rhode Island somehow managed to win a charter from Parliament in 1644; a statue of the Independent Man sits atop its statehouse.

## The Connecticut colony

The Connecticut River valley is one of the few really fertile spots in New England. A mass migration of Puritans from Boston settled near the river, and some Dutch and English immigrants followed. In an open meeting, the new colony drafted the *Fundamental Orders* (1639), the beginning of a modern constitution. So-called "substantial citizens" were to democratically control the new government. The Connecticut colony was soon joined by another attempt at godly government in New Haven. Together, these colonies mark the small beginning of the migration of American settlers to the west.

## Dutch colonies in New York and New Jersey

The practical Dutch actually got where everybody else thought they were heading: to the East Indies in Asia. For 300 years, the Dutch had that profitable colony on the other side of the world. When they considered land just across the Atlantic, they sent Henry Hudson (1609) to explore the great Hudson River and eventually Hudson Bay. While Hudson started up what would later be called the Hudson River, his navigator wrote down the American Indian name for an extended island they passed. The American Indians called it "island of many hills," or *Manhattan*. Later, the Dutch bought the island from the American Indians, thinking they'd made a great deal. The American Indians, however, had the last laugh because they didn't really own Manhattan; they'd just stopped by to fish.

---

### The difference between Puritans and Pilgrims

To understand the difference between Puritans and Pilgrims, remember that Puritans wanted to purify the Church of England from within. Pilgrims thought they had to be separate completely (hence, the name "Separatists") and leave the established church.

Puritans believed (rather like modern religious fundamentalists) that the whole purpose of government was to enforce God's laws. Congregations hired and fired their own ministers; thus, congregants could have local control over what the church was saying. Contrary to the image of Puritans now, the Puritans were actually in favor of good food, drink, songs, and married love. A Protestant ethic supported willpower and hard work, but after the responsibilities were taken care of, nothing was wrong with having fun. Because they never had to answer to any central dogma, the Congregationalists eventually evolved into the most liberal Protestant denomination.

*New Amsterdam* (1623), the Dutch city that would become New York City, was not a beacon of liberty. The Dutch ran business for a profit and had no real interest in religious tolerance, free speech, or voting in the colony they called New Netherland. The Dutch had trouble with American Indian attacks in New Amsterdam, so they built a high wall. The street running along that wall was called Wall Street. The uptown country on Manhattan reminded the Dutch of a location in Holland, so they named it Harlem. They booted out a small Swedish settlement (1655) on the Delaware River, but were themselves later booted out when the English came, first as settlers and then in warships.

In 1664, the surrounded and profitable Dutch peacefully surrendered New Netherland to the English, who renamed it New York after the newly restored King Charles II's brother. Ownership of New Jersey accompanied the acquisition of New York. Large landholdings by a few families in New York state discouraged heavy settlement of the inland area during the early colonial period. When the American Revolution occurred, Upstate New York was still a frontier.

**EXAMPLE**

**Question:** Why did the Dutch found New Netherland?

**Answer:** The Dutch had commercial and mercantile goals: They wanted to make money.

# Pennsylvania and Delaware

After the Catholics lost control of England during the reign of Henry VIII, many different ideas of religion sprang up. Among the groups that tried to discern the word of God were the Quakers. They called themselves the Religious Society of Friends, but everybody else called them Quakers because they allegedly became so full of the Holy Spirit that they quaked. Quakers had no mandatory beliefs and no preachers; they took turns speaking in their Sunday meetings when the spirit moved them: They refused to fight or join the military and tried to live peaceful lives.

This behavior made everybody hate them. William Penn, a serious-minded English boy from a family with money, decided to become a Quaker and worked to get a colony where Quakers could live in peace. Surprisingly, King Charles II owed Penn's father some money, so he gave William a choice piece of land that the king called *Pennsylvania* (1681). Thinking the name too egotistical, Penn tried to change it but eventually settled down to work on attracting good settlers. He carefully laid out Philadelphia, "the city of brotherly love," which quickly became the largest and most beautiful city in the colonies.

The Pennsylvania government was fair, with freedom of religion, no church tax, and a representative legislature elected by all male landowners. The death penalty was levied only for treason or murder; by comparison, more than 200 offenses could result in beheading in England at the time. Within 19 years of its founding, Pennsylvania was the third-richest colony in British America. The Quakers treated the American Indians so fairly that some tribes from the South tried to move to the colony.

Pennsylvania had only a minority of Quakers, however, and trouble soon began.

After the English ousted the Dutch from New York, the future Delaware became the Lower Counties of Pennsylvania and became independent in time to be the first state to ratify the Constitution after the Revolution.

# Colonial Maryland

The rich English Catholic Lord Baltimore founded *Maryland* (1634), located just up the Chesa-peake Bay from Virginia. He hoped to make a profit and provide a haven for his fellow Catholics, who were still heavily discriminated against in England. He was thinking of vast feudal estates, but colonists didn't want to come unless they personally got to own some land. New residents planted tobacco. To work the fields, the Maryland settlers imported *indentured servants,* generally poor white Englishmen who agreed to work for four to seven years for free in exchange for pas-sage to the New World. In the early days, three of every four English immigrants to the Chesa-peake Bay came as indentured servants.

Despite the promise of eventual freedom, only 40 percent of the indentured servants lived to win their freedom, due largely to the early death rate from disease. As indentured servants died out in the late 1600s, Maryland began to import larger numbers of slaves. Even with servants working and slaves on the way, Maryland managed to make a stand for freedom with the adop-tion of the *Act of Toleration* (1649). The act guaranteed freedom of religion to all, Catholic or Prot-estant, as long as they believed in Jesus. The Toleration law didn't help much if you were Buddhist or Jewish, though; the act threatened nonbelievers in Jesus with death.

# The Virginia colony

When he wasn't bankrolling colonies, Sir Walter Raleigh liked to smoke a pipe. Back then, people called it "drinking tobacco," but by any name, the habit has always been hard to quit. Smoking really took off in England after John Rolfe, the husband of Pocahontas, figured out a way to grow smoother-tasting tobacco in the Jamestown colony. He made so much money that pretty soon people were planting tobacco in their front yards and even in the street. As the market for the "bewitching weed" grew, colonists pushed for more land to grow it on. With more land, they needed more labor: Virginia finally had an economic hit.

Just in time, a Dutch ship appeared off Jamestown and sold a cargo of 20 Africans to work for hungry Virginia planters. It was still a year before the Pilgrims came to New England seeking freedom. In the same year that the slave ship arrived, London authorized the *House of Burgesses* (1619) in Virginia to be the first representative government in the New World. America was already on a two-track system. Early Africans were indentured servants, just like Europeans on contract for a limited number of years. Slavery replaced indenture in the late 1600s.

# The Carolina colony

*Carolina* (1670) was the third Middle colony in a row named in honor of the then-current English ruler: Charles II had replaced Charles I, who lost his head. The colony served as a supply station for the hugely profitable sugar plantations of the West Indies. Carolina even tried its hand at supplying slaves. Over the objections of its London proprietors, the colony shipped as many as 10,000 American Indians to the cane fields of the sugar islands. Carolina officially adopted a version of the Barbados slave code in 1696 and learned to grow rice with the help of West African slaves; by 1710, the colony had more Africans than whites.

Carolina divided into North and South Carolina in 1691. In North Carolina, people farmed small plots, often just claiming land, building a cabin, and planting a few crops. They were rugged individualists, hiding out between the landed aristocracies of Virginia and South Carolina. The North Carolina folks were even accused of harboring pirates along stormy Cape Hatteras, the "graveyard of the Atlantic." When the local Tuscaroras Indians attacked a North Carolina town, the settlers fought a bloody war and ended up selling hundreds of the American Indians into slavery. The survivors traveled north looking for protection and became the sixth tribe in the Iroquois Confederacy.

South Carolina had larger plantations and a slave population that helped develop crops of rice and indigo by building up the land. In addition to fertile land, South Carolina had the major port city of Charleston.

## Georgia

*Georgia* (1733) was the last of the original 13 colonies and the only one founded in the 1700s. Named for the foppish King George II, Georgia was a buffer against the Spanish in Florida and the French in Louisiana whom the English feared would attack their colonies. Georgia's founder was James Oglethorpe, a fair-minded reformer who used his own money to develop a land that would let debtors get a new start. Oglethorpe helped design the beautiful city of Savannah, banned slavery, and fought off Spanish attacks. He invited reformers to visit, including the young John Wesley, who would go on to found the Methodist Church. Over Oglethorpe's objections after he left the colony, Georgia allowed slavery in 1750. Oglethorpe lived long enough to be a friend of the American Revolution in England.

# EARLY CHALLENGES TO THE NEW COLONIES

The early days of the colonies were far from smooth sailing. Settlers had problems with American Indians, autocratic English government, diseases, slavery, the economy, and even witchcraft. The following sections summarize topics that may come up on the AP exam.

## American Indian troubles

American Indians resented being driven off their land, and they fought back from time to time with counter attacks. Shortly before the Pilgrims arrived, an epidemic swept through the New England coastal tribes and wiped out three-quarters of the native people. With no strength to repel even the weak Pilgrim settlement, the local American Indians were friendly. *Squanto* (1620), who had been kidnapped by an English ship's captain years before, greeted the Pilgrims in perfect English, asked them if they brought any beer, and helped them through to the first Thanksgiving.

As the settlers pushed the American Indians off their land over the next 50 years, the son of the chief who had welcomed the Pilgrims lost his patience. The settlers called him King Philip because they couldn't be bothered to learn his American Indian name, Metacom. Backed by an alliance of fed-up American Indians, he launched *King Philip's War* (1675). By the time the war ended a year later, King Philip's forces had attacked 52 towns. The settlers responded with a brutal massacre of Indian men, women, and children. One out of ten settlers of military age was a casualty; families were sometimes carried off by American Indians. Even Plymouth itself, site of the Pilgrims' landing, fell victim.

*Bacon's Rebellion of 1676*, an uprising of white settlers against American Indians, had tied down the Virginia government, the only other significant English presence in North America. Canada was still mostly French and rooting for the Indians. The New England colonies had to defend themselves on their own.

In the end, the settlers fought together under the direction of the *New England Confederation* (1643) and held on. In the south, the first capital of Virginia, Jamestown, was burned in 1676, but the government eventually regained control. Although nightmare fears of Indian attacks lasted for years, actual Indian power in New England ended with the death of Metacom. For the first time, settlers in separate colonies began to think of themselves as Americans.

## The Navigation and Molasses Acts

The colonists needed to cooperate to survive. The first colonial union was the *New England Confederation* (1643), a partnership of the Massachusetts Bay Colony, Plymouth, and two Connecticut colonies for mutual defense and problem-solving.

About 40 years later, the royal government in London imposed a very different *Dominion of New England* (1686). The head of the new dominion was Sir Edmund Andros, whose job was to enforce the law, especially the *Navigation Acts* (1660), which made it illegal to send anything to the colonies that hadn't first passed through and been taxed by England. The Navigation Acts and the later *Molasses Act of 1733* supported a policy of *mercantilism*, which forced colonies to buy and sell with England so that England could profit off the colonies.

 EXAMPLE

> **Question:** What did the Navigation Acts (1660) and the Molasses Act (1733) support?
>
> **Answer:** These acts furthered the policy of *mercantilism*.

The colonists hated Sir Edmund, and he responded by closing down meetings, schools, the courts, and the press, and revoking land titles. He issued taxes without consulting the local assemblies. The colonists were on the verge of revolt when the English, in what was called the *Glorious Revolution* (1689), dethroned the unpopular James II and brought on the easier rule of William and Mary. Sir Edmund was caught trying to sneak out of town dressed as a woman, and he was sent back to England.

## Disease and money

The Chesapeake area was a money-maker but not a very healthy place to be. Disease and death were a constant fear of even the well-to-do in 1600 and early 1700 Virginia and Maryland. Half the people born in the early years of these colonies didn't live to see their 20th birthdays. Few of those who lived past 20 made it to 50, and women were lucky to see 40. Most marriages ended in the death of a partner within 7 years. Without many parents or any grandparents for moral guidance, more than one-third of the girls were pregnant when they got married.

Still, the money kept rolling in to those who survived to spend it. In the 1630s, Chesapeake Bay shipped 1.5 million pounds of tobacco a year; by 1700, the colony shipped 40 million pounds a year. Both Virginia and Maryland employed the *headright system* (1670), which encouraged the importation of servant workers. Whoever paid to bring in a servant received the right to 50 acres of land. Hungry for land and labor, big planters brought some 100,000 indentured servants into the region by 1700; most of those servants didn't live long enough to serve out their contracts. In all, these indentured servants represented three-quarters of all newcomers to the region in the 1600s.

# Early rebellions

*Leisler's Rebellion* (1689) was an uprising in colonial New York City in which militia captain Jacob Leisler seized control of lower New York from 1689 to 1691. The uprising, which occurred in the midst of Britain's Glorious Revolution (see the earlier section "The Navigation and Molasses Acts"), reflected colonial resentment of the policies of King James II. British troops sent by James' successor William III restored royal authority in 1691.

In Virginia, its governor, William Berkeley, was doing well with the Indians. To keep his personally profitable fur-trade monopoly with the local Indians flowing, he looked the other way when American Indians killed settlers on the frontier. In *Bacon's Rebellion* (1676), a group of about 1,000 planters took on the American Indians; they then drove Berkeley from his capital at Jamestown and burned the place. After Bacon died of dysentery, a common disease of the time, Berkeley defeated the rebellion and hanged the surviving leaders. This small rebellion sent a wake-up call to the big planters; they needed to find workers who lived longer and couldn't fight back. The answer was slaves.

# Slavery before the Revolution

Only about 5 percent of the 8 million human beings stolen from Africa to be enslaved in the New World during the 1600s and 1700s went to the colonies in America (or, later, the United States itself). One-third of the slaves went to Brazil; most of the rest worked the sugar plantations of the Caribbean.

As late as 1670, slaves made up less than 10 percent of the population of Southern plantations, a situation that started to change as indentured servants died off. By 1750, half the population of Virginia was African. Many slaves in the Deep South died from hard work in the rice and indigo fields (cotton came a century later) and had to be replaced with new workers. In the Chesapeake Bay, the very place that killed so many white indentured servants, slaves lived much longer. By the mid-1700s, the slave population of this area was capable of sustaining itself without importing more human beings.

Slaves brought more than just labor to the New World. Without call-and-response singing, the rhythmic ring shout dance, hand drums, and the banjo, all of which came from Africa, America may still be doing the minuet. With African influence, the United States started jazz, blues, and rock-and-roll. Much of the early U.S. economic system was based directly or indirectly on the unpaid labor of slaves. They provided much of the hard work and often the know-how to grow crops that aided the development of and enriched the United States.

Slaves fought back when they could. A revolt in New York City in 1712 cost the lives of a dozen whites and 21 Africans. The *Stono Revolt* (1739) saw 50 self-liberated slaves marching toward Florida to be free, only to be stopped by the militia.

# Life in New England

In contrast to the middle Southern states, New England added 10 years to the average life span of new settlers. The first generation of Puritan colonists lived an average of 70 years — pretty close to a modern life span. Because of this unprecedented longevity, some say New England invented grandparents, who were still around to get to know their grandchildren.

Family morality is reflected in the low premarital pregnancy rate, again in stark contrast to the experience in the South. Massachusetts started the first college, Harvard, in 1636, just 8 years after the colony's founding. It took Virginia 83 years after staking out Jamestown to found the College of William and Mary in 1693.

## Witches and religion

The Puritan light burned bright, but it also could be blinding. After about 40 years of accepting only the select, Puritan churches had to offer a *Half-Way Covenant* (1662), which opened church attendance to people who couldn't prove they were among God's elect. As time went on, the doors of the churches opened wider, perhaps sometimes even admitting sinners.

At about this time, a new type of sermon began to appear — something that speakers called a *jeremiad* after the always-scolding Old Testament prophet Jeremiah. Preachers thundered about the wrath of God and the hellfire that awaits the sinner, just as though sinners walked among the elect. This kind of angry shouting soon showed its ugly face in the town of Salem, north of Boston.

A group of teenage girls, under the influence of voodoo talk by a West Indian slave, claimed to have been bewitched by certain older women in the town. This claim triggered a hysterical witch hunt that led to the execution of 20 people. Most of the victims were hanged, but one was pressed to death under a huge rock. The girls claimed they could see devils in the courtroom ceiling, and Puritan judges believed them.

The *Salem Witch Trials* (1692) lasted for 16 months and died out when opposition to the unfairness of the trials became stronger than the fear of witches. The experience introduced the phrase *witch hunt* into the language, meaning a campaign directed against people who hold unpopular views but are otherwise innocent.

# 8

# The Road to the Revolution: 1691–1775

## KEY CONCEPTS

- The growing populations in colonial America
- Religion, politics, and commerce in the colonies
- The French-Indian War and other pre-Revolutionary conflicts
- Events that set the stage for rebellion against Britain

From shaky settlements clinging to the edge of a wild continent, the 13 colonies grew to become prosperous and increasingly independent. Surviving colonial wars with the French and their American Indian allies gave colonists confidence. Being able to make a good living by farming, building ships, and trading showed the early residents of British North America that they could take care of themselves. Life was good, and as land and income grew, so did the population: More than five times as many people lived in the colonies in the 1770s as had made their homes there in the 1690s. With growth came opposition to being told what to do by England.

# POPULATION EXPANSION IN THE COLONIES

The early colonies of New England, including Massachusetts, Rhode Island, Connecticut, and New Hampshire, supported themselves by fishing and small family farms. The early Southern colonies of Virginia, Delaware, Maryland, North Carolina, South Carolina, and Georgia made their money on large plantations growing rice and tobacco. The Middle colonies of New York, Pennsylvania, and New Jersey were also in the middle economically, with medium-sized farms growing medium-sized crops of grain and raising cattle.

Between 1691 and 1775, the American colonies grew quickly, thanks mostly to immigration. In 1700, the 13 original colonies had only 250,000 people. Just 50 years later, the population had quintupled to 1.25 million. The colonists had plenty of children, but America also attracted immigrants by the thousands, including people from outside of England as well as 200,000 slaves from Africa. Canada was the largest British colony, and Jamaica was the richest, but the 13 colonies were the most popular places to settle because their good land grew rich crops. The colonies were 90 percent farms; the population of New York City in 1700 was only 5,000 people.

In the early days, around 5 percent of the settlers were other Europeans, such as Germans, Swedes, Dutch, Irish, Welsh, and Scots. None of these non-English people felt any great love for their English rulers. Even early on, the new land was the most multicultural area in the world, especially the ethnically rich Middle colonies of Pennsylvania and New York. Beyond the fittingly named New England, by the time of the Revolution, half the people of the colonies weren't from England — about a third of the signers of the Declaration of Independence originated from the world beyond that island nation. The following sections list the most prominent groups to move to the American colonies during this time.

>  **TIP**
>
> England, Britain, the United Kingdom . . . how many names can a little-but-mighty island have? England is the biggest part of the island called Britain, which is about the size of California and is a few miles off the west coast of Europe. Great Britain evolved politically from the gradual union of England and Scotland, which started in 1603 with the Union of Crowns and slid into the Acts of Union in 1707, when the parliaments of the two nations merged into the Kingdom of Great Britain. Over time, the kingdom added Wales and Ireland and took the name United Kingdom. After 1700, the mother country of the colonies can be referred to by either the more inclusive Britain or by its original name, England.

## The Scotch-Irish

Perhaps the most aggressive immigrants to carve out the frontier for farms were the Scotch-Irish. The United States has had 12 presidents with a Scotch-Irish background. These English-speaking people were originally from the Scottish lowlands (not the more picturesque Scottish highlands). The only thing high about the lowlands was the land rents charged by greedy Scottish lords. Many of the Scotch-Irish moved to Northern Ireland, where their Protestant descendants still make up the majority of the population. Some kept going to America.

With little money, the Scotch-Irish didn't stop traveling until they found cheap land on the frontiers of Pennsylvania, Virginia, and Maryland. Having been pushed around plenty themselves, they tended to solve potential American Indian problems by shooting first and asking questions later. By 1750, the Scotch-Irish had spread out along the *Great Wagon Road,* a path for immigration they helped build through mountain passes from Philadelphia to Georgia. By the Revolution, they represented 7 percent of the population of the colonies.

Having moved more than once, the Scotch-Irish didn't originally build to stay. They threw up rough log cabins, chopped down trees, and planted crops between the stumps. As they gained title to their lands and confidence that no lords would boot them off, the Scotch-Irish built Presbyterian churches.

The rough-and-tumble Scotch-Irish caused heartache for the original Quaker settlers of Pennsylvania (see Chapter 7) when they killed peaceful American Indians and led the *Paxton Boys'* (1764) march on Philadelphia to protest lenient treatment of the natives. The Paxton Boys wanted to punish American Indians in general, regardless of whether they'd actually done wrong; luckily, Ben Franklin and the Philadelphia militia stood up to the Paxton Boys and protected the friendly American Indians. The Scotch-Irish also shook things up with the *Regulators' Uprising* (1764) against aristocratic domination of their rural settlements in North Carolina. Many of the Regulator hotheads, including a young Andrew Jackson, later joined the move toward revolution.

## The Germans

Germans were the largest non-English-speaking immigrant group in the colonies. Faced with war and oppression in their homeland, they were delighted to find the rich soil of Pennsylvania. They built sturdy homes and barns, some of which are still used today. German Americans eventually became one-third of the population of the Quaker State (Pennsylvania); some neighborhoods in Philadelphia had German street signs. German Americans brought the Lutheran religion, adding to the Protestant mix of religious toleration. By the time of the Revolution, German Americans were about 6 percent of the population of the colonies as a whole. The Pennsylvania Dutch are so called because English-speaking Americans got confused by *Deutsch,* the German name for *German.* Actually, Pennsylvania Dutch are of German heritage.

## The French

French Canada had about 1 person for every 20 in the 13 colonies, but it helped form what would become the United States. *La Salle* (1682) was a French explorer who navigated down the Mississippi, establishing French claims to the Louisiana territory that the French government would eventually sell to the young U.S. French *courers de bois* (runners of the woods) ranged over North America trading animal pelts with the American Indians. French Acadians resettled by the British from Canada would become the Cajuns of Louisiana. The French founded Detroit, New Orleans, Pittsburgh, and other towns. French settler Crèvecoeur observed in his *Letters from an American Farmer* (1782) that the "strange mixture of blood, which you find in no other country" was an "American, this new man."

## Africans and the ongoing issue of slavery

Africans made up 20 percent of the population by the time of the Revolution, mostly in the South but also with at least a few representatives in all the other early colonies. Slaves worked all their lives with no pay, and their children automatically became slaves, too. Slavery grew because slaves made money for their masters, who then could buy more slaves. Because of slavery, the agricultural output and profits of the early South grew rapidly.

When they could get together at the end of long workdays, slaves created their own African American culture that melded African cultural traditions with the realities of their new home. Africans were brought to America in chains, but when they could, they fought for their freedom. Slaves revolted in New York in 1712 and 1741; during the *Stono Rebellion* (1739) in South Carolina, slaves under a flag of freedom fought a pitched battle with white slaveholders. This rebellion led slave owners to tighten the rules so that slaves found it hard to get together or even learn to read. Slaves who revolted were tortured and/or killed.

**EXAMPLE**

**Question:** Where was slavery legal in the colonies?

**Answer:** Slavery was legal in all British North American colonies in the 1700s.

**EXAMPLE**

**Question:** What did slaves do besides hard work?

**Answer:** Slaves in early America maintained some African social customs and even created a hybrid African/American culture.

**EXAMPLE**

**Question:** Why did slavery grow in the colonies?

**Answer:** Slaves made money for their owners, which increased the owners' social and political power.

**EXAMPLE**

**Question:** How did owners' power over slaves change in the colonies?

**Answer:** In the 1700s, slave laws became more repressive, and owners expanded their legal power over slaves.

**EXAMPLE**

**Question:** Name some slave rebellions that occurred in the colonies.

**Answer:** The Stono Rebellion (1739) in South Carolina and the New York slave conflicts (1712 and 1741) are examples of slave rebellions.

# DAILY LIFE IN THE COLONIES

Colonial Americans lived in drafty houses heated in the winter by fireplaces in one or two rooms. Bedrooms, churches, and schools had no heat, air conditioning, or even fans. The bathroom was an outhouse 20 feet out the back door, and baths, when they happened, meant boiling a lot of water and pouring it into a tin tub barely big enough to sit in. Garbage disposal meant tossing garbage out the window, where it was taken care of by hogs or buzzards. Light at night may be a flickering whale-oil lamp, and everybody had to ask whether whatever they were doing instead of going to bed was worth the candle. Going to bed early was easy, because most people were tired from a workday that ran 12 hours from first light until sundown, when they couldn't see anymore.

Entertainment meant getting together with a good excuse like a *militia muster,* when citizen soldiers drilled and partied, or a barn-raising, quilting bee, funeral, or wedding. All these events could be accompanied by a good deal of drinking and flirting. Northerners liked sleigh rides and skating; Southerners went for fox hunts and playing cards. Southerners thought that plays and dancing were just fine; Northerners took a few years to warm up to those ideas.

The Middle states were, as usual, in the middle when it came to entertainment. Not much fox hunting happened, but plays and dancing were okay with most people. Everybody played the lottery. Lotteries were used to fund churches, hospitals, and colleges like Harvard.

## The relative prosperity of the colonies

The idea that anybody had a chance to make a good life in America started in the early 1700s. It was true; by the time of the Revolution, the early states had some of the most prosperous people in the world.

In fact, unless you were one of the growing number of slaves, America in the 1700s was the place to be. Most people were farmers, but jobs were always available in towns for skilled craftsmen. Even if you were an indentured servant, you could potentially earn your freedom and rise to prominence, which is what two originally indentured signers of the Declaration of Independence did. George Walton was only 26 when he risked hanging by the British to sign the Declaration; he was an orphan who had been indentured to a builder. George Taylor had to indenture himself to earn his ticket from Ireland, but as an old guy of 60, he was important enough to sign the Declaration.

Although every free person had a chance for success, the number of rich people who earned far more than the average farmer grew over time. That doesn't mean life was easy. Between the late 1600s and the Revolution in 1776, the colonies were dragged into one European war after another. Wars burn up lots of military supplies, so the merchants in the big cities made big money by supplying the troops. By 1750, the richest 10 percent of the people in Boston and Philadelphia owned more than half of the property. They got reserved seats in the churches and schools.

Although a few poor people in the cities were supported by charity and sometimes had to wear a large red P (for *Poor*) on their clothes, poverty in the colonies was nothing like it was in Britain in the 1700s, where as many as one out of three people lived with next to nothing. The colonies were full of land that could be farmed and opportunities in trade and skilled jobs.

The colonies prospered despite British attempts to use them as a dumping ground for British problems. The government in London tried to drop its problems on the colonies by sending over 50,000 convicts. These convicts included real hard cases as well as plenty of people who received harsh sentences for little more than stealing a loaf of bread. Some of them became upright citizens in the New World, but they had no love for their British persecutors.

The worst poverty was within the growing slave population. White people were afraid of slave violence like the Stono Rebellion in 1739 and made periodic attempts to limit the importation of more slaves, but British leaders vetoed these attempts. Thomas Jefferson tried to put language opposed to slavery in the Declaration of Independence, but he was overridden by Southern slaveholders (see Chapter 9).

## Education and vocations

Most people were farmers, but colonists learned technical skills on the job. This didn't always mean you had to be an indentured servant to gain a skill; Ben Franklin (the youngest boy of 16 children) learned to be a printer by working for his brother.

In England, education was a privilege of the elite, not a basic right for everyone. Things were different in New England, where public elementary schools supported by towns and counties started in the 1600s. In the Middle colonies, schools were sometimes free and sometimes private, for-pay institutions. In the South, where distances between plantations could be large, families tended to rely on private tutors.

Early Puritan religion taught that everyone should be able to read the Bible. Students went to school when they could spare time away from their chores on the family farm. In all schools, whipping was the rule. Students memorized Latin and Greek and didn't talk back to their teachers for fear of being whipped.

Christian ministers were the most respected professionals in the colonies. Harvard, Yale, Princeton, Brown, and almost all the other original colleges were established to train ministers. Lawyers weren't universally loved in the pioneer societies; a few colonies even passed laws against them. Some early settlers even thought that lawyers deliberately made disputes worse just so they could make money from them. Physicians learned their trade from hanging around other doctors in the early days; the first medical school in the colonies wasn't founded until 1765. *Bleeding* (deliberately draining blood from the patient in order to eliminate an "excess of humors" thought to be the cause of the illness) was a favorite form of treatment, and epidemics were common.

Smallpox affected one in five people; George Washington was a heavily pockmarked survivor of the disease. The first crude inoculation for smallpox was given in 1721, but it took a hundred years to catch on. An epidemic of diphtheria in the 1730s took thousands of lives and helped scare people into the First Great Awakening, covered in the later section "Changing Attitudes toward Religion."

# AMERICAN ARTS

The 1700s brought more than just independence to the colonies; during this period, American art, architecture, and writing took off. The following sections describe the cultural flourish of this era.

## American painters

Fine-arts painters got their start in America during the 1700s. At first, colonial artists focused on portraits — settlers wanted to be remembered, and cameras weren't an option. Benjamin West was the first American artist to train in Europe; when he saw a statue of Apollo, he realized it was no more handsome than an American Indian warrior. The following are a few prominent painters of early America:

- **John Trumbull (1785)** painted pictures of the American Revolution, in which he served briefly.

- **Charles Willson Peale (1780)** served in the Revolution, painting all the while. Peale could accurately be described as a Renaissance man, being good at carpentry, dentistry, optometry, shoemaking, and taxidermy.

- **Benjamin West (1770)** painted large-scale historic pictures. He said that when he was young, American Indians showed him how to make paint by mixing clay from the riverbank with bear grease in a pot.

 **TIP**

You can check out early American art at the National Gallery of Art website (http://www.nga.gov).

## Architecture

Early American architecture styles were imported from Europe; even the log cabin is based on a Swedish model. Nobody lived in log cabins in most of Europe; the idea came from the northern Swedes during their short-lived colony in America.

The popular *Georgian architecture* (1750) was named after the Georges who were kings of England in the 18th century. Georgian style usually is defined by red brick walls that contrast with the white used for window trimming and cornices. A small porch often emphasizes the entrance. *Regularity* was a term of praise for Georgian architects, who used mathematical formulas to figure the proportion of windows to wall size. Georgian is the architecture of Williamsburg, Harvard, and many colonial buildings.

## Literature, libraries, and the birth of American journalism

Colonial literature was very much in the shadow of the mother country; for years, many Americans assumed that only the English had the sophistication to write. This assumption began to change with the prejudice-shattering poetry of *Phillis Wheatley* (1772), a slave who had learned to write. Her memorial poem for George Whitefield (see "Changing Attitudes toward Religion" later in this chapter) caused such a stir that John Hancock and others examined her to make sure a black person could actually write such a work.

*Benjamin Franklin* (1776) would be remembered even if he weren't a famous Revolutionary War leader. His *Poor Richard's Almanack*, which he began editing 45 years before the Revolution, contained gems of thought quoted throughout the colonies. Among them is his reaction to the Great Awakening: "Serving God is doing good to man, but praying is thought an easier service, and therefore more generally chosen." Franklin proved that lightning was electricity and invented bifocal glasses, the efficient Franklin stove, and the lightning rod. He also started the first privately supported library in the country.

By the Revolution, around 40 simple newspapers were published in the colonies. Most of these papers were one-page weeklies, but they begin to reflect and mold public opinion. *Peter Zenger* (1734) was a New York newspaper printer who attacked the corrupt royal governor. He was hauled into court and charged with libel. The government didn't deny the truth of what he said but planned to throw him in prison anyway. In a landmark day for freedom of the press, the jury set Zenger free. Ever since, newspapers have had the right to publish the truth even if it upsets the government.

# CHANGING ATTITUDES TOWARD RELIGION

The problem with all the education that ministers received in the American colonies (see "Education and vocations" earlier in this chapter) is that they started to question what their own churches believed. The predestination doctrine got harder to support; fewer and fewer people wanted to believe that nothing they could do in life would alter God's judgment about whether they were going to heaven or hell. The Puritans' (see Chapter 7) original belief that predestination meant only a small group of people preselected by God for salvation should get to be in their church didn't leave a lot of room for free will or more church members. They tried the *Half-Way Covenant* (1662) to let in a few new members who couldn't swear they were members of the elect, but the churches were losing their power over a people busy making a living in the early 1700s.

The *Great Awakening* was a spiritual revival complete with preaching and conversions that occurred all over the colonies. Spiritual awakening was so important that it actually happened at least twice. The *First Great Awakening* (1734) began in the 1730s, when the colonies were becoming well established; the *Second Great Awakening* occurred in the 1820s. First Great Awakening ministers were set up for their success by the toil, loneliness, and heartbreak of life on the frontier. The movement had more power in the country than in the cities, but America was practically all country in the early 1700s. Great Awakening preachers left in their wake a spiritually charged citizenship eager for change. By traveling throughout the colonies, they gave the separate sections a sense of belonging to a whole nation. The Great Awakening set the emotional stage for the American Revolution. Two men in particular were very influential in this movement:

- *Jonathan Edwards* **(1734):** The First Great Awakening began with Edwards, a well-educated theologian and Congregationalist minister from Massachusetts. Edwards came from Puritan roots but spoke with the power of immediate, personal religious experience. His fiery sermons, including "Sinners in the Hands of an Angry God," attracted a large following.

- *George Whitefield* **(1738):** Whitefield was even more electric than Edwards. He traveled across the colonies and spoke in the dramatic, emotional style of a modern revival preacher, often in outdoor camp meetings. He was the first nationwide American superstar, accepting everyone into his audiences and preaching a simple message of the power of God. He gave more than 18,000 sermons. Whitefield was the most widely recognized public figure in the 100 years before George Washington.

Edwards, Whitefield, and others who used a similar style started a new trend in American religion. Previously, so-called *Old Light* ministers droned on in their sermons, using only rationality and arguments from theology. Modern *New Light* preachers spoke with emotion and showmanship. Princeton, Brown, Rutgers, and Dartmouth were all founded as *New Light* schools.

On the more open end of spirituality, the Quakers (see Chapter 7) believed God was so close to love that people should be free to worship him in the way that was best for them. Quakers supported women's rights and freedom of worship. They opposed slavery and war, but they did pay taxes and worked to influence local governments. Although some Quakers were actually put to death in New England for their tolerant beliefs, more worked to build a peaceful society in Pennsylvania, the colony established by Quaker William Penn.

As freedom in the colonies grew, so did tolerance for neighbors who may have a different ways of worshiping God. The colonies in the 1750s represented many religious denominations, generally liked the king, opposed aristocrats from England, and were open to settlement by non-English people.

> **EXAMPLE**
>
> **Question:** Who were the biggest followers of the First Great Awakening?
>
> **Answer:** The First Great Awakening of the 1730s and 1740s appealed more to poor and rural people and less to rich urbanites.

> **EXAMPLE**
>
> **Question:** What did the Quakers believe?
>
> **Answer:** Quakers were against war and slavery; they paid taxes, tried to influence local governments, and supported women's rights and freedom of worship.

> **EXAMPLE**
>
> **Question:** Was Quakerism the official religion of Quaker Pennsylvania?
>
> **Answer:** Because it was founded by Quakers, who believed in freedom of worship, colonial Pennsylvania had no established official church.

> **EXAMPLE**
>
> **Question:** What was the political and social atmosphere of the colonies by the 1750s?
>
> **Answer:** In general, the colonies in the 1750s represented many religious denominations, disliked aristocrats from England but were okay with the king, and were receptive to settlement by non-English people.

# EARLY POLITICS

Three colonies had governors appointed by their official proprietors, and two colonies elected their own governors. In the other eight colonies, the king appointed usually competent governors (not counting the dunderhead governor Peter Zenger exposed in New York — see "Literature, libraries, and the birth of American journalism" earlier in this chapter). The colonies had two legislative bodies like the modern U.S. Senate and House of Representatives (see Chapter 9). The Senate-type legislators usually were appointed, and the House-type representatives were elected by all the people who had the right to vote, generally white men who owned property.

Property wasn't too expensive in a land with miles of open space, so getting the right to vote wasn't hard. The House, elected by the people, had some major power over the governor; it controlled his salary. The colonies had the most democratic government known in the world up to that time.

# MAKING MONEY IN COLONIAL AMERICA

Due in large part to the plentiful goods they produced and traded, the colonies also provided the highest average standard of living people had ever seen. The most profitable goods of the period included the following:

- The Middle colonies produced enough wheat to make all the bread the colonists could eat and still export thousands of barrels of flour. The United States was (and is still) the world's leading wheat exporter.

- Tobacco was a big money-maker for Virginia and Maryland. Taxes on tobacco made up one-third of U.S. government revenue until long after the Civil War.

- With a seemly unending supply of codfish off the coast of New England, boatloads were exported to Europe. Although cod is no longer as plentiful, the fish was so important to the growth of New England that a "Sacred Cod" still hangs in the Massachusetts House of Representatives.

- New England fishing led to shipbuilding and provided training for thousands of Yankee sailors to man American ships. With a plentiful lumber supply, by the time of the Revolution, the colonies were building a third of all the ships in the British trading fleet.

- North America had a lock on beaver pelts, and any man who was fashionable in Europe just had to have a beaver fur hat.

- Making cloth at home, American women outfitted their families for free and often had extra linen to sell.

- Before the Revolution, America had more small iron forges than England did. One famous place — Valley Forge, Pennsylvania — was even named for its iron works.

## The triangular trade

From the earliest days, rum and other forms of alcohol had an enthusiastic following in the New World. Early Americans could drink most modern people under the table. The infamous *triangular trade* was the shipping of New England rum to Africa in exchange for slaves, who were sold in the West Indies for money and molasses, which was taken back to New England to make more rum. This three-legged voyage was hugely profitable but made up only a minority of New England trade. Most Yankee traders exchanged food and lumber for manufactured goods, which they sold in the colonies.

## Mercantilism

The colonies made more money per person on average than anyplace else in the world. Long before they knew it, the colonies were on a collision course with the interests of their mother country due to England's policy of *mercantilism*. Under this policy, the colonies were supposed to supply England raw materials and buy expensive manufactured stuff only from the mother country. If the colonists wanted to sell anything to another country, the trade was supposed to go through England. England controlled trade, got the markups, and treated the colonists like cows. After the colonists got organized, they couldn't afford to let this practice continue.

## Trade tension

America was growing fast; Britain was growing slowly. Pretty soon, the British had all the American food and other stuff they needed, and Americans wanted European finery that Britain didn't produce. Yankee businessmen wanted to trade with other countries, especially the rich French West Indies. This situation produced the beginning of trade tension between the colonies and their mother country — tension that would eventually become one of the leading causes of revolt.

Beginning in 1650, the English passed a series of Navigation Acts to support mercantilism. The *Navigation Acts* (1650) tried to regulate trade with the colonies to make more money for England. As part of the program, Parliament passed the *Molasses Act* (1733), which imposed a tax of sixpence per gallon on molasses (about $1 in modern money) to make English products cheaper than those from the French West Indies. Colonists largely opposed the tax and rarely paid it; smuggling to avoid it was a huge business. The growing corruption of local officials and disrespect for British law caused by this act and others helped lead to the American Revolution in 1776.

American tobacco filled the pipes of Europe, but the smoking trade was less troublesome; most of the leaf was shipped through England, giving British merchants a nice little profit.

# FIGHTING ACROSS NORTH AMERICA

Special as the colonies felt they were, they were actually pawns in a world-domination power struggle among the great nations of Europe — mostly England, France, and Spain. Spain got the early lead by finding gold and silver all over South America (except for Brazil, owned by Spain's Portuguese neighbors). Mexico and parts of what would eventually become the United States were also part of the Spanish realm. On the East Coast of North America, England started late but was catching up fast, with no gold but plenty of valuable crops in the West Indies and 13 mainland colonies. In Canada and other parts of North America, France ruled a New World empire larger than the English with some valuable furs and fish.

## Frontier fighting

The English colonists got left alone by Britain for their first 30 years, during which time they learned to take care of themselves. Being left alone also meant that, at first, the king didn't bother to send any troops over to help the colonists in their small fights, which he probably viewed as no more important than getting involved in a war between the squirrels in his backyard.

In both *King William's War* (1690) and *Queen Anne's War* (1710), French woodsmen and their American Indian allies raided English settlements. Fighting back, English colonists and their American Indian allies attacked Canada without doing much damage. The French and American Indians managed to kill a lot of settlers in Schenectady, New York, and Deerfield, Massachusetts, but averaging out the rest of the conflicts, the British won. They got frozen northern Canada around Hudson Bay and the peninsula of Nova Scotia, north of Maine, for their troubles.

The *War of Jenkins's Ear* (1739) was fought over British outrage that the Spanish cut off the ear of a British sea captain named Jenkins. During this conflict, great Georgia reformer James Oglethorpe skillfully repelled Spanish raids into the southern Atlantic colonies. (See Chapter 7 for more on Oglethorpe and Georgia.) When the war spread, New Englanders pitched in and, with the help of the Royal Navy, invaded Canada again. This time, they captured a large French fort, but the British gave it back at the end of the war in 1748. The colonists felt betrayed by Britain (and not for the last time).

## The French and Indian War

In 1754, the governor of Virginia gave a 21-year-old surveyor named George Washington a mission to scout out French forces who were building forts on land near the Pennsylvania-Ohio border — land that Virginians (including Washington's family) liked to think they owned. Washington, with 150 Virginian volunteers, spied some Frenchmen resting in the woods and took a shot at them. The Frenchmen called for reinforcements and eventually surrounded Washington. They could have killed him; his men had killed their leader in the sneak attack. Instead, they let Washington and his men go — ironically enough, on July 4. That was the start of the French and Indian War, the largest international war the world had yet seen.

The Americans called the conflict the *French and Indian War,* but it was the *Seven Years' War* in the rest of the world. The war raged so hot and heavy in Europe that the French couldn't do much more in the New World than unleash their American Indian allies. The British, fearing a stab in the back from French people living under British rule in Canada, forced some 4,000 of them to move to New Orleans, where they became the Cajuns.

To unite the colonists and impress the (hopefully) loyal Iroquois, the British called the intercolonial *Albany Congress* (1754). The American Indians stayed mostly loyal, and Ben Franklin got to present his *Albany Plan of Union,* an early attempt to form a union of the colonies. It was a nonstarter, but everybody agreed that the idea was interesting.

The British lost repeatedly early in the French and Indian War. A major British attack against Fort Duquesne (Pittsburgh) was cut to ribbons by a much smaller force of French and American Indians who knew about hiding behind bushes and rocks. In that battle, Washington had two horses shot out from under him, and four bullets tore through his coat. Miraculously unwounded, he rallied his men for an orderly retreat. A later major British attack on outposts all over Canada also failed.

Finally, new Prime Minister William Pitt the Elder directed British forces to make a coordinated assault on the key French fortress at Quebec. In one of the most important battles in British and American history, the British-American force won. The French were thrown completely out of North America, and William Pitt got Pittsburgh named after him.

During this long war, some 20,000 local troops from all the colonies learned to work and fight together. They saw that the British could lose, and they experienced British arrogance firsthand. British General James Wolfe, for example, called members of the American militia "contemptible, cowardly dogs." And despite Washington's heroic war record, the British demoted him to captain — not a good way to make friends.

With the French and most of the hostile American Indians out of the way, the colonies didn't need much protection from mother Britain. When the *Treaty of Paris* (1763) ended the war, the colonies were psychologically on their way to 1776. With the French defeated, the English tried to make peace with the American Indians by prohibiting the colonists from settling west of the Alleghenies in the *Proclamation of 1763*.

 **EXAMPLE**

**Question:** What was the Proclamation of 1763?

**Answer:** The Proclamation of 1763 was a British royal decree that forbade the American colonists from settling west of the Alleghenies. Its goal was to promote peace with the American Indians and a clear line of defense for the British.

# The British halt Western expansion

The Treaty of Paris (see the preceding section) was a tough blow for the American Indians. The warriors who had sided with the French lost an ally, but even American Indians who had been neutral or pro-British had lost the French counterweight to colonial expansion.

## The French empire

In Canada, the French were held up by internal religious and political disagreements, but *Samuel de Champlain* (1608) got a town going in the natural fortress of Quebec. Almost immediately, Champlain got involved in a conflict between two Indian tribes. He helped the local Huron American Indians win a fight over their traditional enemies. Unfortunately, the Hurons' traditional enemies were the very powerful Iroquois nation. Only a few Iroquois were around when Champlain got involved, but tens of thousands more lived farther south, and after Champlain's over reaching, they tended to side with the British.

The mostly Catholic French were pretty comfortable staying in France. The French Protestants who (like the English religious dissenters who founded New England) might have been glad to go to the New World were not allowed to leave. The French who did make it to the New World were more interested in exploring and trading furs than settling down to raise families. This fact made for slow population growth in the French colonies: By 1750, French Canada had only 60,000 settlers, as opposed to the 1.25 million in the English North American colonies. Like the British, French businessmen were getting rich on rum and sugar down in the Caribbean, and most of them were not at all interested in going on freezing beaver hunts in Canada.

Although farming wasn't an important occupation for them, the French managed to float a large amount of grain down the Mississippi to feed their sugar colonies in the West Indies. French fur trappers traveled farther and farther inland. French trading posts were established all across Canada, up to the British settlements in America and down to the Rio Grande in the south of what's now Texas. The French moved around a lot, because when you trap too many beaver, they tend to disappear.

*Antoine Cadillac* (1701) founded Detroit and fittingly enough got a car named for him. *Robert de La Salle* (1682) floated down the Mississippi and named Louisiana for his king. The French also established a well-placed fort at *New Orleans* (1718), named for the French Regent.

In the same year that the French admitted defeat, the great Ottawa American Indian leader Pontiac launched a last-ditch attack against the British advance into the Ohio country. It almost worked. Pontiac's warriors overran all but three British outposts west of the Appalachians, killing 2,000 soldiers and settlers, and coming close to taking heavily fortified Detroit.

Almost as though they were going into extreme defensive mode right after a victory, the British issued the *Proclamation of 1763,* flatly forbidding any settlement west of the Appalachians. The British were trying to be fair to their American Indian allies and to prevent more bloody uprisings like the one Pontiac had led. For the land-hungry Americans, the law was a slap in the face of their long-fought-for dreams. They disobeyed the law and moved West by the thousands. The British were in no mood to put up with insolence. Neither were the Americans. A confrontation was building.

# PRELUDE TO THE REVOLUTIONARY WAR

By 1770, the 13 colonies were no longer just a fringe experiment out in the wilderness; together, they were a country of 2.5 million well-fed, educated, and experienced people. The American population was one-third as big as that of the mother country, and America had a lot more land. The problem was that the English couldn't recognize a grown-up nation when they saw one; they insisted on treating America like a spoiled child. England thought it was time for the child to make himself useful and do his chores.

These chores had to do with raising 140 million pounds (billions of dollars in modern money) to pay for the debt Britain had run up fighting its wars protecting the colonies. Up until this time, the colonies had skated by without paying taxes to the mother country. Now mother Britain was in need of cash and considered the colonies big enough and strong enough to help.

Also, because the American Indians were still kicking up a fuss — and who knew whether the French and the Spanish would stay defeated — Britain believed the time had come for the colonies to pay for the standing army of 10,000 troops that Britain was helpfully sending over.

## New thoughts about freedom

Schools in the colonies spent a lot of time teaching students about classical life in Greece and Rome. Athens and Rome were often viewed as democracies where people helped decide on their own government, and teachers drilled this idea into the heads of the colonists' children.

Settlers also had a selective idea of their rights as Englishmen — rights that had been slowly expanding since the Magna Carta in 1215. The colonists' idea of English liberty was selective because they concentrated on their lack of representation in Parliament without proposing an alternative solution to funding the army that Parliament had sent to defend them.

Finally, the colonists were influenced by the left-wing of British politics — the radical Whigs, who distrusted everything the king did as a potential attack on their freedom. The Whigs saw corruption everywhere in the royal government, and they weren't always wrong. Although the British government hadn't seen a lot of tax revenue from the colonies, it had enjoyed a fair amount of profit. This profit made the colonies worthwhile based on the theory of mercantilism (discussed earlier in this chapter), which held that the power of a country can be measured by how much money it has.

London was a long way away, and the colonists had no trouble slipping a little trade to other places where they could make a profit. No matter how many Navigation Laws the British passed, they couldn't control the colonies. As the colonies got richer, their side business of trade around the Navigation Laws got larger. Britain felt as though it had paid to take a date to a dance, but that date was dancing with everybody else.

## The Stamp Act

With victory in their pockets and billions of dollars of debt making holes in their purses, the British decided to tax the colonists directly for the first time and took these legal actions, presented in chronological order:

- The prime minister ordered the British navy to start strictly enforcing the Navigation Laws to end the colonies' profitable side trade.

- London enacted the *Sugar Act* (1764), the first law for raising revenue for Britain in the New World. The Sugar Act taxed the sweet stuff Americans were just as addicted to as everybody else. When the colonists screamed, the government lowered the duties, and the outcry died down.

- The *Quartering Act* (1765) attempted to give the 10,000 British soldiers in the New World places to stay: with the colonists. Nobody wanted soldiers crowding into the house and bothering their families. Colonial legislatures dragged their feet and refused to cooperate.

- Parliament passed the *Stamp Act* (1765). People in Britain had already been paying stamp taxes for almost 100 years, but to the colonists, shelling out a few cents to the king for every newspaper, playing card, lease, will, and marriage license seemed to be a major insult.

Colonial legislatures had passed plenty of taxes without trouble, but in those cases, the colonists were taxing themselves. Now a bunch of snooty big shots an ocean away were reaching into the colonists' pockets without permission. Chanting "No taxation without representation," the colonists were fighting mad.

 **TIP**

> To remember all the legislation in order, consider this scene: You navigate to the store (Navigation Laws) to buy some candy (Sugar Act), but a soldier stops you (Quartering Act) and stamps your hand (Stamp Act). This analogy is silly, but it works.

With years of experience in self-government and the precedent of the Albany Congress setting them up for cooperation, nine colonies quickly assembled the *Stamp Act Congress* (1765) in New York City. The congress mostly just talked and passed some resolutions, but it did get 9 of the 13 colonies working together.

More to the point of protest were the unofficial *nonimportation agreements* (1765). Americans agreed among themselves not to buy products from England. These local agreements were enforced by a gang called the Sons of Liberty, which wasn't above applying tar and feathers to the bodies of people who tried to break the strike by buying imported goods. The British were hit hard by the boycott; one quarter of their exports had gone to the colonies, and now almost nothing was selling.

The Stamp Act was never effective. Under mob persuasion, all the stamp sellers had been forced to resign before the act took effect. Because the law wasn't working anyway, Parliament revoked the Stamp Act in 1766. Although this repeal could have been an occasion to make nice, the British government instead petulantly enacted a resolution called the *Declaratory Act* (1766), which declared that although it may be cutting some slack now, Parliament had the power "to bind" the colonies "in all cases whatsoever." It wasn't long before Parliament tried a little more binding.

> **EXAMPLE**
>
> **Question:** What was the purpose of the Stamp Act?
>
> **Answer:** The purpose of the Stamp Act of 1765 was to raise money to support British troops in America.

# The Townshend Act

If the colonists wouldn't pay direct taxes, why not skim a little more off the top before the products got to the New World? The *Townshend Act* (1767) put a light import tax on glass, lead, paper, paint — and, most importantly, on tea. The Townshend Act had everybody so upset and produced almost no revenue, and the cost to the British of occupying the colonies continued to rise.

# The Boston Massacre

In 1768, the British landed about 1,200 troops in Boston — 1 soldier for every 4 residents. *The Boston Massacre* (1770) occurred when citizens started throwing rocks at 10 British troops and the troops fired back, killing or wounding 11 citizens.

# The Boston Tea Party

The Townshend Act (see the earlier section) tax eventually led to the *Boston Tea Party* (1773). When the injury of the tax was combined with the insult of granting a monopoly on tea to the British East India Company, citizens responded by dumping shiploads of tea into Boston Harbor.

# The Intolerable Acts

A year later, the British passed what the colonists called the *Intolerable Acts* (1774), designed to punish Massachusetts in general and Boston in particular. The acts closed Boston Harbor until Boston paid Britain back for all the tea lost in the Tea Party. The acts also took away the rights of the legislature and of town meetings, and allowed any English officials who killed Americans to be tried back in friendly Britain.

Showing little political sensitivity to the feelings of America, the British also passed the Quebec Act. This act expanded Canada down into Ohio on land the colonies thought they owned. Something had to give.

## The first Continental Congress

Samuel Adams was a Boston hothead with shaky hands but a firm resolve. While talking revolution in the bars at night, he organized the first *Committee of Correspondence* (1772). Soon, Committees of Correspondence were exchanging revolutionary ideas in and among all the colonies. They had lots to talk about.

The Committees of Correspondence set the groundwork for the first *Continental Congress* (1774). After seven weeks of drinking and deliberation, the first congress passed a Declaration of Rights and sent appeals to the British king and people. The congress also established something called *The Association* to oversee a boycott of everything British. Americans weren't going to buy, sell, or even use British goods.

## Lexington and Concord

Determined to slap down growing resentment with a surge of strength, in April 1775, British troops marched out of Boston to seize some arms and to arrest protest leaders Samuel Adams and John Hancock. They met colonial militia in the towns of Lexington and Concord. After taking some casualties, the militia fought back, and with American *minutemen* (1775) running in from the hills in all directions, the militia pushed the outnumbered British back to Boston. With 300 total casualties for both sides, the British had a war on their hands.

War wasn't going to be easy for the Americans. They had one-third of the population of the British and not one-tenth of the money, and they were facing the most successful fighters in the world. The British had an experienced standing army of 50,000 men, which they made even stronger by hiring 30,000 German mercenaries. In addition, the colonies were far from united: The British had as many as 50,000 American loyalists ready to fight their fellow colonists to stay linked to Great Britain.

Contrary to some modern National Rifle Association beliefs, America in 1775 wasn't a nation of dead-eye marksmen. Only a small minority of households owned firearms. The colonies had no gun factory, and an imported rifle cost the modern equivalent of $5,000. Only 1 out of 12 colonists reported for duty with their own rifles.

The colonists had the advantage of fighting on their own ground. Eventually, they would get help from the French and other nations. But mostly, the American advantage was that a dedicated minority of the citizens of the New World colonies believed in freedom so much they were willing to die for it.

# COLONIAL HISTORY ESSAY SUBJECTS

Social-history themes make great essay material for the AP U.S. History exam. This section covers a couple of ideas that historians love to discuss, which the information in this chapter addresses. There is a fair chance an assigned essay subject will deal with this area.

- **The impact of the Great Awakening:** The Great Awakening seems to be about religion and, thus, about following cosmic rules, but it also really shook things up socially. Public emotion wasn't something that had been big in Britain, but it was the common experience of religious deliverance in the Awakening. This swept-away feeling helped set the stage for the emotion connected to the Revolution, which would be fought by the grand-children of the people who attended the Awakening. Awakening preachers often came from congregations outside the religious mainstream. Their very presence outside the church implied that people could be true to God without following all the cues of the established churches. In fact, maybe people had to follow their own hearts to be con-nected with God's will. The Awakening led to new schools and the beginning of new light ministers. Could a new country be far behind?

■ **The slavery/freedom paradox:** One of the greatest questions in U.S. history is the slavery/freedom paradox. How can one country be the light of freedom in the world *and* a major exploiter of African slaves? One answer is to see New England as the tower of freedom and abolition and to view the South as the basement of slavery and reac-tion. But what about Patrick Henry, Washington, Jefferson, and Madison, all Southern slaveholders? Another answer is that slavery blurred the boundaries between rich and poor whites in the South and made the idea of equality possible (for everybody but the slaves, of course). This idea gets some support when you consider two other slavehold-ing beacons of democracy in the ancient world: Greece and Rome.

Historian Edmund Morgan said, "Americans bought their independence with slave labor." A more balanced statement may be that America got economic power from a large-scale application of the system of slavery that was legal in most of the world and far larger in the West Indies and South America. The North and the Middle states didn't need large-scale slavery to make money; they were quite capable of winning their freedom without it. Only four generations after the Revolution, while slavery was making more money than it ever had before, the United States fought the bloodiest war in its history — the Civil War — to free the slaves. That war is one of the only times in history when one peo-ple (white Northerners with freed black help) fought for the rights of another people (enslaved black Southerners) — not for conquest or glory, but to put an end to slavery.

# 9

# From Revolution to Republic: 1776–1815

> **KEY CONCEPTS**
>
> - ■ Important steps to the Revolutionary War
> - ■ The patriots' fight for survival
> - ■ America under the Articles of Confederation and the Constitution
> - ■ The struggles and triumphs of the early union

**W**hen George Washington heard the news about the fighting at Lexington and Concord (see Chapter 8), he wrote from Mount Vernon to a friend, "[T]he once-happy and peaceful plains of America are either to be drenched in blood or inhabited by slaves. Sad alternative! But can a virtuous man hesitate in his choice?" Washington didn't hesitate. The *Second Continental Congress* (1775) met in Philadelphia a month after the battle and appointed Washington to command the 30,000 militia troops then bottling up 8,000 British soldiers in Boston.

The patient 43-year-old Washington was a good choice. He may not have been history's most brilliant general, but he was competent and sometimes even daring. Most important, he had the strength of character to hold the army together through hard times, and he had the aristocratic bearing to assure people with money that the rebels were more than just an angry mob. Those tough times, and their aftermath, are covered in this chapter.

> **TIP**
>
> Exciting as they are, battles and military campaigns seldom appear in the big AP exam. The test writers are more interested in the meaning of conflicts and what social conditions contributed to and came out of the fights. Still, some knowledge of how the Revolution happened can provide handy ammunition for answering political, economic, and social questions.

# *COMMON SENSE* AND THE DECLARATION OF INDEPENDENCE

The Continental Congress could have just mailed King George III a polite letter telling him to get the heck out of America, but educated people know giving reasons is always better when you need support to make some major changes. The job of explaining why the colonists wanted to break away from England went to 32-year-old Virginian Thomas Jefferson, who wrote the Declaration of Independence. Before the Declaration, though, people were talking about the writings of Thomas Paine.

Showing the power of an idea whose time had come, patriot Paine published a pamphlet called *Common Sense* (1776), in which he argued that it just made common sense for the colonies to be separated from Britain. Britain was a small island compared with the vast expanse of the colonies. Where in the universe does a small star control a large planet? Paine had a dream of a new kind of government — a republic in which power came from the people, not from some self-serving king.

America was ready to hear Paine's words. People in Britain had slowly been increasing their freedom for years; many colonists knew the words of progressive British thinkers such as *John Locke* (1690) who supported the theory of a republic. Freedom was no theory in America; New England town meetings and elections throughout the colonies prepared patriots to launch one of the world's first true republics.

In the Declaration of Independence, Jefferson wrote that all men are created equal, with the right to life, liberty, and the pursuit of happiness. He called these *natural rights,* not theoretical, British, or pie-in-the-sky-when-we-die rights. Jefferson's *Declaration of Independence* (1776) has served as a model for progressive people around the world ever since. In the Declaration, Jefferson calmly lists the ways the British king and government had trampled on the natural rights of their subjects in America. The Declaration was officially approved on July 4, 1776.

Notice that both Paine and Jefferson referred to natural rights and common sense. They viewed the world as being rational, made for humans, and capable of being improved by people. They were children of the *Enlightenment* (1760), a giant wake-up call that started in Europe in the early 1700s and spread around the world. Despite the continued presence of fear and intolerance, people today are still working on carrying out the ideas of the Enlightenment.

# EARLY BATTLES BETWEEN BRITAIN AND THE PATRIOTS

The fighting between the patriots and the British loyalist forces began to look like more than just a family feud when the patriots surprised some British forts in northern New York and hauled off their cannons. With the extra firepower, the patriots marched up Bunker Hill (actually, Breed's Hill), overlooking Boston.

The British eventually dislodged the patriots, but not without losing a lot of men. The British burned a couple of seaports; the patriots invaded Canada and beat some Loyalist soldiers in the South. Then the British hired German professional soldiers, the Hessians, to help them defeat the colonists.

Congress didn't officially declare the United States independent until 14 months after the first shots were fired. With both sides shooting away, Congress's hesitation for more than a year shows how close the colonies still felt to Britain. Another sign of how difficult it was to break the bond with Mother England was the fact that around one in six colonial people remained loyal to the British crown. Not only did Loyalists not want to leave Britain, but they were also ready to fight the patriots who did.

## Problems faced by the British

Like any occupying power, the problem for the British army was that it really controlled only the ground it was standing on. Although as many as 50,000 Loyalist colonists fought alongside the British at one time or another, their numbers weren't enough to keep any large part of America loyal to the king after the king's army left town.

Things got pretty hot for Loyalists when the British army wasn't around to protect them. Patriots weren't above going from tar-and-feather parties to destruction of Loyalist property and violence that bordered on terrorism. At the war's end, some 80,000 Loyalists moved out of the country to Canada or Britain.

## Problems the patriots faced

The problem for the patriots was that the British had a larger and better-trained army — at least 35,000 British and Hessian troops supported by 500 ships. Washington had, at most, 18,000 men, mostly poorly trained and equipped. Although by the end of the war, Washington had around 8,000 properly trained regular-army Continental soldiers, many of the minuteman volunteers who made up most of the army were good for little more than a minute in a stand-up battle. Sniping from behind rocks went only so far in a real war; sooner or later, the armies had to face each other across an open field. Minutemen volunteers tended to fire a round or two and then head home to their farms. Developing soldiers who would stand up to British cannon and massed musket fire took years of drilling and combat experience.

## Slaves: Fighting for both sides

Thousands of African slaves fought with the British because they were promised freedom if they did. Many, but not most, were helped out of the country when the war ended. The black Loyalist Colonel Titus Tye became legendary for capturing supplies and patriots. Blacks fought for the Revolution as well: A black soldier is shown right next to Washington in the famous picture of Washington crossing the Delaware.

# THE AMERICAN REVOLUTION: AN OVERVIEW

Surrounded by angry colonists, the British cleared out of Boston and sailed to New York City, where they had a lot more support. George Washington tried to defend New York but was quickly pushed out, almost losing his army and his life in the fallback. As winter closed off the ability of the armies to maneuver, Washington struck back against detachments of the British army in New Jersey after famously rowing across the ice-clogged Delaware River at night on December 26, 1776.

Meanwhile, the British planned to cut troublesome New England off from the rest of the colonies by marching an army down from Canada through New York, a strategy that didn't work. In the important *Battle of Saratoga* (1777), a patriot army forced the British to surrender in northern New York. That victory gave the French the incentive to enter the war on the side of the patriots. French help was a significant factor in the war, because the French had the weapons, navy, and well-trained regular army that the patriots desperately needed. After their loss at Saratoga, the British offered the Americans home rule within the British empire, but it was way too late for that.

**EXAMPLE**

**Question:** What was the most important outcome of the Battle of Saratoga?

**Answer:** The win by the patriots in the Battle of Saratoga gave the French the belief that the colonialists might succeed if the French entered the war to help the rebels.

## Valley Forge and help from France

Another British army managed to take Philadelphia, forcing the members of the Continental Congress to run for their lives. Washington's army stayed gamely nearby, freezing through a terrible winter at its Valley Forge camp. With the French threatening them, the British moved back to the safety of New York City, fighting a hot battle with Washington along the way. For the next three years, Washington stayed close to New York, tying down the British troops there. The French landed a powerful army of 6,000 soldiers to help the patriots.

Obviously, the British couldn't win the war by sitting around New York. Because New England hadn't worked for the British, and the Middle states had proven tough, the British decided to try the South, where a large Loyalist population promised a better welcome.

## Cornwallis and losing morale

British General Charles Cornwallis took the South's most important city, Charleston, forcing the surrender of the entire Southern patriot army. Then he marched through the Carolinas and Virginia, constantly harassed by patriot forces who attacked any time they could isolate a bite-sized British force. Patriots stung Cornwallis but couldn't stop him.

After four years of war, the patriots were running out of steam in 1780. Despite French help, the powerless Congress was so broke that it announced it could pay off patriot debts only at the rate of 2.5 cents on the dollar. Without food and supplies, Washington's army was close to mutiny. Rich American merchants sold the patriots poor quality supplies at huge profits. The South seemed to be going to the British. Many of the once enthusiastic revolutionaries despaired of ever winning their freedom. Soldiers worried about how their families were doing without them, the chronic lack of guns and food, and the fact that they got paid in almost-worthless paper money.

> **EXAMPLE**
>
> **Question:** What were the complaints of the Continental soldiers in Washington's army?
>
> **Answer:** Continental soldiers' discontent came from home worries, not enough weapons, paper-money pay, and little food.

## Victory and the Treaty of Paris

At this point, Cornwallis decided to do something he considered very safe: He marched his army to what he thought was shelter and resupply in Yorktown on the Virginia coast. Instead of being met by the protective, well-stocked British fleet, however, he found the French navy controlling the escape routes by sea. Washington and his French allies marched 300 miles from New York in a few weeks to attack the trapped British.

Cornwallis surrendered with about one-quarter of all the British troops in North America. After another year of small-scale fighting, the British government gave up. The Americans went from despair to joyous celebration.

In the *Treaty of Paris* (1783), the British formally recognized the independence of the United States and, taking a satisfyingly broad view of what the new United States owned, signed over everything from the Atlantic to the Mississippi and from the Great Lakes to Spanish Florida. America began its independence with the largest area of rich land in the world and with a priceless heritage of freedom.

> **EXAMPLE**
>
> **Question:** What were the major parts of the 1783 Treaty of Paris?
>
> **Answer:** Under the Treaty of Paris, the United States was free and owned all the lands to the Mississippi.

# DESIGNING A NEW COUNTRY

The American Revolution introduced the reality, not just the theory, of democratic government to the world. The Revolution challenged the old order in Europe and South America by opposing inherited political power with the democratic idea that government rests on the consent of the governed. The example of the first successful revolution against a European empire provided a model for many other colonial peoples, who realized that they, too, could become self-governing nations. In the 20th century, revolutionaries sometimes even quoted Thomas Jefferson as they fought against American economic interests.

America won its independence with the help of the endless fights between European countries; it provided the model for what would become, 200 years later, the European Union. The United States remains a leading example of the extent to which a country with people from all around the world can become and remain a workable society.

Before America could become a practical reality, however, it had to figure out exactly what would change following independence. In their enthusiasm for new-found freedom, some lawmakers got ahead of the times.

After the Revolution, with 1 out of 30 American people (the most conservative Loyalist residents) leaving permanently for Canada or Britain, the new United States had a distinctly progressive bent. In the old days, for example, the titles *Mr.* and *Mrs.* were reserved only for the upper classes; now everybody got called that. Even more social changes were to come.

## Separation of church and state

Church and state were separated. Although the Congregationalist denomination hung on for a few years as the official religion of Massachusetts, one by one, the states dropped any affiliation with a particular denomination. One of Jefferson's proudest accomplishments was the passage of the *Virginia Statute for Religious Freedom* (1786), which separated religion from government in what was then the largest state. It served as a model for other states.

## Early attempts to abolish slavery

The Continental Congress of 1774 called for the abolition of the slave trade. Some Northern states ended slavery as early as 1776. Even a few forward-thinking Southerners freed their slaves in a burst of Revolutionary zeal. Washington arranged for his slaves to be set free after he and his wife died. Although the U.S. set a deadline of 1808 to abolish the importation of new slaves, a *slave rebellion in Haiti* (1791) scared a lot of slave owners into harsher treatment of slaves. The slave revolt also made Napoleon rethink his involvement in the New World.

**Question:** What was the influence of the slave rebellion in Haiti on the U.S.?

**Answer:** The rebellion scared Southern slave owners into increasingly brutal treatment of slaves and gave Napoleon a reason to want to sell out of his interests in the New World, paving the way for the Louisiana Purchase.

Jefferson was embarrassed that he couldn't free his slaves. Enslaved workers were worth as much as $50,000 each in modern money. A poor businessman, Jefferson had been forced to mortgage his slaves to the bank, which wouldn't let Jefferson set them free. The Polish American Revolutionary war hero Thaddeus Kosciusko spent his army pay to help buy the freedom of slaves.

## Women's gains and republican motherhood

Women made some early gains. New Jersey's Revolutionary constitution of 1776 even briefly granted women the right to vote, 100 years before the rest of the world. Although that early right was overturned, women played a role in the freedom fight. John Adams's wife, Abigail, warned him in her so-called *Remember-the-Ladies letter* (1776) before the Declaration of Independence that women were ready to start their own revolution. During the war, some women, dressed like men, fought in both the artillery and the infantry for the patriots. Two sisters dragged a British messenger off his horse and smuggled his secret dispatches through enemy lines to the Americans.

> **EXAMPLE**
>
> **Question:** What did Abigail Adams, wife of future President John Adams, write about in a famous letter to him?
>
> **Answer:** In an early call for women's rights, Abigail advised John to "remember the ladies."

The idea of *republican motherhood* (1780) elevated women to the role of keeper of the nation's conscience and first educator of future patriots. The concept of republican motherhood resulted in increased educational opportunities for American women. The reasoning was that women had to be educated to raise good members of a free country. By 1837, women had their own source of higher education: Mount Holyoke Female Seminary, the predecessor to Mount Holyoke College.

> **EXAMPLE**
>
> **Question:** What was the meaning of republican motherhood?
>
> **Answer:** Republican motherhood meant that it was the important responsibility of women to raise the next generation of freedom-loving patriots.

Although republican motherhood kept women at home rearing children, it also began to legitimize political activity for women. The Abolitionist movement, which started to gain strength in the 1830s and 1840s, found many of its strongest voices among educated Northern women. The *Seneca Falls Convention* (1848), which began the women's rights movement in the United States, owes some of its origin to the emphasis on republican motherhood at the time of the Revolution.

## Trade, industry, and economic democracy

The rich Loyalists who fled the U.S.A. left behind some large pieces of good land that were divided among deserving patriots. Although land that the king and his unrepentant subjects had owned was sold to help pay off the war debt, few attacks were made on former Loyalists who chose to stay in the new country. Because America didn't have royalty or an aristocracy, there was some measure of economic democracy even before the political democracy of the Revolution got going. That may be one reason why the United States didn't experience as much violence after its change of government as France did a few years later.

Commerce and industry got off to a good recovery after the Revolution. Although the United States was outside the British family, it still had the whole non-British world with which to trade. American ships were landing in China as soon as they could get out of port after the peace treaty was signed. River-powered industry was encouraged in New England as soon as the restrictions of old England were gone. Building a business wasn't always easy. The new country had to compete with British manufacturers who were dumping, for cheap prices, products that had been bottled up by the war.

## Expanding the country

The ink had barely dried on the Treaty of Paris when Congress sat down to plan for the expansion of the United States into its western lands. *The Land Ordinance of 1785* provided that the land in the old Northwest Territory — covering what are now Ohio, Indiana, Michigan, Illinois, and Wisconsin — should be sold to help pay off the national debt. The proceeds from the sale of 1 out of 36 sections went to support local schools, a gift to education that was unheard of in the rest of the world.

Then even more important, the *Northwest Ordinance* (1787) let the new lands pass quickly from dependent territories to full partnership as states as soon as any given territory had 60,000 residents. It also banned slavery in the Northwest Territory.

> **EXAMPLE**
>
> **Question:** What was the major purpose of the Northwest Ordinance?
>
> **Answer:** The Northwest Ordinance of 1787 provided rules for admission of new states and prohibited slavery in the Northwest Territory.

# THE LEGAL FOUNDATION OF A NATION

To get a fresh start, the Continental Congress in 1776 asked the states to rewrite their state constitutions as republican documents. Written constitutions serve as the fundamental rules — laws that don't change with the day-to-day ideas of ordinary legislation. Most of the state constitutions were similar, being contracts that defined the powers of government and the rights of citizens.

Massachusetts came up with the new idea of having the people of the state ratify any amendments to the state constitution. The amendment process for the U.S. Constitution still works that way: The legislatures of three-quarters of all the states must approve any changes. After the states began to think in a new citizen-friendly way, almost half of the 13 original colonies decided to move their capitals to be closer to the people in the center of each state.

## The Articles of Confederation

To set some permanent rules for the new nation, Congress drafted the *Articles of Confederation* (1777). The major issue at first wasn't so much how to govern the new country as how to handle the land it was sitting on. Most colonial governments liked to think of themselves as extending all the way over the Appalachian Mountains to the Mississippi, if not to the Pacific. They each had claims on Western land. The new central U.S. government got the states to give up these claims so that new states could be formed and land sold to settlers to support the national government. The individual states pooled their Western land resources for the common good.

This was an important start, because the Articles of Confederation gave no power to Congress to collect taxes. Congress established a tax quota for each state and then used the time-honored negotiating strategy of begging and pleading to get the states to pay up. How well this system worked is reflected in the number of Continental soldiers who were never even supplied with shoes by the government. And tax collecting wasn't the end of the Confederation government's weakness. Congress wasn't allowed to regulate commerce and set tariffs; each state did that individually. Apples could be taxed at 10 cents in New York and $10 in Pennsylvania — possibly both ways if a cargo moved across state lines.

> **EXAMPLE**
>
> **Question:** What was the major government revenue weakness of the Articles of Confederation?
>
> **Answer:** Under the Articles of Confederation, the United States couldn't levy taxes or control commerce.

The Articles of Confederation was an anti-King George agreement; whatever the colonies didn't like about the British government, they left out of the Articles of Confederation. Dictatorial administration? The articles allowed for no president, king, or executive at all. Crooked judges? The articles established no national judicial system; each state did its own thing. The central government got to negotiate treaties and run a postal system, though it was a little unclear where it would get the money to print the stamps.

The Articles of Confederation contained good things as well. First, the articles existed, giving the states a unified platform to work with. Second, weak as they were, the articles clearly spelled out the powers of the government. Unlike the unwritten, hard-to-define British Constitution, the articles were right there in black and white. They held the union together through a tough war and gave the states a stepping stone to something stronger and more permanent.

## Shays' Rebellion

When the war was over, the states' attentions drifted back to their own interests. Quarrels over boundaries generated minor battles between discharged state militias. A large but mostly peaceful uprising in western Massachusetts, led by a captain in the war, scared the government and the local courts.

*Shays' Rebellion* (1786) was a series of armed demonstrations led by small farmers angered by debt and taxes. Failure to repay debts often resulted in imprisonment in debtor's prisons or loss of the family farm. The rebels freed their friends from prison and stopped courts from ordering evictions. The rebellion lasted about six months before it was violently put down by a private army paid for by rich landowners. Without a standing army, the national government could do nothing. This scare helped lead to support for the *Constitutional Convention* (1787), which began a few months after the rebellion.

**EXAMPLE**

**Question:** What was Shays' Rebellion?

**Answer:** In Shays' Rebellion, debt-ridden Massachusetts farmers attacked courts. The Rebellion helped show the need for a more powerful federal government.

## The Constitutional Convention

Delegates from all the states came to the Constitutional Convention, including Revolutionary superstars Ben Franklin (then 81 years old), Alexander Hamilton, and James Madison. George Washington chaired the meeting.

The delegates knew they needed a strong central government, but they wanted to preserve the maximum rights to states and their individual citizens. Proposals broke down into a large-state plan and a small-state plan. Under the Articles of Confederation, the rule had been one state, one vote. The big states wanted representation by population size. In the end, the great compromise split the difference. Big states got the House of Representatives, based on population; the small states got the U.S. Senate, with two senators for every state, no matter how small. As a tip to the big states, all tax and revenue bills had to start in the House. The many compromises took years to be finally approved.

**EXAMPLE**

**Question:** Did all the delegates agree with the new Constitution at the first meeting?

**Answer:** No, the Constitution was controversial and required compromise and years of discussion to be ratified by all 13 states.

Getting over King George and their fear of despotism, the delegates established a strong president who could appoint judges and other officials, serve as commander in chief of the military, and veto legislation. This strong president was to be chosen by the people indirectly through an electoral college as a supposed safeguard against mob rule. The *executive* president branch of government was balanced with the *legislative* Congress and *judicial* Courts branches. The deal including both the House of Representatives and the Senate was called the *Great Compromise* (1788).

## Slavery: Reduced but not gone yet

The Southern states wanted to count slaves as part of their population to get more representatives in the House and the electoral college, which elected the president. The North said it was nice that the South finally wanted to count slaves as people, but the way Southerners treated slaves, Northerners may as well request representation for their horses.

The two sides split the difference: In writing the new Constitution, Southern slaveholders got a *Three-Fifths Compromise* (1789), in which slaves were partly counted. All but two of the states wanted to shut down the African slave trade; the compromise was to stop stealing people from Africa in 20 years (1807).

**EXAMPLE**

**Question:** What was the Three-Fifths Compromise?

**Answer:** The Three-Fifths Compromise said that, in determining Congressional representation, slaves counted but only partially. Five slaves counted as three people for the purposes of assigning members of the House of Representatives and the Electoral College, which officially selects the president.

## Reining in the states

The Constitution needed the approval of nine states to get going. Eventually, it was approved by all 13 states, but it took three years and some mighty close votes. In general, wealthy, well-educated people liked the strong central government called for by the new Constitution; people who supported the federal Constitution were *Federalists* (1788). They wrote the *Federalist Papers* (1788), arguing that a large republic can best protect minority rights.

In the end, the laws that didn't change in the Constitution served all the people. You can count on one hand the countries in the world that have had stable governments for the past 200 years. Although it's far from an economic democracy, the United States has provided a shield for freedom and a chance for success to millions of people.

> **EXAMPLE**
>
> **Question:** What was the main point of the Federalist Papers?
>
> **Answer:** The Federalist Papers argued that a large republic best protects minority rights.

As weary old Ben Franklin was leaving the convention hall, a woman asked him, "Well, doctor, what have we got — a republic or a monarchy?" The elder statesman replied, "A republic, madam, if you can keep it."

# The first president: George Washington

George Washington became the first U.S. president in 1789. His ride from quiet Mount Vernon to the nation's temporary capital of New York City was one big party: Bells rang, bands played, and the roads were strewn with flowers. Washington took the oath of office on a balcony overlooking Wall Street — something that some people have seen as a bad omen, foreshadowing the control of government by big money. Washington appointed the first Cabinet: Thomas Jefferson (State), Alexander Hamilton (Treasury), and Henry Knox (War).

# The Bill of Rights

The *Bill of Rights* (1791), the first ten amendments to the Constitution, was approved by all the states to guarantee that the new Constitution would mandate basic rights for all citizens. Spelling out these rights put critics of the new Constitution at ease by mandating freedom of speech, religion, and other liberties.

> **TIP**
>
> Although the AP exam probably won't trick you with individual amendment numbers, the Bill of Rights makes excellent essay material and can come in handy on multiple-choice questions. Here's the short version:
>
> - **First Amendment:** Freedom of religion, speech, and press
> - **Second Amendment:** Right to keep and bear arms
> - **Third Amendment:** Protection from mandatory quartering of troops in private citizens' homes
> - **Fourth Amendment:** Protection from unreasonable search and seizure
> - **Fifth Amendment:** Due process under the law
> - **Sixth Amendment:** Right to criminal trial by jury and other rights for the accused
> - **Seventh Amendment:** Right to civil trial by jury
> - **Eighth Amendment:** No excessive bail or cruel and unusual punishment
> - **Ninth Amendment:** Establishes that amendments don't limit rights and that more rights can be conferred
> - **Tenth Amendment:** Establishes that powers not listed in Constitution belong to the states and the people

# THE YOUNG REPUBLIC

The population of the United States grew rapidly. By the time of the first official census in 1790, approximately 4 million people lived in the U.S., almost double the 1770 population of just over 2 million. Although business was picking up, the government was still deep in debt from the Revolutionary War.

Treasury Secretary Alexander Hamilton wanted to pay off the national debt. Even though the United States had won the war, investors still didn't think government bonds were worth much more than 10 cents on the dollar. Hamilton proposed to pay the investors all back. To raise the money, he got Congress to approve a duty on foreign imports and U.S.-made luxury items such as whiskey and carriages. The credit of the United States improved. Hamilton supported the development of a national bank, partially funded by the government, that could keep money in circulation and help boost the economy. He also wanted to give subsidies to business, but Congress wouldn't buy that. Jefferson argued against the Bank of the United States, but it passed anyway. Although he got the nation on a firm financial footing, Hamilton's policies were seen by poorer farmers as serving the rich Eastern merchants.

> **EXAMPLE**
>
> **Question:** What was Alexander Hamilton's economic policy?
>
> **Answer:** Alexander Hamilton's economic program included a Bank of the U.S., plus excise and tariff taxes. Congress rejected his idea of direct subsidies to manufacturers.

> **EXAMPLE**
>
> **Question:** How was Hamilton's financial program viewed by poorer voters?
>
> **Answer:** Alexander Hamilton's fiscal policy was seen as favoring Eastern merchants.

As a states' rights *strict-constructionist,* Jefferson believed that anything not specifically mentioned in the Constitution was prohibited to the federal government. Hamilton took a broad interpretation, or *loose-construction,* view of the Constitution. He thought the Constitution had *implied powers,* which allowed the government to do whatever was necessary to carry out the general tasks assigned in the Constitution. A modern example of implied power is the federal road-building program; the only power enumerated for this in the Constitution is the maintenance of postal roads. Therefore, every freeway is officially a postal road.

## The Whiskey Rebellion

Whiskey was distilled money for the frontier farmers, who had little cash and almost no transportation; whiskey was the easiest and most profitable thing to do with a crop of grain. Even preachers got paid with jugs of liquor, which they could then exchange for food or supplies. The *Whiskey Rebellion* (1794) was a protest on the western Pennsylvania frontier against the tax Hamilton had gotten passed on liquor. At almost $4 a gallon in modern money, the tax was more than most self-respecting moonshiners could come up with in a barter economy.

Hamilton's tax may have raised money, but it really hurt small-time farmers/distillers. With local protests spreading throughout the states, Hamilton and Washington personally led an army of 13,000 armed men on a fruitless search for whiskey criminals near Pittsburgh. They didn't catch many people, but they made their point. The whiskey business paid up for a while in Pennsylvania. On a larger scale, the new federal government showed it could use force to back up laws. But in places without soldiers, the tax was difficult to collect, and it was repealed in 1803.

## Forming political parties

Hamilton's ambitious big-government programs created opposition from people like Jefferson, who believed in more individualism and less government. Political parties began to form around these opinions. People who liked Hamilton's ideas were called *Federalists* (1795), and Jefferson's followers called themselves *Democratic-Republicans* (1800). The Federalists died out around 1816. After trying silly party names like *Whigs* (1834) and *Know-Nothings* (1855), American's factions divided the names of Jefferson's party. Political parties weren't an idea of the framers of the Constitution, but they've been a handy addition to democracy, always shifting just to the right or left of whoever is in power.

## Staying out of other people's wars

The French had a bloody revolution of their own starting in 1789, occasioning yet another French war with Britain. The *Franco-American Alliance* (1778) that was key in helping the United States win its independence was still on the books, but Washington decided not to take sides and issued his *Neutrality Proclamation* (1793). That was okay with the French, who figured that the baby United States wouldn't be much help anyway.

Meanwhile, on the Ohio frontier, some American Indians had gotten together in the *Miami Confederacy* (1790) and had twice beaten small U.S. armies sent against them. The British were still staying in forts on American soil, arming the American Indians. Finally, a serious U.S. force beat the American Indians at the *Battle of Fallen Timbers* (1794), and the American Indians sold most of their lands in the *Treaty of Greenville* (1795).

Rolling along the treaty trail, trying to stay out of trouble, the United States signed *Jay's Treaty* (1794) with Britain to stop the British from staying in forts on American soil. The agreement didn't stop Britain from seizing American ships at sea and forcing U.S. sailors to join its navy, but it did let the United States into the valuable trade with the British West Indies. Spain helped the United States with *Pinckney's Treaty* (1795), giving the new country all the land down to Florida and free use of the Mississippi. America was getting a little respect.

EXAMPLE

**Question:** What was Pinckney's Treaty?

**Answer:** Pinckney's Treaty of 1795 with Spain fixed Southern boundaries and gave U.S. ships the right to use the Mississippi River.

## Washington leaves office

Facing criticism and tired of politics, Washington left office at the end of his second term. His *Farewell Address* (1796) warned the nation to stay out of permanent alliances and asked people to be governed by moral and spiritual principles.

Washington himself was a freethinking Freemason who welcomed all religions and avoided being a formal member of any church in his later years. He was an example of good behavior; after 200 years, his character still shines. He liked a good time, however; his major retirement project was the construction on his property of one of the largest whiskey stills in the country. His last words were "It is well."

# JOHN ADAMS

John Adams (1797), the second American president, sent envoys to France to try to solve a disagreement. Angry that the Americans would be agreeing with the British under Jay's Treaty when they should be loyal to the French under the Franco-American Alliance, the French had begun seizing American ships at sea. After an aborted negotiation called the *XYZ Affair* (1797) for the coded names of three French envoys who tried to extort a bribe from the United States, both sides got over their bad feelings and signed the *Convention of 1800,* which ended their formal alliance.

> **TIP**
>
> Don't miss the forest for the trees. The AP exam cares about trends, not a whirlwind of treaty names. The individual names are like a bonus round: You get extra points for remembering. The main trend to understand from all the early U.S. diplomacy is that the new nation was wisely avoiding war and slowly gaining respect. If the United States had fought a war with France in 1800, the French surely wouldn't have sold America the Louisiana Purchase in 1803.

What with all the international and domestic political tensions, the ruling Federalists in Congress went overboard and passed the *Alien and Sedition Acts* (1798). These acts made criticizing the president a crime, raised the waiting time for citizenship from 5 to 17 years, and allowed the government to deport any noncitizens it didn't like.

The U.S. appeared to be on the path to becoming a police-state, but Jefferson fought the repressive laws every step of the way, and they expired at the end of Adams's one term as president. Jefferson and James Madison secretly wrote the *Kentucky and Virginia Resolutions* (1798), which were passed by these states to protest the repressive Alien and Sedition Acts. In fighting the laws, Jefferson took an extreme turn in the antigovernment direction and introduced the concept of nullification, saying that any state could refuse to follow a federal law it didn't like. This concept would come back to haunt the country in the run up to the Civil War.

> **EXAMPLE**
>
> **Question:** What were the Kentucky and Virginia Resolutions?
>
> **Answer:** Kentucky and Virginia Resolutions championed states' rights against the Alien and Sedition Acts.

# THOMAS JEFFERSON AND THE 1800S

*Thomas Jefferson* (1801) narrowly squeaked past Federalist attacks to become the third president. This election marked the first change in political parties for the United States and was an important landmark for peaceful political transition. Jefferson believed in small government. He reduced government programs, pardoned the martyrs to the expired Alien and Sedition Acts, and had the government return many of their fines. A new naturalization act again let immigrants become citizens after only five years.

In 1804, Alexander Hamilton was killed in a duel with Jefferson's Vice President Aaron Burr; Burr fled the country.

**EXAMPLE**

**Question:** What was Thomas Jefferson's political approach?

**Answer:** Jefferson reduced the activities of the federal government.

## Empowering the Supreme Court

During his last days in office, Adams had appointed a new chief justice of the Supreme Court, John Marshall. Marshall had only six weeks of formal legal training; he was President Adams's last choice after three other men couldn't take the job. President Jefferson didn't like Marshall's strong-government views but couldn't get rid of him.

John Marshall had suffered from hunger and cold as a soldier at Valley Forge; he knew governments had to be strong enough to deliver for their people. Marshall's first landmark case was *Marbury v. Madison* (1803). In rejecting an appeal from a fellow Federalist, Marshall overturned a previous law as unconstitutional because it didn't agree with the 15-year-old U.S. Constitution. This set the precedent that the Supreme Court can review all laws for their constitutionality.

**EXAMPLE**

**Question:** What was the importance of the case of *Marbury v. Madison*?

**Answer:** This decision gave the Supreme Court the power to review all laws for their constitutionality.

Jefferson's small-government followers tried to strike back by filing impeachment charges against a judge they didn't like. Congress dropped the charges, and the principles of independent judicial review and separation of powers became the law of the land.

## The Louisiana Purchase

In France, Napoleon Bonaparte had two troubles on his mind: He was fighting almost every other country in Europe, and he had just lost a war to an island of slaves. Haiti was a rich sugar island where thousands of slaves had risen up in revolt against their French masters. Napoleon's troops could shoot their way in, but diseases and guerilla warfare meant they really couldn't stay. Napoleon needed money and wanted out of the New World.

Jefferson had sent negotiators to France to try to buy New Orleans. They had authorization to pay as much as $10 million (half a billion dollars in modern money) for the city. Napoleon surprised them by offering all of France's holdings in North America, from the Mississippi to the Pacific Ocean, for $15 million. What the heck? They bought a wilderness to get a city.

**EXAMPLE**

**Question:** What was the background of the Louisiana Purchase?

**Answer:** The Louisiana Purchase resulted from Napoleon's loss in Haiti, opened the whole trans-Mississippi area, and showed Jefferson's flexibility with his own strict-constructionist views.

## The Lewis and Clark expedition

*Meriwether Lewis* and *William Clark* (1804) explored the new territory with the help of the American Indian woman Sacajawea. They wouldn't have survived without her. By traveling with a woman and her child, Lewis and Clark showed the American Indians that their expedition wasn't a hostile war party. Their two-and-a-half year adventure pointed the way west for future settlers. Other early explorers, including *Zebulon Pike* (1805), brought back reports of the immense and unknown new territory of the United States. Pike showed the value of publicity; although Pikes Peak was only one of over 50 tall mountains in Colorado, it became the one everybody knows.

# EVENTS LEADING TO THE WAR OF 1812

After winning a landslide reelection victory in 1804, Jefferson and the nation were caught between France and Britain in the two countries' seemingly endless war to control Europe. Jefferson was temporarily unpopular for keeping the United States out of an early war with the great powers; America couldn't trade with either power without facing the other's guns. Both sides grabbed American merchant ships and sailors. The British forced some 6,000 American sailors to join their navy between 1808 and 1811 alone.

**EXAMPLE**

**Question:** How was Jefferson's policy of avoiding war received by the public?

**Answer:** Jefferson was unpopular for neutrality toward Britain and France.

Too weak to fight, the United States passed the *Embargo Acts* (1807), which were meant to stop all trade with foreign nations. While the United States held its breath and turned blue, the British and French managed to do without American goods. American exporters either smuggled goods or went out of business; many saw the acts as attacking Americans to fight foreigners.

To the extent that they kept foreign goods out, the Embargo Acts helped infant U.S. industries grow without competition. Some traders actually liked the cops-and-robbers aspects of the smuggling business; it was exciting, and the profits were great if you didn't get caught. Just before Jefferson left office, Congress passed the *Non-Intercourse Act* (1809), which limited the embargo to Britain and France.

## James Madison steps in

*James Madison* (1809), friend and follower of Jefferson, took over as president of a nation still caught in the French/British nutcracker. The 15-year U.S. headache of foreign entanglement without any foreign alliances showed the impossibility of separating the United States from the world, as both Washington and Jefferson had wished. As a trading nation, America couldn't avoid the crossfire of belligerents.

Congress made an effort to address the situation: *Macon's Bill No. 2* (1810). This bill said that, if either Britain or France would end its commercial blockade, the United States would restore its embargo against the nation that didn't stop blocking trade. In other words, America would take sides, but it was first come, first served. France promised to be good; Britain didn't. America was drawn closer to another conflict with Britain.

## Britain's deal with Tecumseh

Meanwhile, in the green forests of the frontier, a strong Shawnee leader named *Tecumseh* (1811) united tribes from Canada to Mexico and prepared to push the settlers back. The British were more than happy to supply guns to the American Indians. William Henry Harrison, U.S. governor of Indiana, led a band of militia toward Tecumseh's headquarters on the Tippecanoe River while the chief was away gathering together his allies.

Tecumseh's brother unwisely attacked the militia before the American Indians could get together, telling the braves that his medicine-man powers would keep them from being wounded. When magic didn't stop the militia's bullets, the American Indians fled, and Tecumseh's rebellion was over before it started. Tecumseh fought on, eventually charging alone into the middle of an American army. An old American frontiersman helped the American Indians give Tecumseh's body an honored burial.

## The War of 1812 against Britain

After being pushed around for years, the United States declared war on Great Britain in 1812. The United States could hardly have been more divided; war resolutions barely passed in Congress. The war was most popular in the South and in the Middle and Western states. New England greeted the news of war with mourning.

The young United States faced a war with its old enemy Britain, still the most powerful empire in the world. Faced with the experienced British military, the young United States was in trouble trying to go to war without the support of the whole country. New England refused to let its militias fight and probably loaned more money to Britain than to the U.S. government. New England even helped supply food for the British invaders from Canada.

How could New England, the hotbed of freedom and revolution, as well as a major shipping area, turn against an American government that was determined to preserve the freedom of international shipping? A lot of the answer was politics. New England was Federalist territory; the people there would rather lose a war than see Jefferson's Republicans win.

Like slipping on a banana peel and sliding into a gold mine, the *War of 1812* was an embarrassment that turned out fine. New England didn't want to fight; inexperienced American troops often ran from a British army hardened by years of combat with Napoleon, and old generals from the Revolutionary War proved that they needed to retire. U.S. invasions of Canada failed miserably; the British army burned Washington, D.C., and the British navy raided and blockaded American ports.

The good news was that the United States achieved some victories to remember:

- The *USS Constitution* (Old Ironsides), with a crew that was one-sixth free blacks, blew away proud British ships.
- The star-spangled banner continued to wave over Baltimore Harbor and inspired the national anthem.
- A thrown-together force of sailors, frontiersmen, free blacks, Frenchmen, and pirates smashed a larger force of experienced British regulars to save New Orleans.

When the smoke cleared, the United States and Britain signed the *Treaty of Ghent* (1814), without any formal gains for either side. The United States gained respect for standing up to the great British Empire, and Americans felt a new sense of national pride.

It had been a close thing. Toward the end of the war, at the *Hartford Convention* (1814), angry New England states demanded more power but shut up when news of the victory at New Orleans reached the capital at about the same time as their complaints. Ironically, New England started all the talk about nullification and secession that would become popular in the South with respect to the issue of slavery.

# THE ERA OF GOOD FEELINGS

With so many years of embargo and blockade, the United States had time to develop its own industries, and the government was involved in the growth of American business from the beginning of the country. Following the war, Congress passed the protective *Tariff of 1816,* which taxed foreign imports to make American goods more competitive. Congressman Henry Clay championed the *American System* (1820), which included easy credit, increased tariffs, and support for roads and canals to move American products. An added bonus: Roads and canals were the most important way to encourage settlement of the West.

> **EXAMPLE**
>
> **Question:** What were the most important new forms of transportation in the early United States?
>
> **Answer:** Roads and canals were the most important new avenues of transportation.

*James Monroe* (1817), the last of the Revolutionary War heroes to be president, served two terms that were free of enough controversy to be called the *Era of Good Feelings*. Of course, nothing involving humans is completely without controversy; Monroe faced plenty of debate about tariffs, the Bank of the United States, where and how to build canals and roads, and how much to charge for the sale of the millions of acres of public lands that were up for grabs.

Whatever its political challenges, the nation continued to build transportation. The Cumberland Road began in 1811 and eventually stretched from Maryland to the frontier at Illinois. The first steamboat to make it down the Ohio River and on to New Orleans also sailed in 1811.

# 10

# The United States Grows Up, 1816–1845

The years between 1816 and 1845 were a time of tremendous growth and expansion for the United States. In this chapter, you find out about events that changed the landscape of the country, pointing the U.S. in the direction it still follows today. AP tests always have questions on *Jacksonian democracy*; this chapter helps you get ready for them.

> **TIP**
>
> Don't just memorize names, dates, and places. *When you see themes, connect them:* Manifest Destiny was a social trend connected to American Indian removal. The *Gibbons v. Ogden* decision on interstate commerce was the economic reality brought about by the invention of the steamship and better transportation. Jacksonian democracy was a consequence that stemmed from the shift toward more universal male voting rights. Connect themes as you review so that you'll be ready to connect to a high score on test day.

# MANIFEST DESTINY

You're almost sure to see a question on the AP test about Manifest Destiny, a theme that runs through much of U.S. history. *Manifest Destiny* means that lots of Americans felt God intended for the United States to control all the land between the Atlantic and Pacific Oceans. With the giant Louisiana Purchase speeding America toward the West Coast while the country was on only its third president, the U.S. seemed to be on a transcontinental roll. (See Chapter 9 for more on the Louisiana Purchase.)

The word *manifest* refers to an obvious fact, and a *destiny* is an unavoidable fate. Because of the practical implications of Manifest Destiny — that U.S. citizens would have to fight not only the British but thousands of American Indians and Mexicans as well to achieve the country's destiny — a substantial minority of citizens opposed the idea at any given time and would have been just as happy to pass up the honor. Many more thought America was doing non-Americans a favor by forcibly inviting them to be part of the U.S.A.

> **TIP**
>
> For the AP exam, remember that Manifest Destiny showed up early in the 1800s, encouraged by Thomas Jefferson's huge Louisiana Purchase, and remained part of the national thinking until the U.S. finished grabbing land during the Spanish-American War at the end of the 1800s. That is almost 100 years. This concept fits as part of the official AP theme of American exceptionalism: Americans thought they were so special that they deserved to rule the continent and, being on a mission to fulfill this destiny, were ready to run over anything that got in their way.

Manifest Destiny is part of the larger topic of *American exceptionalism*. Consider this when writing the inevitable social history essay involving Manifest Destiny: All nations think they're special; powerful nations have in the past expressed their exceptionalism by taking over more land. Manifest Destiny was an American expression of exceptionalism. Exceptionalism can be good; feeling moral has inspired America to help other nations, and feeling free has led the U.S. to support freedom for other people. You can still hear the ghost of Manifest Destiny exceptionalism in talk of using force to bring American values — democracy and civil liberties — to other countries.

TIP

> To show this strong trend on an essay question, you could mention Manifest Destiny in the context of the Trail of Tears (covered later in this chapter), the long trail West (Chapter 11), the willingness of both sides to fight to the death in the Civil War (Chapter 12), and as a cultural influence on America becoming a world power (Chapter 16). Relating a trend to later events wins the approval of test-grading teachers.

On multiple-choice questions, watch out for wrong choices that tie Manifest Destiny to slavery, independence, or an overseas empire. Manifest Destiny is just about territorial expansion from the Atlantic to the Pacific, sometimes called *overspreading the continent.*

Manifest Destiny hit the *Oregon Trail* in the 1840s as settlers begin to drive their wagon trains west toward rich land in the Pacific Northwest. The *Oregon Treaty* (1846) with Britain officially gave most of the territory to the U.S.

# KICK-STARTING POLITICAL ACTION

History shows how social developments influence political outcomes. Factories allowed for the growth of towns. The growth of towns provided a place for social movements like abolition, labor unions, and temperance organizations. Women who came together for the Second Awakening got interested in women's rights and abolition, often at the same time. (See "Transcendentalism and the Second Great Awakening" later in this chapter.) The U.S. grew and changed rapidly, which may explain why the country went through so many different presidents, and why the Supreme Court gained so much power during this era.

EXAMPLE

> **Question:** Some artists say, "I don't care who makes the laws as long as I can write the songs." How did social developments in the 1820s and 1830s influence the development of the United States?
>
> **Answer:** In addition to the connections outlined just before this sample question, you can also point to the growth in Jacksonian democracy that brought down the Bank of the U.S. (see "War on the Bank of the U.S."), the cotton farming that pushed American Indians off southern land (see "Slavery Grows with Cotton" and "The Trail of Tears"), and the improvements in transportation that allowed the spread of culture (see "Feeling in Art, Education, and Belief").

## Presidents during this period

Besides Andrew Jackson, only one other president in this period stuck around for a full two terms: *James Monroe,* who governed during the Era of Good Feelings (1817 to 1825). Other than presiding over the Missouri Compromise and issuing the Monroe Doctrine, Monroe was the first president to ride on a steamboat.

---

### The Adams-Jackson race of 1824

Andrew Jackson was a popular guy who had actually won the most votes for president in 1824, the first time the whole country voted directly for the presidential electors. Unfortunately for him, he didn't have a majority. The three other candidates, one of whom was John Quincy Adams, pooled their support in the House of Representatives to elect Adams, who had ties to the beginning of the country: His father was the second U.S. president.

---

Other presidents of this era include

- *John Quincy Adams (1825–1829):* During Adams' one term, the U.S. developed the Erie Canal and the Baltimore & Ohio railroad, revolutionizing transportation. Adams also had the honor of losing to Andrew Jackson twice. The first time Jackson ran for president, Adams squeezed into the White House with the help of the House of Representatives.

- *Andrew Jackson (1829–1837):* Jackson was the superstar of this era and the godfather of Jacksonian democracy. He threw such a big populist party on inauguration day that he had to crawl out a back window of the White House to find a place to sleep. Check out "Andrew Jackson: Bringing Tough-Guy Democracy to Washington" later in this chapter for more information.

- *Martin Van Buren (1837–1841):* Van Buren had the bad luck to be president during the depression economy following the Panic of 1837 and during the infamous Trail of Tears. With experiences like that, one term was enough.

- *William Henry Harrison (1841):* Harrison didn't even have time to get settled in the White House. He delivered an almost two-hour inauguration speech, caught pneumonia, and died.

- *John Tyler (1841–1845):* Tyler, William Henry Harrison's vice president who became President at Harrison's death, annexed Texas, fought against a national bank, and found time to have 15 children. The population of the nation grew almost as fast as Tyler's family.

- *James Polk (1844–1849):* During the first year of expansion-minded James Polk's presidency, Texas got added to the nation.

## The Marshall Court

The Supreme Court became a powerful third branch of government largely through the 34 years of service of John Marshall. Marshall was chief justice from 1801, when the United States was still new, until 1835, when the country and its government were pretty grown up. In Chapter 9, you can find information about the establishment of judicial review with the *Marbury v. Madison* decision in 1803. Following are a few more key decisions from the Marshall era.

### McCulloch v. Maryland: 1819

Maryland didn't much like the Bank of the United States doing business in its state, and so it decided to tax the bank out of existence. James McCulloch, the bank's cashier, refused to pay tax to Maryland because his bank was chartered by the United States government. Maryland said that it didn't see anything in the U.S. Constitution about a national bank and that the bank was therefore illegal and certainly couldn't hide behind the robes of the U.S. Supreme Court.

In its 1819 decision, John Marshall's court held that the Constitution doesn't have to flat-out specify everything the government can do; Congress has implied powers for passing laws. After all, the Constitution says the U.S. government can do anything "necessary and proper" to carry out its specifically listed duties. In this case, the specific duties were to tax, borrow, and coin money.

*McCulloch v. Maryland* held for *implied powers* in 1819. If the Marshall court hadn't established implied powers, the federal government wouldn't be building roads or flying rockets because these and a thousand more activities are not specifically listed in the Constitution.

## Cohens v. Virginia: 1821

Lotteries were big business even in the early days of the U.S. The Cohens were jailed for selling illegal lottery tickets, and they appealed their Virginia criminal conviction to the Supreme Court. The Marshall court heard the appeal and thus established the principle that state criminal decisions could be appealed to the federal Supreme Court. This allows mobsters to yell: "Mess with me, and I'll take you all the way to the Supreme Court!"

## Gibbons v. Ogden: 1824

*Gibbons v. Ogden* held that the U.S. government has the right to regulate interstate commerce. Imagine if everybody in New York had to pay one person to get to New Jersey. Aaron Ogden had that kind of a deal with New York state; before the area had bridges, crossing the river meant taking Ogden's boat or swimming. The problem was that Thomas Gibbons had a license from the federal government for the same route. Ogden sued Gibbons, and the New York state court said that Ogden had the power to stop Gibbons. The federal Supreme Court overturned the state court's ruling, claiming that federal law is supreme, especially in interstate commerce (trade that crosses state lines).

> **TIP**
>
> You will see questions on Supreme Court decisions on the AP exam. Memorize the key decisions, which you can find in Chapter 23.

> **EXAMPLE**
>
> **Question:** What Supreme Court decision established the principle of federal regulation of interstate commerce?
>
> **Answer:** *Gibbons v. Ogden* determined that the federal government had jurisdiction over trade that crossed state lines.

# THE MISSOURI COMPROMISE OF 1820

As early as the beginning of the 1800s, the increasingly industrial Northern states and the slaveholding agricultural Southern states were anxiously watching the balance of power between them. Because each had exactly 11 states, the balance of power in the U.S. Senate was even. The problem, however, was that Missouri wanted to be admitted as a slave state, which would throw the balance of power to the South. Henry Clay, the Great Compromiser, was seen as neutral because he came from what was then the slave holding Wild West of Kentucky. He came up with the *Missouri Compromise* (1820).

The compromise stated that Missouri would come in as a slave state, but Maine would enter as a free state to keep the balance. From then on, an imaginary line would cross the middle of the U.S. Any territory north of that line would be free; anything south would be open to slavery. This was called the *Mason-Dixon line* (1820).

 **EXAMPLE**

> **Question:** What new free state was added as the result of the Missouri Compromise?
>
> **Answer:** Under the Missouri Compromise, Maine entered the Union as a free state.

Neither the North nor the South liked the Missouri Compromise, but both sides lived with it for the next 30 years. The Compromise led to fights within the previously united Democratic-Republican party, which, up until that time, had been the only political party in the U.S. Because things had been so mellow before the compromise, the period was called the Era of Good Feelings. Afterward, the good feelings wore off in a political fight between Andrew Jackson and John Quincy Adams. The states' rights issue had been hidden in the closet with the failure of the Articles of Confederation (see Chapter 9). Now it came out of the closet and became the subject of continuing compromise to avoid the threat of succession.

> **TIP**
>
> The Missouri Compromise is a cinch to be on the AP test. Remember, that it's early (1820) and deals directly only with Missouri and Maine. It helped divide, not unite, the political process, but it remained the general law of the land for 30 years. After that, the new Compromise of 1850, which dealt with the Western states and the Fugitive Slave Law, took over.

# THE MONROE DOCTRINE (1823)

Although it had once been the property of the European powers (see Chapters 7 and 8), North and South America were relatively free of colonial ownership by 1820. Following the American Revolution, most countries gained their independence from foreign masters.

As a small but aspiring power, the United States wanted to keep it that way. To this end, President James Monroe posted a stay-out warning on the Western Hemisphere to the rest of the world. The *Monroe Doctrine* (1823) said the United States wouldn't tolerate further attempts by European powers (the only powers there then were) to colonize the New World. That it worked in the 1800s was more bark than bite since the U.S. lacked the power to back it up, but the Monroe Doctrine established a precedent still cited to this day.

 **EXAMPLE**

**Question:** What was the Monroe Doctrine?

**Answer:** The Monroe Doctrine was a declaration issued by President James Monroe warning European powers not to establish any more colonies in the New World.

# THE TRAIL OF TEARS (1838)

American renewal usually meant American Indian removal. In fact, President Andrew Jackson made his reputation as a frontier American Indian fighter and signed a bill called the *Indian Removal Act* in 1830. The act set aside a big share of the federal budget to have the Army force all the American Indian tribes out of the fertile river valleys the settlers wanted and into dusty prairies west of the Mississippi River. By 1850, most of the American Indians east of the Mississippi were gone, forced to either move west or die along the way. For more than 100,000 American Indians, including Americanized tribes who had their own schools, newspapers, and farms, this journey west was called the *Trail of Tears* (1838), a black mark in U.S. history.

In 1832, in the case of *Worcester v. Georgia,* the Supreme Court struck down the Georgia law that limited the authority the Cherokee had over their own lands, stating that only the federal government, and not the states, had authority in Indian affairs. A lot of anti-Manifest Destiny people applauded this decision, but that didn't stop President Jackson. While *Worcester v. Georgia* might have given the tribes the right to fight eviction, President Jackson wanted none of that. Jackson declared that Chief Justice John Marshall "has made his decision; now let him enforce it."

After gunpoint negotiations, Cherokee families were forced to leave their homes in 1838 to 1839 and walk the 1,200 mile Trail of Tears to barren land in Oklahoma. With no supplies, half of the families died on the forced march to what was then called Indian Territory. Later on, even that would be taken away from them (see Chapter 14).

# ANDREW JACKSON'S PRESIDENCY

Andrew Jackson never went to college, and he's in good company — neither did Washington, Lincoln, or Truman. Although he wasn't as nice a guy as Washington or Lincoln, he did usher in the *age of the common man*. The emphasis here is on the word *man,* because Jacksonian democracy certainly didn't include women. Nor did it include blacks. But under Jackson, a majority of white men voted for president for the first time; previously, you had to own property to vote in many states.

## Jackson's Kitchen Cabinet

Jackson was a self-made Western fighter with few sophisticated ideas but strong frontier convictions. He ignored his appointed cabinet officers and relied on the advice of a shifting group of buddies known as the *Kitchen Cabinet*. He had no problem appointing friends to government jobs in what was called the *spoils system,* as in "to the victor belong the spoils." According to Jackson, any man should be equal to doing any job. The Founding Fathers said they believed in equality, but those were just words — most of them, including Washington, were rich guys. Jackson made the little guys feel like they owned the government.

After the U.S. allowed greater voting participation under Jacksonian democracy, it started to have issues that, until then, had been swept under the parlor rug. These problems included the right of individual states to nullify or ignore federal laws, fights within the administration, and the future of an unpopular national bank.

# Jackson's response to nullification

John Quincy Adams, the president before Jackson, did what he could to protect the American Indians, but the pressure from Jackson and his followers never let up. Plus, Adams had his hands full with a Civil War prequel led by his own vice president (John Calhoun), who protested *tariffs* (federal taxes on imports). Southerners called the 1828 tax the *Tariff of Abominations* because it made stuff that Southern planters bought from overseas more expensive. By beginning to challenge the right of the national government to make laws the South didn't like, Southerners came up with a political time bomb that would tick for 30 years until it blew up in the real Civil War of 1861.

According to the South, the federal government was a collection of independent states that had united under the catchy name "United States" to get a few things done. If states felt like disuniting over a certain issue, they could just sit that game out (or even leave the team if necessary). *Nullification* (1830) meant any state could just refuse to follow (as in nullify or declare null and void) any federal law with which it didn't agree. When states talked about nullification if they didn't get their way, famous Congressman Daniel Webster spoke against it, crying, "Liberty and Union, now and forever, one and inseparable!"

The nullification time bomb ticked on in a debate over selling cheap land to settlers in the west. Jackson supported cheap land. He was the first president from outside the original 13 colonies, the first tough-guy frontiersman with no ties to the polite, educated founders of the country.

Jackson was stuck with the same uncooperative vice president John Calhoun that his rival John Quincy Adams had endured (you can see why presidents now pick their own vice presidents). Calhoun quit over a new tariff bill and went home to South Carolina, where he got an *Ordinance of Nullification* passed, ordering federal customs officials in that state to stop following federal law.

Old General Jackson never blinked; he had Congress authorize a Force Bill to use the army to enforce the collection of taxes. Jackson talked loudly about hanging his former vice president. Having learned a few things in politics, he also offered some cuts in the tariff. South Carolina backed down, and both sides claimed victory.

# Abolishing the Bank of the U.S.

Currently, the U.S. has a Treasury Department that works with independent banks, but when Jackson was president, there was an official Bank of the United States with financial power many in government did not like. Jackson hated the national bank because it was tight about loaning money that expansion-minded Americans needed. He abolished the bank and sold Western land to settlers on a low payment plan. When money and good land started to run out, Jackson changed the rules to cash-only. That move burst the real-estate bubble, and the country went into a recession that lasted for years beyond Jackson's presidency (and made voters think twice about tough-guy presidents).

**EXAMPLE**

**Question:** Which event best illustrates Andrew Jackson's idea of expanded democracy?

**Answer:** Jackson saw the Bank of the U.S. as a rip-off by rich guys (and he wasn't too far off). His abolition of the bank is an example of his view of expanded democracy.

> **TIP**
>
> Watch out for smart-aleck professor questions on Jackson. He marks a turning point in U.S. politics because he's the first president to come from a Western state (Tennessee looked Western back then), and he fought the American Indians, nullification, and the Bank of the United States. Because we teachers like to have our cynical little laughs in the teacher's lounge, we often try to fool you with a multiple-choice question that has Jackson as a founder of the country or in favor of one of the issues he fought. Don't fall for it.

# MODERN CONVENIENCES

In the days before modern transportation, telephones, and TV, messages and products had to arrive on foot. Consider that the Battle of New Orleans took place after the War of 1812 was over — the news of peace was a little slow getting around. You could own the best crops or raw materials in the world, but having stuff to sell wouldn't do you any good if you couldn't get it to where somebody was ready to buy it. In the early days of the U.S., transportation moved as slowly as it had thousands of years earlier in the Roman Empire.

Several inventions helped the U.S. grow. In 1838, an Illinois blacksmith named John Deere invented the steel plow, good for helping grow crops. For harvesting crops, Pennsylvania farmer Cyrus McCormick invented a mechanical thresher that did the work of 15 men. A New York painter named Samuel Morse invented the telegraph in 1844, and the world became instantaneously connected. In new factories, the same kind of steam engines that chugged along in boats and trains helped run manufacturing equipment.

These inventions changed the world more than battles, bills, or presidents did. They're concrete examples of the non-political *themes* that will be the key to your success on the AP U.S. History exam.

## Factory jobs and the American Dream

Commuting wasn't really an issue before the Civil War. Most people worked where they lived: down on the farm. Sounds nice now, but back then for a lot of people it meant boredom and little money. With improved transportation for products and steam power to run machines, factories in New England began making cloth, tools, and guns. For example, the whole town of Lowell, Massachusetts, popped up around a cloth factory that supplied jobs for hundreds of *Lowell girls* who came from farms and immigrant ships beginning in 1813. The *Lowell system* (1815) guaranteed these girls safe living conditions and food as long as they worked from dawn to dusk six days a week, almost twice as long as people work today.

People chose to work in factories and stores because, hard as the work was, it gave them some freedom to change their lives. Before the Industrial Revolution, most of the money and power belonged to the people who owned land. People were stuck where they were born: lucky landholder or landless farm laborer. The Industrial Revolution gave people the chance to move around, change jobs, and maybe even save up enough money to start a small business. Most poor people stayed poor, but some of them managed to get ahead; in the U.S., no fixed social classes held them back. The Industrial Revolution, with all its pollution and overwork, was the beginning of the American Dream.

# Advances in transportation

Transportation was important in the early United States for moving products as well as people. Growing great crops did no good if there was no way to get them to the people who wanted to buy them. New forms of transportation led to the growth of the new United States.

## The canal system

The Dutch, French, and British all had big canal systems before the American Revolution. The United States was late to the party but made up for its slow start with enthusiasm. First came the completion of the *Erie Canal* (1825), which connected over 300 miles between the Hudson River in New York and Lake Erie. Between 1825 and 1840, the United States dug more than 3,000 miles of canals. Making an artificial river may not seem that high tech, but canals were a hundred times faster and stronger than trying to get little wagons down muddy and often-frozen dirt roads. Before canals, crops and resources never got far from home; after canals, the idea of a national marketplace seemed possible.

## Steamships and water travel

In 1807, American inventor *Robert Fulton* (1810) built the double-paddle-wheeled steamboat *Clermont* which traveled up the Hudson River from New York faster than traveling via a canal or horse-drawn wagon. By the mid-1850s, steamboats driven by large paddle wheels were carrying passengers on all major U.S. rivers. Oceangoing steamships, constructed with strong iron hulls, reduced the time needed to travel to Europe from weeks to days. The *Savannah* in 1819 was the first ship equipped with a steam engine to cross the Atlantic Ocean. By 1838, several steam-powered paddle wheelers were crossing the Atlantic, and in 1840, the first regularly scheduled steamship service began.

## Railroads

Canals got to be the latest thing for only a few years, because railroads were faster and could go anywhere. In 1830, the first little American steam engine pathetically lost a race with a horse. Getting it right didn't take long: By 1840, the U.S. boasted 400 railroads and more miles of track than canal. By the time of the Civil War, America was the world railroad leader with close to 30,000 miles of track.

# The Industrial Revolution

Industrial work was a new way of life — not exactly fun, but at least a way to get off the farm. Men, women, and children worked 12-hour days, six days a week. The first labor unions originated to fight for better working conditions, but that battle took a hundred years to win. Factories made products people wanted, and people made money they needed to buy the products. *Skilled workers* like steam engine builders, printers, and carpenters did much better than the more common *unskilled workers,* who had to take any job they could get and were easy to replace.

The first *Industrial Revolution* in the United States started off, humbly enough, making thread in small water-powered mills at the time of the American Revolution. Fast forward 30 years, and steam-powered factories provided jobs off the farm for around 5 percent of the people. This was the small beginning of the get-ahead capitalist spirit that still drives Americans.

# SLAVERY GROWS WITH COTTON

There was no American Dream for slaves, only an endless nightmare of working all their lives without pay. They were beaten, raped, and killed with no legal protection and no hope for the future; they'd work until they died, and their children were doomed to be slaves like them.

The irony of proclaiming freedom in a land where one out of four people were slaves wasn't lost on the leaders of the American Revolution. The U.S. banned the importation of new slaves from Africa after 1808 and waited for what they called the "peculiar institution" to go away, much like people now wait for someone else to fix global warming. Slavery was too much a part of the country to deal with right away; eight of the first ten presidents owned slaves. Enslaving people while fighting a revolution for freedom was bad enough, but then it got worse.

## The cotton gin and expanding slavery

While George Washington was president, a teacher named Eli Whitney invented a cotton engine (*cotton gin* for short) that removed seeds from cotton balls and allowed Southern plantations to grow 50 times more cotton than they ever had before. Trouble was, without ready labor or machinery, every 10 acres of cotton needed another slave to grow it.

The technical invention of the cotton gin led to millions of people being enslaved, and that growth in slavery plus the social movement of abolition eventually brought about the Civil War, which I discuss more thoroughly in Chapter 12. (**Note:** The link between the cotton gin, the growth of slavery, and the beginning of the abolition movement is an example of how trends fit together. Noting connections like these will help you on the AP exam.)

## The increasing power of pro-slavery factions

Slavery became big money; by the Civil War, the U.S. had five times more enslaved people than it did during the Revolution. A good slave was worth as much in modern money as an SUV costs today. The slave states had extra political power grandfathered into the Constitution — slaves counted as three-fifths of a person in determining representation for slave states. This kind of power forced careful balancing legislation like the Missouri Compromise outlined earlier; slave state representatives wouldn't even let the subject of abolition come up in Congress. The few slave rebellions like that of Nat Turner in 1831 were put down with devastating force. Most Southern states made it illegal for a slave to learn to read and write.

## The anti-slavery movement

Northern blacks lived with racism even though they weren't technically slaves. Free blacks had trouble finding jobs, schools, or places to live in the North. Eventually, as ex-slaves learned to write and speak about conditions in the South, they began to gain Northern white supporters. Important people in the anti-slavery movement included

- *Frederick Douglass (1850)* escaped from slavery in 1838 and wrote his moving life story.
- *Harriet Tubman (1860)* escaped slavery in 1848 and went back to help more than 300 other slaves (including her parents) make it safely to freedom.

- **William Lloyd Garrison (1855),** the white editor of the abolitionist newspaper *The Liberator,* was a founder of the Anti-Slavery society.
- **Sojourner Truth (1851),** a freed slave woman, spoke eloquently in support of abolition.

Both races opposed to slavery worked together on the *Underground Railroad* (1855), sheltering former slaves on the way to freedom. Although most white Southerners were too poor to own slaves, many were willing to fight for slavery anyway. In the North and West, opposition to slavery grew steadily stronger.

# EDUCATION AND THE ARTS

For the first time, ordinary people could learn about culture in free public schools. Before the 1830s, schools were mostly for rich kids; if you wanted to get an education, your parents had to pay. Horace Mann started the *common school movement* (1850) of tax-supported mandatory free education for all children. By the end of the 1850s, every state outside the South had free education and teacher training.

In the 1820s, America got its own art after years of looking up to Europe as the only seat of real culture. The Hudson River School produced artists like Thomas Cole, who painted man and nature in harmony along the Hudson River in rural upstate New York. George Caitlin painted American Indians in natural settings, and John James Audubon became famous for his paintings of birds.

The U.S. cut a fine trail in literature as well; James Fenimore Cooper, Washington Irving, Nathaniel Hawthorne, Edgar Allan Poe, Herman Melville, and Henry David Thoreau (among others) wrote influential works during this period that are still popular today.

# TRANSCENDENTALISM AND THE SECOND GREAT AWAKENING

Strong feelings about spirituality were part of the *Second Great Awakening* (1830), which encouraged the idea that religion should be felt as well as thought. *Henry David Thoreau*, author of *Walden*, shared a philosophy with his New England neighbor *Ralph Waldo Emerson*: Transcendentalism. The *Transcendentalists* believed God was an inner voice, leading people to do the right thing and live in harmony with nature, if they'd just listen.

Evangelists traveled the country speaking at emotional revival meetings. Ministers like Charles Finney preached that how people lived helped decide whether they would go to heaven — a big change from the predestination of the Pilgrims (see Chapter 7). For the first time in America, women took an active part in church, which led to growing female influence in social movements. The Second Great Awakening also saw the birth of Mormonism and the spread of the Methodist church, as well as the beginning of groups devoted to abolition, education, and temperance.

# 11

# From Sea to Shining Sea: 1846–1854

**KEY CONCEPTS**

- Technological advancements and their impact on a growing America
- Territorial expansion across the continent
- Social changes and the continuing problems with slavery
- Controversial laws that led to the Civil War

America was bursting at the seams in the 1840s. In one ten-year period, the country suddenly had 35 percent more people, including almost a million immigrants from Ireland and half a million from Germany. The Irish mostly settled in Eastern cities and brought a motivated labor force willing to do a lot of work for low pay. The Irish also expanded Catholic churches and schools, making the mostly Protestant United States stretch to include the Church of Rome into its accepted religious mix. The Germans went straight for the good farmland of the Midwest and brought along the Christmas tree, German beer, opposition to slavery, and support for public education, including kindergarten (a German word).

The population surge was driven by *revolutions in Europe* (1848) and the *potato famine* (1845) in Ireland; people were drawn to the United States by the promise of opportunity and good land. Much of this opportunity was created just by people who were looking for it, especially because the United States needed both workers and consumers, and new inventions were ready to be used.

> **TIP**
>
> Social history, like much of the information covered in this chapter, is useful for scoring points on the AP exam. Knowing the leaders of the women's rights and abolition movements, for example, is important. You'll encounter multiple-choice questions in these areas, and you should be able to use these topics in essay answers. The authors and poets mentioned in this chapter and elsewhere in the book are extra-credit items. The test probably won't have many multiple-choice questions about art, but showing that you know how literature fits into the American story in essays rings college bells. **Hint:** American literature gets more up-front on issues of race and gender as Americans challenge the conventions they inherited from the Old World.

# NEW INVENTIONS

Eli Whitney was only getting started when he invented the cotton gin in 1793 (see Chapter 10). He went on to be one of the pioneers of *interchangeable-parts manufacturing* (1800) by making musket guns with identical parts for the Army. Until then, guns were handmade, with each part machined to fit only its own rifle. After Whitney popularized the manufacture of interchangeable parts, factories could become assembly lines rather than disparate workshops for individual craftsmen. This practical idea led to a surge of inventions that led to the rapid growth in manufacturing by the "American System" that would become prevalent during the 1840s and 1850s.

Whitney's cotton gin allowed the South to become a rich slave empire and spurred him on to greater inventions. His interchangeable parts supported mass production, which Northern factories perfected by the 1850s. As a result, the North became an even richer manufacturing empire, complete with the rifle power the North would need to defeat the Southern slavers in the Civil War. You could say that Whitney's rifle solved the problem his cotton gin created in the first place.

## The advent of mass production

The North wasn't just making guns. The *Singer sewing machine* (1846) revolutionized clothes-making; it was the first practical way to sew clothes without making everything by hand. You pumped the first sewing machine with your foot; electrical power hadn't been invented. Even though it was made with interchangeable parts, however, the sewing machine was still expensive, which led to another big change, this time in the way products were sold.

Before the mid-1800s, most purchases had to be made with cash up front. Singer revolutionized this system by allowing families to buy the new sewing machine on time payments. Consumers could justify the purchase with what they would save in clothing. This system linked the first must-have home technology with the first must-pay credit debt.

Mass production also sped the introduction of *the grain reaper* (1834), manufactured by Cyrus McCormick. This reaper enabled one man riding on a horse-drawn machine to cut as much wheat as five men swinging the hand scythes, previously the only way to harvest grain since the days of the Romans. This invention allowed the extensive large-scale agriculture that made the Midwest rich. Even an invention as humble as John Deere's *steel plow* (1837) greatly improved food-growing by reliably turning the soil for better crops.

## The telegraph

Samuel Morse was the first person to put electricity to work with the invention of the *telegraph* (1844). For the first time, news could travel across the nation in seconds, not weeks. The "talking wire" drew opinions closer together in the decade before the Civil War. Getting instant feedback may actually have heightened the disagreements between North and South. Morse's telegraph got an international boost with the laying of the Atlantic cable to Britain. The cable broke before the Civil War but was restored permanently right afterward. The telegraph reached the West Coast in 1861.

# STRIDES IN TRANSPORTATION

In the early years after the Revolution, you could get out and walk if you didn't like the roads. Or maybe you could swim; early roads turned to giant mud puddles when it rained. Horses and wagons got stuck up to the middle, and drivers would have to crawl through mud to get food to feed the stuck animals while they waited for help. Once in a while, a carriage would just sink out of sight. But highways, canals, and railroads soon came along, allowing farm products to get to big-city markets and urban inventions to get to people everywhere. By the 1850s, stage-coaches and the Pony Express crossed the country. Clipper ships sailed the oceans faster than steamships could. The world was getting more and more connected.

## Traveling the long and winding road

Most roads at the time were dirt trails or logs placed side by side (resulting in very bumpy rides). Even city streets were mostly unpaved. During a particularly wet and muddy time in San Francisco, a citizen erected a sign that warned his city street was "not passable, not even jackass-able." The first break in transportation came with the privately owned *Lancaster Turnpike* (1795), 60 miles of hard-surface road heading west from Philadelphia. In 1811, the federal government began to build the Cumberland (or National) Road from Maryland. By 1852, the road stretched across the old Northwest territory to Illinois and was the beginning of many a wagon train.

## Creating canals

Robert Fulton's pioneering idea of the *steamboat* (1807), first launched on New York's Hudson River (see Chapter 10) proved even more valuable on the great Mississippi. As early as 1820, 60 steamboats regularly traveled on the Mississippi; by the time of the Civil War, the big river had the regular service of 1,000 boats. This type of transportation led to settlement; people could get their crops to market, and the local stores could get manufactured goods to make life a little easier.

With the completion of the *Erie Canal* (1825), Americans started to make the rivers come to them. Hooking up to the Hudson River at Albany, the Erie Canal went all the way to the Great Lakes. What used to cost a dollar to ship now cost a nickel. Rocky New England farms couldn't compete with the lush produce of New York and Pennsylvania floating into town on canal boats. New England farmers either moved west to the land along the canal path or worked in growing industries — the first sign of how better transportation could hurt as well as help local producers.

Having made their own rivers with the canals, the states began to get over the need for a water path. The *first railroad* (1828) chugged along three years after the Erie Canal was finished. By 1850, the northern United States was more interconnected by rails than it was by canals. The cotton-growing South started to build late; by the Civil War, the South had just a skeleton of railroads, whereas the North had a spider web. For more about railroads, see Chapter 13.

# SOCIAL CHANGE

With all the freedom and change, utopia societies seemed to spring up around every American corner. But these perfect worlds were a little hard to live in — not surprisingly, because *utopia*, from Thomas More's fantasy novel *Utopia* (1516), meant *no place*.

Improved communication brought about by the telegraph and more efficient travel (discussed earlier in this chapter) didn't always lead to improved understanding. The South saw strengthened trading ties along the Mississippi and across the Atlantic as economic insurance that outsiders would have to allow slavery to continue to support Northern and British profits. Northerners were afraid expansion of the slave system and cheap imports would put them out of a job. Moving in what they perceived to be the right direction put the two sections of the United States on a collision course.

## Key social movements of the 1800s

Here are some of the major social movements that started in the mid 1800s:

- **Women's rights:** The *Seneca Falls Convention* (1848) was the first women's rights conference, held in Seneca Falls, New York, in 1848. At the time, state law prevented women from inheriting property, signing contracts, serving on juries, and voting in elections. Seneca Falls participants were connected to both the Second Great Awakening and the early Abolitionist movement. Conference participants went on to work for women's rights and against slavery.

- **Labor unions:** The first large labor unions started in the 1840s and expanded after the Civil War.

- **Mental health treatment reform:** *Dorothea Dix* (1845) published reports that led to many reforms in mental institutions throughout the South. She was made superintendent of nurses for the Union Army during the Civil War. With her example, intrepid women and men worked to reform treatment of prisoners and the mentally ill.

- **Temperance:** *Neal Dow* (1851) got a prohibition law passed in Maine and ten other states; these laws were rescinded when the stress of fighting the Civil War made lots of people need a drink.

- **Utopian communities:** Named for Thomas More's novel *Utopia*, utopian communities were established in several places in the U.S. Utopian dreamers tried to create a new social structure by building societies where people could live and work together in perfect harmony. Among the hopeful utopias were

  - *New Harmony* (1825): On the Wabash River in southern Indiana, New Harmony produced limited community but lots of education. The progress of entomology, geology, and the Smithsonian Institution in Washington are all associated with this attempt by Welsh industrialist Robert Owen to build a better world.

  - *Brook Farm* (1841): Located near Boston, this community had a literary influence from authors like Henry Thoreau and Nathaniel Hawthorne. They were better at writing than at farming.

  - *The Oneida Community* (1848): This commune in New York practiced community marriage and shared jobs and child raising. Although the commune broke up, the members went on to found Oneida Silver, one of the largest silverware companies in the world.

- *The Shakers* (1840): At one time, under the guidance of Mother Ann Lee, the Shakers established 19 different communities organized around groups with men and women living separately but working together. Each village was governed by two men and two women. The Shakers made a simple style of furniture and other housewares that are still in demand today. Since Shakers didn't have children, they largely died out. The Shaker song "Simple Gifts" is still sung to remind people of quiet peace.

# Moving from farm to factory

Workers were needed almost everywhere during the fast-growing 1840s and 1850s; they were rewarded with wages that grew slowly but steadily. But life wasn't all domestic bliss, of course. Thousands of hungry workers shifted from job to job and city to city. Factory owners, trying to meet increased demand and improve their own incomes, worked factory employees for 13 or 14 hours a day, often under unsafe conditions. Unions, under state law, weren't legally allowed to organize until the 1840s, and the "easy" 10-hour day, long fought by employers, slowly started to be accepted.

The willingness of single men to do whatever it took to earn a living and support the nation without turning into a mob was a key reason the United States grew so much during this time. Peaceful, willing workers without families — an often-overlooked strength of any society — made up half the labor force.

# Public education

Public schools were growing against a very real backlash among people who thought education was wrong, at least if they had to pay for it.

As late as 1860, the United States had only about 100 real high schools. Education got a boost from *Noah Webster* (1828), whose reading lessons and dictionary taught Americanism as well as letters. *McGuffey's Readers* (1850) presented patriotism along with language and were used all over the country for 100 years. *Horace Mann* (1850) established the model for free public education that eventually spread across the land.

> **TIP**
>
> Don't confuse Noah Webster (1758–1843), the teacher and dictionary-maker, with Daniel Webster (1782–1852), legendary congressman and leader of national compromise. Noah brought people together with a common approach to language; Daniel tried to keep the Union together with common laws. Noah got his name on almost every American dictionary; Daniel was no longer alive to see his compromise laws fall apart in the years before the Civil War.

As the country expanded, public education was a proud part of most new settlements. The little, red one-room schoolhouse got its start teaching farm kids the three Rs: reading, 'riting, and 'rithmetic. All the grades were in one room, and some kids could spare only a few months of learning in between helping out with the crops. The idea of assigning students by grade didn't really get going until after the Civil War.

*Oberlin College* (1837) in Ohio was the first college to admit women and blacks; Ohio's *Antioch College* (1852) had the first female faculty member. The fact that Oberlin College's second president was the famous Great Awakening preacher *Charles Finney* (1840) (a committed abolitionist, early champion of women's rights, and the most powerful revivalist in an age of renewed faith) and

Antioch's first president was Unitarian educator Horace Mann demonstrates the connection between religious revival and social action at that time. The great Northeastern universities were then still segregated: no women and no blacks.

# Expanding religious diversity

In 1850, three out of four Americans attended church, usually a Protestant one, every Sunday. The idea that one sect contained all the unique and chosen people and that everyone else was going to hell had loosened up as the United States learned to live with many different Protestant denominations. The Enlightenment-inspired founding fathers hadn't been all that big on religion, but they — and members of new American movements like the Unitarians and Transcendentalists — certainly did believe that spiritual and material life could be improved right here on Earth.

The *Second Great Awakening* (1830), a powerful nationwide spiritual movement put the emphasis on salvation through personal change (see Chapter 8 for information on the First Great Awakening). Both the spirit of the movement and the connections that people made at tent meetings helped found several middle-class movements, often led by women, including those for temperance, prison and asylum reform, abolition, and women's rights. Methodists, Baptists, Mormons, and members of other new religious denominations gained strength, and members of America's first religions, such as the Congregationalists and Anglicans (see Chapter 8), loosened up. The Second Great Awakening stressed *perfectionism*, the belief that free will can create a better life on Earth. Free will perfectionism encouraged reform movements and was directly opposed to the original Puritan belief in predestination. It was during the Second Great Awakening that women were first allowed to lead prayers in church.

> **EXAMPLE**
>
> **Question:** Why was the belief in perfectionism important in the Second Great Awakening?
>
> **Answer:** Perfectionism supported social movements, presented the idea that free will could improve life, and marked a departure from the Puritan belief in predestination.

> **EXAMPLE**
>
> **Question:** What were the social movements that came out of the Second Great Awakening?
>
> **Answer:** The women's rights, antislavery, temperance, and education movements were all supported by middle-class women coming out of the Second Great Awakening.

The notion of predestination (see Chapter 7) faded away in favor of emotional activism. Middle-class women were enthusiastic revivalists, charged up by spiritual services and the community of believers. Their awakened talents helped spur both religious and social causes. No social cause received more attention than abolition of slavery. By 1845, the issue of slavery split national denominations like the Methodist and Baptist churches into Northern and Southern branches. First the churches split, then the political parties, and finally the nation.

# EXPANDED ROLES FOR WOMEN

Women didn't get much education in the early days beyond what they would need to run a home. Male physicians said that too much learning could injure the female brain. By 1850, around 20 percent of all women had worked outside the home by the time they were married. After they married, women didn't work for wages; they were locked inside the household. Women seemed to be trapped on a pedestal of domesticity: They were supposed to be more morally refined than men but were limited to being the keepers of families. They got some input on social responsibility with the *cult of domesticity (1850)*, which held that, by being virtuous, women could change the world through their families.

## Gaining control of their own lives

Of little breakthroughs is freedom made. Under the belief in *republican motherhood (1780)* at the time of the Revolution (see Chapter 9), women were valued as teachers of children, especially the sons who were needed for the new democracy. With the *cult of domesticity*, however, women began to use their power as queens of the household to make decisions about things that mattered outside the family as well. They gained more power to plan children and choose their own mates; families arranged fewer marriages.

 **EXAMPLE**

> **Question:** What were the positive benefits of the cult of domesticity for women?
>
> **Answer:** American women gained power from the 1700s to 1860 as they moved from republican motherhood to the cult of domesticity. Changes in women's rights over this time included their own choice of husbands, activism outside the home, and more control over childbearing.

As the 1800s progressed, more women worked in factories, and they participated in early union activities. As public education spread in the 1840s, the hitherto male profession of teaching began to admit some females. Women could also work as cooks or maids. About one Northern family in ten was rich enough to pay a domestic servant to help with the housework.

Women had only half as many children during the 1800s as during the 1700s; family planning was beginning to take hold. Couples used timing and early barrier methods to keep from getting pregnant. These methods had been passed down for hundreds of years; in the mid-1800s, women just got more assertive about using them. With fewer children, mothers could spend more time rearing their kids. The idea of helping children develop began to take hold; parents no longer just survived the kids until they could be sent out into the fields.

## Women's rights

As women got some power, they wanted more. *Lucretia Mott* and *Susan B. Anthony* were Quakers who stood up for women's rights. Mott fought for women and abolition from the 1820s until after the Civil War, and Anthony carried the movement into the 1900s. *Elizabeth Cady Stanton* was a mother of seven who insisted, with the full support of her husband, on leaving the word *obey* out of her marriage ceremony. Stanton and Mott were leaders of the groundbreaking *Seneca Falls Convention (1848)*, which proclaimed the rights of women. Seneca Falls was the first meeting of women to adopt a program designed to lead to votes for women. The Convention's *Declaration of Sentiments (1848)* echoed the U.S. Declaration of Independence.

# ARTS IN MID-19TH CENTURY AMERICA

Art defines a culture, and culture is a pretty good predictor of the actions people as a group will take. In the 1800s, the United States developed a national culture of music and writing that helped the young country identify its own character.

## Stephen Foster and the American songbook

*Stephen Foster* (1850) was one of the most popular composers in American history and the only songwriter to try to make a living from the art until the 1900s. He wrote "Oh! Susanna," "Camptown Races," "My Old Kentucky Home," "Beautiful Dreamer," and "Old Folks at Home (Swanee River)" — songs so popular 150 years after their composition that an album of them won a Grammy award in 2005.

Showing how thoroughly mixed American culture was on the eve of the nation's tearing itself apart in the Civil War, Foster, who was from the North, wrote about the South. The man who wrote the music used in the North's "Battle Hymn of the Republic" was from South Carolina. "Dixie," the theme song of the South, was written in New York City by a Northerner.

## The rise of American literature

American literature came onto its own with the increased popularity of Henry Wadsworth Longfellow, Walt Whitman, Ralph Waldo Emerson, and many others:

- **Ralph Waldo Emerson:** Emerson was a giant of American letters for almost 50 years. His *Transcendentalist* (1840) philosophy stressed self-reliance and personal spiritual unity.

- **Henry David Thoreau:** Emerson's friend and colleague Thoreau wrote *Walden* (1854), about man's connection to nature, and *On the Duty of Civil Disobedience* (1849), a book that influenced Mahatma Gandhi and Martin Luther King Jr.

- **James Fenimore Cooper**: Cooper brought American Indians as well as frontiersmen, women, and black Americans to life in novels such as *The Last of the Mohicans* (1826).

- **Washington Irving**: Irving is famous for his short stories such as "The Legend of Sleepy Hollow" and "Rip Van Winkle."

- **Walt Whitman:** Whitman wrote *Leaves of Grass* (1855), a collection of poems that broke down the conventions of poetry with bold language:

    Fresh and strong the world we seize, world of labor and the march,

    Pioneers! O Pioneers!"

- **Henry Wadsworth Longfellow:** Longfellow was an American poet who was also widely popular in Europe. He wrote "Paul Revere's Ride," "A Psalm of Life," "The Song of Hiawatha," "Evangeline," and "Christmas Bells."

- **John Greenleaf Whittier:** A poet of human freedom, Whittier stood up to angry mobs for the abolition of slavery.

- **Louisa May Alcott:** Alcott showed the man-centered Victorian world that women can write beautifully with *Little Women* (1868).

- **Emily Dickinson:** Dickinson demonstrated the universality of even a quiet human heart with more than 1,000 poems published after her death.

Not all writers saw much good in human beings. The following writers, whose themes were darker, served a useful purpose in helping the world see that good and evil are never pure and that living well means making moral choices every day:

- **Edgar Allan Poe:** Poe lived on the dark side of madness and evil with stories like "The Fall of the House of Usher" and poems like "The Raven."

- **Nathaniel Hawthorne:** Hawthorne wrote *The Scarlet Letter* (1850), about a woman who had a secret affair with a minister, bore his child out of wedlock, and had to wear a scarlet A for adultery.

- **Herman Melville:** Melville's *Moby-Dick* (1851), one of the greatest American novels, tells the story of a sea captain's obsessive hunt for a great white whale.

Painting began to show the beauty of the American landscape. The *Hudson River School*, active from 1850 to 1875, painted dramatic American landscapes, especially featuring the Hudson River area in northern New York. This movement made people stop to appreciate the wonders of nature.

**EXAMPLE**

**Question:** What was the Hudson River School of painting?

**Answer:** The Hudson River School painted dramatic American landscapes, mostly featuring the Hudson River area in northern New York.

# THE ECONOMICS OF SLAVERY

As a nation founded on the ringing words of freedom, the United States was never proud of slavery, even though many of its founding fathers owned slaves. Like a bad habit you mean to give up next year, slavery just kept getting bigger and harder to shake. Opposition to the peculiar institution (as slavery was politely called) grew in the North, which didn't have any slaves. In the South, it was considered too profitable and too vital an institution to be publicly debated.

The cotton trade did not just enrich a few southern planters. It was a money-maker, directly or indirectly, for the North and the South. Northern ships carried Southern cotton to market in Britain and New England. To a large degree, the extra profits of many merchants in all parts of the United States before the Civil War depended on the crushing work of slaves.

Cotton represented half the value of all U.S. exports in the years before the Civil War. The profits of slave labor didn't stop at the border: About one of five jobs in Britain was tied to manufacturing cotton cloth, most of it from raw cotton grown in the American South. Southerners assumed that Britain would have to support them in any break with the North to keep Britain's vital supply of cotton raw materials coming. The South called it *King Cotton* (1860).

Fewer than 2,000 families in the South owned more than 100 slaves. Three of four families owned no slaves at all. Because the South was basically a three-crop economy, even large landowners could suffer reversals when their crops did poorly. In fact, some of the strongest supporters of slavery were small Southern farmers who owned no slaves. These small farmers looked down on the black slaves who lived around them and felt a shallow brotherhood with their rich, white neighbors. Poor whites could look forward to the day when they could buy a slave or two. It was a sick application of the American dream of upward mobility.

> ## "I tremble for my country..."
>
> Thomas Jefferson, slaveholder, said this about slavery: "The whole commerce between master and slave is a perpetual exercise of . . . despotism on the one part and degrading submissions on the other. . . . I tremble for my country when I reflect that God is just; that his justice cannot sleep forever." People often see more than a little moral disconnect between Jefferson's proclamations against slavery and the fact that he kept slaves. Sadly Jefferson — a good president but a poor businessman — couldn't free his slaves in his will. He had mortgaged them to get enough money to live on.

In addition, the South was at the mercy of the North for basic manufactured supplies; even cotton clothing came from New England.

Slavery could be a money-loser. A slave cost as much as $80,000 in modern money. If slave traders missed the market or some of their charges died, they were in trouble fast. Economically as well as morally, the slavery/cotton empire was a bet with the devil. On average, it continued to be profitable right up to the time of the Civil War, but it was a house of cards.

# EARLY ETHNIC GROUP ISSUES

America in the days before the Civil War was a society that talked a good talk about democracy, equality, and freedom but still used the slavery of black people to make money. Immigrants who came to America's shores faced prejudice and discrimination. Meanwhile, as America grew, settlers needed more territory, and this prompted what essentially became a land grab that uprooted Native Americans and forced them from their ancestral homes, and that led to the Mexican-American War.

Liberty during this early period was too often limited to freedom for white, Protestant men. There was not as much freedom for Catholics, especially Catholic immigrants from Ireland and Germany. Nor was there freedom for blacks who lived in slavery in the South and in segregated poverty in the North. Nor was there complete freedom for women locked into bonds of domesticity. American Indians were not citizens, and Mexicans lost their land in the drive for Manifest Destiny. Freedom in America had a long way to go.

## The relocation of Native Americans

A similar moral double standard affecting the "peculiar institution" also affected the land grabs from American Indians and foreign governments. What started out as 13 states grateful for their own freedom turned into a continent-wide rush for territory. See Chapters 9 and 10 for more information.

The *Indian Removal Act* (1830) provided federal assistance to move more than 100,000 American Indians from their ancestral homes east of the Mississippi to the specially created Indian Territory in what is now Oklahoma. The government was supposed to supply food and transportation help with the forced migration, but many Native Americans died on the long treks.

In the *Trail of Tears* (1838), 17,000 Cherokee were forced to travel 1,200 miles to Oklahoma from their homes in Georgia. More than 4,000 American Indians died in make-shift camps or on the trail itself. From the southern U.S., the Choctaw, Creek, Chickasaw, and Seminole tribes were also relocated. In the north, evicted tribes included the Shawnees, Ottawas, Potawatomis, Sauks, and Foxes. Chief Black Hawk led American Indians back to their homes in Illinois to fight for their land, but they were defeated by the army and state militias.

## The treatment of immigrants

Immigrants rushed in. Irish, German, Polish, and Italian immigrants weren't always welcomed in the land of the free. The Know-Nothing Party campaigned against Catholic immigration in the 1850s. Signs for jobs often said, "No Irish Need Apply." When Irish workers hungry for jobs replaced striking women textile employees in New England, prejudice against the new immigrants soared. Irish, Italian, and Polish immigrants often spent generations living in ethnically isolated communities. In the years before the Civil War, multi-ethnic neighborhoods and towns were relatively rare.

Most immigrants avoided the South so they wouldn't have to compete with slave labor on the one hand and rich landowners on the other. That situation left the South short of new blood and of any kind of cheap labor except slaves.

**EXAMPLE**

**Question:** How did textile mill owners inflame prejudice against the Irish?

**Answer:** New England textile mills replaced striking local workers with Irish immigrants.

## Problems faced by free blacks

About 250,000 free blacks lived in the South and another 250,000 in the North. Blacks gained freedom through Northern emancipation laws and the occasional goodwill of Southern owners; their children were then free as well. They were in a precarious position. Free blacks couldn't testify in court. If they were assaulted by whites, unless other whites showed up to defend them (which was rare), the blacks never got justice. In the South, they were in constant danger of being kidnapped into slavery. In the North, mobs of poor Irish and other immigrants who resented the competition from free blacks for low-wage jobs often beat them up. Blacks couldn't go to most white schools, stores, or churches. Frederick Douglass, the distinguished black abolitionist, was beaten by Northern rowdies more than once.

**EXAMPLE**

**Question:** How did some blacks become free before the Civil War?

**Answer:** The number of free blacks in the United States grew because Northern states ended slavery, some Southern slaveholders freed their slaves after the Revolution or in their wills, and freed blacks had children who were then themselves free.

## Slave revolts

Blacks fought for their own freedom whenever they could. They didn't have much opportunity to fight back; slaves were guarded and whipped for the slightest infraction. Informant slaves who brought news of any trouble were rewarded, and potential troublemakers were punished without justice or mercy. Even walking on the road at night could spell death to a black man who didn't have clear permission. Despite these barriers, at least 11 slave revolts occurred between colonial times and the Civil War, including these:

- In 1800, an armed insurrection in Richmond led by a tall, strong blacksmith slave named Gabriel was foiled by informants. Gabriel had carefully planned to take Virginia's governor (later president) James Monroe hostage and ask for freedom for slaves in the name of the American Revolution. He was questioned under torture but refused to submit. He, two of his brothers, and 24 others were hanged. After Gabriel's bid for freedom, Virginia kept slaves under extra-tight surveillance.

  In 2007, Virginia governor Tim Kaine informally pardoned Gabriel and his co-conspirators. The modern governor said that Gabriel's motivation had been "his devotion to the ideals of the American Revolution; it was worth risking death to secure liberty." The governor noted that "Gabriel's cause — the end of slavery and the furtherance of equality of all people — has prevailed in the light of history." He added, "It is important to acknowledge that history favorably regards Gabriel's cause while consigning legions who sought to keep him and others in chains to be forgotten."

- In 1822, Denmark Vesey, who had managed to buy his freedom after winning a city lottery, was within days of launching a revolt that could have included more than 1,000 slaves in Charleston. Vesey had been able to plan the revolt because he was a free black who worked as a carpenter. He had tried to live with whites, but he was angry because they had repeatedly closed the black church he had helped start. Betrayed by frightened slaves, Vesey and more than 30 of his followers were hanged. Vesey's son survived to reopen the black church after the Civil War.

- Nat Turner was a black slave who could read and who served as a preacher. He had visions that told him to fight for freedom, and in 1831, he led a rebellion of at least 100 slaves in Virginia. The slaves fought for two days, killing around 60 white civilians, before they were defeated by an overwhelming force of soldiers, sailors, and militiamen who rushed in from all directions.

  After the battle, Virginia actually debated proposals to end slavery but decided to go the other way instead. The state forbade teaching a slave to read and instituted regular slave patrols that stopped any blacks found on the roads.

## Abolitionists in the North

The movement for the abolition of slavery began with calls for freedom from Quakers and Mennonites before the Revolution. An American Colonization Society was formed in 1817 to send blacks back to their now-forgotten home in Africa; a few years later, the society founded the Republic of Liberia on the west coast of Africa.

In 1832, a rare group of people got together at Lane Theological Seminary in Cincinnati and held an 18-day debate on slavery. They included Theodore Weld, who had been evangelized by Charles Finney, the same Great Awakening preacher who would go on to be president of Oberlin College. Based on what he learned from slaves just across the river from Cincinnati in Kentucky, Weld wrote *American Slavery As It Is* (1839). He greatly influenced a young lady whose father was the head of the seminary.

That young lady was Harriet Beecher Stowe, and twenty years later she would write the best-selling novel of the 1800s: *Uncle Tom's Cabin* (1852). That book burst upon society like a star shell, lighting up thinking all over the North. It sold more than 300,000 copies in its first year. Watching thousands of stage productions in every little town in the North, people in the audience gasped as Eliza carried her son across the shifting river ice to freedom and cried at the death of kindly Uncle Tom. Showing the power of an idea whose time has come, *Uncle Tom's Cabin* crystallized opposition to slavery in the North. (For more information about *Uncle Tom's Cabin,* see Chapter 12.)

On New Year's Day 1831, uncompromising publisher William Lloyd Garrison, another spiritual child of the Great Awakening, launched the antislavery newspaper *The Liberator.* He said, "I will be as harsh as truth and as uncompromising as justice." The cause soon had black heroes:

- Sojourner Truth, a freed black woman from New York, fought for both emancipation and women's rights.
- Frederick Douglass, an eloquent escaped slave, wrote his early life story in *Narrative of the Life of Frederick Douglass* (1845). He went on to be a respected spokesman for blacks through the Civil War and for years after.

**EXAMPLE**

**Question:** Who was William Lloyd Garrison?

**Answer:** Garrison was the uncompromising abolitionist who founded the anti-slavery newspaper *The Liberator* (1831).

Abolitionists were beaten, burned out of their houses, and sometimes killed, but they didn't back down. At first, careful politicians like Abraham Lincoln avoided them, but by the 1850s. the abolitionist cause was beginning to be accepted in the North. With the birth of the Republican Party in 1854, that cause found a national voice. See Chapter 12 for more information on the rise of abolition.

# MORE LAND FOR AMERICA

Destiny hadn't finished manifesting itself at the beginning of the 1840s, but shortly thereafter, the United States picked up a lot of land in a short time.

First came the *Aroostook War* (1842). These lumberjack battles in northern Maine were settled with the British masters of Canada in a way that left Maine with plenty of north woods, Canada with room to build a winter road to Quebec, and the U.S. with the nice surprise of major iron deposits in Minnesota.

Then Texas won its independence from Mexico in 1836, but between then and 1845, Texans had to stand by while Congress debated whether to admit it as a slave state. In 1845, Texas switched from being the Lone Star Republic to being the 28th star in the American flag. Mexico couldn't stand the transition of its former territory to the United States, and war broke out soon after American provocations in disputed south Texas.

One of Andrew Jackson's last political acts was recommending his friend and neighbor James Polk as the Democratic presidential nominee in 1844. Polk was victorious over a terminally frustrated Henry Clay and efficiently carried out his four-point presidential agenda: lower tariffs, establish an independent treasury, grab California (looked beautiful even before gold was discovered in 1848), and settle the Oregon border. Polk got legislation to lower the tariffs and restore an independent treasury. Then he went to work on grabbing California and the Oregon Territory.

In 1846, the British settled the Oregon Territory question by splitting the difference with the United States on the northern border of what became the state of Washington.

Then Polk managed to stir up border incidents with an angry Mexico down on the Rio Grande in Texas, and the *Mexican-American War* was under way in 1846. After some tough fighting, the U.S. defeated Mexico and in 1849 got California and all of the Southwest. At the time, California's inhabitants included around 13,000 Mexicans, 1,000 Americans more or less poaching on Mexican territory, and 100,000 American Indians. The war was unpopular in New England; Henry David Thoreau spent a night in jail to protest it. Abe Lincoln opposed it.

Most of the rest of the country was spoiling to finish off Manifest Destiny with a good fight. Renegade Americans in California seized the province, aided by Captain John Fremont, who just happened to be in the neighborhood with an armed patrol.

An American army fought its way into Mexico City by September 1847. Mexico reluctantly signed the *Treaty of Guadalupe Hidalgo* (1848), turning over an area that amounted to about a third of the United States in exchange for $18 million (offered rather guiltily by the United States). When the treaty was signed, neither side knew that gold, ultimately worth billions of dollars, had been discovered nine days earlier on the American River in California.

# SLIDING TO CIVIL WAR

This enormous new addition to the United States meant an enormous fight over whether it would be slave or free. Almost all the free states passed resolutions supporting the *Wilmot Proviso* (1846), an anti-slavery move calling for all the new land to be admitted as free states. This contentious amendment easily passed the U.S. House of Representatives but couldn't get through the carefully balanced Senate.

> **EXAMPLE**
>
> **Question:** What was the first resolution to split the North and South on the slavery issue?
>
> **Answer:** The Wilmot Proviso of 1846 was the first purely sectional vote (which never passed) to block extending slavery to territory acquired from Mexico.

Politically, the South was fighting with its back to the wall. The free-state population now far outnumbered that of slave states, even with the three-fifths provision for nonvoting slaves (see Chapter 9). Therefore, the North had more votes in the House, and if more free states were admitted, it soon would have more votes in the Senate as well. The South couldn't back down.

Meanwhile, hatred for slavery had reached the point in the North at which many people couldn't stand the thought of creating another state under the grip of slaveholders. The Mexican land was becoming a gigantic poison pill for compromise in the Union.

In the election of 1848, the Whigs ran a hero of the Mexican-American War, General Zachary Taylor. Taylor had no political liabilities, having never held public office or, for that matter, having ever voted in a presidential election. The Democrats ran an old veteran of the War of 1812 who believed in *popular sovereignty* (1850), the principle of letting the people of any territory decide whether they wanted the territory to be slave or free.

**Question:** What is popular sovereignty?

**Answer:** Popular sovereignty allowed local voters to choose whether their state would be slave or free.

A new Free Soil Party came out squarely against the extension of slavery to even one more square inch of the United States. The Free Soilers diverted enough votes from the Democrats to elect Zachary Taylor of the Whig party. Taylor hadn't made any speeches about slavery during the election, but he was a slaveholding plantation owner from Louisiana. That was enough to attract most Southern votes.

With the discovery of gold, California rushed toward statehood as a free state. The territory had plenty of people, had written its own constitution, and was ready to more than pay for itself. But if California were admitted, the balance in the Senate would swing to a majority for the nonslave states.

The Southerners were also worried about the issue of runaway slaves. Even the loss of a small number of slaves upset the South:

- *Harriet Tubman* (1849), a fearless runaway slave, had helped rescue more than 300 other slaves from the South, including her aging parents.

- *The Underground Railroad* (1850), a series of safe houses and hiding places for escaping slaves, was helping a small number of slaves escape. The total number of slaves who made it North in a year was around 1,000 — a small loss to freedom from a slave population of 4 million.

The South was also angry about the North's nonstop campaign to outlaw slavery in the nation's capital, Washington, D.C. The South was looking for a fight almost as though it had a guilty conscience.

# The Compromise of 1850

The situation didn't come to fighting yet. Most Northerners in 1850 were willing to let slavery remain in the South, as long as it didn't spread to other states. The old peacemakers of the Congress, Henry Clay (73), Daniel Webster (68), and Southerner John Calhoun (also 68), cobbled together the *Compromise of 1850*. They'd been working tirelessly to hold the nation together for 40 years, but now they were running out of time, both in their own lives and in the lifespan of compromise. Some highlights of the Compromise of 1850:

- The North got California as a free state, finally tipping the balance toward free-state votes in the Senate.

- The slave trade, but not slavery itself, was outlawed in Washington, D.C.

- New Mexico and Arizona could join the Union under popular sovereignty by deciding to be slave states if they wanted to.

The big Southern win in the Compromise of 1850 was the *Fugitive Slave Law*, which allowed slaves who had escaped to the North to be grabbed by federal marshals and hauled back South in chains. When a Boston runaway slave was dragged off in 1854, the shocking scene made previously peaceful compromisers into instant abolitionists.

> **EXAMPLE**
>
> **Question:** What was the most common Northern position on slavery in 1850?
>
> **Answer:** For most Northerners in 1850, slavery could remain in the South as long as it didn't spread.

> **EXAMPLE**
>
> **Question:** What was the most pro-slavery part of the Compromise of 1850?
>
> **Answer:** The Fugitive Slave Law required captured escaped slaves in the North to be returned to the South.

The Fugitive Slave Law was a public-relations disaster for the South, delivered in spite of the few slaves returned. The South became even more angry when Northern states refused to enforce the law.

Democrat Franklin Pierce won the presidency in 1852 and pledged to enforce the Fugitive Slave Law. This election was the end of the road for the Whigs; they had too many abolitionists to do well in the South and not enough antislavery zeal to win the North.

The South looked desperately for new slave-state territory, even sending private military expeditions to Central America and Cuba; these expeditions were easily beaten back, to the embarrassment of the United States. The United States tossed another $10 million Mexico's way for a chunk of desert containing Tucson — the Gadsden Purchase — which made for a good southern route for a railroad west, which the South preferred.

## Stephen Douglas and the Kansas-Nebraska Act

Stephen Douglas, senator from Illinois, wanted the western railroad to go from the North (specifically, from his state's big city, Chicago). To do this, the United States would have to organize the Nebraska Territory such that a railroad could be run across it. The South wasn't going to settle for any more free states, but the Missouri Compromise of 1820 had said that slavery was banned from Nebraska.

Douglas, a Northerner from Abe Lincoln's home state, proposed that the compromise be disregarded and the Nebraska territory opened to popular sovereignty. That could mean that Kansas, due west of slaveholding Missouri, could become a new slave state. Over angry opposition from the North, Douglas rammed the *Kansas-Nebraska Act* (1854) through Congress, doing away with the Missouri Compromise.

The Kansas-Nebraska Act was a self-defeating victory for the South. The North felt betrayed: The Missouri Compromise clearly said that there would be no slavery in the Nebraska territory, but now Southerners were flooding into Kansas to claim it for the South. The North hadn't liked the Compromise of 1850 in the first place; from now on, they would openly ignore it.

A new political party sprang up spontaneously in 1854 in the Midwest to fight against slavery. Within two years, the Republican Party would have enough strength to elect the speaker of the House of Representatives. The compromises were over.

# 12

# The Fight over Slavery: 1855–1865

**KEY CONCEPTS**

- The real causes of the Civil War
- Key battles and their impact on the course of the war
- Important changes resulting from the war

The Civil War involved four years of brutal fighting for a clear cause with tremendous bravery on each side. The first cuts of the Civil War were delivered with medieval broadswords near a peaceful river in Kansas, a thousand miles from the debates in Washington. The political decision that made the war inevitable came not from the divided Congress or the compromising president, but from the one place where the South had complete control: the Supreme Court.

When John Brown and his sons hacked five Southern slavery advocates to death in Kansas in 1856, Northerners showed that at least some of them would shed blood to defeat slavery. A few months later, the Supreme Court's Dred Scott decision blew the lid off the Missouri Compromise of 1820 and all the other compromises which had temporarily bought time by dividing the country into slave and non-slave sections (see Chapter 10). With the 1857 Dred Scott decision, middle-of-the-road peacemakers no longer had a place to meet. When the new Republican Party elected a worried-but-determined antislavery president in 1860, Southern guns were already being moved into position.

> **TIP**
>
> Although the political, economic, and social focus of the AP exam limits your need to know the Civil War's specific battles, you may be asked about the *causes* of the Civil War. While the South talked about states' rights and the North talked about keeping the Union together, the real cause was clearly slavery. Also be sure to mention the political impact of the polarizing 1860 election, the economic influence of cotton profits, and the social dynamic of Northern immigrants wanting more free land in the West. Most of all, the growing Northern population threatened to swamp the South with more voters and more free states.

# *UNCLE TOM'S CABIN* AND THE SHIFT IN PUBLIC OPINION

In 1852, author Harriet Beecher Stowe had an unexpected hit on her hands. *Uncle Tom's Cabin* (1852) was the most popular book in the United States and a best seller, not only in the U. S. but also in England and France. It went on to become the best-selling novel of the entire 1800s. One copy of the book was in print for almost every voter in the North; *Uncle Tom* was banned in the South.

*Uncle Tom's Cabin* followed the format of then-popular writing called *domestic* or *women's fiction*; it could have been a hit even if it didn't have so much meaning. Increasing its impact was the fact that *Uncle Tom's Cabin* was the first novel many people had ever read: Literacy was just becoming common for average people due to the growth of public schools. It would also be the last book many young Northerners read before they went off to fight and sometimes die in the Union Army.

The book not only helped start the war but also helped win it by causing Europeans to side with the North. Because of the book's popularity in Britain and France, those governments were morally afraid to intervene on the side of the South. The book was translated into languages around the world, including Chinese. Stowe had a simple answer when asked how her book came about. "God wrote it," she said.

People didn't even have to read the book to get the message; *Uncle Tom* appeared in thousands of plays performed in every Northern town before the Civil War. The message was so popular that *Uncle Tom's Cabin* was still in theaters during the 1900s, 50 years after the Civil War was over.

Another book, *The Impending Crisis of the South* (1857), written by middle-class Southerner Hinton Helper, argued that slavery was bad for the Southerners who didn't own slaves. The book was banned in the South but used by the Republicans in the North as campaign publicity. Southerners were fighting mad about exposés they considered to be false and libelous.

> **EXAMPLE**
>
> **Question:** Why was *Uncle Tom's Cabin* important?
>
> **Answer:** The book turned Northern opinion firmly against slavery.

## Why *Uncle Tom's Cabin* was so influential

What made Harriet Beecher Stowe's book so powerful? *Uncle Tom's Cabin* (1852) put a human face on slaves for the first time in literary history. Most people don't like to see other people suffer. The way Americans coped with the cruelty of slavery was to pretend, without thinking too hard, that slaves were work animals without feelings. In *Uncle Tom's Cabin*, the slaves have names, families, hopes, and spiritual souls. Uncle Tom is never the kiss-up that his name has come to signify in modern times; he stands up for his beliefs and his friends even though he doesn't have the power to fight back physically against the slave masters.

Tom is an older Christian slave separated from his wife and children when his master falls on hard times and is forced to sell Tom literally down the river to a life of hard labor and punishment on a cotton plantation in the Deep South. Eliza, a young mother who also belongs to Tom's master, is about to have her own son torn away from her and flees North, finally crossing into freedom in a harrowing scene in which she carries her small child across the dangerously shifting ice of the Ohio River. On his way south, Tom saves a 6-year-old white girl named Eva from drowning. Eva's family buys Tom. By the time young Eva dies of natural causes several years later, she and Tom have developed a faith in goodwill that inspires everyone around them. Eventually, Tom is sold to an evil slave owner named Simon Legree. When Tom refuses to tell about two slaves who have escaped from the plantation, Legree has Tom beaten to death. Like Christ on the cross, as Tom is being killed, he forgives the slave drivers who are whipping him. The slaves who escaped from Legree meet the slaves who escaped from Tom's first master in Canada and realize they're all from the same family. Moved by Tom's story, the son of Tom's first master frees all his slaves.

Part of the power of *Uncle Tom's Cabin* for contemporary audiences came from readers' feeling that they were learning the truth about the taboo subject of slave life. The subtitle of the book is *Life among the Lowly*, making the cause sound plaintive and nonthreatening. The main title is a poem in three words. *Cabin* is the humble home familiar to all Americans; several U.S. presidents benefited in elections because they'd been born in log cabins. *Tom* is as simple as any male name; it was the name of both Thomas Jefferson and Thomas, a disciple of Christ. *Tom* incorporates the *ohm* sound used in meditation and as part of *Amen*; the name means *twin* in Latin and Greek. *Uncle* is a favorite relative, kindly without having to carry the emotional baggage of a mother or father.

# FROM WORDS TO BULLETS IN BLEEDING KANSAS

After the *Kansas-Nebraska Act* (1854) opened new territory for settlement, with popular sovereignty deciding whether the states to be formed would be slave or free, settlers poured into Kansas (see Chapter 11). Most of the Northern settlers just wanted land, but they included some well-armed partisans who were ready to fight to make Kansas a free state. At the same time, the South sent tough gangs of men to raid Northern settlements and fix elections with the goal of making Kansas a slave state. Northerners fought back, and the resulting sporadic violence won the area the name *Bleeding Kansas* from 1854 to the beginning of the Civil War in 1861.

For several years, Kansans lived under the proslavery *Lecompton Constitution* (1857), a railroaded partisan document forced through by crooked votes and supported by the U.S. president but not accepted by Congress.

Responding to raids by proslavery Southern bands, militant abolitionist John Brown and his sons brutally killed five Southern sympathizers in 1856 (see the discussion on John Brown later in this chapter). Brown wasn't arrested and continued to lead antislavery defenders in pitched battles with Southern forces. Although plenty of property destruction and beatings occurred, fewer than 60 people were actually killed during the years of Bleeding Kansas.

Having let the genie out of the bottle by pushing through the Kansas-Nebraska Act, Senator Stephen Douglas threw away Southern support for the Democratic Party in general and for his presidential campaign in particular by insisting on an honest vote for Kansas. Douglas was from Illinois, like Abraham Lincoln, but he was willing to compromise on slavery. That made him a popular opponent, but Lincoln beat him in the presidential election of 1860.

Violence even reached the Senate floor when a Southern congressman named Preston Brooks beat abolitionist Senator Charles Sumner almost to death in 1856 over a virulent speech Sumner made against Southern-sponsored Kansan "hirelings picked from the drunken spew and vomit of an uneasy civilization." It is easy to see why that speech made Southerners mad, but outrage over the beating of Sumner contributed to the growth of Sumner's antislavery Republican Party in the North.

In the end, Kansas settlers were allowed to vote in a fair election in which they supported a free-state constitution by a margin of two to one. The territory never had more than a few slaves; no slave owner would risk his valuable property on such dangerous ground. Kansas was admitted to the Union after the beginning of the Civil War and was the scene of raids and reprisals by both sides during the war. Kansas contributed more than its share of volunteers to the Union Army.

# THE DRED SCOTT DECISION

In the presidential election of 1856, the Democrats cast around for someone nobody knew enough about to hate and came up with James "Old Buck" Buchanan, who had been out of the country serving as ambassador to Britain. Buchanan beat John Fremont, the first presidential candidate of the new Republican Party.

Had Fremont won, the Civil War could have been off to an early start. Fremont believed in action and was so antislavery that when he later served as a Union general during the Civil War, he had to be recalled for freeing slaves prematurely. Buchanan, on the other hand, generally supported slavery and its extension to the territories under popular sovereignty, so the South stayed put during most of his presidency. He couldn't have done much else to save the Union, though; sectional conflict was barreling down the tracks like a runaway freight train.

As he took the oath of office, Buchanan was looking forward to the Supreme Court's decision on the Dred Scott case, issued only two days after he became president.

## Background

*Dred Scott* (1857) was a slave whose master had taken him to live in free Illinois and Wisconsin. Scott sued for his freedom, because he had spent years living with his master in places where slavery was illegal. The Supreme Court could have just ruled that Scott couldn't sue because, in the twisted world of pre-Civil War law, Scott wasn't a person with legal standing. Legally, he could no more sue for freedom than your cat can sue for cat food. The law, bad as it was, was clear on a slave's lack of standing to sue in court.

# The ruling

The Supreme Court may be the highest in the land and presumably above partisanship, but that doesn't mean the judges are blind to politics. Having lost its majority in the Senate and with abolitionists nipping at Southerners' heels in the House, the South still ruled in one place: the Supreme Court. Most of whose justices were Southern sympathizers. They took this opportunity to strike a legal blow against anybody who questioned slavery.

The Supreme Court ruled that because slaves were private property and because the Fifth Amendment prohibited Congress from depriving people of their property without due process of law, every restriction on slavery, every hard-fought compromise, and every choice of the people in any state or territory was null and void. *Due process of the law* means that lawmakers must respect all of a person's legal rights, not just some or most of them, when passing laws. If a slave owner had an unrestricted legal right to own a slave (and of course the slave, being property, had no rights at all) then the slave owner could take his slaves anywhere he wanted and work them as slaves as long as he wanted.

The ruling in the Dred Scott case probably is the worst decision the Supreme Court ever made. First, it was an irrational interpretation of the Fifth Amendment to the Constitution, the amendment that protects life, liberty, and property. Due process of the law is exactly what the Congress and the territorial and state legislatures had gone through in debating and passing laws banning slavery from jurisdictions under their control. The legislature clearly had the right to legally deprive people of their property for the public good; that's exactly what taxation and eminent domain are. Second, the ruling on the Dred Scott case virtually guaranteed that civil law would lead to civil war; the Supreme Court was stripping the power of the law by making it politically absurd.

# The ramifications

The fallout from the Dred Scott decision didn't take long to hit. Stephen Douglas, the Democratic cheerleader for popular sovereignty, felt stabbed in the back and fought back furiously in the Senate. The Republicans had a field day, calling the previously respected Supreme Court nothing but a Southern debating society. The South was first delighted and then aghast that the North wouldn't follow the ruling of the august Supreme Court when the South was winning. Talk on both sides moved farther in the direction of "We can't live with these people."

> **EXAMPLE**
>
> **Question:** What was the overall legal importance of the Dred Scott decision?
>
> **Answer:** The Dred Scott decision meant Congress could put no limits on slavery in the territories, or technically, anywhere else in the United States

> **EXAMPLE**
>
> **Question:** What laws did the Dred Scott decision overturn?
>
> **Answer:** The Dred Scott case effectively repealed the Missouri Compromise of 1820, the Compromise of 1850, and the Kansas-Nebraska Act of 1854.

# FINANCIAL COLLAPSE: THE PANIC OF 1857

Just in time to increase the misery index in the North, the short but sharp Panic of 1857 brought financial collapse and unemployment. The South rode out the down market on the back of King Cotton, figuring that its relative prosperity was further proof that God was on its side. Hungry people in the North renewed their cries for the federal government to make cheap land available for settlement. Congress passed a Homestead Bill in 1860 to do just that, but President Buchanan vetoed it. Buchanan's friends in the South didn't want more settlers to vote against slavery in the territories.

# THE ELECTION OF 1860: WIDENING THE DIVIDE

With fights brewing in all branches of government, everyone looked anxiously toward the presidential election of 1860. Would the Democrats find a bring-us-together candidate? Could the Republicans possibly win when they weren't even allowed south of the Mason-Dixon line? Who was going to save democracy?

## Abraham Lincoln runs for president

Abraham Lincoln described himself as ugly. He towered above the short but determined fireplug figure of Stephen Douglas during their debates for the Senate in 1858, which turned out to be a prequel of the 1860 presidential race between the two. (See "Turning Words to Bullets in Bleeding Kansas," earlier in this chapter.)

Lincoln had risen from his humble beginnings on the Indiana frontier to become one of the better-known local lawyers in Illinois. In the House of Representatives, where incumbents usually kept getting reelected, he had managed to serve only one term. Up until the passage of the Kansas-Nebraska Act in 1854, he didn't stand out from a thousand other lawyer-politicians.

Although against slavery, Lincoln shied away from the troublemaking abolitionists. When the passage of the Kansas-Nebraska Act threatened to extend slavery, the Republican Party rose in opposition, and Lincoln, the party's nominee for President, became a tiger. He debated the famous Senator Douglas all over Illinois and came close to knocking him out of the Senate.

## John Brown

During this time, the abolitionist anger of John Brown could wait no more. Brown had been the bad-boy hero of peaceful-but-well-funded abolitionists since he killed a few slavery supporters during the war for Bleeding Kansas (see "Turning Words to Bullets in Bleeding Kansas," earlier in this chapter). His purpose in going to Kansas was to help protect the free-state settlers, including some of his adult children, from violent Southern raids.

Brown had a legitimate concern for the welfare of his sons and the free-state settlers in their vicinity, especially because the sacking of the free town of Lawrence seemed to signal an all-out campaign of violence by proslavery forces. After he murdered five proslavery men, he skillfully led the free-state settlers in defending themselves. When he captured a detachment of armed slavery raiders, he treated them well and negotiated for the return of two of his own sons who were being held by the slavery forces.

Brown put together a plan to start a slave uprising by marching through Virginia, handing out guns that he would steal from the federal armory at Harpers Ferry, north of Washington, D.C. Brown and a few men took the armory but were quickly arrested after a shootout with an army detachment under the command of then Union colonel Robert E. Lee. Brown's Harpers Ferry idea could never have worked. During the Civil War, slaves didn't revolt even when the Union Army was near.

Brown was quickly tried and hanged, but his spirit electrified the antislavery North and completely angered and frightened the slaveholding South. His last words as the noose was being tied around his neck were "This is a beautiful country." His death raised a spirit in the North that helped elect antislavery Abraham Lincoln.

> **TIP**
>
> When a guy like Brown does something violent, labeling him crazy is natural. Maybe he was crazy, but how crazy and violent was the slave system he hated? People seem to have more tolerance for institutionalized violence than they do for attacks against violent institutions. Brown just thought *somebody* had to do *something;* he was driven to his actions by the crazy system of slavery.

## Lincoln's election and Southern succession

It took two conventions for the Democrats to nominate Stephen Douglas for president in 1860. The Southerners walked out of the first convention and nominated John Breckinridge, a moderate from Kentucky who was willing to run on a Southern Democrat platform calling for the extension of slavery. The Northern Democrats who were left behind nominated Douglas. Desperate compromisers threw together a Constitutional Union Party, to put a fourth candidate in the race, John Bell of Tennessee. The Republicans thought they were playing it as safe as possible by picking Abraham Lincoln; their other choices were better known but more radically anti-slavery.

During a bitter campaign, the Southerners announced that if "that baboon" Lincoln became president, they were going to start their own country. Although Lincoln scored less than 40 percent of the popular vote, he got electoral votes from every free state. Even with Lincoln elected, the South was under no real danger of having its slavery institution taken way. That would take a constitutional amendment, and the slaveholders had almost twice as many states as they needed to defeat an amendment. The Republicans were a minority in both the House and Senate, and the Southerners still controlled the Supreme Court. But the South was fed up.

Within days of Lincoln's election, Southern states started to secede. Eventually, 11 states left the Union, taking with them most of the U.S. Army guns and supplies on Southern soil. To tell the truth, the army didn't have many supplies to grab. The entire U.S. Army consisted of only 15,000 men, and lots of them were scattered across the frontier, looking out for American Indians. The Union held on to one major fort guarding the approach to the hotbed of the rebellion: Fort Sumter in Charleston harbor.

Even as soldiers drilled, the sides made one final attempt at compromise: the *Crittenden Amendments* (1860), which would have allowed slavery in the Southwest and in territories to be acquired (watch out, Cuba). That law was a nonstarter.

# THE CIVIL WAR ERUPTS

Most Southerners actually thought they could just say, "Well, it's been a nice country, but gotta go," and the North would wave a peaceful goodbye. Although three-quarters of the soldiers from the South owned no slaves, they were still ready to fight for those who did. Southerners figured that Northern businessmen would want to hold on to Northern middleman profits from the cotton trade and the millions of dollars owed to them by the South. The South believed that a need for what they called *King Cotton* (1860) would force the British to come to their aid. They found out that money talks, but not as loud as a cause does. For the North, saving the Union and opposing slavery were causes worth fighting for.

Five border slave states chose to stay with the Union — luckily for the North, because border-state people, manufacturing, and horses would have added more than a third to Southern Confederate strength. As it was, the North had more than twice as many people as the South, three times as much money, and ten times as many factories.

Those figures didn't mean that the North was sure to win though; Britain had that kind of advantage over the colonies, and the Revolution still triumphed. As in the Revolutionary War, the South didn't really have to win; it just had to not lose. The North was forced to attack the South on the South's own soil; the South mostly fought from behind prepared defenses with short internal lines of supply and communications. The Union Navy blockaded Southern ports, but the South had enough food and weapons to last a few years.

The hotheads of South Carolina fired on *Fort Sumter*, the key to Charleston harbor held by the Union, thereby rousing Northerners into feeling that their nation's flag was under attack. Lincoln asked for 75,000 volunteers.

## The battles at Bull Run (1861 and 1862)

After the Union troops had a few months of training, they marched off to take the Confederate capital of Richmond, Virginia, and end the war quickly. At *First Bull Run* (1861) in Northern Virginia, the first battle of the war, one unit of Confederates held firm like a stone, earning their talented general the nickname "Stonewall" Jackson and buying the South enough time to win the fight.

The Union regrouped under Gen. George McClellan, who was good at organizing parades but not too good at actually fighting. About a year after Bull Run, McClellan lost the *Peninsula Campaign* (July 1862) to the Confederate Army under Robert E. Lee. Lee beat the Union again at *Second Bull Run* (August 1862) and headed into Union territory, only a few miles from Washington, D.C.

## The battle at Antietam (1862)

In one of the two most important fights of the Civil War (the other was the battle at Gettysburg), Lee was turned back, barely, at *Antietam* (September 1862). Second Bull Run and Antietam showed that both sides could defend their own territory.

Britain and France might have been tempted to get involved on the Southern side, but Antietam (and their opposition to slavery) made them stay away.

# The Emancipation Proclamation

Antietam also gave Lincoln the backing he needed to announce his plan to free the slaves in the states then fighting the Union. On New Year's Day, he officially issued the *Emancipation Proclamation* (1863). With the Union on record as fighting for the cause of freedom, average people in Britain and France made sure their governments wouldn't help the South. They had read *Uncle Tom's Cabin* (see "How Reading Led to Fighting" earlier in this chapter).

> **EXAMPLE**
>
> **Question:** What was the significance of the Battle of Antietam?
>
> **Answer:** It helped convince England and France not to support the Confederacy, and it gave Lincoln the political strength to issue the Emancipation Proclamation.

> **EXAMPLE**
>
> **Question:** What was the most important immediate impact of the Emancipation Proclamation?
>
> **Answer:** Issuing the Emancipation Proclamation showed that the North was fighting to end slavery, not just to preserve the Union. This increased support from ex-slaves and from foreign nations opposed to slavery.

# Blockade of southern supply lines

Meanwhile, the North tightened its *Anaconda Plan* blockade to cut off Southern supplies. Southerners had figured that Britain would have to help them because something like one out of five jobs in Britain was tied to Southern King Cotton. Even though some British working people went unemployed and hungry, the British refused to help. The Northern states shipped Britain extra food; they had plenty to share.

The South tried to break the blockade with a homemade iron-sided ship called the *Merrimack*. Just in time, a Union ironclad arrived to fight. The *Monitor* and the *Merrimack* (1862) fought to a tie. After this first fight between metal ships, it was clear that warships of the future would be made out of steel, not wood.

# The battles of Fredericksburg (1862) and Chancellorsville (1863)

The Union lost badly at *Fredericksburg* (December 1862) by attacking an unbeatable Southern entrenchment and at *Chancellorsville* (May 1863). They were suckered by a brilliant flank attack by Lee. Up to that time, the Union commanding generals (McClellan, McDowell, Burnside, Hooker) deserved a grade of about F+.

## The battles at Gettysburg and Vicksburg (1863)

Lee was feeling his oats and decided to have another go at invading the North. At *Gettysburg* (July 1863) in Pennsylvania, he attacked Union troops who would not be moved. For three days of ferocious fighting, the Union held. The battle was very close; the South had peace commissioners ready to take the Union's surrender. Instead, Lee's army was forced to retreat to Virginia. Gettysburg, the South's last real chance to win the Civil War, joined Antietam as the other key battle of the conflict.

**EXAMPLE**

**Question:** What were the two key battles of the Civil War?

**Answer:** Antietam, where the North held the line against the South, and Gettysburg, where the South was defeated in Northern territory.

The day after Gettysburg, General Ulysses S. Grant took the Confederate fortress at *Vicksburg* (1863), splitting the South at the Mississippi River. With the twin victories at Gettysburg and Vicksburg, Britain and France even stopped taking Southern money to build them warships. The Confederacy was on its own. Union General William Tecumseh Sherman marched across the Confederacy from *Atlanta to the sea* (1864), leaving a 60-mile-wide path of destruction and freeing 25,000 slaves. His tactics were brutal, but they helped shorten the war and save lives. He said, "War is all hell."

## Extending freedom

Although the Emancipation Proclamation of 1863 technically only freed slaves in the Confederacy (which was out of the reach of the law), more and more slaves were freed as the Union Army rolled up Southern territory. More than 200,000 freed slaves joined the Union Army and fought to free those still held in bondage.

Paid less than whites until the last year of the war, they fought bravely in difficult battles. About 10 percent of Union forces were black, and they suffered more than their share of casualties. Southern slaves never rose up against their masters, but they did run away to freedom when they could.

## The presidential election of 1864 and the end of the war

Lincoln won reelection in 1864 on the Republican ticket, cleverly including a loyal border-state Democrat as vice president. When Lincoln won, desertions from the Confederate Army increased. General Grant, now in command of the main Union Army, hammered relentlessly at Lee throughout 1864. Finally, in April 1865, the Confederacy surrendered. Lincoln visited the defeated Southern capital of Richmond. When grateful slaves tried to kneel in front of him, he pulled them up and said, "You must kneel to God only, and thank Him for the liberty."

> **TIP**
>
> People will tell you the AP never asks about battles, but that isn't necessarily true. Don't get lulled into studying nothing about the way the Civil War unfolded. At a minimum, remember Antietam, which kept out foreign intervention and let in the Emancipation Proclamation. The battle of Gettysburg stopped the South's invasion of the North and marked the last real chance for the South to win the war.

> **EXAMPLE**
>
> **Question:** How many Southerners owned slaves?
>
> **Answer:** Only about one quarter of Southern whites owned slaves.

> **EXAMPLE**
>
> **Question:** What was the role of black troops in the Civil War?
>
> **Answer:** Black soldiers made up 10 percent of the Union Army. They suffered more than their share of casualties and by the end of the war were paid the same as white troops.

## The loss of Lincoln

A few days after he knew the war would end, Lincoln was assassinated by John Wilkes Booth, an actor with Southern sympathies who thought he could somehow revive the Confederacy by killing Lincoln. Actually, killing Lincoln hurt the South. Lincoln had planned to let Southern states rejoin the Union on relatively easy terms. With Lincoln gone, Democratic Vice President Andrew Johnson would have to try to manage *Reconstruction,* the rebuilding of the South with free blacks (see Chapter 13), through a Republican-controlled Congress eager to make sure that the South learned a lesson.

> **EXAMPLE**
>
> **Question:** What was the impact of the assassination of President Lincoln?
>
> **Answer:** Without the forgiving Lincoln to guide the process, Reconstruction of the South after the war became a partisan political controversy.

# THE AFTERMATH OF THE CIVIL WAR

More than 600,000 men died in the Civil War — close to the total for all the other wars the United States has ever fought. Family members fought one another. Mary Lincoln, the president's wife, had three brothers killed fighting for the Confederacy. Four million slaves were freed, although real social freedom took another 100 years to accomplish. Extreme states' rights were abolished, and the twin national challenges of nullification and secession, which first threatened the Union when George Washington was president (see Chapter 9), were finally laid to rest.

The Union's victory in the Civil War expanded federal power. The first 12 amendments to the Constitution, in place before the war, all limited the power of the government. The next three amendments, passed after the war, all expanded national power.

The Civil War led to a national banking system with national currency; the first income tax (3 percent, starting in 1861); the first draft (1863); and, through attempts to help freed slaves, the *Freedman's Bureau (1865)* was the beginning of a national welfare system.

Before the Civil War, the term *United States* was plural. People said, "The United States — *they* have decided to expand." After the war, *United States* was singular, as in "The United States — *it* has decided to grow." Small words can make a big difference.

# 13

# Reconstruction and the Move Westward, 1866–1880

> ## KEY CONCEPTS
>
> - From Reconstruction to segregation in the South
> - Republican Presidents Grant and Hayes
> - Technological, industrial, and social advancements in the Gilded Age
> - The expansion westward

**B**ecause everyone who died on both sides was an American, the Civil War cost as many U.S. lives as all the other wars the country has ever fought combined. Both sides lived for years with chips on their shoulders. And what about those 4 million newly freed slaves? The Civil War resulted in Reconstruction and also set the stage for U.S. expansion west.

After the Civil War, industry grew, and even farmers started using machines. More people moved to the cities, trading all-day farm chores for nighttime bright lights. Railroads crossed the country, American Indians were pushed onto reservations, and immigrants streamed onshore. Hard-to-remember presidents debated about hard-to-remember things like tariffs and silver coinage. Meanwhile, the rights of women and labor advanced in fits and starts. This chapter covers the beginnings of all of these things. Pay special attention to social trends that can be useful for both multiple-choice and essay success on the big test.

# RECONSTRUCTION

What with the actions of Union Generals Sherman and Grant, plus the South's own destructive fighting (see Chapter 12), the Cotton Belt was badly torn up after the war. Southern plantations needed five years to get back into full cotton production. The *Reconstruction* (1865–1877) of the South was done by new national and local governments, as well as by charitable helpers. And the *Thirteenth Amendment* (1865) turned Lincoln's Emancipation Proclamation into a national ban on slavery.

Slaves who were worth billions of dollars to plantation owners before the war were now officially free, so how was the South going to plant and harvest its valuable cotton? After the Civil War, blacks with only the clothes on their backs and no education, food, or places to live weren't really all that free. Former slaves often didn't have any choice but to sign up to work for very low wages, often for their former masters.

The issues of Reconstruction included the changes that Southern states would have to make to be readmitted to the Union, how much help the former slaves would have from the federal government, and how Northern troops could contain Southern terrorist attacks by groups like the Ku Klux Klan.

> **TIP**
>
> Expect a question about Reconstruction on test day, especially about the amendments that I discuss in this section. Remember that the amendments were passed in the order you would expect if you freed someone: The Thirteenth abolished slavery, the Fourteenth granted citizenship, and the Fifteenth provided the right to vote.

## The Freedmen's Bureau

A month before the Civil War was even over, Congress created the *Freedmen's Bureau* (1865) to help educate and take care of freed slaves. By the time the bureau stopped work, it had taught 200,000 former slaves to read with the help of volunteer teachers from the North. In one classroom, four generations of a family, from child to great-grandmother, all learned to read together. Union Gen. Oliver Howard ran the Freedmen's Bureau and later started Howard University in Washington, D.C.

# The Radical Republicans

With Abraham Lincoln gone (see Chapter 12), his Democratic vice president, Andrew Johnson, took over as president. Lincoln had generously planned to let the Southern states rejoin the Union on easy terms. Johnson went even farther with the generous policy; he issued pardons to hundreds of ex-Confederates.

That wasn't what the *Radical Republicans* (1866) in Congress wanted; they wanted to change the South radically, punish the former slave masters, and protect the blacks with federal power. To the disgust of these Republican lawmakers, new delegates from the South came knocking on the Capitol door in December 1865 — the very same year in which the South was finally defeated and Lincoln was shot.

And who should be there asking for admission as congressmen but several Confederate generals, members of the Confederate Cabinet, and even the Confederate vice president? The Radical Republicans threw them out. The radicals had two reasons for hanging tough:

- The unreconstructed Southerners had passed ugly *Black Codes* (1866) that made blacks almost into slaves again. Blacks had to sign one-year labor contracts, and if they didn't come through, they could be fined and put so deeply in debt that they would never earn anything. They could be punished for "idleness" by being sent to work on chain gangs.

- Now that the slaves were officially free, the South actually got more representatives in Congress than it had before the war, when a slave counted as only three-fifths of a person. Working with Northern Democrats, the South could even take control of Congress and undo all the progress that the North had fought to gain.

# The Thirteenth, Fourteenth, and Fifteenth Amendments

The Thirteenth Amendment (1865) prevents slavery in the United States. To nail down blacks' rights, Congress passed the *Fourteenth Amendment* (1866) to the Constitution. It guaranteed the citizenship of freed slaves, reduced the representation of Southern states if they kept blacks from voting, disqualified anyone who had left public service in the North to join the Confederacy from ever holding office in the Union again, and guaranteed the debt of the Union while repudiating the debt of the Confederacy. The Fourteenth Amendment also encouraged universal male voting.

Congress was determined to not let any Confederate state back in unless it endorsed the Fourteenth Amendment. President Andrew Johnson told the former rebel states not to sign it. Johnson had been the only senator from a Southern state to remain loyal to the Union; now that the fighting was over, he wanted to go easy on his Southern buddies. Even though Johnson was from a different political party, Lincoln had made him vice president as a show of national unity. Now Lincoln was dead and Johnson was unexpectedly president. The Republican Congress headed for a showdown with the president they never wanted.

Johnson had hoped to pick up some support in the fall congressional elections, but the Republicans won big. After whites attacked blacks in vicious riots in the South, Congress divided the South into five military districts and sent in the Army to keep order. It also passed the *Fifteenth Amendment* (1869) to guarantee blacks the right to vote. To get back into the Union, representatives of former Confederate states had to sign both amendments.

> **EXAMPLE**
>
> **Question:** What was the purpose of the Fourteenth Amendment?
>
> **Answer:** The Fourteenth Amendment guaranteed citizenship and civil rights for former slaves.

> **EXAMPLE**
>
> **Question:** What was the most serious constitutional issue following the Civil War?
>
> **Answer:** How the former Confederate states would be readmitted to the Union.

# Women, former slaves, and the limits of freedom

Women's rights leaders like Susan B. Anthony and Elizabeth Cady Stanton put their own cause on hold to work tirelessly for emancipation of the slaves. Although women's rights was a growing concern before the Civil War, most politically involved women were even more concerned with ending slavery and preserving the Union. Women from outside the women's rights movement also served during the war. For example, Dorothea Dix was the leader of Union nurses. The Woman's Loyal League gathered nearly 400,000 signatures on a petition for a constitutional amendment banning slavery. Many of these socially involved women were more than a little upset that the new Fourteenth and Fifteenth Amendments gave black males the right to vote, but not white or black women. Women would have to wait almost 60 years before their election rights became part of the Constitution.

Meanwhile, more and more Western states acted on their own to let women step up to the ballot box, starting with Wyoming ("The Equality State") in 1869. Black women, voting or not, helped rally black political participation in the South until they were silenced by the heavy hand of segregationist governments.

> **EXAMPLE**
>
> **Question:** Name a female leader who was not greatly involved in the women's rights movement.
>
> **Answer:** Despite being the leader of the Union's nurses, Dorothea Dix wasn't a women's rights pioneer.

Northern troops in the South supported "radical" state governments that allowed blacks freedom and passed public education bills to help everyone. But by the time federal troops finally withdrew from the South in 1877, Southern state governments were quickly seized by *Redeemer* or home-rule segregationist groups, which took as many rights as they could away from blacks. Before these groups struck, however, blacks enjoyed a brief period of being elected to Congress and local offices, which outraged former slave masters.

White Southerners called anyone from the North who helped Reconstruction a *carpetbagger* (1870), taking a dig at the image of outsiders arriving with cheap luggage made out of carpets. Southerners who cooperated with Reconstruction were called *scalawags* (1870). The most important and lasting contribution of the carpetbagger governments was the establishment of a system of education in the South.

Although Reconstruction Southern state governments did have their share of mismanagement, they were no more outrageous than the scams going on in some Northern capitals at this time. Reconstruction governments got some important work going in public education and road repair.

Blacks as well as poor whites in the South were forced into sharecropping. In a system reminiscent of feudalism, they worked their small parts of a large plantation owned by a landlord and turned over a third or more of their crops to the landlord. Worse, sharecroppers were required to buy supplies from the landowner and sell their own crops to the landlord at prices that the landlord set. Because the landlord kept all the accounts, any halfway crooked landlord could make sure his sharecroppers stayed perpetually in debt.

> **EXAMPLE**
>
> **Question:** What lasting accomplishments of carpetbagger governments remained even after the Redeemers took over?
>
> **Answer:** The greatest accomplishment of the carpetbagger Southern governments that survived the Redeemer segregationist takeover was a lasting public education system.

> **EXAMPLE**
>
> **Question:** How did blacks earn money after the Civil War?
>
> **Answer:** Most of them were sharecroppers close to where they'd been slaves.

## Southern opposition to Reconstruction

Southerners struck back at Reconstruction with violence through terrorist organizations such as the *Ku Klux Klan* (1867). The original Ku Klux Klan lasted only for about six years before federal troops put it down, but its terrorist hatred did a lot of damage. Hundreds of blacks and their white helpers were beaten and murdered. Congress passed the *Force Acts* (1870), which used federal troops to largely stamp out the Klan, but white intimidation of blacks lasted well into the 20th century (see Chapter 14).

### Frederick Douglass on the end of Reconstruction

"As the war for the Union recedes into the misty shadows of the past, and the Negro is no longer needed to assault forts and stop rebel bullets, he is in some sense, of less importance. Peace with the old master class has been war to the Negro. As the one has risen, the other has fallen. The reaction has been sudden, marked, and violent. It has swept the Negro from all the legislative halls of the Southern States, and from those of the Congress of the United States. It has, in many cases, driven him from the ballot box and the jury box. The situation has much in it for serious thought, but nothing to cause despair. Above all the frowning clouds that lower about our horizon, there is the steady light of stars, and the thick clouds that now obscure them, will in due season pass away."

By the 1890s, blacks were blocked from voting in the South by technically legal methods like rigged literacy tests and poll taxes. A hate-filled white minority didn't limit itself to legal methods; lynching and beatings of innocent blacks continued for 100 years after the Civil War.

After the Civil War, President Andrew Johnson made himself so unpopular with the Republican Congress that it moved to impeach him. Fearing that Johnson would fire the Republican members of the Cabinet he had inherited from Lincoln, Congress passed the *Tenure of Office Act* (1867), which made that move illegal. Johnson fired Republican Secretary of War Edwin M. Stanton anyway because Stanton wanted strong Reconstruction measures. The House of Representatives voted to impeach Johnson. Amid much drama, the Senate came just one vote short of voting Johnson out of office. Tempers ran high, but the country stuck to democracy. No violence broke out among the Union and former Confederate leaders.

The national government's attempts at Reconstruction lasted until the disputed election of Rutherford Hayes as president in 1877 caused the Republicans to make a deal to pull the last Union troops out of the South. Even while it was going on, Southerners pushed back.

The political gains that blacks made during the 12 years of Reconstruction didn't last much longer than the last federal soldier on the scene to defend them. Powerful Southern whites refused to allow the status of blacks to change from slave to citizen in one generation. In fact, it took 100 years for blacks to be really free to vote, go to school, and live as Americans with the rest of Southern society.

The legacy of poverty had a lot of staying power. In the words of the distinguished ex-slave Frederick Douglass, a freedman was "free from the individual master, but still a slave to society . . . free from the old quarter that once gave him shelter, but a slave to the rains of summer and the frosts of winter. He was, in a word, literally turned loose, naked, hungry and destitute, to the open sky." Delayed but not forever denied, the gains of the 1960s civil-rights movement had their basis in the faltering reforms of Reconstruction in the 1860s.

## The end of Reconstruction

The political fight that ended Reconstruction was the *Hayes-Tilden Compromise* (1877). Hayes was a Republican political hack running under the burden of Grant-administration corruption. Samuel Tilden was the Democratic reformer who had cleaned up the Boss Tweed scandal. Tilden racked up more popular votes, but the numbers in the Electoral College were about even.

The Democrats made a deal to let their opponent Hayes win in return for the Republicans' agreeing to withdraw the last federal troops from the South. In reality, the determination of the North to protect blacks in the South had faded with time.

The last-gasp *Civil Rights Act* (1875) was mostly overturned by the South-leaning Supreme Court in the *Civil Rights Cases* (1883). Even the Fourteenth Amendment was found by the court to apply only to government violations of civil rights, not to the denial of rights by individuals. Blacks were pretty much on their own in a hostile society for the next 100 years.

# THE PRESIDENCY OF ULYSSES S. GRANT

In 1868 (before the end of Reconstruction), former Union Gen. Ulysses S. Grant ran for president as a Republican under the slogan "Vote as you shot" and was elected by a grateful nation and an army of Union veterans. Although Grant had most of the electoral votes, his popular-vote majority came from former slaves. The Republicans, on only their second elected president, realized that they would have to play politics carefully to stay in office. Unfortunately, politics (then as now) meant hanging around with rich people who were out for their own good.

Grant proved to be better at fighting battles than watching over money. He had been in office for only a few months when speculators tried to corner the gold market on *Black Friday* (1869), causing a business panic. Other problems followed Grant through his presidency:

- The *Crédit Mobilier scandal* (1872), which involved Union Pacific railroad payoffs to politicians.
- The *Whiskey Ring scandal* (1875), in which politicians robbed the U.S. Treasury of excise taxes on alcohol.
- The forced resignation of Grant's secretary of war William Belknap in 1876 after he was caught pocketing bribes from suppliers to American Indian reservations.

Although Grant himself was not personally dishonest, he did enjoy drinking Old Crow whiskey and had complete trust in his relatives and friends. The crooks who always hang around politics took advantage of Grant's easygoing character. After *Boss Tweed* (1872), leader of the Tammany Hall ring in New York City, was finally sent to prison, one of his cronies explained how it worked: "I seen my opportunities, and I took 'em."

# LIFE IN THE GILDED AGE

Author Mark Twain (see "Increasing literacy" later in this chapter) called the period of the 1800s after the Civil War the *Gilded Age* (1875), for all the gold-painted furniture and fancy living. The country was evenly split between Republicans and Democrats; although the Republicans won most of the presidential races, control of Congress changed hands in more than half of the elections.

Most people voted, and the issues, though deeply felt at the time, seem pretty small in retrospect. Republican voters tended to be rural Protestants, believers in personal morality, and veterans of the Civil War. Democrats tended to be more easygoing in their judgments, to live in big cities and in the South, and to be recent immigrants.

The self-betterment dreams of early modern Americans were modest; people didn't dream of a mansion, just a home. Even so, the country grew and changed in ways that many people found surprising.

## The change in currency to paper money

An economic panic that started in 1873 introduced an issue that would continue for the rest of the 1800s. During the Civil War, the Union had issued millions of dollars in paper money. People who owed loans wanted more paper money, because that would increase inflation. Inflated cheap money would make the debt they owed easier to repay. The cheap-money people also supported the coinage of silver to bring about more inflation. Businessmen who loaned money wanted all paper money paid off in gold, so that the money they loaned would be worth more when it was paid back. The U.S. Treasury, backed by businessmen, redeemed paper money for gold so regularly that, after a while, people got tired of carrying jangling coins and just used paper money instead.

# Immigration

When a country loses 600,000 men in a war, you'd expect the population to go down for a while. The South lost 1 out of 10 adult males, the North 1 out of 30; the equivalent loss in today's U.S. population would be 6 million people. But the United States was the most popular immigration destination in the world. The population of the country actually went up by more than 25 percent during the Civil War decade; by 1870, the United States had almost 40 million citizens. Lots of these people were moving to Eastern cities or opened Western land. With no real danger of foreign attacks or internal dissolution, the United States turned to wrangling about money and voting rights.

The history of the post–Civil War United States centered on moves to the cities and to the West. The Civil War was a fight among farm boys; 80 percent of Americans at that time lived in the country. But by 1900, the United States was only 60 percent rural and boasted several cities over 1 million in population. New York had become the second-largest city in the world.

Europe was growing too. Thanks in part to food imported directly from America and to European cultivation of that New World wonder food, the potato, the population of Europe doubled in the 1800s.

Many Europeans were moving around that continent, looking for new opportunities. For some people — like the Irish living in famine — the choice was immigrate or die. Aided by the ease and cheapness of steamship travel, 20 million Europeans made the jump across the Atlantic to the United States between 1820 and 1900.

As in the Know-Nothing days before the Civil War, the increase in immigrants and the growth of cities worried some traditionalists. As the 1870s drew to a close, calls to restrict immigration grew louder.

# Industrialization and the birth of labor unions

The world's petrochemical future began with the first rickety oil well in Pennsylvania in 1859. Cars didn't exist yet, but kerosene made from petroleum oil burned brighter than the expensive whale oil that had been the only thing used in lamps since before the days of *Moby-Dick*. The oil business was off to a good start; within a few years, kerosene was the fourth-leading export of the United States.

Slowly, American products begin to show up all over the world. Among the first to arrive were five-gallon kerosene cans from the Standard Oil Co. The growth in industry was trailed by a growth in labor unions. The National Labor Union was formed just after the Civil War and helped to win the first eight-hour working day, initially just for federal government employees. Workers in the period after the Civil War were often made to work ten or more hours a day, six days a week, without overtime.

By 1872, labor unions had hundreds of thousands of members, and more than 30 national unions represented typesetters, hat-makers, cobblers, and other skilled craftspeople. Business depressions in the 1870s and the inability of unions to raise wages while profits were shrinking caused the union movement to lose momentum for a while. In the 1870s, a new national union coalition called the Knights of Labor gained strength. The Knights tried to unite all laboring men behind a program of worker-owned stores; health and safety regulations; and, most important, the eight-hour working day (which didn't become standard until the 1900s).

> **TIP**
>
> Older U.S. history texts (and some older U.S. history teachers) may not pay enough attention to the labor-, women's-, and minority-rights movements that the politically up-to-date AP U.S. History exam expects you to know. Don't get caught short. Because this exam gets you the college credit you want, take this opportunity to memorize some key names and dates from the evolving history of people's movements. Progress is like a dance between the leaders and the people: Sometimes the rulers lead; sometimes the people do.

# Increasing literacy

Public schools spread throughout the nation in the 1870s. The change was especially important in the South, where public education was not available until it became a lasting benefit of Reconstruction. Adults too old for school were so eager to learn that they flocked to public lectures called *chautauquas* held in hundreds of locations all over the country. The number of Americans who couldn't read dropped from 20 percent in 1870 to about 10 percent in 1900, despite the influx of millions of initially poorly educated immigrants. However, in 1900, almost half of nonwhite Americans still couldn't read. Only 40 years before, it had been against the law to teach slaves to read in much of the South.

College education got a big boost from the *Morrill Act* (1862), which reserved some of the proceeds from the sale of public lands to found land-grant colleges in new states. *Land-grant colleges* are state schools with public backing in all of the United States that allow people to get higher education even if they come from poor families. In another higher education development, *Johns Hopkins University* (1876) provided the first serious graduate-degree programs in the United States.

More people could read than ever before. They chose books with stories that seemed to speak to their own lives and dreams. The books they read then proceeded to reshape the way readers saw the world:

- Horatio Alger wrote more than 100 novels with titles like *Luck and Pluck* (1869) and *Tattered Tom* (1871). The young heroes of Horatio Alger stories advance through hard work and honesty from poverty to middle-class economic safety, not from rags to riches, as people who have never read the stories have come to believe.

- Walt Whitman continued his poetic tributes to human nature, loosened social restraints, and his native land through the 1870s. His work expanded the understanding of poetry.

- America and the world found a new literary friend when a failed silver miner named Samuel Clemens took the pen name Mark Twain. His writing, from *The Innocents Abroad* (1869) to *The Adventures of Tom Sawyer* (1876) to *The Adventures of Huckleberry Finn* (1884), helped make reading widely popular and broadened the meaning of great literature.

# The impact of Charles Darwin

Charles Darwin's theory of evolution upset religious traditions as it spread through America after the Civil War. Darwin said that all living things have evolved to their present form through a dazzling process of natural selection. The Bible says literally that God created the world in six days, but evolution covers millions of years. Religious fundamentalists felt that their faith would be shaken if they didn't take those six days in the Bible literally. Religious modernists, on the other hand (including followers of Catholicism, Judaism, and most of the mainstream Protestant denominations), saw evolution as just an advance in understanding the grand workings of God.

The fight over human evolution that started during this period is part of an evolutionary battle between literal and spiritual interpretations of religious teaching that has been going on since the writing of the first holy books. In the United States, evolutionary theory led to political, educational, and religious polarization. *Social Darwinists* (1875) carried natural selection to a literal extreme and taught that survival-of-the-fittest competition was the law of society. Speakers toured the U.S. to promote science and Darwin's theory. Toward the end of the 1800s, fundamentalist churches increasingly opposed evolution.

>  **EXAMPLE**
>
> **Question:** How was Darwin's theory of evolution used to explain society?
>
> **Answer:** Social Darwinists said society functions on Darwin's survival-of-the-fittest theory.

## Censorship and women's rights

The forces of new morality took on the forces of censorship in the 1870s. Winning the right for women to vote was a crusade for eloquent *Victoria Woodhull* (1872), who became the first woman to run for president (with the amused support of rich industrialist Cornelius Vanderbilt). She and her sister published a magazine that crusaded for equal rights and exposed respected minister Henry Ward Beecher for having an affair with a female parishioner.

Armed with the *Comstock Laws* (1873), Anthony Comstock tried to arrest Woodhull for indecency. The *Comstock Laws* include federal and state laws against indecent material. For 50 years, these laws were also used to suppress information about birth control. Woodhull escaped Comstock's clutches and represented progressive causes for the rest of her life. Comstock's censorship laws survived into the 1960s, when they no longer seemed necessary to a free society. Family planning information and most kinds of literature are no longer prohibited in the U.S. Woodhull's feminism is still alive today in books, movies, songs, and politics.

## The temperance movement

People on the frontier often drank too much, and the United States had been a frontier society for all its existence. The National Prohibition Party organized in 1869 and the more-moderate Women's Christian Temperance Union (WCTU) in 1874. Temperance allows a little social drinking for those who can control it; Prohibition bans alcohol for everyone.

Throughout the late 1800s and early 1900s, people against drinking gained political strength. In the early 1900s, the Prohibitionists won big. With the passage of the *Eighteenth Amendment* (1920), alcohol became illegal in the U.S. America's "dry" period lasted only 13 years. In 1933, the Eighteenth Amendment was repealed, because making alcoholic beverages illegal seemed to lead to more problems than it solved. (Read more about the Eighteenth Amendment in Chapter 15.)

# THE PUSH WESTWARD

After the Civil War, the country was bursting with energy. Industries developed, immigrants poured in, railroads crisscrossed the land, education spread, wealth increased, and the West was settled. The country began to look abroad for new frontiers.

## The railroad and economic growth

At the end of the Civil War, most of the railroads were in the North and east of the Mississippi; none of them crossed the West. California could be reached only by weeks of sailing or riding in a bumpy stagecoach. By 1900, the United States had more railroads than Europe, and people could ride the rails to the West Coast in a matter of a few days.

Beginning right after the end of the Civil War in 1865, a crew of 5,000 (mostly Irish) workers pushed the rail lines west from Omaha, while 10,000 Chinese workers labored over the Sierras from Sacramento. By 1869, the railroad across America was complete.

The *Crédit Mobilier* (1872) scandal tainted the westbound-from-Omaha owners of the Union Pacific Railroad. The Central Pacific Railroad from Sacramento made a lot of money but avoided the large-scale political bribery of the Crédit Mobilier gang.

*Cornelius Vanderbilt* (1870) had made a fortune in steamboats. In his late 60s, when he should have been happily enjoying the money, he decided to build some railroads. He pioneered the use of steel instead of iron rails for the important New York Central, making train tracks safer and less expensive to build. In the years after the Civil War, the railroads finally agreed on a standard width or *gauge* for rails so that people didn't have to keep getting off and changing trains. Westinghouse air brakes helped trains stop, and Pullman cars made them comfortable.

Railroads made the United States the largest integrated market in the world. Food, resources, and products could move anywhere in the country, which stimulated growth. Building the railroads also helped develop the U.S. steel industry. When Vanderbilt first used steel rails, he had to buy the steel from England — soon the U.S. had a strong steel industry. Settlements sprung up like strings of pearls along the railroads, just as they'd done in the past along rivers. Corn, wheat, and cattle replaced tall-grass prairies and buffalo. Forests were cut down and became lumber carried on rails to build cities.

> **EXAMPLE**
>
> **Question:** How did the railroads contribute to economic growth?
>
> **Answer:** Transportation sparked growth from 1860 to 1900 by creating the world's largest connected market system, by allowing settlers and businessmen to reach any part of the country quickly, and by fueling the business involved in the very act of building the world's largest railroad system.

Quick profits attracted rip-off artists. Jay Gould made a fortune buying railroads, inflating their stocks, and then selling them. The scam was called *stock watering*, after the farmer's trick of getting cattle really thirsty and then letting them fill up with heavy water just before they hit the scales to be sold by weight.

Railroad stock wars led to bare-knuckle fights between capitalists. Tough old Vanderbilt said, "I won't sue you; the law takes too long. I'll ruin you." Railroads had almost unlimited political power; they bought influence by giving out free passes to politicians and reporters. Without competition on most routes, they could charge whatever they wanted. They angered small shippers and farmers by demanding more money from them than from their large business cronies.

# The cultivation of the West

The *Homestead Act* (1862) allowed half a million settlers to buy 160 acres of land from the federal government for the bargain price of $30 (about $900 in modern money). Around two out of three of these families couldn't make a go of farming marginal Western land. Another 2.5 million settlers bought land from the railroads, land speculators, or state governments.

Farming increased everywhere. As with any real estate, location was everything. Land west of the 100th meridian, the imaginary dividing line that runs north from the Texas Panhandle, was just too dry for regular farming without irrigation. Ranchers held on by planting tough strains of wheat and fencing their land with the new barbed wire invented in 1874.

Cattle drives moved beef to the nearest railroad terminals all over the West. The spectacular Long Drive covered 500 miles from Texas to Kansas, with crews of black, white, and Mexican cowboys moving herds as big as 10,000 head to market. The Long Drive was just one of thousands of trails that connected cattle range in the farthest corners of the West to railroad lines and finally dinner plates. These cattle drives built the real-life legend of the cowboys. The cattle drives died out in the 1880s as the open range was broken up by homesteaders, but by that time, more than 4 million steers had made the big roundup.

**TIP**

> Historian Frederick Turner, who specialized in the American West, thought that the constant push against the Western frontier defined America. Although Turner's specific conclusions are no longer current, his overall approach to looking at how social and economic issues influence history is very important.

The frontier spirit of tough self-sufficiency and belief in the power of new directions wasn't limited to the West. As the 1800s drew to a close, the formerly rural United States moved closer to world leadership in social and industrial development (see Chapter 14). By the end of the 19th century, the once-little republic on the edge of the New World forest began to move toward center stage in world affairs.

**EXAMPLE**

> **Question:** What was the biggest change in the agricultural landscape in the post–Civil War era?
>
> **Answer:** Settlers cultivated more and more land to grow crops.

**EXAMPLE**

> **Question:** What was the role of the federal government after the Civil War with regard to race relations, economic development, and Western expansion?

**Answer:** The Homestead Act and quick admission of new states supported Western expansion; a strong dollar, railroads, and high tariffs boosted economic development; Reconstruction and the Freedmen's Bureau were federal efforts in race relations.

# Further assaults on Native American holdings and rights

At the end of the Civil War, close to half a million American Indians were scattered across the West — 1 American Indian for every 60 Americans. Twenty-five years later, the Western homes of the American Indians were on reservations, and their homelands were carved into states and territories.

Most American Indians didn't really live in tightly organized tribes, and they mostly didn't stay put for long. Tribes were made up of family-based bands that numbered as few as 25 people. They came together with other bands that spoke the same language for periodic hunts, wars, or parties.

The various tribes also often had no permanent leaders, which frustrated the settlers who were looking for a chief to negotiate with. American Indians not only didn't have permanent leaders, they also lacked obedient followers who could be made to stick to treaty agreements. Most of all, the American Indians lacked any political or long term military power to make the United States stick to its own agreements. Many treaties were signed by compromised and self-appointed leaders on behalf of tribes that barely knew what was going on, except for the obvious fact that their life of freedom was being ruined by relentless settler aggression.

Settler inroads pushed American Indians into being aggressive with one another as well as with the whites, resulting in a sort-of domino effect:

- Before the settlers arrived, the Comanches had driven the Apaches off their land on the central Plains in the 1700s.

- Pushed by other tribes, the Cheyenne abandoned their villages along the upper Mississippi and Missouri rivers in the early 1800s.

- The Sioux, displaced from the Great Lakes, learned to ride horses and, like the Cheyenne, became skilled buffalo hunters.

Far more American Indians died from diseases than from the bullets of settlers; explorers are biological weapons even if they don't want to be. But the pressure of settlement of the West by white Americans in the late 1800s ended the independence and cultural vitality of the remaining free Indian nations.

In the 1860s, the U.S. Army pushed to move American Indians either to the Sioux Reservation in Dakota Territory or to Indian Territory in Oklahoma — the end of the trail for Eastern American Indians from the 1830s on. Mounted Plains Indians resisted skillfully when they could and tried to live in peace when they were surrounded.

In one of the most brutal and cowardly acts in the West, Colonel John Chivington's Colorado Militia murdered almost 200 women, children, and elderly men in an attack on an American Indian encampment living under the American flag on Sand Creek in Colorado. Because the camp was at peace, the warriors were off hunting. Reaction to Chivington's massacre turned public opinion away from a general war against the American Indians and toward a somewhat more even-handed treatment of peaceful natives.

The Sioux struck back a couple of years later, wiping out a detachment of 81 soldiers who were building a trail through their land in Montana. Stung, the federal government actually signed the *Treaty of Fort Laramie* (1868), with the Sioux. The U.S. government agreed to stop the trail and guaranteed a Great Sioux reservation on the land around it.

Within years, Colonel George Custer's Seventh Cavalry was back on Lakota Sioux land for a "scientific exploration." Custer announced that he had discovered gold, and, treaty be damned, greedy miners rushed onto land given to the Indians forever in the treaty signed only a few years before. Custer attacked the Sioux and got killed, along with 264 officers and men. The Sioux were eventually hunted down and returned to the reservation.

Also hunted down by settlers were the Plains buffalo that fed the American Indians. Buffalo were 15 million strong at the end of the Civil War. Twenty years later in 1885, fewer than 1,000 buffalo were left.

# 14

# The U.S. Grows Up, 1881–1899

**KEY CONCEPTS**

- The great capitalists
- Progress for women and working people
- The movement of business toward the modern corporation
- The U.S on the international stage

The 33 years between the end of the Civil War in 1865 and the beginning of the Spanish-American War in 1898 was the longest period of peace in U.S. history, and America used the time to grow. New inventions transformed the country. Industry, pushed originally by flamboyant capitalists, began to take on the look of modern big business. Women and working people fought to make progress. Blacks endured endless persecution, but they weren't slaves anymore. Lost causes like the Populist Party and protests by laborers and farmers sowed the seeds for later reform.

As the United States grew more powerful, it played a bigger role in the world. The country that started as colonies gaining their own independence ended up fighting Spain to take over its colonies and, a little embarrassed, eventually set those colonies free. The United States became strong and stable enough to help lead the world into the 1900s.

# SOCIAL CHANGE IN THE GILDED AGE

Some see the time after the Civil War as a time of complacency, when the U.S. caught its breath and concentrated on making money and inventing things. Mark Twain called this period the *Gilded Age* because he thought people were covering up reality in gold paint. Even though the pace of change slowed down, people who saw injustice often worked to improve society.

- The American Society for the Prevention of Cruelty to Animals was founded in 1866.

- Clara Barton, a beloved nurse from the Civil War, founded the American Red Cross in 1881 .

- The Anti-Saloon League (1893) won some temporary victories, but Prohibition, when it came in 1919, lasted little more than a decade (see Chapter 16).

## Separate but not equal

Politics didn't help blacks in the closing years of the 1800s. They weren't slaves anymore, but society was still holding them down. According to the chilling phrase used until the 1960s, keeping blacks "in their place" meant, for many Southern whites, that blacks would be kept poor, segregated, and unable to vote. *Jim Crow laws* (1890) prohibited blacks from mixing with whites in Southern schools, buses, trains, and parks. These restrictive laws also erected phony literacy tests and poll taxes to keep blacks from voting. The laws didn't apply to anyone whose family was eligible to vote before 1866 and therefore exempted all white people from a test designed to be nearly impossible to pass.

Despite many challenges, Jim Crow laws were finally cleared away only by the Civil Rights Act of 1964. An early attempt to appeal to the Supreme Court, *Plessy v. Ferguson* (1896), failed when the court ruled that "separate but equal" facilities were legal under the Fourteenth Amendment. This ruling was a good day for the segregationist South but a bad day for justice. (See Chapter 23 for the best Supreme Court rulings.) The lives of blacks were separate but almost never equal. Just to make sure blacks and their Northern supporters were too frightened to fight back, whites lynched more than 1,000 blacks during the 1880s and 1890s.

> **EXAMPLE**
>
> **Question:** What was the significance of the Supreme Court decision in *Plessy v. Ferguson* (1896)?
>
> **Answer:** The decision said that "separate but equal" public facilities were acceptable under the civil-rights laws.

Blacks were left to pull themselves up by their own bootstraps, and they did so:

- **Booker T. Washington (1885):** Booker T. Washington taught hundreds of blacks to make a living at his Tuskegee Institute in Alabama. His *Atlanta Compromise Speech* (1895) called for blacks to better themselves through education even while they remained separate but linked to whites, like the individual fingers of a hand. Blacks mostly attended special black colleges until they began to be admitted to traditionally white institutions in the 1960s.

- *George Washington Carver* **(1900):** George Washington Carver was a respected agricultural chemist who publicized many uses for peanuts and sweet potatoes at a time when the South needed a crop to replace cotton.

- *W. E. B. Du Bois* **(1910):** W. E. B. Du Bois earned a PhD from Harvard and helped found the National Association for the Advancement of Colored People (NAACP).

- *Paul Dunbar* **(1900):** Writer Paul Dunbar made the literary world appreciate the experience of blacks through poetry and dialect in *Lyrics of Lowly Life* (1896).

> **EXAMPLE**
>
> **Question:** What did Booker T. Washington support in his Atlanta Compromise Speech?
>
> **Answer:** He favored black self-help and accepted separate but cooperative development with whites.

## Dealing with change on the railroads

Railroads were so important that they actually changed the time. Before the 1880s, every major city had its own local time, based on calling it noon when the sun was right over city hall. Noon in Philadelphia was a few minutes later than noon in New York; when the clocks in St. Louis said 11:50, the clocks in Chicago said noon. This customized time didn't matter much in the days of stagecoaches, but railroads needed to run on a schedule that everybody understood. In 1883, the major railroads laid out four time zones for the United States; these time zones are still basically what Americans set their watches by today.

The year 1877 was a bad time for many white railroad workers. The four largest railroads in the United States cut their pay by 10 percent. When union members went on strike, federal troops were called in to break up the picket lines. In the fighting that followed, more than 100 people died. During this time, the last federal troops protecting blacks were withdrawn from the South.

Chinese workers also faced trouble. After they finished building the Central Pacific railroad west from Sacramento, the jobs for low-paid Chinese far outnumbered those for other workers. When the Chinese population of California reached nearly 10 percent of the state total, jobless white residents launched violent attacks against the competitive Asians.

Under pressure, Congress passed the *Chinese Exclusion Act* (1882), barring all further settlement from China; this first law to limit national immigration stayed in effect for 60 years. Some exclusionists even tried to take away the citizenship of Chinese born in the United States, but the Supreme Court slapped them down in *U.S. v. Wong Kim Ark* (1898), saying that all people born in the United States are citizens.

## Progress for immigrants

Immigrants brought progress as well as strong backs. They were willing to challenge entrenched interests, if necessary, to better working conditions. Most immigrants came from European towns and farms, and some newcomers took the money they earned and went back to their home countries. Almost half the Italian immigrants returned to Italy; perhaps 20 percent of other immigrants eventually went back home in the 1800s. But most stayed to work on building a better life in the U.S.

The new Americans who stayed had help from urban settlement houses like *Jane Addams' Hull House* (1889) in Chicago and Lillian Wald's *Henry Street Settlement* (1893) in New York. Florence Kelley worked at both places and for 40 years led the fight for the welfare of ordinary people. Reformers slowly got laws passed to improve the treatment of the poor.

> **EXAMPLE**
>
> **Question:** From what social and economic background did most late-1800s immigrants come?
>
> **Answer:** They came mostly from rural and small-town Europe.

# The growing women's rights movement

In 1820, the United States didn't have a single female college graduate. By 1900, however, one out of every four college graduates was a woman.

The women's rights movement got support in *Women and Economics* (1898), written by feminist thinker Charlotte Gilman. Gilman said that women have no biological differences that necessarily keep them from full participation in the world. She called for child care and takeout food 100 years before fast food and drop-off preschool became a staple of working parents.

In 1890, pioneer feminists Elizabeth Cady Stanton and Susan B. Anthony passed on the torch of the Seneca Falls Convention of 1848 (see Chapter 11) by founding the National American Women's Suffrage Association.

Women cleverly linked their role in the family with getting the vote. The concept had its roots in *republican motherhood* (see Chapter 9), but the arguments were now both clear and not about to go away. Hull House hero Jane Addams said men were as sloppy at running government as they were in the home and that voting needed a woman's touch. Carrie Catt said the growth of city life meant that women couldn't confine caring about the future of their families to their houses: Family life now extended into the community, and women needed to be represented there. The movement gained strength; most Western states allowed women to vote even before the passage of the women's suffrage amendment in 1920.

>  **TIP**
>
> The AP exam will include questions on women's rights and other social issues. Knowing the names of the primary leaders of these movements in the 1880s will help your score. At minimum, remember from the women's movement Abigail Adams, Harriet Tubman, Elizabeth Cady Stanton, and Susan B. Anthony. From the black freedom movement, keep in mind W. E. B. Du Bois, Booker T. Washington, William Lloyd Garrison, and Frederick Douglass. For labor (discussed later in this chapter), remember Samuel Gompers, Eugene V. Debs, and Terence Powderly.

# Educating the population

The Morrill Act of 1862 (see Chapter 13) provided money from the sale of public land to state universities; the Hatch Act of 1887 added agricultural experimentation and education to the government-supported mix. College and high school graduation both tripled between 1870 and 1900, although those increases still meant that only 6 percent of the U.S. population stayed in school long enough to get a high-school diploma.

## Bicycles: Providing transportation for everyone

Before the automobile, bicycles set people free. Riders could tear along on dangerous-looking high-wheel bikes at speeds that are hard to reach even today. "Safety bicycles," with two equal-sized wheels like the ones ridden today, made riding the rage for both men and women. By 1893, the United States had as many bicycles as horses.

# ARTS AND ENTERTAINMENT IN THE LATE 19TH CENTURY

Greater education meant greater interest in reading and in entertainment in general. Newspapers grew as most people learned to read. The invention of the linotype (1885), which automatically set type for newspapers reduced the price of papers and made them more colorful.

The Associated Press, founded in the 1840s, allowed newspapers all over the world to share stories from reporters on the scene. Unfortunately, newspapers sometimes resorted to sensational and often misleading yellow journalism (1895) to grab readers. The term yellow journalism comes from an early color newspaper comic strip featuring a character called the Yellow Kid.

The rise in newspapers also led to a boost in literature and in access to art and music, because news on these items was suddenly more public. Following are some other notable achievements in art and entertainment:

- Henry Richardson designed massive civic buildings decorated with Gothic arches.
- The Chicago World's Fair of 1893 presented the dream of a beautiful future city and sold enough tickets to admit almost half of the population of the United States.
- Buffalo Bill's Wild West Show (1885) brought cowboys and Indians to the world. Among the stars of the extravaganza was crack shot Annie Oakley.
- The Barnum and Bailey Circus hit the road in 1881.
- Professional baseball got its start in the 1870s; college football was big by the 1880s; and basketball was invented by YMCA instructor James Naismith in 1891.

## Literature leading to action

Civil War General Lew Wallace thought that Christianity needed defending from attacks by Darwinists (see Chapter 13), so he wrote a moving book called Ben-Hur (1880) that became, like Uncle Tom's Cabin, a best-selling, international hit. The book's main character, Judah Ben-Hur, accidentally injures a high-ranking Roman commander, for which he suffers a life of punishment, and is redeemed in the end by an encounter with Jesus. Ben-Hur was the first work of fiction to be blessed by the pope.

Following are other notable authors and works of the period:

- Low-profile but still beloved was the reclusive *Emily Dickinson* (1886), whose poetry still moves people.

- *Henry James* (1889) used authentic characters to explore the worlds of Americans and Europeans and even women's rights in *Daisy Miller* and *The Bostonians*.

- California writers brought fresh Western ideas:
  - Jack London wrote about nature in *The Call of the Wild* (1903).
  - Frank Norris took on the railroad monopoly in *The Octopus* (1901).

- Theodore Dreiser pioneered social realism with *Sister Carrie* (1900).

- Upton Sinclair created public uproar with his novel *The Jungle,* a muckraking exposè of the meatpacking industry. Books like *The Jungle* led to the passage of the *Pure Food and Drug Act* (1906).

- Jacob Riis took pictures that changed society's view of the poor in *How the Other Half Lives* (1890). His book led a young police commissioner named Teddy Roosevelt to close dangerous rooming houses.

> **EXAMPLE**
>
> **Question:** What was Jacob Riis's *How the Other Half Lives?*
>
> **Answer:** The book was a photographic study of poverty in New York in the 1890s.

## Arts and music

Music and art grew in popularity. Now competing with photographers, artists mixed feeling with realism:

- **Thomas Eakins (1895)** ignored Victorian fashion to paint a world he considered beautiful beyond the need for idealization.

- **Winslow Homer (1890)** painted life near the sea in beautiful watercolors.

- **Augustus Saint-Gaudens (1890)** made moving sculpture, including memorializing the heroics of blacks in the Civil War.

Symphony orchestras and opera houses were founded in major American cities in the late 1800s. As black musical traditions merged with white folk and country music, "ragged music" became ragtime, spirituals became blues, and rhythm became jazz (and, eventually, rock-and-roll).

# PRESIDENTS OF THE PERIOD

Although the plump, stuffy, walrus-mustached presidents who ran the country from the Civil War to the end of the 1800s may not seem very heroic, their very lack of conflict gave the nation time to heal and grow. Their ability for dramatic action was limited by Congress, which was usually pretty evenly divided between Democrats and Republicans.

# James Garfield, Chester Arthur, and William McKinley

James Garfield didn't get to be president long; he was shot in the back by a man from one of the factions in Garfield's own Republican Party. After that, even the corruption-challenged Republicans had had enough.

With the help of Chester Arthur, a newly reformed vice president turned president, Republicans surprised even themselves by passing the Magna Carta for civil-service reform, the *Pendleton Act* (1883). This law required people to have qualifications and pass tests to get government jobs. Extorting political "contributions" from government workers became illegal, even if the president *had* appointed them.

William McKinley got to preside over the Spanish-American War and the annexation of Hawaii at the turn of the 20th century. He rolled back civil service reforms to benefit his own Republican party. Civil-service reform was great, but it had two drawbacks:

- Politicians couldn't fire incompetent government employees who had slipped through the system.
- Because elected officials couldn't pay back political contributors with jobs, these politicians had to pay them back with legislation.

## Grover Cleveland

The voters thanked the Republicans for finally getting honest by electing a Democrat for the first time since the Civil War. Grover Cleveland was no progressive, but he was honest. He vetoed a bill to provide seeds to drought-stricken farmers. "Although the people support the government," he said, "the government should not support the people."

Cleveland lowered the tariff to save citizens money on imported goods and force American manufacturers to compete. The big industrialists didn't like competing. In the next election, they raised a war chest and managed to beat Cleveland by a few votes. It was the first big-business-money election in American history; many more would follow.

## Benjamin Harrison

The businessmen got what they paid for. New Republican President Benjamin Harrison pushed through the highest tariff bill ever passed, the *McKinley Tariff Act* (1890). The McKinley bill set a record by taxing the average import almost 50 percent. As an example, this tax made an imported coffeepot worth $10 cost $15.

U.S. industrialists were delighted because they had less competition. U.S. manufacturers could raise their protected prices and make more profit. Regular people couldn't help noticing they were paying high prices for both imported *and* protected domestic goods.

## The return of Grover Cleveland

Voters took most of the seats away from the Republicans in the House of Representatives and brought honest Grover Cleveland back again — the only president to win reelection after being out of office.

While Cleveland was making his comeback in the 1892 election, the new Populist Party managed to get more than 1 million votes. The party's platform called for a graduated income tax, government ownership of railroads and telephones, the direct election of U.S. senators, an eight-hour workday, and immigration reform. They never elected a president, but the Populists saw much of their program become law. The Populists also tried to help Southern blacks, which made white Southerners angry. The whites tightened the Jim Crow laws so that almost no blacks got to vote in the South.

Cleveland had to face the Depression of 1893, the worst economic downturn of the 1800s. Strapped for cash to run the government, he turned to J.P. Morgan, the richest banker in the country. Morgan and his banker friends came up with the money, but they charged a commission of more than 10 percent. In the face of economic troubles, Cleveland couldn't get the tariff reductions he had promised through Congress, and the Republicans took control again in the next election.

# GETTING DOWN TO BUSINESS

The United States went from also-ran to Number One among the manufacturing nations of the world in the 30 years after the Civil War. This amazing growth was based on *profits*, *people*, and *products*:

- The Civil War was terrible where the bullets were flying, but the North came through with almost no destruction and a lot of money earned by supplying the army. It invested much of that profit in new businesses.

- People kept coming to America. Many of them were hard workers willing to put in 12-hour days if that's what it took to move their families up the economic ladder.

- The United States almost burst with inventive ingenuity, creating new products like Alexander Bell's *telephone* (1876), the typewriter, the cash register, and the electric street car. Thomas Edison's *electric light* (1879), combined with the distribution system he designed to power it, changed the world. Before bright lights, people used to sleep at night. Edison also invented the phonograph (the ancestor of music players) and the movies that still entertain us.

## The rise of the big businessman

Ambitious businessmen learned how to take advantage of all this profit, people, and product innovation to become rich.

## Andrew Carnegie

*Andrew Carnegie* (1890) ran a steelmaking operation that proved the power of *vertical integration* — controlling everything you need to make a product. Carnegie miners dug iron ore out of frozen northern Minnesota and loaded it onto Carnegie ships, which steamed across the Great Lakes to Carnegie trains, which took the ore to Carnegie blast furnaces running night and day in Pittsburgh.

Carnegie also helped fund thousands of public libraries, thus spreading "the poor people's university" all over the country. By 1920, the United States had thousands of free public libraries — more than in the rest of the world combined — and half of them were built with help from Carnegie. Carnegie wrote *The Gospel of Wealth*, a book that said rich people had a responsibility to spend their money in a way that would help poor people better themselves.

## John D. Rockefeller

*John D. Rockefeller* (1885) built Standard Oil into a company by using *horizontal integration* — controlling all the outlets for selling a product. Standard Oil drove retail and wholesale competitors out of business. Rockefeller said, "The day of combination is here to stay. Individualism has gone, never to return."

Rockefeller did whales an unexpected favor when he organized Standard Oil in 1870: The kerosene he made from petroleum gave much better light than the expensive whale oil that people had previously burned in lamps. Cans of kerosene from Standard Oil were invariably one of the first American products to arrive as U.S. commerce spread all over the world. Electric lights soon made kerosene obsolete, but freeways would lead to other uses for oil.

## J.P. Morgan

*J.P. Morgan* (1895) controlled banks he didn't even own with *interlocking directorates,* people who shared seats on many boards of directors. When a group of businesses conspired to fix prices, it was called a *trust.*

# North versus South in business

The South took a long time to do much manufacturing; it was farther behind the North in industrialization in 1900 than it had been before the war. Even making cloth from cotton lagged in the South; although Southerners had built a few textile mills by 1900, two-thirds of the cloth was still being made in the North.

The only manufactured product that was good for the South was bad for people: cigarettes. The invention of the cigarette-manufacturing machine in the 1880s got Americans smoking in a big way. The machine meant more tobacco production and a cigarette-manufacturing industry for the South.

Breaking in against Northern firms on established products was tough. Birmingham, Alabama, just happened to have iron ore, coal, and limestone close to town — perfect for making steel. Northern railroads slowed this competition on behalf of their Pittsburgh steelmaking buddies by charging Birmingham steelmakers inflated shipping rates, as though they were sending their steel from Pittsburgh.

# Private enterprise and antitrust laws

State governments tried to regulate the railroads but were pushed aside when the Supreme Court ruled in the *Wabash Cases* (1886) that states can't regulate interstate commerce, meaning that the states had to keep their hands off any business that worked between two or more states.

In response, Congress passed the *Interstate Commerce Act* (1887), which set up the Interstate Commerce Commission (ICC). Although the ICC didn't have much power to take on the powerful railroads, it established the principle that the public has an interest in private enterprise that the government has a duty to protect.

Besides the transportation companies, a number of other virtual monopoly trusts like steel and telephones took advantage of the public. To deal with companies so big that they stopped competition, Congress passed the *Sherman Anti-Trust Act* (1890). This (and other such laws) was designed to make sure that consumers get fair prices based on competition, not price-fixing by businesses. (The term *antitrust law* has persisted in the United States; the rest of the world calls such laws *competition laws*.)

Attacking the victims, the Anti-Trust Act was even used against union organization in its early days, until the Clayton Act stopped it in 1914 (see Chapter 15). As with the ICC, the Anti-Trust Act took years to be fully put into effect to stand up to business.

# HARD TIMES AND LABOR UNIONS

Even with some brave efforts, the working face of America wasn't what the founding fathers had imagined. The century started with Thomas Jefferson's dream of independent farmers creating a democratic utopia and ended with most Americans working for other people.

During the last 20 years of the 1800s, several hundred thousand unskilled workers a year landed on America's shores, looking for work. This influx of workers made it easy for bosses to hire people at low wages — pay so low that whole families had to work, kids included. Child labor went on until the 1930s, when photographs of children as young as 8 in dangerous jobs, taken by pioneering documentary photographer *Lewis Hine* (1910), finally made the government take action. Some employers also took advantage of workers by charging them high prices in company stores and threatening them if they tried to organize.

Labor-union organizations grew as a response to bad treatment and low wages. The *Knights of Labor* (see Chapter 13) had close to 1 million members by 1886. *Terence Powderly* of the Knights denounced multimillionaire businessmen for "laying the foundation for their colossal fortunes on the bodies and souls of living men."

A demonstration in that year in Chicago's *Haymarket Square* (1886) turned to violence when a bomb was thrown, killing a policeman. Eight union leaders were arrested. Even though no evidence showed that any of the leaders had anything to do with the bomb, five were sentenced to death and three to stiff prison terms.

Association with violence, even though the Knights of Labor didn't cause it, cooled support for the organization. When a new organization of skilled workers called the *American Federation of Labor* (AFL) was formed later that year, it gradually took over the union fight from the Knights. AFL President *Samuel Gompers* concentrated only on skilled workers organized by specialty. Gompers knew how to work within the system to improve the position of working people gradually.

**EXAMPLE**

**Question:** What kind of labor unions made up the AFL?

**Answer:** Only skilled worker labor unions were admitted to the AFL.

*Coxey's Army* (1894), a small band of determined protestors, marched across the country to Washington, D.C., to demand jobs and federal help. During the *Pullman strike* (1894), in which workers blocked the railroad tracks to protest cuts in pay without cuts in company-housing rent, federal troops moved in against striking laborers for the first time. Union leader Eugene Debs, realizing that the system had to change, later ran for president.

For the time being, big business and big government appeared to have joined to keep poor people in their place. When progressive William Jennings Bryan ran against conservative William McKinley in 1896, the conservatives triumphed decisively. People with jobs and unmortgaged farms didn't want to take a chance of losing them to free silver and free trade. The *Dingley Tariff Bill (1897)* made imported goods cost more than ever, enabling domestic industries to charge more without foreign competition. Gold stayed the standard, but new gold discoveries in Alaska, Canada, and elsewhere helped the money supply. Although progressives had lost the election, the causes of women, workers, and blacks slowly edged toward acceptance in the public mind.

 **EXAMPLE**

> **Question:** What was the cause of the Pullman strike?
>
> **Answer:** Pullman cut workers' pay without a corresponding cut in workers' rent.

## Hard times for farmers, too

Major machinery became available to farmers in the 1880s. If you had a place big enough that you could afford it, a single machine could plow, plant, and work the seeds into the soil. The amazing combine coupled a machine that cut grain with another machine that threshed the grain off the stems and into bags, ready to sell. Impressed by these machines but naïve about the cost, a lot of landowners got caught in a financial squeeze by over-borrowing and overproduction.

Pushed by the banks and exploited by big business, farmers fought back in almost every way they could, trying to regulate railroads, organize cooperatives, form a political party, and even inflate the currency. But they never did what the trusts did every day: limit production to raise prices. That strategy would have taken more organization and trust than independent farmers could muster.

 **EXAMPLE**

> **Question:** What did farmers do to improve their financial situation?
>
> **Answer:** They tried to lower railroad charges, organize production cooperatives, and get political help. Unlike monopoly capitalists, however, they never held down supply to increase demand and price.

Because more land and better farm equipment were available, the price that farmers got paid for a bushel of wheat fell from $1 at the time of the Civil War to 50 cents in 1890. Loans that farmers had taken out to grow more wheat cost twice as much wheat to repay.

Meanwhile, the nation got used to paying cheap prices for beautiful California produce, harvested by poorly paid Mexican and Chinese labor, and shipped east in the railroads' new refrigerator cars. Small family farmers went deeper into debt.

 **EXAMPLE**

> **Question:** How did farms change in size and equipment in the late 1800s?
>
> **Answer:** More and bigger farms were available, with better equipment.

## Third parties

Farmers joined with laborers to support cheap money and progressive causes through the *Greenback Labor Party* (1878) and the *Populist Party* (1892). Neither party won the presidency, but each polled as much as 10 percent of the votes and elected enough legislators to sway the Democrats in their direction.

Third parties have played a big part in American history; don't get them confused. Here's a run-down of major third parties in the 1800s:

- In 1832, the Anti-Masonic Party, seeking the eradication of the Freemasons and other secret societies from the United States, received a few votes.

- In 1848, the Free Soil Party, a precursor of the Republican Party, nominated former President Martin Van Buren as its presidential candidate, splitting the vote in New York and causing the election of Zachary Taylor.

- In 1856, parts of the disintegrating Whig Party teamed up with the Know-Nothing Party, which opposed foreign immigration. Even as a team, the parties came in third behind Democrat James Buchanan and John C. Fremont of the newly formed Republican Party.

- In 1860, four major candidates ran for president, including candidates from the break-away Southern Democratic Party and the last-ditch-compromise Constitutional Union Party. Republican Abraham Lincoln was elected with only 39 percent of the vote and wasn't even on the ballot in many Southern states.

- In 1892, the Populist Party won 22 electoral votes and 8.6 percent of the popular vote. The Democratic Party eventually adopted many Populist Party positions, making this contest a good example of a delayed vote for change.

# SETTLING THE WEST

Settlers rode the railroads to new homes in the West as American Indians were driven out of their wide-open country to try to survive on confined reservations. Said one American Indian, "The antelope have gone; the buffalo wallows are empty. . . We are like birds with a broken wing."

James Earle Fraser's famous statue *End of the Trail* (1915), an image of an American Indian on horseback with bowed head and downcast lance, was reproduced so many times that it seemed to symbolize the end of wide-open-spaces freedom for urbanized settlers as well as the free life of Great Plains American Indians.

In one of the few times a professional historian actually made history, Frederick Turner gave a speech called "The Significance of the Frontier in the American History" at the Chicago World's Fair of 1893. Turner said that the American character was formed by the possibilities of the open frontier — a frontier, he announced, that was closing.

It was unclear at the time what was to replace the challenge of the frontier, but plenty of challenges requiring work existed both at home and in the rest of the world. Actually, the frontier was as much a state of mind as a place. At the same time Turner was announcing the end of the West, the government was creating permanently open land with the world's first national parks in Yosemite, Yellowstone, and Sequoia. These preserves were the first of hundreds of national parks and forests — a good idea from the U.S. that has spread around the world.

## Pressure on American Indians

Even American Indians' small reservations were threatened under the *Dawes Severalty Act* (1887), which tried to break up tribes and split up land for ownership by individual American Indian families. By 1900, American Indian tribes had lost more than half of the limited land onto which they'd been crowded 20 years before. Native families were forced to accept private allotments of poor land on which they'd be separated from their tribal culture. When this resulted in surplus land, the government sold it off at bargain prices to settlers.

The shortsighted policy of trying to make American Indians into settler farmers on land that wouldn't support crops lasted until the American Indian New Deal of the 1930s recognized American Indians as full U.S. citizens. One last American Indian massacre occurred in 1890, when federal troops opened fire with machine guns on American Indians gathering for a sacred dance at *Wounded Knee* (1890), South Dakota. Two hundred men, women, and children were killed.

From a low of fewer than 250,000 American Indians at the close of the Western frontier in 1890, the U.S. American Indian population rebounded to 3 million urban and rural American Indians by 2010 — 1 out of 100 Americans. And millions of white, black, and Hispanic Americans have some American Indian ancestry.

**EXAMPLE**

**Question:** What was the main policy of the United States toward American Indians from 1877 to the New Deal?

**Answer:** To break up tribes and give individual American Indians their own land.

## Helen Jackson's Ramona

People who fought for American Indian rights included Helen Jackson, who wrote the factual story of mistreatment in *A Century of Dishonor* (1881) and then the popular fiction novel *Ramona* (1884).

*Ramona* is the story of a part-American Indian, part-Scottish girl in California. With black hair and blue eyes, Ramona is reared in a privileged ranch family until she falls in love with the poor son of an American Indian chief. The book sold 600,000 copies and spawned plays, movies, and even towns.

People loved the story so much that they named towns for Ramona; localities competed with claims to be the inspiration for her homeland. Unfortunately, the story missed its immediate goal of winning widespread sympathy for the plight of American Indians; instead, it touched off the American love of Spanish mission architecture that lives on today in many Mexican restaurants. *Ramona* did encourage the trend toward thinking of the defeated American Indians as being somehow noble and worthy of humane treatment. Long after the story was forgotten, its meaning moved society.

# BACKING PAPER MONEY WITH PRECIOUS METALS

After the California gold rush that began in 1849 and lasted into the 1850s came the Nevada Silver bonanza of the 1860s. Scattered gold and silver discoveries also popped up in other Western states. All this glittering metal allowed the U.S. Treasury to back paper money with gold by 1879 (see Chapter 13).

The many senators who represented the few people living in the low-population, high-treasure West pushed for the government to buy more precious metal. This push encouraged inflation, which was good for debt-ridden workers and farmers who could see that silver-based money would ease their woes by making loans easier to repay (see Chapter 13).

At the Democratic Party convention in 1896, presidential candidate William Jennings Bryan made his famous *Cross of Gold* (1896) speech, which emotionally compared the Republicans, who demanded money tied only to gold, to the Romans who crucified Jesus. Poor people were elated; rich people were horrified. Backed by middle-class fear and upper-class financing, the Republicans easily beat Bryan.

**EXAMPLE**

> **Question:** What was William Jennings Bryan's Cross of Gold speech?
>
> **Answer:** Delivered to the Democratic convention that nominated him for president, the speech called for the inflationary use of silver money to keep poor people from being crucified by golden hard money on the bankers' "cross of gold."

# AMERICAN IMPERIALISM

As the 1800s drew to a close, America was bursting at the seams. It had been the longest time in U.S. history without a major war, and the country needed something to distract itself from its economic troubles. The European powers were in a final imperialistic feeding frenzy, gobbling up the chunks of Africa and Asia they'd overlooked before. The U.S. had peacefully purchased Alaska from Russia in 1867.

Could the United States, founded on anticolonialism, stay out of the game? As the *Washington Post* editorialized, "The taste of Empire is in the mouth of the people even as the taste of blood is in the jungle." Some people believed social Darwinism proved that the United States *must* rule because it *could* rule.

The old Monroe Doctrine (see Chapter 10) got enforced in 1896 when the United States offered to mediate in a conflict between Venezuela and Britain on the border of British colony British Guiana in South America. After blowing America off at first, the British agreed when they found themselves fighting in the Boer War in Africa. This was a small diplomatic victory for the United States.

## The annexation of Hawaii

Hawaii had been flirting with the United States since it became a whaling supply station in the early 1800s and the site of a major American missionary effort. Thanks to missionaries, Hawaii actually had the first printing press west of the Mississippi in 1822. Thanks to the king of Hawaii, John Sutter founded Sacramento (and set the stage for the gold rush) with the help of Hawaiian workers. The sons of the first missionaries planted sugar cane, and the Hawaiian government granted Pearl Harbor to the United States as a naval base.

When the McKinley Tariff made selling Hawaiian sugar in the United States more expensive, the American sugar planters in Hawaii had an easy solution. They deposed Queen Liliuokalani and asked to be admitted to the United States; Hawaii wouldn't be subject to the tariff if it were part of the United States. For five years, the United States held Hawaii off as a point of honor — it didn't want to be associated with land-grabbing. With the outbreak of the Spanish-American War, the United States got over national worries about honor and annexed Hawaii.

# The Spanish-American War

Sugar also made problems in Cuba when high U.S. import duties caused fewer sales and more hardship for the sugar workers. The workers rose in revolt against the Spanish colonial government, which suppressed them violently.

The United States was sympathetic to the workers' plight, and yellow journalists egged the country on toward war with Spain. Sensationalist newspaperman William Randolph Hearst sent famous Western artist Frederick Remington to Cuba to draw pictures of the atrocities. When Remington cabled that conditions weren't bad enough for a war, Hearst cabled back, "Please remain. You furnish the pictures and I'll furnish the war."

## Losing the battleship Maine

At the worst possible time for the Spanish, the U.S. battleship *Maine,* which had been sent to Cuba on a "goodwill" visit, blew up in Havana harbor. Four independent investigations over the past 100 years have come to four different conclusions about what caused the explosion, but at the time everybody but the Spanish believed that Spain had torched it. Congress voted to invade Cuba, but also passed the *Teller Amendment* (1898), which promised to free Cuba after the island was free of the Spanish.

Using some tricky fighting, the United States first attacked the Spanish not in Cuba but in Spain's Philippine Islands colony, halfway around the world. The U.S. fleet sailed into Manila harbor, pulverized the Spanish fleet, and then sat around sweltering through the tropical summer, waiting for American troops to get there and take the islands. With the help of Filipino insurrectionists, the American army made short work of the Spanish troops.

Cuba was the same story. The American navy smashed the Spanish without losing a ship, and the American army, with Teddy Roosevelt leading the Rough Riders, quickly defeated the Spanish troops. The army still had a few Civil War veterans from 33 years before; Northerners and Southerners felt good about fighting on the same side.

## Letting Cuba go but keeping the rest

To end the one-sided Spanish-American War, Spain agreed to give the United States control of Cuba, the Philippines, and Puerto Rico. The United States, feeling a little guilty, generously kicked in $20 million for the Philippines, because they were kind of a bonus for freeing Cuba. Puerto Rico came as a free bonus, which America decided to keep.

> **TIP**
>
> U.S. expansionism at the end of the 1800s is a natural stopping place for any essay discussion on Manifest Destiny you may have to undertake on the AP U.S. History exam. Remember: *Imperialism* is keeping colonies; *expansionism* is adding land that becomes a real part of the mother country. With the Philippines free, Hawaii a state, and Puerto Rico regularly voting to stay with the United States, the end of the United States's 1890s overseas adventures came out as expansionism.

The United States set Cuba free as promised, keeping only a naval base at Guantanamo Bay, which was a little bigger than Manhattan. Having successfully invaded once, the United States felt free to intervene in Cuba any time it wanted to — until Fidel Castro took power in 1958.

## Fighting in the Philippines

The Philippines were trickier. European countries, especially Germany, were still sniffing around the world for colonies. The United States decided to keep the Philippines for a few years to establish a government and build some schools and roads. That meant fighting a bloody war against the same Filipino revolutionaries who had just finished helping America get rid of the Spanish.

The Philippines conflict lasted for five years and led to the deaths of thousands of soldiers on both sides and hundreds of thousands of civilians caught in the crossfire. The United States finally freed the Philippines in 1946, after World War II.

# Rejecting the idea of empire

The U.S. flirtation with empire, especially keeping the Philippines, was opposed by a lot of Americans, including Mark Twain, Andrew Carnegie, former President Grover Cleveland, Jane Addams, and the presidents of Harvard and Stanford universities.

Eventually, the imperialist eagle came to rest with the release of Cuba and the Philippines; Puerto Rico and Hawaii were mostly agreed about staying part of the United States. As the United States increasingly became a world power, the temptation to push smaller nations around never went away.

> **EXAMPLE**
>
> **Question:** What was the biggest controversy following the Spanish-American War?
>
> **Answer:** Americans debated whether freedom-loving America had any right to keep the Philippine Islands as a colony.

# 15

# America on the International Stage, Ready or Not: 1900–1919

## KEY CONCEPTS

- America's forays into imperialism
- The presidencies of Theodore Roosevelt, William Howard Taft, and Woodrow Wilson
- The politics and policies of the Progressives
- World War I

At the beginning of the 20th century, the U.S. was ready to become more important to the rest of the world. America's somewhat-reluctant empire extended halfway around the globe, so the country was beginning to look like an international power. But people still remembered the Founding Fathers' warnings to stay away from entangling foreign alliances, and they were more concerned with the economic and social work to do at home.

After years of holding off change, the U.S. begin to make major reforms under the Progressive movement with the beginning of the new century in 1900. With domestic reform at a high point, the U.S. got dragged into World War I. After tipping the balance toward victory for the Allies in this war, the U.S. president proposed an international League of Nations which his own Congress would not support. By not quite agreeing to sign on for its own ideals of international democracy, the U.S. unintentionally ensured that it would have to fight for them again.

# THE UNITED STATES IN ASIA

In 1899, the Americans and the Filipinos were standing side by side waving goodbye to the Spanish colonists when the native independence fighters realized something was wrong: The Yanks weren't leaving.

After five years of the U.S. Army slogging through the jungle led by ex-American-Indian-fighters from the American West, the Americans managed to knock out all the major rebel armies at a cost of thousands of soldiers and hundreds of thousands of civilian lives. The eventual rewards to the U.S. were an independent Philippines that is generally pro-American, a naval base, and a jumping-off place for activity in Asia. The Filipinos learned some English in the schools Americans helped build but were quite happy to finally get their freedom on July 4th, 1946 — see Chapter 17.

## China and the Open Door Policy

Colonialism benefited European countries politically, so they pushed to acquire Hong Kong (Britain), Macau (Portugal), and Tsing Tao (Germany) from large-but-weak China. The U.S. didn't want to rule China, but it also didn't want other countries to set up permanent shop and exclude them from trade. So the U.S., consulting more or less with the other major European powers, issued the *Open Door Policy* (1899). All foreign nations in China were supposed to respect Chinese rights and let other countries bid fairly on commercial contracts. To the Chinese, this policy felt like an agreement among the bullies about how to fairly divide the lunch money they stole.

> EXAMPLE
>
> **Question:** What was the Open Door Policy?
>
> **Answer:** A U.S.-sponsored agreement among Western nations to respect Chinese rights and let other countries bid fairly on commercial contracts.

## The Boxer Rebellion

Chinese anti-Westerners called the Boxers murdered Western missionaries and besieged Western diplomats holed up in the capital of Beijing. Western governments quickly threw together an eight-nation rescue/invasion force of 20,000 soldiers to put down the *Boxer Rebellion* (1900).

The United States contributed a couple thousand troops who were already on hand in the Philippines. The Western diplomats barricaded their offices into one big fort and held out for 55 days with nothing but one old cannon until help arrived.

China had to pay a huge amount of money for the trouble some of their citizens had caused the Westerners. Shame over their weakness led the Chinese to get rid of the ancient Empress Dowager and start a more modern government. The U.S. used some of its share of the money to educate Chinese students in America.

# THEODORE ROOSEVELT

A nation happy to be a world power without having to do much fighting overwhelmingly reelected William McKinley for a second term. In this election, plump and popular McKinley was almost overshadowed by his rambunctious running mate, Theodore Roosevelt, hero of the Spanish-American War. Neither man could know that Roosevelt would ascend to the highest office in the land just a few short months after McKinley's victory.

## Early life

Theodore Roosevelt was a whirlwind. One of the greatest and toughest presidents in American history, Roosevelt was so sickly as a child that he had to sleep sitting up to keep from dying of asthma. His father insisted that he exercise and take up boxing to keep from being beaten up by bullies. When a doctor told him that his heart condition would keep him at a desk job, Roosevelt just exercised more.

Roosevelt was brilliant, graduating from Harvard magna cum laude. He wrote books about U.S. Navy battles in the War of 1812 and a four-volume history of the West, both of which scholars still cite today. Roosevelt's first presidency was as leader of the American Historical Association.

When his mother and his young wife both happened to die on the same day, Roosevelt headed west. He built a ranch in the Dakota Territory and learned shooting, riding, and roping. Elected deputy sheriff, he single handedly brought in three desperados, guarding them without sleeping for almost two days by reading Tolstoy to keep awake. He later married his childhood sweetheart and took her on a honeymoon to Europe, where he climbed Mont Blanc, the highest peak in the Alps.

## Appointments and positions

Appointed to the Civil Service Commission, he served with such fairness that even after the Democrats won the White House, they kept Progressive Republican Roosevelt at his post. As the police commissioner of New York, he cleaned up the police department, often calling officers in the middle of the night to make sure they were sober and awake.

Roosevelt had always loved the ocean, so Republican president William McKinley appointed him Assistant Secretary of the Navy. Assistant was enough power for Roosevelt; he pretty much ran things over the head of his boss and modernized the U.S. Navy.

When the Spanish-American War broke out, Roosevelt quit his desk job and organized a regiment of volunteers called the Rough Riders, whose members included cowboys, American Indians, polo players, and policemen. Fighting alongside a black regiment, they did well in the key battles of the fight for Cuba. See Chapter 14 for more on the Spanish-American War. Later in that year of 1898, war hero Roosevelt was elected governor of New York state.

## The McKinley-Roosevelt election of 1900

When McKinley campaigned for a second term as President, he chose Theodore Roosevelt as his running mate. The political bosses in New York State were so happy to see their reform-minded, high-energy governor leave the state to run for vice president that they would have bought him the office if they could have, just to get rid of him.

During the campaign, Teddy toured with cowboys and cut into the rural and Western support for the Democratic nominee, well-known "Cross of Gold" speaker William Jennings Bryan. In the end, the election wasn't even close. McKinley and Roosevelt won because, although a lot of people didn't like imperialism, they were more afraid of Bryan's unconventional economic theories.

The U.S. didn't get much time with newly reelected President William McKinley; a crazy anarchist gunned him down at the 1901 World's Fair in Buffalo. Although the fair displayed an early X-ray machine, doctors didn't know how to use it, so they never removed the bullet, which could have saved McKinley's life. Worse, they had to operate in a room without electric lights. Electricity was relatively new, and although the outside of the building had beautiful lights all over it, no one had thought to put one in the medical department on the inside. At 42, Rough Rider Teddy Roosevelt became the youngest president ever.

## The Roosevelt presidency

Teddy Roosevelt's policies and personality guided the United States into the 20th century realities of a more active national government and a bigger role in world affairs.

### Roosevelt's Big-Stick philosophy

Even before becoming president, Roosevelt talked in favor of speaking softly but carrying a big stick. He set an example as an activist president that influenced both national and local politics for years to come.

Roosevelt worked to carry out McKinley's careful policies, but he began to use his famous Big Stick to support progressive laws. Like the Teddy bear named for him at this time, Roosevelt's policies combined inherited power with humanizing grace. Progressives believed that it was their job as the elite to remake social rules for the benefit of ordinary people. Roosevelt charmed his opponents with talk and threatened them with the *Big Stick* (1903) of power. Roosevelt began the practice of busting up *trusts* (1904) (corporations that controlled whole industries so they could fix prices) to encourage competition and lower prices for customers. See Chapter 14 for more on trusts.

TIP

Don't get mesmerized by Theodore Roosevelt's Big-Stick philosophy and think that he made all the progress in the 1900s. Roosevelt's successor, William Taft, actually busted more trusts. Roosevelt set the tone, but he was balanced and opportunistic in his politics.

## Building the Panama Canal

One place Theodore Roosevelt didn't settle for incremental progress was in dealing with other nations. When the nation of Colombia wouldn't let the United States build a canal through its Panama district, Roosevelt helped set up a revolution in which the Panama part of Colombia became an independent country. The new country was — no surprise — quite willing to have a U.S.-owned canal run through the middle of it.

Roosevelt became the first president to leave U.S. soil when he dashed down to Panama to help with the digging. Health workers figured out how to protect people from yellow fever and malaria as the result of America's interest in both the canal and in Cuba. The *Panama Canal (1914)* was a big success, cutting sailing time between the Atlantic and Pacific by more than half. The U.S. finally turned the canal over to Panama in 1999 after owning it for almost 100 years.

## The Roosevelt Corollary

Roosevelt also created the aggressive *Roosevelt Corollary to the Monroe Doctrine* (1905), also known as *preventive intervention*. The original *Monroe Doctrine* (1823) said that the United States would defend the New World from any further attempts at Old World colonization.

The Roosevelt Corollary said that to keep the little countries of South America from being taken over by Europeans or local despots, the U.S. would step in with American troops, but only to help them. Usually in the process some big U.S. businessmen were helped as well. U.S. troops intervened in six Latin American countries but kept none of them as colonies.

**EXAMPLE**

**Question:** What was the Roosevelt Corollary to the Monroe Doctrine?

**Answer:** The U.S. would prevent the intervention of Old World powers in Latin America by intervening itself as necessary.

## Nativism and the Great White Fleet

Still squabbling over the China situation, Japan and Russia fought a war in 1904. Roosevelt got them to a conference table in the U.S. and hammered out a peace agreement for which he won a Nobel Peace Prize. Roosevelt sent the entire U.S. Navy, painted white, on an around-the-world cruise as *The Great White Fleet* (1908), symbolizing both American purity and strength.

In 1906, he made a secret deal with the Japanese to limit immigration, thus reassuring California, which was beginning to work up an Asian paranoia again after having previously excluded the Chinese. The movement to limit immigration, called *nativism*, grew in the early 1900s due to increases in the foreign-born population, competition for jobs, paranoia about imported radicals, and economic racism toward Asians.

**EXAMPLE**

**Question:** What influenced the rise of nativism in the early 1900s?

**Answer:** Increases in the foreign-born population, competition for jobs, and paranoia about imported radicals. California was a center of anti-Asian feeling.

# EXPOSING THE SHORTCOMINGS OF SOCIETY

Although change sometimes begins slowly, it can be pretty strong after it gets going. The U.S. had always had a Progressive movement, even as early as Abigail Adams's "Remember the Ladies" letter before the Revolution. Although "walrus" presidents (with their slow-moving politics and big business connections) seemed to dominate the post-Civil War 1800s, the Greenback Labor party of the 1870s and the Populist party of the 1890s had an influence on popular opinion if not elections. Progressive thinkers rejected the Social Darwinism of unregulated business and called for government action because concentrations of wealth were hurting, not improving, society.

Women and working people may not have won their crusades at first, but they didn't give up. Upper-class suffragettes worked for the women's vote and improved living conditions through urban settlement houses like Jane Addams's *Hull House* (1889) in Chicago and Lillian Wald's *Henry Street Settlement* (1893) in New York. Women's clubs blossomed from 100,000 members in the 1890s to more than 1 million by World War I.

**EXAMPLE**

**Question:** Why did Progressives reject Social Darwinism?

**Answer:** Because the natural competition of unregulated business resulted in monopolies that hurt people and did not help society to improve.

## The era of the muckraker

As the circulation of newspapers, popular magazines, and books grew in the early 1900s, exposing the shortcomings of society became a major occupation. Authors seemed to be able to dredge up almost any hidden secret. *Lincoln Steffens* (1902) wrote *The Shame of the Cities,* detailing municipal corruption in leading towns. *Ida Tarbell* (1904) exposed the monopolistic practices of the Standard Oil Company that had ruined her father. *Thomas Lawson* (1905), himself a major stock manipulator, tattled on the trust scammers in *Frenzied Finance.* Other socially conscious authors examined legislative corruption in *The Treason of the Senate* (1906), the slow progress of the blacks in *Following the Color Line* (1908), and child labor in *The Bitter Cry of Children* (1906). Teddy Roosevelt called these reformers *muckrakers* (1904) because they insisted on cleaning up the country by looking down at the mucky mess.

**EXAMPLE**

**Question:** What helped muckrakers publicize their investigations?

**Answer:** The growth in the popular press, magazines, and books.

## Food safety

Dr. Harvey Wiley, working from within the government with a Poison Squad, uncovered enough evidence of the dangers posed by unsafe food to lead to the passage of the *Pure Food and Drug Act* (1906), which forced manufacturers to use safe ingredients and honest labels.

*The Jungle* (1906), by muckraker *Upton Sinclair,* sickened the public with its description of what went on inside the food industry and led to the *Meat Inspection Act of 1906.* To protect people from being poisoned by their own food, federal inspectors visited packing houses. Like the novel

*Ramona* (see Chapter 14), which intended to save American Indians but ended up initially saving Mission architecture, *The Jungle* was intended to save workers but ended up saving the food they processed.

## Achievements of the Progressives

Forward-thinking attempts to clean up politics became a cause for both political parties. The *Progressives* (1910) succeeded because they weren't marginalized as dangerous radicals: Progressives were middle- and even upper-class reformers working to fix the system from within.

**EXAMPLE**

**Question:** Why were the Progressives so successful?

**Answer:** They were respectable middle-class reformers with popular support.

To get around the influence of political bosses, Progressives introduced the *initiative* system so that voters could propose and vote on new laws without going through the legislature. The still-ongoing attempts to limit campaign contributions and the corruption they can bring began when the Progressives passed campaign financing laws in a few states in the early 1900s. Previously, the rule in elections had been that voters marked ballots in public, and party bosses could see how people voted; the early Progressives made the secret Australian ballot the national standard. Often-corrupt state legislatures got to choose U.S. senators until Progressives passed the *Seventeenth Amendment* (1913), which mandated the election of senators by the people.

In the key Supreme Court case of *Muller v. Oregon* (1908), Progressive attorney *Louis Brandeis* convinced the court that states have a right to protect employees in the workplace; in *Muller,* that meant protecting women from having to work more than 10 hours a day. Brandeis went on to become one of the first Jewish high officials when he joined the Supreme Court in 1914.

The tragic industrial *Triangle Shirtwaist Fire* (1911) claimed the lives of almost 150 women workers but led to legal regulation of workplaces. By the time of World War I, more than half of the states had laws providing some worker's compensation to people injured on the job. Prohibition was also a popular cause; by 1914 more than half of the country had prohibited the sale of liquor.

## Roosevelt's Square Deal

Theodore Roosevelt promised Americans a *Square Deal:* He would control the big corporations, protect consumers, and conserve the environment. When coal miners stayed on strike for almost half a year, the many people who heated their homes with coal were facing a frozen winter. Roosevelt called employers and workers into the White House and became the first president to hammer out a labor agreement. He threatened to use federal troops against the mine *owners* if they didn't compromise — a big change from previous government actions, when the troops were always ordered in to punish the workers. Congress created the *Department of Commerce and Labor* (1903) to oversee both business and workers.

**EXAMPLE**

**Question:** How did President Roosevelt handle the coal strike?

**Answer:** He became the first president to arbitrate a labor settlement.

The all-powerful railroads got slapped around a bit when the *Elkins Act* (1902) prohibited rebates that kept rates high for little shippers and the *Hepburn Act* (1906) ended the practice of giving free passes to anyone who could politically help the transportation companies. The heretofore weak Interstate Commerce Commission actually got the power to take action against fares that gouged the public.

Roosevelt busted his first big trust with the *Northern Securities Company* (1904). Famous American financier J.P. Morgan and his friends were trying to monopolize railroads in the Northwest. Roosevelt slapped them down, and the Supreme Court backed him.

> **TIP**
>
> Theodore Roosevelt didn't believe that big business itself was inherently bad. He was against businesses that controlled a market so that they could make people pay unfairly high prices. He probably wouldn't have minded today's big-box stores as long as they allowed real competition.

## Preserving the American wilderness

Before Theodore Roosevelt, the U.S. had the *Forest Reserve Act* (1891), which set aside some land for preservation, but most of the country was open to exploitation by loggers, miners, ranchers, or anybody else with a profitable way to use it up. When Roosevelt went camping with the famous environmentalist John Muir in Yosemite, he became committed to saving beautiful land. Because the frontier was no longer limitless, the U.S. started locking up land for the future in parks and national forests.

First Roosevelt increased the value of Western land by supporting the *Newlands Reclamation Act* (1902), which resulted in damming nearly every river in the West to irrigate nearby fields. Then he set aside almost 200 million acres of land for national forests and parks —much more land than all the previous presidents combined.

Working with farsighted Forest Service head Gifford Pinchot, Roosevelt created 42 million acres of national forests, 53 national wildlife refuges, and 18 areas of special interest like the Grand Canyon. Americans responded by joining new outdoor organizations like the Boy Scouts, Girl Scouts, and Sierra Club (founded by Roosevelt's friend John Muir).

## The financial panic in 1907

The *Banker's Panic of 1907* was caused by Wall Street financial manipulation that led to the beginning of banking regulation. Roosevelt rode out this panic by passing the *Aldrich-Vreeland Act* (1908), which provided for the issuance of emergency currency and paved the way for the *National Reserve Act* (1913) that's still responsible for dealing with national financial problems.

## Roosevelt's legacy

He easily won reelection in 1904, and when his second term expired in 1908, he supported William Howard Taft as his successor. Most of the nation wanted Roosevelt to remain as president, but he went hunting in Africa instead.

Injured in a perilous exploration in South America years later, Teddy Roosevelt died in his sleep in 1919. Said then president Woodrow Wilson's vice president Thomas Marshall, "Death had to take him sleeping, for if Roosevelt had been awake, there would have been a fight." Roosevelt enlarged the presidency and the nation in three ways: He civilized capitalism so that it could survive in a world where people as well as profit mattered; he began to make the environment a concern of government; and he introduced the U.S. to its growing responsibilities on the world stage.

# WILLIAM HOWARD TAFT AND TRUST-BUSTING

President William Howard Taft, elected president in 1908, had a hard act to follow. Fat and jovial but without Roosevelt's vision or charm, Taft tried to stick to Roosevelt's policies. He took on the U.S. Steel trust and a number of other monopolies, carefully following laws passed under Roosevelt.

In 1911, the Supreme Court ordered that Standard Oil Company be broken up. At the same time, the court issued a *rule of reason* that said the law applied only to companies that *unreasonably* restrain trade. This ruling made busting trusts even harder. Even so, Taft went after twice as many monopolies as Roosevelt actually took on.

Republican businessmen generally liked high tariffs on imported goods; it made their products easier to sell at a profit. However , the Progressive wing of the Republican party called high tariffs the "Mother of All Trusts" and vowed to substantially lower the charges. After lots of inner-party wrangling, Congress passed the *Payne-Aldrich Bill* (1909), which lowered tariffs but only on the items people didn't want anyway.

Taft failed to come through for the Progressive wing of his party. Although he acted to protect U.S. business interests in Latin America with a few invasions of small countries, he got in even more trouble with Progressives for firing environmental hero Gifford Pinchot after Pinchot criticized the sale of public lands for corporate development. Taft also established the Bureau of Mines to protect coal land and water supplies, but this measure was too little too late. The Republicans lost big in Congress and then, with Roosevelt running on a third-party ticket, lost even bigger in the presidential election of 1912 to Democrat Woodrow Wilson.

# IDEALISM WITH WOODROW WILSON

The campaign of 1912 was one to remember. Roosevelt's name was put in nomination at the Progressive party convention by Hull House feminist Jane Addams. The convention exploded when Roosevelt declared, "We stand at Armageddon, and we battle for the Lord."

During the campaign, Roosevelt was shot in the chest in Milwaukee by a crazy person. Fortunately, the bullet went through Roosevelt's steel glasses case, but he was still wounded and bleeding. Roosevelt refused all help and went on to make an 80-minute speech after he had been shot. Doctors decided the bullet was too dangerous to remove, and he carried it with him for the rest of his life. He took a couple of weeks off and then was back on the campaign trail.

On election day, Democrat Woodrow Wilson won easily because Taft and Roosevelt split the Republican vote (although Teddy got more of the vote). The country's heart was clearly with the Progressives. Not counting the very unprogressive South, which voted for Democrats just because they weren't Republicans, Progressive votes would have easily won the election. Even the perennial Socialist candidate Eugene Debs racked up 900,000 votes. It was time for change in America. In his own way, Wilson was progressive as well.

# Wilson's New Freedoms

Woodrow Wilson was only the second Democratic president since the Civil War and the first teacher — a professor at Princeton — ever elected president. He promised a program of *New Freedoms,* which included antitrust action, tariff revision, and reform in banking.

A man of serious purpose (and the second great president, after Teddy Roosevelt, to be a historian), Wilson went after a clear program and got what he fought for on the domestic front.

He got real reductions in the cost of imported goods in the *Underwood Tariff Bill* (1913). By taking the unprecedented step of going to Congress himself and appealing to the American people to watch their representatives for last-minute special-interest tricks, Wilson got a bill that really reduced import fees. Because the passage of the *Sixteenth Amendment* (1913) allowed for an income tax, Congress slapped on a modest charge on all incomes over the equivalent of $65,000 in modern money ($3,000 back then). By 1917, income tax passed tariff receipts as the largest share of the federal income.

 EXAMPLE

> **Question:** When did taxes on imports stop being the largest share of federal income?
>
> **Answer:** With the passage of the income tax in 1917.

# The Federal Reserve Act

Clearly, the banking system needed some help. The Banker's panic of 1907 had shown that the government could ease financial downturns if it had some extra cash to throw into the game when times got tough. Wilson went directly to Congress and got the *Federal Reserve Act* (1913), one of the most important economic landmarks in U.S. history and still the law of the land.

What the Federal Reserve Act did was establish a national system of 12 privately owned regional banks under the central authority of the Federal Reserve Board appointed by the president and Congress. In this public/private establishment, the regional banks can issue Federal Reserve System Notes for private money backed by the government, but only under direction from the government-controlled Federal Reserve Board.

With the power of private enterprise and the control of central government policy, the government spaced the regional banks around the country to try to minimize the control of Wall Street New York money. Still, New York remained the financial capital no matter how many solid-looking bank buildings the rest of the country got.

# The Trade Commission and Anti-Trust Act

In early 1914, Wilson made his third appearance before Congress. Moving on from the Roosevelt/Taft program of busting trusts, Wilson encouraged fair competition through the *Federal Trade Commission* (1914), which reduced monopolistic trade practices.

With the addition of the *Clayton Anti-Trust Act* (1914), the practices of price discrimination, agreements forbidding retailers from handling other companies' products, and interlocking directorate agreements to limit competition all became illegal. Even better, individual officers of corporations could be held responsible if their companies violated the laws.

The new business laws set out clear guidelines that corporations had to follow, much better than being penalized with no warning under previous, less clear legislation. As a plus for labor, the law ended the silly business of applying antitrust laws to unions.

## Victories for ordinary people

Wilson made himself even more popular with working people when, in 1916, he approved legislation (the *Adamson Act*) that increased wages and cut working hours of railroad employees, thus avoiding a strike. Other victories for ordinary people included the following:

- The *Federal Farm Loan Act* (1916) and the *Warehouse Act* (1916) let farmers get much-needed loans at low rates.

- The *La Follette Seamen's Act* (1915) guaranteed sailors on American merchant ships decent wages and treatment (and eventually doomed the U.S. merchant fleet, which couldn't compete with low paid foreign sailors).

- The *Workingmen's Compensation Act* (1916) granted help to disabled federal employees.

## Wilson's great shortcoming: Government segregation

Wilson had a moral blind spot when it came to the treatment of blacks. A Southerner who fondly remembered seeing Robert E. Lee as a child, Wilson delivered for his racist South Democratic voters by segregating federal offices for the first time since the Civil War and dismissing many blacks from government work.

His segregation of government lasted until after World War II, when the Democrats under Harry Truman decided to do the right thing for civil rights even if it cost Democrats the next election (which it did). Since that time, the South has moved into the Republican column in most presidential elections.

The most important black leader to stand up to Wilson's segregationist tendencies during the Progressive Era was the eloquent W. E. B. Du Bois, a founder of the NAACP. Du Bois fought for African American progress for most of his 95-year life. He carried the torch until the day he died in Africa, which just happened to be the day before Martin Luther King's "I Have a Dream" speech in Washington, D.C.

> **EXAMPLE**
>
> **Question:** Who was the most important black leader during the Progressive time period?
>
> **Answer:** W. E. B. Du Bois, a founder of the NAACP.

## Wilson's international progress

Wilson tried to apply morality to international relations, but it's hard to be idealistic when other people are shooting at you. He withdrew subsidies for U.S. companies investing abroad and stopped giving American ships free passage through the Panama Canal. He reluctantly continued the Roosevelt Corollary by sending U.S. Marines in to tame violence in Haiti and the Dominican Republic. Wilson bought the Virgin Islands in the Caribbean from Denmark, thus giving Americans another naval ship base and another place to soak up the sun.

Wilson did his best to stay out of Mexican politics as factions maneuvered after a revolution. Standing up to pressure from American businessmen worried about their Mexican investments, Wilson declared that he wouldn't decide foreign policy "in the terms of material interest."

After innocent Americans had been killed on both sides of the border by Pancho Villa's soldiers, Wilson sent General "Black Jack" Pershing on a lightning cavalry raid into Mexico. Pershing chased Villas's army and was swiftly pulled back. He would be needed elsewhere; the situation in Europe was looking grim.

# WORLD WAR I

Germany and Austria-Hungary (the Central Powers) were locked in a war with Britain, France, and Russia (the Entente). The actual fighting started in August 1914 after Franz Ferdinand, the prince who was set to become emperor of Austria-Hungary, was assassinated on a visit to Serbia. However, the endless fight to be the leading nation of Europe had been brewing for hundreds of years. This was exactly the kind of war the United States wanted to avoid.

The natural tendency of English-speaking America to side with England was helped along by careful propaganda coming over the only news wire from Europe, which conveniently ran through Britain. Plus, Germans looked like bad guys with their spiked helmets, upturned mustaches, and habit of tromping through neutral countries.

The millions of Americans of German heritage did little cheering for their old homeland; one of the reasons they left Germany in the first place was to avoid all that military bluster. Americans even changed the German names of foods: sauerkraut became victory cabbage, and more Americans started saying "hot dog" instead of "wiener."

Germany paid a penalty for not having a navy as strong as the British. America proclaimed her neutral rights to the seas, in hope of continuing trade with the warring parties who were very much in need of supplies. Meanwhile, Germany and Britain both blockaded each other. Britain used surface ships that could gently force American cargo ships away from Germany and into British ports. Germany used submarines, which could only wave at passing ships or sink them; they weren't big enough to shepherd the American ships to distant German ports or even take on extra passengers if the ships sank. Because this war was the first with submarines, the whole undersea attack policy seemed unfair to many Americans.

## The sinking of the *Lusitania*

Germany said that it would try not to sink any neutral ships but that mistakes could easily happen. The first so-called mistake wasn't a neutral ship but the British liner *Lusitania* carrying ammunition as well as passengers. The Germans sunk it off Ireland in 1915, killing over a thousand people, more than a hundred of them Americans.

Germany agreed to stop sinking passenger liners but reasonably asked that Britain respond by lifting its blockade, which was starving the German people. Britain refused, so safety on the sea was definitely up in the air as the U.S. got ready to vote for president in 1916. Wilson barely squeaked through to reelection on a platform that said, "He kept us out of war," but he made no guarantees for the future.

## America enters the Great War

At the beginning of 1917, Wilson made one last, moving speech asking the fighting powers to come to the peace table. Meanwhile, the Germans made a large and dangerous tactical decision. Figuring that it would take the U.S. longer to get to France than it would take Germany to win the war with full submarine warfare, the Germans announced that all bets were off. They were blockaded, and they intended to blockade Britain by sinking any ships headed that way.

The Germans sent a note called the *Zimmermann telegram* (1917) to Mexico, inviting them to invade the United States with the help of Japan. This harebrained scheme would never have worked, and the Mexicans knew it. Britain, who had been happily reading diplomatic mail from other countries that passed through their island along the transatlantic cable, intercepted the telegram and excitedly showed it to the United States. The Germans had already started sinking ships, and the telegram was the last straw for even peace-loving Wilson. The United States declared war on Germany.

## Wilson's 14 points

Forced to resort to cold steel, Wilson turned fighting into an idealistic crusade. He declared that this was a "war to end all wars" and a "crusade to make the world safe for democracy." Wilson outlined the 14 *Points* (1918) he felt should be the righteous aims of the Allies. In short form, they included

- No secret treaties (like the spider webs of undercover alliances that started the war)
- Freedom of the seas
- Free trade
- Fewer weapons
- National *self-determination* (a people's right to choose its own form of government without interference)
- An international organization to keep the peace

**EXAMPLE**

**Question:** What were the main issues in Wilson's 14 Points?

**Answer:** Open treaties, freedom of the seas, national self-determination, and an international peace keeping organization.

## Laws repressing anti-war sentiment

As a propaganda machine led by George Creel talked up America's peaceful war aims, an ugly set of repressive laws, the *Espionage Act* (1917) and the *Sedition Act* (1918), led to the arrest of virtually anyone who spoke up against the war.

Most of the 2,000 wartime prosecutions were against union leaders, including Socialist presidential candidate Eugene Debs, who had been putting up with persecution for 24 years since the Pullman Strike of 1894.

## War preparations

America never got into full production for World War I. The draft supplied lots of soldiers after the War Department issued a work or fight declaration. Labor was kept under control by the National War Labor Board chaired by former president William Howard Taft. Unions made solid gains in membership, and pay improved with lots of wartime work.

For the first time, blacks (who had for years stayed in the South) began to move North to take wartime jobs; 500,000 made the move by 1920. This Great Migration led to violence on the part of whites, especially when blacks helped break white labor actions like the great steel strike of 1919.

**Question:** When did blacks start to migrate to the North?

**Answer:** They made the move during and after World War I.

## Women's progress during the Great War

President Wilson learned how determined women were to get the vote when police arrested 20 suffragettes who were trying to storm the White House. During the war, he came out in favor of women's suffrage (voting) as "a vitally necessary war measure." Most Western states had given women the vote before 1914 (see Chapter 14). New York, Michigan, Oklahoma, and South Dakota jumped on board during the war. After only 130 years of waiting, Abigail Adams' pre-Revolution wish finally came true: With the passage of the *Nineteenth Amendment* (1920), all American women got the right to vote.

With men gone to fight, some women took temporary so-called men's jobs in railroads and factories, but they quickly gave up their positions when the war was over. Still, by the end of the war, one out of four women had a job outside the home.

## Wartime food production and Prohibition

Food was no problem for America during the war; farm production increased by 20 percent. An effective humanitarian engineer named Herbert Hoover had already led a food drive to help Europe; now he headed the national food effort.

People grew victory gardens and patriotically observed meatless Tuesdays and wheatless Wednesdays. *Liberty Loan* drives got ordinary citizens to buy government bonds and raised billions of dollars to finance the war.

> **EXAMPLE**
>
> **Question:** What was the Liberty Loan program?
>
> **Answer:** Liberty Loan was a government bond program in which ordinary citizens helped raise money to finance the war.

Congress restricted the manufacture of alcohol, and that set the already half-dry country up for its national experiment with Prohibition. Lots of brewers were a little suspect anyway, what with all the German names like Budweiser, Schlitz, and Pabst. Progressives were under fire from prohibitionists to try a perfect alcohol-free society.

In 1919, the *Eighteenth Amendment* prohibited the legal sale of alcoholic beverages in the United States, thus opening the door for lots of profitable illegal sales. (In 1933, the *Twenty First Amendment* repealed Prohibition; see Chapter 16.)

> **EXAMPLE**
>
> **Question:** What led to the passage of Prohibition in 1919?
>
> **Answer:** Years of Prohibition campaigning, war shortages, the belief that human beings could be perfected, plus the spreading passage of state anti-liquor laws.

# Entering the fight — reluctantly

At first, the U.S. hoped to just send the Navy and let the Europeans do the ground fighting. The British and French quickly admitted their problem: They were almost out of men. The United States drafted a minimally trained army of 4 million men and began to ship them to Europe.

A year passed between the time America declared war and the time an effective U.S. fighting force assembled in Europe, and it was none too soon. Russia, which had been fighting on the Allied side, was swept by a Communist revolution and dropped out of the war.

Experienced German troops shifted to fight in France. By May of 1918, the Germans were within 40 miles of Paris. The first large American contingent was thrown right into a breach in the French line. In July, the German advance ground to a halt. By the fall, over a million American troops were helping to slowly push the Germans back.

Heroes came from the strangest places: Sergeant York, an American soldier raised in an anti-war church, singlehandedly killed 20 Germans and captured 132 more.

# The Great War ends

In October, the Germans asked for peace based on Wilson's 14 Points. At 11:00 a.m. on the 11th day of the 11th month (November 11, 1918), the Great War was over.

The Allied forces won because Germany knew what was going to happen if it continued fighting; Socialist revolutions were going on back in Germany, and lots of German (and Allied) troops were dying from a worldwide flu epidemic. Germany had given up before it was completely defeated, something that would come to bother a hard-fighting, wounded corporal in the German army named Adolf Hitler.

The United States was far from the arsenal of democracy it would become in World War II; Britain and France actually supplied most of the planes, big guns, and transport ships used by American troops.

Leaders of the world hurried to Paris in January of 1919 to conclude a peace treaty while revolutions were tearing apart Russia and central Europe. Woodrow Wilson was the hero of the day. People expected freedom and peace from the 14 Points. Unfortunately, most of the points' good ideas didn't end up in the Treaty of Versailles, a compromise Wilson had to make with broke, tired, and angry European victors.

Wilson tried to move the world toward fairness, and he did succeed on getting a few new nations established and some more reasonable boundaries drawn. In the end, Wilson got a treaty with too much reparation money due to be paid by a too-poor Germany. He took what he could get to preserve his pet project, the *League of Nations*.

# The peace that cannot hold

Back in America, powerful conservative forces had taken over Congress. They refused to ratify the Treaty of Versailles as written, and Wilson refused to accept anything less. The misunderstood final warning from George Washington to "avoid foreign entanglements" hovered over the hall like an outdated ghost.

George Washington had been speaking to a small, weak nation of farmers in a world where crossing the ocean took weeks and America didn't have to trade with anybody. Now the U.S. was the one nation with the strength and moral position to make the League of Nations work, but it wouldn't take the responsibility. Wilson's moral position worked against him — some senators had just *had* it with the do-gooder.

## Wilson's attempt to save the peace

Wilson went on a speaking tour to try to get people to put pressure on Congress to accept the treaty. In Pueblo, Colorado, with tears streaming down his cheeks, he pleaded for the League of Nations as the only way to avoid another war. That night he collapsed. Hit by a stroke, Wilson didn't make public appearances for months afterward. The political strategy he followed from his sick bed was not successful.

Wilson's Democratic Party had lost control of Congress in the 1918 elections. Senator Henry Cabot Lodge, the great Republican enemy of the League of Nations, attached some reservations to the treaty that Wilson didn't like. Wilson ordered all the Democratic senators to vote against the treaty rather than compromise. Having been so successful in the past, Wilson seemed to think he could turn the upcoming presidential election of 1920 into a referendum on the treaty.

EXAMPLE

**Question:** How did President Wilson try to convince Congress to vote for the Treaty of Versailles?

**Answer:** He appealed directly to the people to put pressure on Congress.

## The League of Nations falls

The Republicans nominated affable and empty-headed Warren Harding of Ohio for president. He trounced the Democrats who supported the League of Nations by saying he would work for a vague Association of Nations and played to the postwar wish to get back to normal. The Republicans got almost twice as many votes as the too-serious Democrats.

The failure of the United States to join the League of Nations was one of the factors that led to World War II. The United States didn't create Hitler, Mussolini, or the poverty, greed, and hatred that sparked World War II and caused the deaths of at least 72 million people, including 418,000 Americans. But because of outmoded isolationism and an almost-adolescent fight between people who were too righteous to work together, the United States did nothing to stop it. As the saying goes, if you're not part of the solution, maybe you're part of the problem.

# 16

# The Jazz Age and the Great Depression: 1921–1939

## KEY CONCEPTS

- Business growth and changing society in the 1920s
- Problems facing minority groups and immigrants
- Causes of and responses to the Great Depression
- Franklin Roosevelt's New Deal

When Republican Warren Harding took over as president in 1921, the nation was ready for happy days after all the preachiness of Woodrow Wilson. Harding's Cabinet members weren't about to preach; in fact, they included a den of thieves.

President Harding wasn't a bad man, but he was suspiciously lazy in his choice of political friends. His Secretary of the Interior leased America's emergency *Teapot Dome* (1923) oil reserve to private businessmen in exchange for a $400,000 bribe ($4 million in modern money). His head of Veteran's Affairs stole the modern equivalent of $2 billion by allowing shady work on veterans' hospitals. His

Attorney General — the man who was supposed to enforce the laws — was charged with the sale of pardons and liquor permits. Harding didn't have to face the ugly scene his friends had created: He died of an illness in the middle of his first term.

That's the way it went in the Roaring '20s: high times with a big bill coming later. Kicking off the 1900s, activist presidents Theodore Roosevelt, William Howard Taft, and Woodrow Wilson had tackled serious problems with the belief that progressive reform would help America live up to its high ideals (see Chapter 15). After all that progress and the trauma of World War I, people were tired of idealism — they just wanted to return to normal. Trouble is, you can never get in the same river twice — the current moves on without you. Normal in the 1920s was a whole new world. Unfortunately for the people of that era, the Great Depression was right around the corner.

# U.S. VERSUS COMMUNISM: THE EARLY YEARS

With the Communist revolution taking over in Russia, the United States had the terrorist jitters. The U.S. sent troops to Siberia toward the end of World War I to help maintain order, but they were soon withdrawn. President Wilson expanded the federal police with a new FBI under the leadership of a young J. Edgar Hoover. Before the *Red Scare* (1921) was over, more than 10,000 people had been arrested in the *Palmer Raids* (1920) named for the Attorney General who led them. People were beaten and held illegally, and no evidence of a real conspiracy was ever found.

Real terrorists did actually strike: A bomb in Washington D.C. just missed a young Franklin Delano Roosevelt, and another killed 38 people and wounded hundreds on Wall Street. The actual bombers escaped, and almost all the people arrested were guilty of nothing more than being radical union members or recent immigrants from Eastern Europe. Immigrants suspected of troublemaking were often deported.

Scared for their lives and property, most Americans supported the anti-Communist raids at first. But when the police issued a red alert for a Communist takeover on May 1 that never materialized, public support for police-state tactics started to fade. Factory owners kept the Communist issue going as long as possible by trying to link unions with Communists.

During the hysteria, five legally elected members of the New York legislature and one U.S. Congressman weren't allowed to take their seats because of their left-wing views. Two immigrant Italians, *Nicola Sacco* and *Bartolomeo Vanzetti* (1921) were executed for murder on evidence that had more to do with their radical views and their immigrant status than proof of their alleged crime.

**EXAMPLE**

> **Question:** What happened to immigrants suspected of being trouble makers during the *Red Scare* (1920)?
>
> **Answer:** They were deported.

# THE RETURN OF THE KLAN

The Ku Klux Klan (KKK) that had terrorized blacks and their Reconstruction allies in the post-Civil-War South re-emerged during the 1920s. This time, the Klan was much larger than it had been after the Civil War, and it had more than blacks to hate: The new Klan was also against booze, international cooperation, Jews, Catholics, evolution, gambling, immigrants, and sex.

### The Birth of a Nation

The pioneering 1915 film *The Birth of a Nation* follows the family of Northern abolitionist Congressman Stoneman (based on real life abolitionist leader Congressman Stevens.). Before the Civil War, the Northern Stoneman family visits their Southern friends the Camerons, who live on the perfect South Carolina plantation, complete with happy slaves.

When the Civil War breaks out, the children of the two families support their respective sides, but young Northern soldier Phil Stoneman can't forget his love for Southerner Margaret Cameron. The only surviving Cameron son is Ben. Wounded while fighting bravely for the Confederates, Ben is recovering in a Northern hospital when a lovely young nurse comes by. To their mutual delight, she is his childhood love, Elsie Stoneman.

After the war, Ben creates the Ku Klux Klan, inspired when he sees white children dressing up like ghosts to scare black children. The Klan is born just in time, because black ex-slaves are menacing white women, including Ben's sister Flora, who jumps off a cliff to escape. When Elsie is also threatened, Ben and the Klan arrive in the nick of time to save her. Phil Stoneman and his Union army friends realize they must work together with the Klan to save what the movie calls their "Aryan birthright."

A title slide has an authentic quote from Woodrow Wilson about "the great Ku Klux Klan." The movie ends with a double Cameron/Stoneman wedding as the world lives happily together under a picture of Christ.

Because it used lies to sell tickets and inflame hatred, *The Birth of a Nation* was boycotted in many cities and states. Unfortunately, for millions who did see it, many of whom had never known a black person, the movie solidified the evil stereotype of lazy, happy slaves who turn into dangerous animals unless kept in their place by white vigilantes.

Change always brings out reaction, and the 1920s version of the Klan had millions of aggressive and frightening hood-wearing members that included senators, mayors, and perhaps even a president. Although the original Klan died out some 20 years after the Civil War ended, the new Klan sprung out of the popularity of one of the first story movies, *The Birth of a Nation* (1915). Showing the power of popular culture, the movie, which made up Klan traditions different from those actually started by the original KKK, inspired the new Klan organization. The KKK of the 1920s, in other words, basically learned it at the movies.

The reconstituted Klan fizzled out in the late 1920s when the corruption of their leaders and the shamefulness of their tactics became obvious even to people with sheets over their heads. Although the new Klan made lots of temporary converts among people frightened by change, the KKK also faced something it never had in the old South: stand-up opposition from ordinary people who wouldn't let hate win.

# IMMIGRATION ACT OF 1924

In the 1920s, new laws to slow immigration relieved the nativist fear of being overwhelmed by immigrants. (See Chapter 15 for more on nativism.) The *Immigration Act of 1924* capped the number of immigrants allowed in the U.S. each year at 2 percent of the number of a home nation's citizens already in the United States as of 1890. For example, if 3 million Americans of German descent lived in the U.S. in 1890, 60,000 Germans (2 percent of 3 million) could come to the country each year under the 1924 act. This quota barred the door to many hopeful immigrants from countries that didn't have a lot of people in the U.S. in 1890.

One such country was Italy. Lots of Italian people wanted to come to America, but the whole country was only able to send fewer than 6,000 people a year. This number still made the Italians better off than the Japanese, who were completely locked out of the U.S. The various groups that actually got into the U.S. tried to maintain their national cultures, but their children learned to speak English and made friends with kids from all over. Radio and movies accelerated the melting pot by teaching standardized language and culture. The number of immigrant children who were forced into child labor declined as individual states began to require school attendance and forbid underage employment.

> **EXAMPLE**
>
> **Question:** Why did fewer immigrants come to the United States in the 1920s?
>
> **Answer:** The *Immigration Act of 1924* limited new Americans to a low quota of 2 percent of the number of citizens by national origin in the United States by 1890.

> **EXAMPLE**
>
> **Question:** What reduced child labor in the 1920s?
>
> **Answer:** States passed laws that required children to attend school and prohibited underage labor.

# THE JAZZ AGE

During the 1920s, radios, record players, magazines, and movies began to bring the world to average working people who could never have afforded to go to plays, concerts, or college. Telephones, electricity, and indoor plumbing all made life more comfortable. More people had cars than bathtubs. (After all, you can't drive a bathtub to town.) Young people left the farm; for the first time in history, more people lived in cities than in the country. The 1920s were called the Jazz Age because popular music shared influences from big band, ragtime and rhythm, and songs that encouraged dancing.

## Prohibition: High demand and high crime

Prohibition, implemented by the *Volstead Act* after the passage of the *Eighteenth Amendment* (1919), may have cut down on drinking by 10 percent, but it increased crime by 50 percent. Because booze was illegal but in demand, liquor made great profits for organized crime. For every large saloon that closed, at least three small *speakeasies* (illicit pubs) opened.

Because low-alcohol beer and wine were bulky and hard to transport, potent hard liquor cocktails became the quick-acting drink of choice. Lots of hard liquor was smuggled, but desperate drinkers learned to make gin in their bathtubs or bought special grape juice that turned to wine with minimal effort.

Arrests for drunken driving and public intoxication went up more than 50 percent. The law made millions of otherwise-law-abiding Americans into criminals, and it gave real criminals so much money that they fought ugly wars over territory in big cities.

The king of the mobs in Chicago was Al Capone, a symbol of the gangster era. After more than 500 deaths in the Windy City, Capone was finally sent to prison for tax evasion. At their height, illegal liquor mobs took in more money than the federal government. Finally, after 13 years, the *Twenty-First Amendment* (1933) repealed Prohibition.

# Changing morals

A lot of people had fun in the *Roaring '20s* (1925). People did crazy dances to the new music of the *Jazz Age*. Anything seemed possible with the new-found freedom provided by women's suffrage, cars, radio, movies, and — Prohibition be damned — easy-to-get alcohol. The scene also included well-known gay clubs, but they disappeared at the end of the 1920s and didn't reappear until the 1970s.

Because Sigmund Freud had explained sex drives as a natural part of being human, the subject of sex was less taboo. *Margaret Sanger* (1921) risked arrest to get birth control information to women.

**EXAMPLE**

**Question:** Who was Margaret Sanger?

**Answer:** Margaret Sanger was an early advocate who publicized information about birth control.

# Mass production and mass consumption

Prosperity was the thing that made the Roaring '20s roar. Mass production made new inventions and former luxuries available to almost everybody, especially with the financially dangerous new invention of time payments. Henry Ford lowered the price of his Model T to a few hundred dollars, cheap enough that most working people could get a loan to buy their car on time. By the end of the decade, the U.S. had one car for every five Americans, far more than all the automobiles in the rest of the world.

The growing advertising industry convinced people they needed more and more. Advertising got good at making people want things they didn't need through the mass media of radio, billboards, and popular magazines. *Frederick Taylor* (1922), the father of scientific management he called Taylorism, broke work assignments down into tasks and figured out the most efficient way to get jobs done. Unions lost membership as employers used government support and fear of radicals to break up strikes.

**EXAMPLE**

**Question:** What happened to the Progressive political movement in the 1920s?

**Answer:** Progressive reforms all but disappeared as conservative Republican government slowed immigration, relaxed the regulations on business, and weakened unions.

## Advances in transportation

Motor vehicles were good for more than just joy rides. Trucks moved goods to market more cheaply and quickly than trains; produce farmers made more money, *and* city people got better fruit and vegetables. People didn't have to live right next to where they worked anymore; the first suburbs appeared. Buses allowed schools to consolidate and reach more students.

Women took to driving right from the start; it gave them independence from men. Cars were so handy that people didn't even begin to notice the cost in dollars, accidents, and pollution until years later.

Automobiles were fast, but planes were faster. The Wright brothers flew the first plane in 1903. After that, it took 20 years and countless crashes for aviation to become practical. The first transcontinental airmail route began from San Francisco to New York in 1920. Few passengers flew in the 1920s; most airliners concentrated on carrying the mail.

After Charles Lindbergh became a hero by single-handedly flying his *Spirit of St. Louis* (1927) from New York to Paris, aviation was on everybody's mind. The first flight attendant stepped on board a regularly scheduled commercial flight in 1930.

## Radio

The first radio breakthrough occurred when original station KDKA in Pittsburgh broadcasted the news of Warren Harding's election in 1920. As more and more families gathered around the early radios, commercials for products soon began popping up.

Radio broke down local accents by providing a national standard of speech. It also affected politics by carrying the words of candidates and the sound of their speaking voices, something only a small proportion of the population had ever heard before the 1920s. This development hurt squeaky-voiced politicians like Al Smith and helped great radio personalities like Franklin Roosevelt.

## The Harlem Renaissance

The *Harlem Renaissance* (1926), with writers like Langston Hughes and Zora Neale Hurston and musicians like Louis Armstrong and Duke Ellington, expanded the urban culture of black Americans.

*Marcus Garvey* (1921) tried to raise money for black-owned businesses and the African American colony in Liberia. He galvanized black pride but was set up by the first black employees of the FBI and deported. For the first time, blacks and whites mingled in the nightspots. The Renaissance basketball team was the best in the world. Ongoing racism was highlighted by the death sentences of the innocent black *Scottsboro Boys* (1931) by an all-white jury in the South.

EXAMPLE

**Question:** Who was Marcus Garvey?

**Answer:** Garvey was an organizer who raised African American pride with plans for black owned businesses and an African colony.

# Movies and their influence

Movies changed history during this period, whether it was through an overt message like *The Birth of a Nation* or the shared experience of just going to the movies together.

As one of the first feature films, *The Great Train Robbery* (1903) excited the inexperienced audience so much that some of them ducked when the train went by. The earliest movies were silent and included explanation signs; the cowboys would be galloping silently away and suddenly everything would stop for what looked like a PowerPoint slide. In 1927, *The Jazz Singer* contained the first synchronized dialogue (and singing) in a feature film. After sound was possible, nobody wanted to read written explanations in films again, and from then on movies could talk. A little later, color movies began to appear. Films largely replaced ethnic theater and united the country in shared dramatic experiences. Movies helped white ethnic Americans become regular Americans.

# Flappers

The most beautiful woman in films was the "It-girl," Clara Bow, whose brassy personality was a model for the *flappers* (1925), newly liberated women who made up their own rules about clothes (including short dresses and hair) and behavior. Females could afford to be more independent because the number of women with jobs increased by 25 percent in the 1920s. People called them wild, but flappers didn't care what people thought.

 **EXAMPLE**

> **Question:** Who were the flappers in the 1920s?
>
> **Answer:** The flappers were women who felt liberated to make up their own minds about appearance and behavior. Their style was short hair, short dresses, independence, and wild dancing.

# Controversy over evolution

The idea of evolution scared a lot of conservative religious people who thought that it didn't fit with their idea of God. The state of Tennessee banned the teaching of evolution, but a young high-school football coach named John Scopes taught it anyway and landed in court in the *Scopes Monkey Trial* (1925).

## William Haines

The most famous movie actor of 1925 was handsome William Haines, who lived openly with his gay lover. Pushed to cover up by the studios, the pair switched to interior decoration and lived together the rest of their lives, more than 50 years — in the words of Joan Crawford, "the happiest married couple in Hollywood." They decorated the houses of the stars, including Ronald Reagan's governor's mansion.

The trial starred famous defense attorney Clarence Darrow as Scopes' lawyer and former presidential candidate William Jennings Bryan as the prosecutor. Bryan took the stand to explain why the Bible was always right, and Darrow made him look foolish. Even though the *Scopes Trial* didn't immediately repeal the law, it began to change the way most people thought, which eventually changed the law.

Laws against teaching evolution stayed around until the 1960s, when the Supreme Court ruled that such bans violate the First Amendment because their primary purpose is religious. Fundamentalists still try to get what they call "intelligent design" recognized in schools, but now they're trying to get into the classroom instead of keeping science out.

**EXAMPLE**

**Question:** Who were the key attorneys in the Scopes Trial?

**Answer:** William Jennings Bryan and Clarence Darrow.

## The power of the pen

The sharpest pen of the 1920s belonged to H.L. Mencken, who was the Jon Stewart of his generation. As a Baltimore newspaperman and editor of the *American Mercury* magazine, Mencken took on the backward establishment of America. He defined a puritan as someone with "the haunting fear that someone, somewhere, might be happy."

Other writers stirred the dark coals of the happily roaring '20s:

- F. Scott Fitzgerald wrote *The Great Gatsby* (1925) about the hopeless social climbing of an also-ran who could never reach success because glamor isn't life.

- Theodore Dreiser wrote *An American Tragedy* (1925), a novel about the murder of a pregnant girl by her social-climbing boyfriend.

- The poet e.e. cummings wrote verse so direct that it didn't need capitalization.

- Ernest Hemingway stripped away all the Victorian prose and wrote in deceptively simple English. His *A Farewell to Arms* (1929), a novel paralleling his own experience in World War I, combined toughness with feeling.

- Sherwood Anderson's *Winesburg, Ohio* (1919) contained the touchingly pathetic stories of small-town Americans lost in their own private suffering.

- Sinclair Lewis wrote *Main Street* (1920) and *Babbitt* (1922) about the limits of sophistication in early 1900s America. The character Babbitt became a synonym for the shortsighted, self-serving boosterism encountered in any club or city.

- William Faulkner described the South, prejudices and all, in *The Sound and the Fury* (1929).

On the whole, the writers of the 1920s were surprisingly gloomy for a roaring decade. Maybe they saw trouble coming, or perhaps they just valued honesty more than uplift. So did the many Americans who chose to read their books. Many 1920's authors were called the *Lost Generation* (1925) because they had lost their innocence in the fires of World War I. In a sense, the writers of the '20s were the worthy successors to the early-1900s muckrakers. Unlike the early muckrakers, however, these writers were living in a political world that, for the time being, valued wealth more than progress.

**Question:** What was the spirit of critically acclaimed writers of the 1920s?

**Answer:** Writers generally reflected a gloomy questioning of society.

## Architecture

*Frank Lloyd Wright* (1928) was something of an architectural poet. If architecture is frozen music, he made that music new, stripping off tired classical references to build for a new world.

The soaring Chrysler Building and Empire State Building in New York were further proof of late-1920s architectural exuberance. The International style began to emphasize glass and light as modern building techniques allowed more openness.

# SIGNS OF ECONOMIC TROUBLE AHEAD

Even as the 1920s roared, signs that America's fast growth was running on empty began to appear:

- U.S. manufacturing output rose by 50 percent, but even in good times, hundreds of banks failed every year.

- Buying on credit was rare at the beginning of the decade, but by the end of the 1920s, more than half of the purchases for cars and appliances were on time payments. If people lost their jobs, they couldn't make the payments.

- A Florida land boom so hot that people even bought lots that were under water turned to bust in one 1925 hurricane.

The stock market went up for so long that everybody forgot it could ever go down. Ordinary working people bet their life savings on stocks, buying them *on margin* — a kind of time payment, just like the financing scheme they used for their cars.

The Republican-controlled Congress cut the taxes on rich people: What was three dollars in tax for the rich in 1920 became only one dollar. Wealth-friendly politicians said this money would trickle down to the poorer people.

**Question:** What was the Republican position on taxes for the rich?

**Answer:** Republicans cut taxes on the rich, claiming benefits would trickle down to poorer people.

A little trickling down would have been good, because 40 percent of the whole nation (and a much higher percentage of farmers and blacks) lived below the poverty line, even in the good times of the 1920s. While the poor people lived without government help, cheap taxes for the rich made the economy blow up like a big balloon.

> **EXAMPLE**
>
> **Question:** Which groups had it hardest during the 1920s?
>
> **Answer:** The most economically-depressed groups were farmers and blacks. They didn't share much in the 1920s boom times.

# POLITICS LEADING TO THE DEPRESSION

The three Republican presidents in the 1920s really thought people should take care of themselves. Even after the stock market crashed in 1929, Herbert Hoover quoted the cold-hearted words of President Cleveland from 50 years before: ". . . though the people support the Government, the Government should not support the people."

The same hands-off governmental philosophy guided the three 1920's Republican presidents in international affairs; the U.S. was isolationist and unprepared for war. Antitrust laws passed by earlier progressive presidents, both Republicans and Democrats, went unenforced. Businesses soon learned that they could get away with forming trade associations that limited competition:

- The *Esch-Cummins Transportation Act* (1920) allowed the private combination of the railroads and committed the Interstate Commerce Commission to help them make a profit.

- *The Merchant Marine Act* (1920) sold off ships built by the government at bargain prices to big businessmen. A railroad strike protesting a 12 percent pay cut during boom times was put down with harsh measures by the government in 1922.

International efforts were mostly symbolic:

- The U.S. called the leading powers together to sign the *Washington Naval Treaty* (1922) where they agreed to limit warship construction at an easy-to-meet high level.

- Harding helped American companies grab *oil concessions* (1923) in the Middle East that would eventually lead to international trouble.

- The *Nine-Power Treaty* (1922) made an Open Door policy to China an official international agreement, but it didn't keep Japan and Russia from trying to sneak in to grab some territory for themselves.

- The *Kellogg-Briand Pact* (1928) proved how easy it is to say good words by "outlawing war."

All these agreements sounded good, but with only a weak League of Nations, there was no power to enforce them.

Republicans hiked the tariffs, as they had done in the past, under the *Fordney-McCumber Tariff Law* (1922), which also gave the president the power to raise or lower tariffs by himself. The Republican presidents sent the tariffs even higher on 32 important commodities like dairy products and iron. They lowered taxes on only five items nobody wanted anyway, including paintbrush handles and bobwhite quail.

## Calvin Coolidge: "Silent Cal" stands by

After president Harding escaped facing his administration's corruption by dying in office, Vice President Calvin Coolidge took over and governed in a straightforward manner. Coolidge specialized in keeping his remarks simple. A famous story tells of a dinner guest who said, "Mr. Coolidge, I've made a bet against a fellow who said it was impossible to get more than two words out of you." Coolidge's reply: "You lose."

Although Coolidge had little to say, he supported business like it was a religion. In fact, he believed that "the man who builds a factory builds a temple" and "the man who works there worships there." Coolidge had never worked in a factory.

Although Coolidge came from a New England farm family, he stood by and did nothing as one out of four families lost farms to debt in the 1920s. He just said that farming had never paid much and that the government couldn't do anything about it. Coolidge got elected once in his own right and then decided not to run again.

## Herbert Hoover: Good intentions, bad mistakes

Herbert Hoover had a great reputation as a humanitarian and a problem-solver for three earlier administrations. Then he actually became president and lost his reputation in the Great Depression. Elected in a landslide in 1928, he started by trying to do something for the desperate farmers.

The *Agricultural Marketing Act* (1929) lent money to farmers' organizations to manage their crops for maximum profit. It didn't work very well; prices for grain and cotton just kept dropping because farmers kept growing an oversupply of crops.

# THE STOCK MARKET CRASH OF 1929

On *Black Tuesday* (1929) in October 1929, the stock market crashed. Stocks kept sliding until they reached a point in 1932 when they were down 89 percent, lower than they'd been since the 1800s. Prudent investors who bought slowly over their lifetime would have been protected from the worst market fluctuations by the law of averages. However, anyone who bought stocks only at the highest and therefore worst time in mid-1929 and held on to them saw most of his adult life pass by before finally breaking even in 1954.

## The Smoot-Hawley Tariff

Responding to business pressure, Hoover did exactly the wrong thing by signing the dangerous *Smoot-Hawley Tariff* (1930). A world economy teetering on the brink of economic collapse certainly didn't need the highest peacetime tariff in U.S. history. The rest of the world viewed the tariff as a sign that they had to protect themselves too. Economic walls went up all over the world.

Tariffs certainly didn't help the United States get over the crisis that started with the Wall Street meltdown in 1929. Unemployment was at 9 percent in 1930 when the Smoot-Hawley tariff passed, but it jumped to 16 percent the next year and 25 percent two years after that.

# The millionaires' dole

As people's jobs evaporated and families started to go hungry, Hoover's response was to assist businesses so that their wealth would trickle down to the poor.

After the Depression had gone on for three years, Congress finally passed the *Reconstruction Finance Corporation (RFC) Act* (1932). The RFC lent money to businesses, agricultural organizations, and local governments. Many called it *the millionaires' dole*.

Actually, Hoover had come a long way from the take-care-of-yourself position of earlier 1920s Republicans, including himself. Realizing that they would have to do something for worried laborers whose union membership had gone down by a third in the union-busting 1920s, Congress passed the *Norris-La Guardia Anti-Injunction Act* (1932), which forbade court interference in peaceful strikes and stopped management from forcing workers to sign anti-union pledges.

> **EXAMPLE**
>
> **Question:** What national program did Herbert Hoover establish to help fight the Depression?
>
> **Answer:** Hoover established the Reconstruction Finance Corporation (RFC) at the end of his term in 1932 to loan money to businesses, organizations, and state and local governments.

A march on Washington by 20,000 hungry veterans called the *Bonus Expeditionary Force* (1932) asked for the bonus ($15,000 in modern money) promised them in the *Adjusted Compensation Act* (1924) when they really needed it, which was *immediately*. General Douglas MacArthur broke up the march with force, but using force on hungry veterans didn't make Hoover any more popular.

Meanwhile, Japan chose the time of economic troubles in the U.S. to take over Manchuria. The United States did nothing but shake its finger.

While his own country was in trouble, Hoover did manage to make some conciliatory gestures in Latin America that later formed the basis of the *Good Neighbor Policy* (1933) under Franklin Roosevelt. At home under Hoover, the situation just kept getting worse.

> **EXAMPLE**
>
> **Question:** What did the government do when the Bonus Expeditionary Force marched on Washington during the Great Depression?
>
> **Answer:** The government used the army to break up the march and send the marchers home.

# The height of the Depression: 1932

By 1932, one in four Americans — more than 11 million people — had no job. Most people didn't want to hear any more Republican philosophy about how it was good for the poor to have to struggle on their own. As opponents pointed out, Hoover's RFC could pay to feed a pig but not a human child.

Shantytowns of displaced people called *Hoovervilles* sprung up near big cities. The Depression was cause for a great internal migration of transient people traveling from town to town looking for work; 2,000 applicants would show up for a single job interview.

> **EXAMPLE**
>
> **Question:** What was the impact of the Depression on where people lived?
>
> **Answer:** Transient people travelled from town to town in a great internal migration around the United States looking for work.

# FRANKLIN D. ROOSEVELT AND THE NEW DEAL

Franklin Delano Roosevelt (FDR) was the Democratic candidate for president. Roosevelt, a wealthy aristocrat, was a distant cousin of Teddy Roosevelt, and his wife was Teddy's niece Eleanor. FDR had been the Democratic nominee for vice president in 1920 — tall, athletic, and maybe just a little stuck up. Beaten for vice president in the Harding landslide, in 1921 he was struck by a disease that paralyzed his legs for life. He didn't give up, but he did begin to see what a struggle life could be for what he called the *forgotten man*.

FDR was governor of New York when the Depression hit, and he immediately launched relief programs that reached worried people. His campaign song is still a theme for the Democratic party: "Happy Days Are Here Again." People believed in his hope and determination, and Roosevelt beat Hoover in a landslide.

His inaugural address contained now-famous words, quoted here in a slightly extended version to show their serious context: "The only thing we have to fear is fear itself — nameless, unreasoning, unjustified terror which paralyzes needed efforts to convert retreat into advance."

Roosevelt's *New Deal* (1933) program centered on three R's: relief, recovery, and reform:

- First, FDR wanted to provide immediate relief from hunger and homelessness, very real problems in 1933 when one out of four Americans was unemployed.
- Second, the New Deal hoped to help the economy recover so that people would have stable jobs and businesses with which to support themselves.
- Third, the Democrats planned to reform the system so that no American would have to suffer another Great Depression again.

A newly elected, heavily Democratic Congress passed a great amount of legislation so quickly that it became known as the *Hundred Days* (1933) of the new administration. Roosevelt wanted to fix agriculture, banks, and jobs without nationalizing basic industries.

> **EXAMPLE**
>
> **Question:** What were Roosevelt's key aims with the New Deal?
>
> **Answer:** FDR wanted to save the country and the capitalist system by reforming banks, agriculture, and jobs without nationalizing major industries.

# Attempts to address the greatest needs

The first step was to stop the run on the banks that had people desperately trying to withdraw their savings, thus making bank collapse a self-fulfilling prophecy. Roosevelt temporarily closed all the banks and then reopened them under the Emergency Banking Act, which took only eight hours to pass.

Congress created the *Federal Deposit Insurance Corporation (FDIC)* (1933), guaranteeing bank deposits and thus helping stop the panic. To create more money, FDR purposely caused inflation by increasing the price of gold.

For direct help to starving people, Congress passed the *Federal Emergency Relief Administration* (1933), which handed out billions of dollars in grants and jobs through the states. More help was on the way.

## Civilian Conservation Corps (CCC)

The *Civilian Conservation Corps (CCC)* (1933) created more than 3 million jobs in the nine years of its life, hiring mostly young men from poor families. Civilian Conservation Corps camps were run by the Army in every state in the nation.

The CCC constructed buildings and trails in city, state, and national parks that still exist today. The first CCC recruit was ready for training little more than a month after Roosevelt took office; the program continued until World War II gave young men something else to do.

Most Americans happily endorsed the CCC as a combination of good work and necessary economic support — most of a CCC recruit's small-but-regular pay went home to help his family. Although the national CCC ended, over a hundred state and local work programs still exist today modeled on the Conservation Corps.

## WPA, CWA, and PWA

More jobs were created by the *Works Progress Administration (WPA)*, the *Civil Works Administration (CWA)* and the *Public Works Administration (PWA)*. A regular alphabet soup of well-meaning agencies tried to help America keep working through the nightmare of the Depression.

Trails and roads weren't the only New Deal projects; the PWA built the Grand Coulee Dam on the Columbia River, the largest structure in the world that had been built up to that time since the Great Wall of China. To keep people cheerful and raise needed tax revenue, the nation got rid of Prohibition with the *Twenty-first Amendment* (1933).

## Tennessee Valley Authority (TVA)

The federal government got into the electricity business with the construction of the nine dams of the *Tennessee Valley Authority (TVA)* (1933). Even by Depression standards, the Tennessee Valley area was in bad shape, with exhausted soil, epidemic malaria, and widespread poverty. The TVA brought jobs and low-cost power with what was to become one of the largest electrical utilities in the world. At the same time, state public utility commissions began to control abuses by private power companies.

## Help for agriculture

The *Agricultural Adjustment Act* (1933) helped improve farm income by limiting supply, but the Supreme Court overturned it. The *Soil Conservation and Domestic Allotment Act* (1936) and a reformed second *Agricultural Adjustment Act* (1938) passed court tests to become the beginning of the national farm support program that continues to this day.

>  **EXAMPLE**
>
> **Question:** What was the Agricultural Adjustment Act (1933)?
>
> **Answer:** This act was the first attempt at a national farm policy that included limiting supply to raise farm income.

## Securities and Exchange Commission (SEC)

Because Wall Street had problems in the Great Depression, the Roosevelt government started the first fair trading rules for stocks with the *Securities and Exchange Commission* (SEC) (1934). The SEC is still functioning and gets regularly updated when new corporate problems arise.

## Federal Housing Administration (FHA)

To increase the number of construction jobs and homes, the *Federal Housing Administration (FHA)* (1934) began to back small loans for remodeling and new home construction.

When the FHA started, most home mortgages were short-term, three-to-five-year interest-only loans, with a huge balloon payment for the entire value of the loan at the end of the three or five years. Buyers had to come up with at least 40 percent of the value of the home as a down payment. With the Depression, people couldn't make big balloon payments *or* find 40 percent for a down payment. Banks were stuck with houses nobody could afford to buy, and the housing market bottomed out. With the FHA, home ownership has increased from 40 percent in the 1930s to nearly 70 percent today.

## Social Security

*Francis Townsend* (1936) had a plan for old age assistance (aptly named the *Townsend Plan*), which wasn't practical itself but did help spur the Social Security Act. Certainly the largest, most lasting change in life for older people, the *Social Security Administration* (1935) guaranteed small pensions for the elderly and the handicapped by taxing the income of current workers. In the presidential election of 1936, Roosevelt overwhelmingly defeated his Republican opponent, Alf M. Landon of Kansas. The Democrats controlled two thirds of the votes in both the House and the Senate. No political party had enjoyed this much public support since the Era of Good Feelings (see Chapter 9) more than 100 years before.

>  **EXAMPLE**
>
> **Question:** How was the Social Security Administration funded?
>
> **Answer:** Social Security taxed current workers to pay for retirement benefits.

**EXAMPLE**

**Question:** What was the contribution of Francis Townsend in the 1930s?

**Answer:** His Townsend Plan helped encourage the development of Social Security.

## National Recovery Administration (NRA)

FDR and the New Deal made mistakes. To create more jobs, the government created the *National Recovery Administration (NRA)*, in which participating industries agreed to job sharing and wage and price controls to make more work. It was an administrative nightmare and seemed to legalize cartels. It was soon declared unconstitutional in 1935.

Roosevelt went too far when he tried to add more justices to the Supreme Court to keep it from blocking his legislation. Even his supporters wouldn't go along with this manipulation of the Constitution, dubbed the *court-packing scheme* (1937).

## Wrapping up the New Deal agencies

The Indian New Deal, officially named the *Indian Reorganization Act of 1934,* encouraged tribes to organize their own governments and stopped the breakup of American Indian lands.

A change in government treatment of unions was signaled by the *National Labor Relations Board (NLRB)* (1935), which allowed workers a fair hearing when organizing unions. Even with a more sympathetic government, strikers were killed in San Francisco (1934) and Chicago (1937). The *Congress of Industrial Organizations (CIO)* (1937) was later formed to organize whole industries, including unskilled workers and blacks who hadn't been part of the older AFL confederation (see Chapter 14). By 1938, the CIO had 4 million members.

To keep enthusiastic government employees from campaigning for their boss, the *Hatch Act* (1939) barred political work by government employees.

**EXAMPLE**

**Question:** What did the Congress of Industrial Organizations (CIO) add to the labor-organizing movement?

**Answer:** The CIO offered representation to unskilled workers and blacks across whole industries, going beyond the AFL's push for skilled workers by trade.

# The Dust Bowl

The New Deal tried to give long-suffering farmers a break by paying them not to grow crops, thus limiting supply, conserving land, and raising prices of now more moderately produced food. When things were already bad for farmers, over plowed dry land blew away in the *Dust Bowl* (1935), centered in Kansas and Oklahoma. This led to an exodus of poor farmers who headed west to look for work and food.

### *The Grapes of Wrath*

John Steinbeck's novel *The Grapes of Wrath* (1939) tells the story of the Joad family's trip from barren Oklahoma to California in search of a new life. Enduring death and the desertion of family members, the Joads push on, learning that their only hope lies in solidarity with other poor people. A New Deal relief program tries to help, but in the end their daughter Rose of Sharon gives up the milk she had for her stillborn baby to save a starving man.

Steinbeck won the Pulitzer Prize and the Nobel Prize for Literature, and the film version won two Academy Awards. *The Grapes of Wrath* showed rural poverty up close and put a face on the bravery it took to confront Depression homelessness. The story built solid support for social programs in the United States, a country that only a few years before had elected presidents who said the government shouldn't help people. Films like *Mr. Smith Goes to Washington* (1939) showed honesty winning through a corrupt political system.

## The legacy of the New Deal

Fighting the Depression before World War II closed in, Roosevelt managed to cut unemployment from 25 percent to 12 percent. His programs literally kept people all over the country from starving. The New Deal also started programs that prevented something as horrible as the Great Depression from happening again. Millions of people got a chance to improve their lives, and the spirit of the New Deal put a safety net under the American people that no president — no matter how conservative — has ever seriously tried to take away.

> **TIP**
>
> You don't really have to memorize all the New Deal programs, but be ready for questions on the Depression. For essay answers, an understanding of the scope of Roosevelt's recovery program and some specific agencies is important. At minimum, you want to know the agencies started in the New Deal that are still part of America: FDIC, TVA, SEC, FHA, NLRB, and Social Security. If you can figure out what the letters mean, the agencies pretty well explain themselves.

# DEMAGOGUES OF THE DEPRESSION

Whenever there is a shortage of money, there is a surplus of people with good sounding schemes about how to change things. The 1930s had its share of demagogues ready to fool the people with big talk:

- *Huey P. "Kingfish" Long* (1934) promised big money bonuses for everyone in his native Louisiana in order to get almost-dictatorial power as governor and senator.

- *Father Charles Coughlin* (1935) was a thorn in the side of the Roosevelt administration, preaching a kind of fascism, anti-Semitism, and isolationism over a national radio network.

# 17

# World War II: 1940–1945

| KEY CONCEPTS |

- ■ U.S. preparation for war despite isolationist tendencies
- ■ Policies to aid the Allies prior to entry into the war
- ■ Social and economic changes on the home front
- ■ The progress of the war in the Pacific and Europe
- ■ America's emergence as a world power

**A**merica's self-absorbed, it's-all-about-me attitude in the 1920s contributed to the nation suffering a severe economic downturn in the Great Depression (see Chapter 16). As if that wasn't bad enough, the same kind of me-first isolationist impulse on an international scale helped get the country shocked into World War II. The U.S. came out of this global conflict stronger than ever because Americans learned to fight back together and take the lead in solving world problems that they couldn't escape.

True to the modern social history approach, the AP exam won't expect you to know all the battles, generals, and airplane names. You do need to understand what led to the biggest war in history, plus the course of the conflict and its main high points. Because of their age, the Test Masters who put the finishing touches on the AP History Exam almost certainly know people who lived through World War II. They'll expect you to take this chapter's topic as seriously as they do.

# THE BRINK OF WAR

After World War I, Americans tried to crawl back into bed and pull the isolationist covers over their heads. With the nightmare of the Great Depression still causing economic pain, the last thing that people wanted was another international war. The U.S. wasn't looking for trouble, but trouble seemed to be looking for them.

## The London Economic Conference (1933)

At first, President Franklin Roosevelt was in favor of the *London Economic Conference* (1933), which convened to get the nations of the world working together on solutions to the Depression. When he discovered the Conference's sole purpose was to fix the value of gold, Roosevelt backpedaled fast. He had been lowering the value of gold in the U.S. to get more dollars in circulation; the last thing he wanted was an agreement that would fix the dollar-to-gold ratio and take away his money-creating ability. Roosevelt refused to go along because the fixed gold price didn't help the United States face its Depression.

Other nations noticed the isolationist stance of the U.S. and started to act in their own interests as well. Not only did the London Economic Conference fall apart without the United States, but it also made countries that much more determined to go it alone. The collapse of the international finance and trade system of the 1920s contributed to the increasing tendency to violence in international relations.

## Latin America and the Good Neighbor Policy

The U.S. was a little friendlier with Latin America. Roosevelt expanded the *Good Neighbor Policy* (1933) that pledged the United States to work with Central and South American nations to protect the hemisphere.

The idea of working together peacefully was a marked departure from previous U.S. policy, which had usually involved sending in the Marines and negotiating at gunpoint. In the 1930s, the U.S. removed troops from Haiti, Panama, and Cuba, holding on to the base at Guantanamo, Cuba, as a naval station. When Mexico grabbed American-owned oil wells in their country, the U.S. gritted its teeth but didn't intervene.

Franklin Roosevelt flew down to Argentina for the *Inter-American Conference* (1936) and received cheers as he announced friendly aid and cooperation. With the beginnings of World War II thundering in Europe, the United States agreed to share responsibility for the Monroe doctrine with Latin American countries in the *Havana Conference* (1940).

## Japan eyes the Philippines

Following through on the promise the U.S. made after taking the Philippines from Spain, Congress passed the *Tydings-McDuffie Act* (1934), which promised the islands their freedom in 1946 after a final 12-year tune-up. Despite the fact that World War II filled up a large chunk of that time with a Japanese military occupation, the U.S. kept its promise to the Philippines.

In the meantime, the United States's willingness to free the Philippines made Japan think the U.S. really didn't care that much about the islands. By promising to leave, the U.S. unintentionally let Japan believe that America might be easy to push around.

# Reciprocal Trade Agreement Act

In another make-nice bid, Congress let the president set tariff-lowering deals with other countries under the *Reciprocal Trade Agreements Act* (1934). This measure reversed some of the self-inflicted damage of the *Hawley-Smoot* law and started the U.S. and the world on a decreasing-tariff trend that led to the free trade policies that most nations enjoy today.

Although reciprocal trade agreements were hardly enough to make the world peaceful, they were a step in the right direction. Over the protests of vehement anti-communists, Roosevelt recognized the Soviet Union in 1933, something that would come in handy later when the U.S. needed allies in World War II.

# Hitler, Mussolini, and Franco

Meanwhile in Europe, bad guys were moving into the neighborhood. Benito Mussolini, the founder and strutting proponent of Fascism, had taken over Italy in 1922. Looking for something strong and glorious to do, Mussolini invaded the independent African empire of Ethiopia in 1935, sending Italian soldiers in tanks and planes to fight people armed with spears. The League of Nations, without American support, did little but bluster to stop Mussolini.

Adolf Hitler, a tyrant with murderous intentions, took over Germany in 1933 through a parliamentary process. After quickly getting rid of his country's struggling democracy, Hitler revived the German economy with dictatorial control, massive military re-armament, and projects like the world's first national freeway system (the *autobahn*) and the first specially created "people's car" (the *Volkswagen*). Ominously, he also began an ever-tightening persecution of Jewish people and other minorities. Some Western democracies tried to overlook Hitler's crimes because they thought he would fight Communism.

In 1936, Hitler and Mussolini aligned themselves as the Axis powers. Soon they had a joint project. The democratic government of Spain was fighting a civil war with would-be dictator General Franco. Germany and Italy jumped in on Franco's side, sending troops, planes, and tanks. The Spanish Republican government got some help from the Soviet Union and individual volunteers from many countries, including the United States. The governments of France, Britain, and the United States refused to help save the Spanish government, but Germany and Italy had no such hesitation about destroying it. After three years of brutal fighting — including the bombing of civilians by Germany and Italy — Franco won (1939).

# The Neutrality Acts

As the dictators increased their power, the United States increased its effort to figure out a better way to stay out of trouble. Congress passed separate *Neutrality Acts* for three years in a row starting in 1935, in an attempt to avoid the kind of economic entanglement that had led to the U.S. being drawn in to World War I.

These neutrality acts said that when the president proclaimed the existence of a foreign war, no American could loan money, sell weapons, or even sail on a ship belonging to one of the fighting sides. These rules were a step back from the freedom of the seas for which the U.S. had fought major wars in the past. The Neutrality Acts made no distinction between good guys and bad guys; the United States wasn't going to help anybody.

By not working for democracy, the Neutrality Acts gave the advantage to dictatorships. The United States's attempts to avoid conflict also included a refusal to prepare for any possible war. Throughout most of the 1930s, the American army contained fewer than 200,000 men, smaller than the armies of Poland or Turkey.

# THE FLAMES OF WAR GROW HIGHER

The military leadership of Japan wanted to control China, and it launched an invasion of that country in 1937. The Japanese sank a U.S. gunboat on a Chinese river, apologized, and the Americans forgave them. In 1936, Japan became a formal ally of Nazi Germany and Italy in the Anti-Comintern pact.

Meanwhile in Europe, Adolf Hitler gobbled up territory from countries on both sides of Germany. At first, his moves were tentative. When Hitler's troops marched into the demilitarized Rhineland region of Germany in 1936, they had orders to turn right around and go home if anybody stood up to them. Nobody did.

In March of 1938, Germany took over Austria without a fight. At the *Munich Conference* (1938) in September of that year, England and France agreed to let Hitler take over the German-speaking part of Czechoslovakia. This sellout by the democracies only bought peace for a few months. Negotiating with Hitler was like trying to stop a wolf by throwing meat at it. In August of 1939, anti-Communist Hitler stunned the world by signing a treaty — a nonaggression pact — with Joseph Stalin, leader of the big Communist Soviet Union. One week later, Hitler invaded Poland and the Soviets marched in from the east.

## Britain and France take a stand

Finally England and France had had enough; they declared war on Germany, and the greatest conflict in history was under way. After several months of preparation, Hitler's well-organized forces swept across Holland and Belgium into France. By the summer of 1940, Hitler and his Italian buddy Mussolini controlled most of Europe except for the home islands of Britain 35 miles across the English Channel.

Hitler pounded Britain with planes to destroy the British Royal Air Force (RAF) and prepare the islands for German invasion. In the *Battle of Britain* (1940), the RAF, down to its last few planes, heroically defended the island nation. As the bombs fell, bulldog Prime Minister Winston Churchill told the British people to conduct themselves so that if Britain "lasts for a thousand years, men will still say, 'This was their finest hour.'" It was.

## Tentative U.S. steps toward war

By 1938, the Roosevelt administration finally acknowledged that trouble may be coming to the U.S., so it started to build up the Navy to keep any attackers away from American shores. With Europe under Nazi control and America's mother country Britain fighting for its life, the U.S. passed its first peacetime draft called the *Selective Service Act* in September of 1940, beginning the process of bringing millions of men into the armed forces.

## Any aid short of war

Also in September, President Roosevelt took the dramatic step of sending 50 old destroyers to Britain in exchange for some defensive bases in the Atlantic. He didn't wait for Congress: His friend Churchill had told him to act *now*. Aid wasn't that easy; an *America First* (1940) organization led by aviation hero Charles Lindbergh opposed any help for Britain that might draw America into the war. A law to continue the draft passed by only one vote. Despite Lindbergh's popularity, a majority of Americans now favored helping the fight with "any aid short of war."

In the middle of the war buildup came a presidential election. Franklin Roosevelt decided he had to run again for an unprecedented third term. He won easily despite some uneasiness about electing any president for a third term; the Democrats also maintained their majority in Congress.

## Lend-Lease Bill

Britain was running out of money as well as supplies. A newly reelected Roosevelt introduced the *Lend-Lease Bill* (1941), which allowed the U.S. to lend or lease military supplies to Britain and other countries America supported without payment. This move was as close to declaring war as the nation could come without actually pulling the trigger; the hope was that other democracies would do the fighting for America. Lend-Lease had the additional advantage of tooling up U.S. defense plants to operate at full production before the country eventually ended up in the war.

EXAMPLE

**Question:** What was the purpose of the *Lend-Lease Bill* (1941)?

**Answer:** The purpose of Lend-Lease was to get desperately needed supplies to Great Britain and other potential allies without payment in advance.

# Hitler invades the Soviet Union

In June of 1941, less than two years after he had shocked the world by signing a peace treaty with his Communist enemy the Soviet Union, Hitler shocked the world again by sending a huge army to invade his Soviet treaty partners. Having conquered most of Europe, Hitler thought he could get away with anything. In addition, he sincerely hated Communism (and anyone who got in his way).

Hitler was sure his genius planning would have the German army safely in Moscow before winter. During the first weeks of the invasion, the Germans won so much territory and prisoners that it looked like those dreams might come true. The Soviet Union seemed to be on the brink of collapse.

Against the nightmare scenario of the Soviet Union folding like Russia did in World War I, Churchill met with Roosevelt on a battleship off Canada. They weren't supposed to be allies; after all, the U.S. was still officially neutral and not at war. The two took the unusual step of drafting the *Atlantic Charter* (1941). The Charter said that all people had the right to choose their own government, especially to reinstate the democratic governments that dictators had taken away. It also called for disarmament and peace overseen by an international organization.

When they had time to catch their breath, the leaders of the Soviet Union signed on to the Charter later in 1941. The United States was in the interesting position of dictating war aims for a conflict it was not fighting. The charade got even thinner when America started to convoy supplies as far as Iceland through the German submarine packs with a shoot-to-kill order against attacking U-boats.

## Japan attacks Pearl Harbor

In the Pacific, the U.S. also managed to twist the imperial tail of Japan without actually attacking. In late 1940, the United States cut off the shipment of scrap iron and other industrial supplies to Japan; in mid-1941, America froze Japan's investments in the U.S. and cut off all gas and military supplies in response to Japan's move into Indochina. The Japanese war machine was going to grind to a halt without either buying supplies from the U.S. or stealing them from the lightly guarded Dutch West Indies.

America said it would turn on the supplies again if Japan backed out of China, but for Japan that would be a loss of both honor and hard-won territory. Japan pretended to negotiate and got ready for a surprise attack against the United States.

Early on the morning of Sunday, December 7, 1941, with most of the U.S. Pacific Naval Fleet rocking gently at anchor in the tropical breezes of Pearl Harbor, Hawaii, Japanese carrier planes flew in low to drop bombs that sank or disabled almost the whole fleet and killed 2,500 Americans. Unfortunately for the Japanese, they missed sinking the most valuable ships in the Pacific navy, three aircraft carriers that weren't in the harbor at the time. In months to come, these ships would come looking for the Japanese. Given that the U.S. had had no experience at being invaded for the last 125 years, the attack on Pearl Harbor came as a shocking surprise. Within days, the United States was at war with Japan, Germany, and Italy.

>  **TIP**
>
> Having trouble remembering who's on what side? The major players in World War II were *JIG* versus *SUB*. The Axis Powers were Japan, Italy, and Germany against the Allies, who were the Soviet Union, the United States, and Britain. This mnemonic may be simple, but it's also useful.

# FIGHTING TO WIN ON THE HOME FRONT

Having had a couple of years to think about it, Britain and the U.S. had already agreed to put most of their efforts into beating Germany first. Although you may be inclined to chase the wasp that has just stung you, you're better off to go after the biggest hive first. Plus, little Britain and the almost-overwhelmed Soviets were politely saying, "Hey, can we get some help over here?" Sure, but first the United States had to figure out how to feed and equip all three countries, plus ship its fighting forces and supplies half way around the world in two directions.

## The treatment of Japanese Americans

The American mainland home front was not really threatened, with no real danger from enemy bombs or sabotage, but people didn't know that at the time. The attack on Pearl Harbor scared everyone. Out of paranoia and racism, the U.S. government herded over 100,000 Japanese Americans into internment camps to make sure they did not cause trouble. Most of them were

American citizens; none of them were ever proven to be a real danger to the United States. They were politely treated for the most part, but many of them lost the small farms they had managed to buy before the war, where they had grown most of the West Coast's green beans, tomatoes, and strawberries. They appealed their internment to the Supreme Court in the case of *Korematsu v. United States* (1944), and the Court ruled that the internment was legal.

Despite their harsh treatment, thousands of Japanese Americans volunteered for the army and fought bravely in Europe. After the war, they went back to their normal lives. Thirty years after the War, the United States apologized and paid the Japanese Americans and their families a small compensation.

**EXAMPLE**

**Question:** What was the Supreme Court decision in *Korematsu v. United States*?

**Answer:** The Supreme Court held that the internment of Japanese Americans on the West Coast of the United States during World War II was legal.

## War production

Production of war material made the United States what President Roosevelt called the "arsenal of democracy." For starters, the U.S. launched almost 3,000 Liberty ships, each capable of carrying 10,000 tons of cargo anywhere in the world. On those ships went more than 2 million machine guns, billions of bullets, four times as many tanks as the dictators produced, twice as many fighter planes, four times as many bombers, and five times as many heavy guns and trucks.

Farmers hauled in record billion-bushel wheat crops by using machinery to replace manpower. Rationing held down domestic consumption to speed food to American soldiers and their allies. Government agencies worked to keep a lid on wages and prices. Labor unions grew, but their leaders mostly kept their men off the picket lines and on the job. To encourage worker cooperation, Congress passed the *Smith-Connally Anti-Strike Act* (1943), which allowed the government to take over industries tied up by strikes.

The federal government took over the coal mines and for a short period even ran the railroads. Most of the time, the federal government did not need to step in: Business and labor worked together for the war effort. Over all, American workers cooperated with the war effort by having even fewer work stoppages than laborers in besieged Britain.

During the war, thousands of Mexican farm workers entered the United States, partly as a replacement for the interned Japanese. Many never left.

Workers built Liberty ships cheaply and quickly. In a break with tradition, they welded the ships together instead of riveting them. Ship building used to take months, but Liberty ships were ready in six weeks.

Women made up a third of the civilian work force; most of these women had never held a job outside their homes before. *Rosie the Riveter* (1943) symbolized the millions of female workers who helped make the weapons that won the war. They also worked to build Liberty ships that carried these weapons to armies all around the world. After the war, two thirds of the women quit their jobs to return to housework, but they didn't forget their successful employment. Working women became a natural part of the United States's economy in the 1960s, about the time the daughters of the women who helped win World War II came of age.

# Fighting discrimination in defense industries

Despite federal investment for industrial plants in the Old South, millions of blacks left the land of their former enslavement to take new manufacturing jobs in the North and in California.

Cotton-picking was over as an occupation in the South after the invention of machines to do the work. Within a generation, a majority of Southern blacks gave up their rural homes and gravitated toward the city. This migration was so large that it rivaled the influx of immigrants at the beginning of the 1900s.

Under pressure from the nation's only black union, the Roosevelt administration forbade discrimination in defense industries. This was the first time black workers had been given a fair shake in major industries, and they responded by going to work in record numbers.

# Minorities in the armed forces

The American record on discrimination was not that good in the armed forces. Blacks fought in segregated units, often in service rather than combat jobs; however, they did have a limited but proud record as fighter pilots, soldiers, and sailors. In 1948, three years after the end of the war, the armed forces became the first major institution in the United States to be officially desegregated.

More than 25,000 American Indians served in the armed forces during World War II. In both Europe and the Pacific, they made special contributions as *code talkers* who relayed radio messages in Indian languages that enemy troops couldn't understand. After the war, American Indians migrated from reservations to cities in record numbers.

Hundreds of thousands of Mexican Americans served in the armed forces, making up around 3 percent of the army. Although they faced discrimination in housing, education, and even veterans services after the war, they fought back through legal organizations.

> **TIP**
>
> Mexican American school children had to attend so-called Mexican schools in California. In 1947, the *Mendez v. Westminster* court ruling declared that segregating children of "Mexican and Latin descent" in the state of California was unconstitutional. This ruling helped lay the foundation for the landmark *Brown v. Board of Education* (1954) case that ended official racial segregation for all minorities in the United States public school system.

# U.S. recovery from the Depression

The United States *gross domestic product* (GDP), the value of its output of goods and services, doubled during World War II. Although the Depression had hit the U.S. harder than most countries, America recovered strongly during the war. People were working decent jobs and had money to spend; average pay by the end of the war was almost twice as much as it was at the beginning.

As the only industrialized nation not being bombed, the U.S. out-produced the rest of the world. Millions of people were either in the armed forces or employed by defense industries supported by federal contracts. The federal *Office of Scientific Research and Development* (1941) spent billions of dollars on university research and technical innovation, including the top secret *Manhattan Project* (1941) to develop the atomic bomb.

This flood of war spending, not the modest streams of help from New Deal programs, was what finally brought a complete end to the Great Depression. The war cost more than the total of every penny the government had ever spent since the American Revolution. As terrible as it was, World War II lifted up the United States both as an international power and as the world's richest economy. The same Roosevelt Democratic administration that started the New Deal in the face of the Depression ran America during World War II.

The optimistic can-do attitude the United States gained from its trials in war and the Depression buoyed the nation for the rest of the century.

**EXAMPLE**

> **Question:** What was the economic condition of the U.S. home front during World War II?
>
> **Answer:** The U.S. home front economy completely recovered from the Great Depression and boomed during World War II.

# THE FIGHT IN THE PACIFIC

After Pearl Harbor, the situation looked bleak for the Allies. Japan had conquered most of the East Asia, including the American possessions of the Philippines, Guam, and the Wake Islands and the European possessions of Hong Kong, Singapore, the East Indies, Burma, and Indochina. The Japanese said they wanted to start an Asian commonwealth run by Asians, but in fact their rule was often more brutal to the natives than that of the Europeans they replaced.

The Philippines fell to Japan in 1942 after five months of resistance; General Douglas MacArthur was taken away from the Philippines at the last minute to lead the U.S. Pacific forces in Australia. The Japanese fought their way to islands just off Australia before they ran into the slowly growing strength of the Allied forces.

In the naval battle of the *Coral Sea* (May 1942), the first battle in history in which the ships never saw each other and all the fighting was done by planes, the combined U.S. and Australian forces fought the Japanese to a standstill and prevented an invasion of southern New Guinea that would have threatened Australia.

## Midway

The tide began to turn for real in the *Battle of Midway* (June 1942). In this second all-carrier battle, the U.S. defended an island outpost west of Hawaii with everything that could float or fly. The Japanese lost four aircraft carriers and many of their carefully trained pilots; the Americans lost just one carrier. With its greater population and production power, America was on the offensive in the Pacific from Midway on.

## Guadalcanal

The first major land offensive was an American attack on the small island of *Guadalcanal* (August 1942), whose occupation by Japan threatened the shipping of supplies to Australia. It took months of brutal battle, but the Americans finally drove the Japanese off the island. The

U.S. hopped from island to island across the South Pacific, refusing to back down from the fight-to-the-death resistance by the Japanese. By the end of 1944, the U.S. had won islands close enough to the Japanese homeland to serve as launching fields for around the clock bombing of Japan itself. American submarines and planes sunk Japanese supply ships at a rapid rate.

# THE FIGHT IN EUROPE

The first challenge the U.S. faced in fighting for Europe was getting supplies through the well-armed wolf packs of German submarines. In the first months of the war, the Germans sunk more than 500 American merchant ships — faster than the U.S. could rebuild them. Without supplies, Britain couldn't continue fighting.

Faced with a high-tech sub threat, the U.S. and Britain devised cutting-edge solutions. The British broke the German codes so the Allies had an idea of where the German submarine packs were hiding. Patrol planes and convoys equipped with sonar attacked the subs.

Over a year, the tables turned. The German subs had to draw back as the Allies sunk more than a hundred of their undersea boats, in some months at the rate of almost one a day. With fewer German subs, Allied supply ships were safer; their losses decreased from the equivalent of 75 Liberty ships sunk a month to fewer than 20. Although the Germans kept up some submarine attacks for the rest of the war, the time for subs to make a real difference had passed.

## British and U.S. air attacks on Germany

The British believed that heavily bombing German cities would break the German will to fight (even though when the Germans bombed Britain, it only made the British tougher). In late 1942, Britain sent more than 1,000 bombers to attack the German city of Cologne.

Now that America was in the war, the Germans were under constant attack from the British at night and the Americans by day. Heavy conventional bombing didn't break the Germans' will to fight or even stop production; the Germans made planes and submarines until the end of the conflict. What bombing did was to open up a second front in the air before the Allies invaded Europe; until that point, in the first front against the Germans on the ground in Russia, only Soviet troops were fighting.

Allied strategic air attacks forced the Germans to spend limited resources on protecting civilians, using their guns and fighter planes. Domination of the air over the battlefield by Allied tactical planes meant the Germans had to give up lightning raids in the open and settle down to trench warfare, much like in World War I. The Allies remained free to move.

## The Soviets fight back

After giving ground to early German attacks into the Soviet Union, the Soviets got help from nature by way of intensely harsh weather. One of the earliest, coldest, and snowiest winters in Soviet memory broke over German troops, who didn't have winter equipment because Hitler had expected them to win long before the weather got cold. When the snows hit in November 1941, the Germans were so close to taking Moscow that they actually stole tickets from the end of the Moscow tram line. Their advance was thwarted when the Soviets threw their last fresh troops (who just happened to include Siberian ski troops) into the battle and pushed the Germans away from their capital.

The Germans held on deep in the Soviet Union for another year, but after a heroic defense of the city of Stalingrad in 1942, the Soviets launched a counterattack that destroyed an entire German army. From then on, it was a slow and costly three-year fight to Berlin. The Soviets lost at least 27 million people in World War II, more than 50 times as many people as the U.S. lost. Through 1943, Britain and the United States had lost only a few thousand soldiers in Europe. The Soviets pleaded for a second front in Europe to take some of the pressure off their army.

## D-day and Normandy

The Western Allies took two and a half years to launch their D-day invasion; meanwhile they nipped away at the outskirts of Europe. The Allies invaded North Africa in November of 1942, and by the following summer, they'd defeated the German and Italian armies there. Churchill and Roosevelt met in the newly liberated city of Casablanca to plan the rest of the war. The Allies next invaded Italy. Although the Italians were happy to get rid of Mussolini and called their participation in the war quits by September of 1943, the Germans occupied most of the country and fought on in Italy until almost the end of the war.

In June of 1944, the Allies launched a massive invasion of Normandy, France. Over 3 million men had assembled in Britain for the cross-channel push. Thousands died on the beaches, but the Allies pushed inland. A second, smaller invasion came from the south of France. Paris was liberated in August of 1944, and the first major German city fell to the Allies in October.

In the U.S., Franklin Roosevelt won reelection for an unprecedented fourth term as the Allied armies rolled toward victory. Hitler counterattacked at the *Battle of the Bulge* (1944) in December, but this move merely hastened the end of the war by using up his reserves. By April of 1945, the Soviets and their Western allies were in Berlin, and Hitler had committed suicide. Franklin Roosevelt died of a stroke a few days before the victory.

## The Holocaust

After Hitler's death, the world began to face the terrible crime of the Holocaust. Six million Jews — almost every Jew the Nazis could find in Europe — had been murdered in cold blood. In addition, Hitler and his willing German and European accomplices had murdered another 5 million political opponents, prisoners of war, Gypsies, Freemasons, disabled children, and Jehovah's Witnesses, among others. Another 3 million Soviet prisoners were starved to death.

The United States struggled with the fact that it had been unwilling to allow refugees from Europe to seek safety in the U.S. before the war. After they knew about the death camps and the killing of families and children, many Americans made a simple pledge: never again. The experience of World War II influences America's international policy to this day.

# THE ATOMIC BOMB AND THE END OF THE CONFLICT

By the summer of 1945, the Allies had defeated Germany, and U.S. forces were within bombing range of Japan. Authorities as diverse as future Nobel Prize winner William Shockley and ex-president Herbert Hoover estimated that the planned U.S. land invasion of Japan would have cost 1 million U.S. casualties and up to 10 million Japanese lives. The Japanese military was training all civilians — including children — to fight to the death.

# The decision to drop the bomb

The United States had just completed the first test of the new atomic bomb. The Soviet Union was attacking the Japanese army in Manchuria, and the U.S. didn't want to give the Soviets time to make territorial claims. After dropping warning leaflets, the U.S. exploded an atomic bomb over the Japanese city of Hiroshima, killing approximately 130,000 people. The Japanese still didn't surrender. Three days later, the Americans dropped another bomb over Nagasaki that killed an additional 60,000 people.

> **EXAMPLE**
>
> **Question:** Why did the United States drop the atomic bomb on Japan?
>
> **Answer:** To end the war, stop Soviet expansion, and ultimately save lives.

The ending was deadly, but it marked the end of years of global suffering during World War II. The dictators' threat to democracy was so serious that some have called the Allies' defense of international freedom the Good War.

# The outcome of World War II

The Allies wrapped up World War II by occupying Japan and Germany. They divided Germany into zones controlled by Britain, France, the U.S., and the U.S.S.R. Although Berlin was technically in the Soviet zone, the parties divided it separately; the Soviets got East Berlin, and the West took West Berlin. Japan was an all-American occupation, with General Douglas MacArthur dictating a democratic constitution.

In both Japan and Germany, 20 or so major war criminals went on trial, and a few were executed. In Germany, these postwar hearings were called the *Nuremberg trials* (1946), and they established the principle that people have the responsibility not to follow orders if those orders violate international law.

Before World War II, only a handful of democracies existed throughout the world. Now, most of the countries in the world hold democratic elections (or at least pretend to). Before World War II, the world was an international jungle — every nation for itself. Now, although pain and conflict are certainly still plentiful, the United Nations and other international organizations at least try to call attention to abuses and occasionally take real action.

The United States was changed as much as any part of the globe by World War II. Thrust into world leadership, America could never go back to the dream of isolationism.

# 18

# Victory and Cold War: 1946–1960

## KEY CONCEPTS

- America after World War II
- The presidencies of Harry S Truman and Dwight D. Eisenhower
- Communism, containment, and the Cold War
- American life in the 1950s

From the outside, the United States seemed like the place to be in the autumn of 1945. With the help of its allies, the nation had won a stunning victory in battles beyond both its oceans' shores (see Chapter 17).

Unlike every other industrialized nation in the world, the U.S. suffered little damage to its cities. American farms and factories were in full production, and labor had never been so highly paid. People finally felt safe. The U.S. was, briefly, the only country in the world with the atomic bomb. Prosperity continued, but the feeling of safety didn't last for long. This chapter covers the years after World War II, particularly the Cold War and its effects on the nation and the rest of the world.

# POST-WWII AMERICA

World War II had been a four-year roller coaster ride of war for the U.S. As exciting and wonderful as it felt to be victorious, however, Americans couldn't forget that before those four years had come more than ten years of economic calamity in the Great Depression. With no more wartime jobs, folks had to wonder whether hard times were going to return.

President Harry S Truman took over when Franklin Roosevelt died just as the war with Germany was ending; nobody knew whether he could fill Roosevelt's shoes. Even more worrisome was the Soviet Union, which seemed to be morphing from ally to enemy even before the last round of toasts at the victory party.

## The baby boom

The baby boom started after World War II. War families were reunited, and people felt optimistic enough about the future to want to bring more children into the world. Before the war, birth rates had been down and suicide rates up, due largely to the corrosive effects of the Depression years on Americans' sense of optimism and resilience.

After victory and years of good pay, people felt much better. The postwar baby boom formed a ten-year population bulge that helped invent '50s rock-and-roll, '60s protest, '70s attitude, and '80s yuppies. By the second decade of the 21st century, the baby boomers were poised to make retirement an active sport.

## A brighter economic outlook

After the removal of wartime government price controls, costs shot up to match higher wages. The annual inflation rate went from 2 percent in 1945 to 9 percent in 1946 and 14 percent in 1947 before it started to level off. Higher costs meant wages bought less, and that led to strikes: More work stoppages occurred in 1946 than during all of World War II.

### The Taft-Hartley Act

Although the country still had a Democratic president, it had elected the first Republican-controlled Congress since Herbert Hoover. Those Republicans managed to pass a bill over President Truman's veto that they said would get strikes under control.

The *Taft-Hartley Act* (1947) prohibited unions from putting pressure on their employers by picketing other companies that did business with their own company. The act also forbade unions from requiring that an employer hire only union members (called a *closed shop*) but it did allow *union shops,* in which everybody had to join the union after they were hired.

The Taft-Hartley Act is still in effect. It allows states to forbid union shops: Several states have established *right to work* laws that prohibit all workers from having to join a union. Additionally, unions have to give 60 days' notice when they're threatening to strike, and the president can put a hold on strikes that he feels will cause a national emergency.

## A shift from blue collar to white collar workers

At the high point of union membership in the early 1950s, a third of the population was involved in some sort of union; by the early 21st century, that number had declined to less than 15 percent. The Taft-Hartley Act itself didn't cause unions to lose membership — what changed was the kind of work Americans were doing.

In the 1950s, America experienced a decrease in the number of blue-collar manual laborers and an increase in the number of white-collar service workers. For the first time in the history of the world, the white-collar desk workers outnumbered laborers who worked with their hands in the United States. This abundance of service workers has increased over the years, and the number of union members has decreased accordingly.

One obstacle for unions is the fact that service workers stay in jobs for a shorter period of time than they used to; the average American now spends less than four years at one job. This rapid turnover makes union organizing difficult.

In addition, unions were victims of their own success. Employment practices and wages have improved so much that many workers don't think they need the kind of protection unions can bring.

## The Employment Act

After the war, the Truman administration sold unneeded defense plants and equipment at bargain prices to help employers grow civilian businesses. Congress passed the *Employment Act* (1946), which set a goal of maintaining full employment and required the president to submit an annual economic report along with the federal budget. The act established the Council of Economic Advisers, which was responsible for supplying the intelligence to keep the economy and the job market rolling.

# The GI Bill

The Servicemen's Readjustment Act of 1944, better known as the *GI Bill* (1944), offered a bigger, more immediate payoff than did the theories offered by the Economic Advisers. The GI Bill provided for college or vocational education as well as one year of unemployment pay for returning World War II veterans, whom everybody called GIs (short for Government Issue). It also provided loans for returning veterans to buy homes and start businesses.

The GI Bill was the last piece of New Deal legislation endorsed and signed by Franklin Roosevelt. (See Chapter 16 for more on the New Deal.) Ex-soldiers couldn't believe their good fortune: The bill paid for education and offered low-interest loans. Although most veterans attended vocational schools to learn a trade, enough GIs opted for college that many universities doubled in size. The proportion of the population with a college degree grew from 5 percent before the war to more than 25 percent in the early 21st century.

> **EXAMPLE**
>
> **Question:** What most influenced the number of men going to college in the United States during the 20th century?
>
> **Answer:** The GI Bill, which paid for the education of veterans.

Millions of young American families moved to small houses in the suburbs thanks to zero-down-payment loans from the GI Bill. This started a housing revolution that took home ownership from 44 percent in 1940 to almost 70 percent in the early 21st century. All this education and house-building also helped stimulate the economy by making more jobs. The GI Bill provided up to one year of unemployment coverage, but few ex-soldiers could resist getting one of the plentiful jobs before that year was up.

## The International Monetary Fund

To help keep away global economic trouble, the Western Allies established the *International Monetary Fund (IMF)* (1944) during a meeting at Bretton Woods, New Hampshire, toward the end of the War. The IMF is an international organization consisting of just about every country in the world, and its mission is to oversee the global financial system by influencing exchange rates and making loans.

Although the IMF's international policy has its critics, cooperation tied a more prosperous world together and helped to lift countries out of poverty to some extent.

## The United Nations

Despite the postwar tensions that would soon erupt, at least one peaceful international political organization was created. The *United Nations* (1945) got going at the end of the war; President Roosevelt was getting ready to speak to the first U.N. session when he died.

Unlike the similarly themed League of Nations (see Chapter 15), the U.N. began with the full support of the United States. The U.N. has a Security Council controlled by the big powers and a General Assembly of all nations. Able to act only when the big powers agree, the U.N. has become an organizing center for some but not all peacekeeping missions around the world.

# TRUMAN, THE UNEXPECTED PRESIDENT

Nobody expected Harry S Truman to be president, least of all Truman. A last-minute compromise candidate as Franklin Roosevelt's third vice president, Truman had only a few months on the job when Roosevelt died. Truman said to reporters, "Boys, if you ever pray, pray for me now."

Truman was an honest man elected by a political machine, a failed men's clothing store owner who joined George Washington, Abraham Lincoln, and Andrew Jackson as a president who never went to college. When the love of his life turned him down when he first asked her to marry him, Truman went off, earned some money, fought in World War I, came back, and asked her again. This time she said yes.

As a senator before World War II, Truman took it upon himself to visit defense plants and push them to be more productive. The sign on his desk said, "The buck stops here"; Truman wouldn't stand for blame-passing. Counted out politically, he ran a give-'em-hell campaign and surprised everybody by winning the presidential election in his own right in 1948.

In his second term, Truman faced an icy freeze of relationships with the Soviet Union, which had been America's warm wartime ally when he first took office.

# THE BEGINNING OF THE COLD WAR

The division of the world into the Soviet Union and its Communist allies against the United States and major capitalist free market countries in Europe and East Asia happened seemingly overnight at the end of World War II. People called it the *Cold War* (1950), although it got pretty hot in Korea and Vietnam.

World War II ended with the Soviet Union in control of Eastern Europe. The Soviets established Communist governments backed by Soviet troops in Poland, Czechoslovakia, Hungary, and other Eastern European nations. Winston Churchill said that an *iron curtain* (1946) had descended across Europe, dividing the free countries that had real elections from the Communist *satellite* countries ruled by party officials.

> **TIP**
>
> Don't get confused when countries change names. The Soviet Union, also known as the Union of Soviet Socialist Republics, also known as the U.S.S.R., was really just Russia with a few client nations on its outer edges that have since left the Russian Federation. When Russia went Communist after World War I, it took several (formerly partially independent) provinces and countries with it and became the Soviet Union. When it got over being Communist in the 1990s, it let some of the provinces go and went back to being called Russia.

## The shift from ally to enemy

Paranoia struck deep after World War II. The Soviet Union had been torn apart by German troops and had lost millions of people fighting alone on the ground in Europe for two long years before Britain and the U.S. finally got around to the Italian and the D-day invasions.

The Soviet leadership saw the world as an anti-Communist conspiracy, and they were on a self-protective and ideological crusade to turn other countries Communist. They especially wanted a protective barrier of Communist satellite countries between themselves and Germany, a country that had torn into Russia twice in 25 years.

The Soviets knew that some in the West had put up with Hitler for years partly because they thought Hitler could kill off Communism. During the war (before he was vice president), Truman had said the U.S. should let the Germans and the Soviets kill each other off and help whichever side seemed to be losing to keep the bloody fight going. Having lost 27 million people (and almost having lost their country as well) in World War II, the Soviets had reasons to worry.

So did the United States. Not only did its so-called Soviet allies become increasingly hostile, but within a few years, the Soviets also developed the atomic bomb. Other countries, including China and Cuba, became Communist. To people in the U.S., it looked like a conspiracy was afoot in the world; how else could the Communists become so powerful?

## The escalation of perceived threats

Like any argument with paranoia on both sides, push came to shove pretty quickly between the U.S. and the U.S.S.R. because each side was sure that it was right and that the other side was out to get them. The United States shut off Lend-Lease aid to the Soviets shortly after the end of the war. The U.S. offered to include the Communist countries of Eastern Europe in the Marshall

Plan to rebuild Europe. The Soviet leadership refused to participate and forced the satellite countries to do likewise, partly due to suspicion of American motives.

The Soviets clamped a lid on Eastern Europe and supported any country that said it was Communist. In response, the United States supported most countries that said they were anti-Communist. The showdown lead to a dangerous arms race, plus a standoff in jointly controlled Germany and shooting wars (officially *police actions* or *conflicts*) in Korea and Vietnam.

# The policy of containment

A diplomat named George Kennan saw it coming. In his influential 1947 paper "The Sources of Soviet Conduct," he maintained that Russian policy, whether under the tsar or the Communist Party, is relentlessly expansionistic but cautious, and he recommended a policy of firm and vigilant *containment*. The United States followed Kennan's policy.

> **EXAMPLE**
>
> **Question:** What was George Kennan's 1947 policy recommendation?
>
> **Answer:** Kennan recommended a policy of firm containment of Soviet Communist expansion.

## The Berlin Airlift

As Cold War tensions rose, the Soviets cut off Western ground access to the West's part of Berlin by closing the road that ran across the Soviet governed part of Germany. The Americans responded with a giant airlift of supplies that kept Berlin alive for almost a year until the Soviets relented and allowed ground access again. The *Berlin Airlift* (1949) landed a plane every minute, using some of the same aircraft that had recently been trying to kill Berliners.

## The Truman Doctrine

President Truman got Congress to approve loans to Greece and Turkey to counter Soviet moves to turn those countries Communist. He launched the *Truman Doctrine* (1947) of containing Communism by supporting non-Communist countries with money and arms if necessary.

# The Marshall Plan

The U.S. supplied a huge financial support package to Europe through the *Marshall Plan* (1947), which lent billions of dollars to rebuild Western Europe. It worked. The total amount of money the U.S. lent former friends and foes alike over the six years before and during the Plan equaled fully 10 percent of everything produced in the U.S. for a year (the U.S. gross domestic product, or GDP). By the end of the 1950s, Western European economies were well on the way to recovery, and the region had begun plans for establishing the European Community. The Marshall Plan helped keep Western Europe on the U.S. side following the war.

Truman also threw American support behind the creation of the state of Israel in 1948, over the heated objection of the Arabs who lived there.

## The National Security Act and NATO

America's anti-Communist international position led to the creation of super agencies to help fight the Cold War. The *National Security Act* (1947) established the *Joint Chiefs of Staff*, which brought together top military leaders, and the *National Security Council*, which brought together intelligence information gathered by the new *Central Intelligence Agency (CIA)*. The next year, Congress reinstituted the peacetime draft, and in 1949, the nation swallowed hard and entered into the very kind of "entangling alliance" George Washington had warned about.

With the birth of the *North Atlantic Treaty Organization (NATO)* (1949), the U.S. allied itself with Western European nations and pledged to respond to an attack on any one of them as an attack on all. NATO kept a wary eye on the Soviet Union and its *Warsaw Pact* treaty allies, the Soviet satellite countries. The Warsaw Pact was the Soviet equivalent of NATO, made up of Eastern European nations under the control of Moscow.

# ANTI-COMMUNISM HYSTERIA

While MacArthur helped Japan turn into a peaceful and prosperous democracy, the Chinese were fighting among themselves. In 1949, Communist leader Mao Tse-tung won, pushing the non-Communist Chinese leadership off the mainland and on to the island of Taiwan.

The Republicans roundly blamed Truman for "losing" China, but in fact the huge country had never had a democratic government to defend. The Soviet Union's detonation of its first atomic bomb around this same time added to America's worry about the world.

## The Loyalty Review Board

President Truman actually launched the anti-Communist hysteria in the United States by appointing a Loyalty Review Board in 1947 that checked to see whether any of the 3 million federal employees were members of supposedly subversive organizations. About 3,000 federal workers resigned under pressure, although very few of them were charged with crimes. Some Hollywood writers were *blacklisted* for political reasons and spent years unable to get work because of their alleged sympathy with Communist and left-wing organizations.

By 1949, supporting those so-called subversive groups *was* a crime, and members of the U.S. Communist Party went to jail for supposedly advocating the overthrow of the U.S. government. The House Committee on Un-American Activities (HUAC) had a field day uncovering suspected Communists everywhere, led by an ambitious young congressman. Richard Nixon became famous for hounding Communists and their sympathizers in high-level government jobs. He didn't mind calling anyone who got in his way a Communist sympathizer.

In 1950, Truman vetoed a bill that would have given the president power to arrest and lock up any suspicious person during a security emergency because it sounded too much like a police state.

In the midst of paranoia, however, Truman did manage to build some public housing, raise the minimum wage, and extend Social Security. He also proposed a national health insurance system which did not pass. Any further social programs were held hostage by the Cold War.

## McCarthyism

Senator Joseph McCarthy made outrageous, mostly unverified allegations that Communists and their sympathizers had infiltrated the federal government. He said that hundreds of known Communists worked in the State Department, and he pretended to have a list of their names. He accused respected officials of being "fellow travelers" with Communists, even picking on George Marshall (former army chief of staff, secretary of state, and defense secretary and author of the Marshall Plan) and President Eisenhower.

Communist actions in China and Korea and the speed with which the Soviets had gotten the atomic bomb scared Americans enough that they sometimes believed McCarthy's wild accusations. Every time he made a charge that proved false, he simply came up with a new charge. His witch hunt was called *McCarthyism* (1952).

McCarthy finally went overboard when he attacked the United States Army. In the great tradition of journalists who would not be frightened away from telling the truth, television's Edward R. Murrow took on McCarthy when politicians were afraid to act. After 35 days of televised *Army-McCarthy Hearings* (1954), many Americans saw who McCarthy really was: a mean-spirited liar who twisted the people's worries to get power. He was censured by the Senate and died of chronic alcoholism three years later.

McCarthyism showed the power of fear connected to conspiracy theory; it still serves as a useful example of the danger of demagogic leadership.

# THE KOREAN WAR

Paranoia on both sides caused the Cold War, but when the war turned hot in Korea (and later in Vietnam, which you can read about in Chapter 19) the U.S. took hits rather than use weapons that could destroy the world. Senior U.S. policy makers believed in the *domino theory* that said if one nation went communist, its neighbor would follow.

Korea was divided between Communist North Korea and capitalist South Korea after World War II. In 1950, the North, prodded by Stalin, invaded the South, and the *Korean War* (1950 to 1953) was underway. The United States called the fighting a "conflict" since war was not officially declared, but it certainly seemed like a war to the people who were getting shot. The Communist North, armed with Soviet weapons, pushed the South Koreans back to a small pocket on the edge of the peninsula.

Taking command from Japan, Douglas MacArthur engineered a brilliant landing behind Communist lines at Inchon and pushed the North Koreans back across their border. MacArthur then made the mistake of taking over all of Korea, right up to its border with Communist China. The Chinese sent in huge waves of soldiers and pushed the Americans and South Koreans back to the South's border.

After years of sniping, both Koreas signed a peace treaty in 1953, putting things back the way they were before the invasion.

The Korean War got a U.S. military buildup going that eventually ate up 10 percent of the gross national product. With Communism in the past, the U.S. defense figure is now less than 5 percent of the GDP, still almost as much every year as the rest of the world combined.

In the 1950s, the U.S. spent money and lives to defend its democratic capitalist system, but it avoided touching off a nuclear war that could destroy the world. When Chinese Communist troops stormed into Korea, General MacArthur wanted to use atomic bombs and risk a global meltdown. President Truman fired him for insubordination.

Short of using nuclear bombs, Truman was aggressive in defending Korea in part to answer critics that his administration had been soft in letting China go Communist. Nonetheless, he wasn't going to let Korea lead to World War III.

> **EXAMPLE**
>
> **Question:** What influenced President Truman in responding with toughness to Communist aggression in Korea?
>
> **Answer:** Truman wanted to correct the impression that his administration had turned soft on Communism because it had watched the Communists take over China without launching military opposition.

The Korean War finally ended after President Dwight D. Eisenhower visited the front and hinted that he might use atomic weapons. Korea had cost more than 30,000 U.S. lives and hundreds of thousands of Korean and Chinese deaths. Troops still guard the border between the two Koreas to this day.

# THE EISENHOWER PRESIDENCY

After the Democrats had a five-term run in the White House, a Republican took over. Actually, the Democrats were thinking of nominating Eisenhower themselves, but after some reflection, Eisenhower decided he was a Republican. To give Ike a tough anti-Communist edge, the Republicans ran Richard Nixon as vice president.

When a corruption controversy about Nixon surfaced, Ike almost dumped him. Nixon made the first dramatic use of national television as a political tool by going on the air to speak about how his wife had only a respectable Republican cloth coat (no minks for her) and how Communist sympathizers next would attack the fact that his kids had been given a dog named Checkers. The *Checkers speech* saved his nomination, and Eisenhower won the election by an overwhelming majority.

Eisenhower had been a mediator of often-contentious military units as the overall head of the Allied forces in Europe in World War II. He used these talents to lead by consensus during the 1950s. Although he was seldom in the forefront on important issues, he usually came through with reasonable compromise solutions.

## Politics under Ike

Eisenhower's legislative record was mild like his personality. He often worked with a Congress controlled by Democrats, and he had to put up with some boneheads in his own administration. When scientists invented a drug to prevent the horrible childhood disease of polio, Eisenhower's secretary of health condemned the free distribution of the vaccine as "socialized medicine."

Old soldier that he was, Eisenhower knew the waste that goes with military spending. He reduced Truman's military buildup, although costs remained high during the tense Cold War years.

The administration participated in a major roundup of illegal aliens called *Operation Wetback* and tried to set back the cause of American Indian identity by temporarily revoking the tribal rights of the Indian New Deal. Otherwise, Eisenhower kept the programs from the New Deal without trying to dismantle or change them. By continuing these programs in a Republican administration, he helped make them a permanent part of American society.

Ike made his biggest change to the American landscape by starting the huge freeway-building program that linked the whole country together under the *Interstate Highway Act* (1956). With climate change and oil politics, those smooth roads that make people slaves to their cars now look dangerous, but when Ike started to build them, they opened up a world of easy travel.

## Tensions with the U.S.S.R.

Eisenhower tried to start peace talks, but the timing just wasn't right. In 1955, the Soviet Union rejected Ike's proposal at a summit conference for open skies over both countries as an obvious espionage trick. The open skies idea got embarrassing when the Soviets shot down a U.S. spy plane over the U.S.S.R. in 1960, just in time to also shoot down another summit conference. The U.S. also had to stand by and watch as the Soviet Union brutally crushed a 1956 uprising in Hungary.

Worst of all, Vietnam was on the horizon. The U.S. tried funding the French fight against Vietnamese Communist rebels, but the French lost. Vietnam was divided, and the U.S. supported South Vietnam because, although it was a dictatorship, it wasn't Communist. America made a similar mistake in Iran, using the CIA to put the Shah in power in 1953. Both cynical moves would later come back to haunt the U.S. (see Chapter 19).

 **EXAMPLE**

> **Question:** Why did the U.S. increase its involvement in Vietnam?
>
> **Answer:** When the French left Vietnam, the U.S. tried to shore up the anti-Communist South Vietnamese regime.

On the friendly side, Ike proclaimed the *Eisenhower Doctrine* (1957), which offered aid to Middle Eastern nations. Under Eisenhower, the U.S. put a stop to the joint Israeli, British, and French takeover of the Suez Canal, winning some thanks from the Egyptians. Ike landed troops to help the government of Lebanon and got out without a single U.S. death. With the GDP and economy up, sunny Ike carried almost the whole country in his 1956 reelection.

# THE PROSPEROUS 1950S

Americans were ready for some grandfatherly reassurance. The Depression and World War II had been a strain, and the Communists, Korea, and the Cold War didn't give anybody much of a chance to relax. Electing Dwight "Ike" Eisenhower, a balding leading general from World War II with a broad smile, as president in 1952 was a relief.

Real income grew at a rapid rate in the 1950s and beyond. Americans — only 5 percent of the world's population — controlled almost 40 percent of the world's wealth. Money was the biggest story in the history of the United States since World War II.

Not all Americans profited equally from the affluence of their country, and the nation experienced both recession and inflation, but overall the economic course was up for most of the people most of the time.

The seeds of future trouble were contained in some aspects of American affluence. Defense spending stayed high, fully 10 percent of the *gross domestic product* (GDP, the value of goods and services) during the 1950s. President Eisenhower warned about the bad influence of the military-industrial complex on U.S. society.

## Doubling the middle class

Cars, houses, and too many stomachs got bigger. The proportion of the population in the middle class doubled from the Roaring '20s; by the end of the 1950s, about two-thirds of Americans were comfortably middle class. Prosperity gave people the space to improve education, civil rights, and medical care. It also gave the country the income necessary to outspend the Soviet Union in the arms race and Cold War.

By 1960, one out of four homes in America was less than 10 years old. People could afford new homes because their jobs were better — more than likely white collar or sales. The first 707 jet passenger planes launched the travel revolution; before the 1950s, most people had never been on a plane.

### Television takes over American households

The 1950s saw the rapid growth of television and fast food. Many now look down on both, but they provided a rich option of experience and convenience that people wanted. Only 3 million people in the country had televisions in 1950; by the end of the decade, they were in nearly every home. In the 1950s, TVs got only three channels; people had to choose from one of the three shows broadcast by the major networks. Originally, television was only black and white on tiny screens — color television was a big deal when it came out in the mid-'50s — and a 21-inch picture tube was considered large.

### Rocking in the U.S.A.

Rock-and-roll changed music and culture starting in 1954. Elvis Presley may not have had the first rock record, but he was there at the beginning with Little Richard, Ike Turner, Buddy Holly, and Jerry Lee Lewis. Rock-and-roll spread like wildfire, bridging the gap between black rhythm and white melody. The open sexuality didn't hurt, either; rock was in the sexy company of Marilyn Monroe, *Playboy* magazine, and the Kinsey report, which detailed how normal lust could be. Victorian times were gone forever.

### Examining alienation and conformity in literature

Literature was actually more dramatic and upbeat in the happy 1950s than in the roaring 1920s. Early-decade social critics like David Riesman in *The Lonely Crowd,* William Whyte in *The Organization Man,* and Sloan Wilson in *The Man in the Gray Flannel Suit* saw the future in terms of alienation and conformity. Later, the 1960s would show them how wrong they could be.

Ernest Hemingway and John Steinbeck turned out career-capping work and won well-deserved Nobel prizes. Playwrights Tennessee Williams (*Cat on a Hot Tin Roof*) and Arthur Miller (*Death of a Salesman*) wrote searing drama. J.D. Salinger captured adolescent angst and its answer forever in *Catcher in the Rye*. Rebellious individualism was personified by actors James Dean and Marlon Brando and by Beat writers Jack Kerouac, William Burroughs, and Allen Ginsberg.

People like Joseph Heller (*Catch-22*), Kurt Vonnegut (*Slaughterhouse Five*), and Philip Roth (*Goodbye, Columbus*) wrote wittily and meaningfully at the same time. Betty Friedan introduced women's issues in *The Feminine Mystique*. Television wasn't killing off culture, at least not yet.

**EXAMPLE**

> **Question:** What did social critics like David Riesman warn was a coming social problem?
>
> **Answer:** Social critics in the 1950s often warned about conformity and alienation from community.

# Women in the workforce

Of the 40 million new jobs that started between 1950 and 1980, 30 million were in clerical and service work — jobs that women often filled. Women didn't displace men in the job market; they just found jobs that were never there before. Working women were nothing new — women had worked as hard as men on the farm for years. The real anomaly in history was the first hundred years of the Industrial Revolution, during which time middle-class women were supposed to just stay home while men went off to work.

Women moved from being less than one quarter of the work force at the end of World War II to being about half the workers in the early 21st century. This change allowed families to stretch their incomes, but it caused some wrenching readjustments at first as women tried to cover being wife, mother, and full-time worker all at the same time (and men learned some parenting skills to take up the slack).

At least the children were in school; in 1950s America, most kids finished high school. This number contrasts with the time before World War I, when only half of school-age children regularly attended classes.

# Addicted to energy

America began its energy addiction in the 1950s; oil consumption doubled and electric energy usage increased 600 percent in the two decades after World War II. Big cars burned more gas, and commutes got longer as people moved out to the suburbs, which were home to 25 percent of the population by the end of the 1950s and more than 50 percent of the people by the 21st century.

The growth of Sunbelt living in the warm Southern climate made air conditioning a regular part of many people's lives. Productivity increased with energy usage on the farm: petroleum based fertilizers, pesticides, hybrid crops, and gasoline-powered harvesters allowed one farmer to feed ten times as many people at the turn of the 21st century as his grandfather could at the turn of the 20th century.

## The first computer

The first commercial computer appeared in the United States in 1951. The UNIVAC (for *universal automatic computer*) was the size of a small house and used 5,200 vacuum tubes and 125 kilowatts of power (equivalent to 160 horsepower) to store its full capacity of only 1,000 words. With less computing power than a toy watch, the UNIVAC sold for almost $10 million in modern money.

## The cost of affluence

One downside of affluence was distance. People moved every few years; adult children often lived thousands of miles from their parents, grandparents, sisters, and brothers. Airplanes could bring people together for a few hours at the holidays, but the sense of nearby extended family was gone. Self-help advice books and psychological counseling barely filled in the gaps. Affluence and mobility could cost a lot in isolation and loneliness.

Because people were cut off from their family roots anyway, they chose to live where it was sunny; Florida boomed and one out of eight Americans ended up in California.

# THE CIVIL RIGHTS MOVEMENT OF THE 1950S

Although many blacks had migrated North for better jobs during World War II, more than half still lived in the South under Jim Crow laws that kept them prisoners of segregated schools, trains, parks, and hotels.

African Americans died because they couldn't be treated at whites-only hospitals. The only place for Martin Luther King Jr. to stay with his bride on their honeymoon was a blacks-only funeral parlor. Only a few African Americans were registered to vote in the South; the rest were disenfranchised by poll taxes, rigged literacy tests, and flat-out threats. The lives of blacks in the South in the 1940s and 1950s weren't much better than they had been in 1880.

The Democratic Party helped poor people, but it had trouble letting go of its historic base of support among white Southern racists — ugly, but handy for winning close elections. This support dated all the way back to the fact that the Democrats were *not* the party that led the North in the Civil War.

## Dixiecrats

Franklin Roosevelt had made the first move for racial fairness when he ordered an end to discrimination in defense employment during World War II. In 1944, the Supreme Court ruled that whites-only primary elections in the South were illegal.

When Harry Truman, a Democratic president from a border state, heard about the murder of six black servicemen returning from the war, he was outraged. Truman supported the first civil rights legislation in years and desegregated the federal civil service.

Southerners opposed to civil rights walked out of the Democratic Party in 1948 to start the short lived Dixiecrat Party, but Truman won reelection anyway. Because millions of blacks had moved to the North and West where they could vote, their voices began to be heard. Jackie Robinson became the first black player in professional sports in 1947. A few years later, the first black winners of the Nobel and Pulitzer prizes were named.

**EXAMPLE**

**Question:** Why did some Southerners form the Dixiecrat Party in 1948?

**Answer:** Dixiecrats opposed President Truman's civil rights legislation.

## Rosa Parks

On a cold day in the winter of 1955, *Rosa Parks* (1955), a college-educated 42-year-old black seamstress, refused to get up from her seat near the front of a Montgomery city bus to make way for a white man. She was arrested. The protests that began with that arrest started the modern civil rights movement. An early leader of the *Montgomery bus boycott* (1955) movement was a young Christian minister from Atlanta named *Martin Luther King Jr.* (1960).

## Brown v. Board of Education

The civil rights movement had legal and social support. In 1954, the Supreme Court ruled in *Brown v. Board of Education* (1954) that segregated public schools are "inherently unequal" and that desegregation must proceed with "all deliberate speed."

Although Southern representatives initially resisted, desegregation has moved ahead with the deliberate speed of any major social change, which means it has taken generations. Legal forms of discrimination were abolished one by one in the decade after the civil rights movement began in the mid-1950s. These cases were the legal decisions that had the most impact on American society.

**EXAMPLE**

**Question:** What kind of legal decisions had the most impact following World War II?

**Answer:** Court cases involving civil rights were the most important in changing society.

## The Civil Rights Commission

Dwight Eisenhower wasn't a revolutionary. He had grown up in the white Midwest and spent his career in the segregated army. But Eisenhower knew his duty. When the governor of Arkansas threatened to use force to keep black students from enrolling in Little Rock, Arkansas's *Central High School* (1957), Ike called out the army to protect the *Little Rock Nine* as they walked into class. Eisenhower also supported legislation to establish a permanent *Civil Rights Commission* (1957) to investigate and report on discrimination.

**EXAMPLE**

**Question:** What is the main purpose of the Civil Rights Commission?

**Answer:** The Civil Rights Commission is responsible for investigating and reporting on discrimination in the United States.

## Sit-in demonstrations

In 1960, four black college students sat down to have lunch in a North Carolina store. Under orders, the servers refused to wait on them. The students refused to leave, starting the first *sit-in demonstration* (1960). The next day, they came back with 19 classmates, the day after, 85 — by the end of the week, a thousand protestors had converged on the store.

Sit-ins spread to segregated lunch counters all over the country; although the protestors often met with violence, they kept coming. Eventually, national laws outlawed discrimination in facilities open to the general public.

> **EXAMPLE**
>
> **Question:** What are some of the major domestic events during the Eisenhower administration?
>
> **Answer:** During Ike's terms the gross domestic product (GDP) was up, the *baby boom* continued to increase population, black families moved from the rural South to the North and West, the civil rights movement got started, and the interstate freeway system was begun.

# THE SPACE RACE

In 1957, the nation got its second technological shock from the Soviet Union. Just eight years after the Soviets developed an atomic bomb, they launched *Sputnik* (1957), the world's first satellite. The supposedly backward and politically challenged Soviets now seemed dangerously ahead of the U.S. After an early attempt to loft a tiny American satellite blew up on the launching pad, the Soviets brazenly sent up another tin moon; this one contained a dog astronaut named Laika.

Science fever swept the U.S.; the nation *had* to catch up. Eisenhower established the *National Aeronautics and Space Administration (NASA)* (1958) to coordinate a program that would take the U.S. from launching pad zero to moon walking hero in just over ten years. In addition, the *National Defense Education Act* (1958) offered almost a billion dollars in science and other scholarships.

# CASTRO IN CUBA

The Americans got another bad surprise when *Fidel Castro* (1959) took over as head of Cuba from a corrupt, U.S.-supported dictator. Castro was a Communist who allied himself with the Soviet Union, and the Soviets threatened a missile attack if the U.S. messed with Castro.

Almost a million Cubans left their island for the United States, where many of them worked without end to keep American policy vehemently anti-Castro.

# THE ELECTION OF JOHN KENNEDY

Despite the Cold War and other problems during his administration, Eisenhower tried to stay positive. In his eight years as president, the country enjoyed unprecedented prosperity and a national unity of purpose that's hard to imagine in the 21st century. Eisenhower was a successful old soldier who, as president, ended one war and avoided all the others. He left trouble on the horizon, but there was peace on his watch.

The 1960 presidential election featured Ike's vice president Richard Nixon against dashing young senator John F. Kennedy. The nation picked Kennedy in a close race, showing that it had become unprejudiced enough to elect an Irish Catholic. Television, the medium that had saved Nixon through his Checkers speech eight years before, now did him in. In the first televised presidential debates, Kennedy looked fresh and Nixon looked tired. That visual was enough to swing a few thousand votes and, in turn, the election.

# 19

# Rock and Roll Living: 1961–1979

**KEY CONCEPTS**

- The continuation of the Cold War
- The presidencies of Kennedy, Johnson, Nixon, Ford, and Carter
- The Vietnam War and anti-war movements
- Social unrest and the expansion of civil and women's rights and the social safety net

The 1960s and 1970s were neither the dawn of a hippie age of Aquarius nor the beginning of the downfall of society. America changed, but America had always been changing.

The youth counterculture hippie movement often associated with the 1960s lasted from the arrival of the Beatles in 1963 until the departure of Richard Nixon in 1974. Actually, the hippies never really left; they just settled down with mortgages and kids, much like their GI fathers and flapper grandmothers had done.

The 1960s and 1970s pushed social changes into the lives of everyone — changes that had been on the way for a century. These social updates included expansion of the role of women, more-equal treatment for African Americans and other minorities, and social freedom in dress and behavior. America got more choices and managed to roll over the rocky ground of Vietnam, assassinations, demonstrations, Woodstock, riots, peace, love, and Watergate. What a trip!

> **TIP**
>
> Although the AP test doesn't cover current events, questions from several decades ago are common.

# KENNEDY: PROGRESS AND THE COLD WAR

*John F. Kennedy* (1960) was only 43 years old when he was sworn in as the youngest elected president in American history. To add to the movie-star freshness of his administration, he appointed his 35-year-old brother, Bobby, as attorney general and surrounded himself with a cabinet of the best and brightest advisers. This strategy was quite a change from the grandfatherly President Eisenhower.

Kennedy was handsome and eloquent; at his inauguration, he uttered still-famous lines like "Ask not what your country can do for you — ask what you can do for your country" and "Whether you are citizens of America or citizens of the world, ask of us the same high standards of strength and sacrifice which we ask of you."

## The Bay of Pigs and the Cuban Missile crisis

Within weeks of his inauguration, Kennedy was embarrassed by the failed *Bay of Pigs* (1961) invasion of Cuba, which the Eisenhower administration had planned.

Ever since Communist Fidel Castro had taken over Cuba two years before, the American CIA and right-wing Cuban exiles had wanted to kick him out. Some exiles stormed ashore, but their invasion was stopped on the beach. It was an international black eye for the U.S., and Kennedy took full responsibility.

A year and a half later, the *Cuban Missile Crisis* (1962) took place. The Soviets had taken advantage of their alliance with Communist Cuba to install nuclear missiles on the island. These missiles could hit the United States (only 90 miles away) in the blink of an eye.

When Kennedy found out about the missiles, he ordered the U.S. Navy to blockade all shipments to Cuba. After a tense standoff on the high seas, the Soviet ships turned around. Kennedy reached an agreement with the Soviets that they would remove the missiles from Cuba if the U.S. publicly promised never to invade Cuba and quietly packed up U.S. rockets stationed in Turkey.

The Cuban Missile Crisis brought the world closer to nuclear war than it had been at any time before or since — one false move on either side could have touched off the bombs. After the crisis, both sides in the Cold War were more cautious about stirring up surprise threats.

## The Peace Corps

Kennedy had a small Democratic majority in Congress, but given that the Southern Democrats were about as loyal as the South had been during the Civil War, he couldn't get much legislation passed. Kennedy-proposed programs for civil rights, health care, and tax reform stalled but would later pass after his death.

## Urban rumors

The story that Kennedy's words unintentionally meant that he was a Berliner jelly donut is an urban legend — funny, but untrue. Nobody misunderstood President Kennedy during his dramatic speech face-to-face with Communist repression in 1963; he was speaking in German, which he didn't understand, but he said the words correctly.

A too-fancy false reading by a non-German-speaking *New York Times* reporter in the 1980s led to the jelly donut story being later repeated by the BBC, *The Guardian*, MSNBC, CNN, and *Time* magazine. It will remain false, as any German-speaker knows, no matter how many times it gets repeated by journalists who don't bother to check their sources.

The same is true for legends that the U.S. somehow faked the moon landings. Few people believe that now, but a new urban legend pops up whenever any unexpected event occurs. Usually, these rumors involve the secret plans and agendas of some mysterious, unnamed group simply referred to as "they." People love conspiracy theories which purport to explain what they can't understand. As with urban legends about 9/11 and alien landings, it's worth doing real research with credible sources before passing along a rumor.

Kennedy did manage to start the *Peace Corps* (1961), which began within months of his inauguration, to send American volunteers overseas to help developing nations. The Peace Corps still has about 10,000 volunteers (making it about 1 percent the size of the U.S. military, which numbers more than a million people), and it continues its humanitarian work in countries around the world.

## The Space Race

Continuing the U.S. response to earlier Soviet space launches, Kennedy declared that America would land a man on the moon before the end of the 1960s. With focused scientific research and billions of dollars, the U.S. sent the first astronauts to the moon in 1969, faster than anybody thought possible before Kennedy became president.

## Kennedy in Berlin

The Soviets wanted the Western allies out of the democratic outpost of West Berlin because people kept defecting from Communist East Germany through Berlin, and it made the Communists look as bad as they really were. The Berlin Airlift had foiled the Soviets' plan to starve the West out of the city (see Chapter 18), so the Communists built the *Berlin Wall* (1961), a jagged fence through the middle of the city.

Kennedy flew to Berlin in 1963 and declared that he stood so firmly behind the freedom of West Berlin that *"Ich bin ein Berliner"* ("I am a Berliner"). Kennedy's speech electrified the surrounded Berliners; almost the whole population was in the streets to cheer him.

# TRADE AGREEMENTS

The first step toward later events like the European Union and the World Trade Organization came when Congress backed international economic cooperation through the *Trade Expansion Act*

(1962). The act allowed import tariffs to be lowered if reciprocal agreements could be reached with other nations. International negotiations under the *Trade Expansion Act* were called the *Kennedy round* in honor of President Kennedy.

The lowering of tariffs was part of the decades long *General Agreement on Tariffs and Trade* (abbreviated GATT) originally created by the *Bretton Woods Conference* (1944) as part of a larger plan for economic recovery after World War II. The GATT's main objective was the reduction of barriers to international trade.

Continuing the spirit of the Trade Expansion Act, Europe took a step to being a confederation like the early United States when it established the European Union in 1993. The functions of the GATT were taken over by the *World Trade Organization* (1995), which was established during the final round of international tariff-lowering in the 1990s.

# THE UNITED STATES AS WORLD COP

The U.S. under Eisenhower had been leaning on its huge nuclear arsenal in eye-to-eye confrontations with the Soviet Union, under the horrifying doctrine of *Mutually Assured Destruction* (aptly known as MAD). The MAD idea was that neither side could start a war because everybody knew both sides would be destroyed.

Under Kennedy, the United States expanded its role as world policeman, even if nobody had actually called the cops. America largely paid for a U.N. force to police violence in the newly independent Congo and helped work out an international agreement to prop up a shaky truce in Laos. These peacekeeping actions called into question the limited military options of the United States; the U.S. military was set up more to defeat other armies than to keep the peace.

Non-nuclear brushfire wars demanded a more flexible response, so Kennedy began to build up elite combat forces such as the Green Berets. These soldiers were supposed to be tough enough to fight anywhere at a moment's notice. They were, but that didn't mean they could control other countries. In the end, having a ready army and a belief that America could do anything led to no-win wars like Vietnam, and later, Iraq and Afghanistan.

American troops could go anywhere, but it was just a waste of lives to have them stay if the local government they supported couldn't win the backing of its own people.

## Early involvement in Vietnam

Perhaps the worst local anti-Communist government in a parade of anti-Communist losers supported by the United States was the corrupt Diem regime in South Vietnam. To support the Diem regime, Kennedy ordered increasing numbers of U.S. advisers to South Vietnam. By the time of his death, more than 15,000 U.S. troops were in South Vietnam, too many to advise but not enough to fight.

Kennedy's successor, President Lyndon B. Johnson, upped the ante to more than 500,000 troops, enough to fight, but not nearly enough to win against a more or less popular Communist revolution.

> **TIP**
>
> If the AP test has an essay question about Vietnam, it may be looking for trends in U.S. foreign involvement. The U.S. has had a hard time learning the same lesson it taught the British during America's own fight for independence: The very presence of a foreign army creates a cause for local rebels. Modern armies can go anywhere, but their weapons let them control only the ground they're standing on, not the minds of the people who live there.

## Kennedy's peacemaking initiative

Along with chest-beating confrontation, however, the U.S. under Kennedy also tried some peacemaking initiatives:

- **The Alliance for Progress (1961):** The Alliance for Progress was an ambitious attempt to offer Marshall Plan–like support to Latin American governments. It failed to transform the area because, unlike Europe, Latin America contained rich elites (including U.S. companies) unwilling to make room for progress by poorer citizens.

  Dictatorships took over 13 Latin American countries during the 1960s, and the *Alliance for Progress* was later forgotten under President Nixon. Only in the 1990s did Latin America see the rise of democratic governments able to remain in power despite the opposition of economic interests in their own countries and (sometimes) in the United States.

- **The Nuclear Test Ban Treaty (1963):** President Kennedy signed the first Nuclear Test Ban Treaty with the Soviet Union. This treaty stopped polluting bomb tests. A Comprehensive Nuclear Test Ban Treaty was signed much later, in 1996, after the dissolution of the Soviet Union, although several nations still don't go along with the agreement.

- **Early support for détente:** Kennedy pushed for a live-and-let-live approach to the Soviet Union and Communist China, a policy that would later be called *détente* (1975), a French word that means "relaxation of tensions." In another move for peace, Kennedy installed a hotline between the White House and the Soviet Kremlin, so that the leaders could talk directly to defuse dangerous confrontations.

# THE SUPREME COURT OF THE 1960S

Throughout the 1960s, the Supreme Court was active in the changes that brought about more American freedom and responsibility:

- **Engel v. Vitale (1962):** In this case, the court ruled that officials can't require prayers and Bible-reading in public schools because these activities may go against the beliefs of some of the students.

- **New York Times v. Sullivan (1964):** In this case, the court held that news media could be sued for libel only if they wrongly attacked a public official out of malice, thus completing a long chain of free-press decisions that went back to the Peter Zenger case before the American Revolution.

- **Griswold v. Connecticut (1965) and Roe v. Wade (1973):** With these cases, the court made birth control and abortion legal. *Row v. Wade* continues to be controversial but has withstood legal challenges to this day.

- ■ **Reynolds v. Sims (1964):** In this case, the court ordered that state legislatures regularly redraw their voting districts to reflect changes in population, thus taking power away from rural counties and giving it to the places where people actually lived. This *redistricting* can be subject to *gerrymandering* as politicians try to draw districts that will let them continue to hold power.

- ■ **Miranda v. Arizona (1966):** In this case, the court ordered police departments to read defendants their rights to remain silent and be represented by an attorney when they are arrested. Although controversial at the time, the concept of rights for suspects has now spread to much of the democratic world.

   Widespread quoting of the Miranda warning in police TV shows and movies has led people in other countries to demand to be read their rights when they're arrested. They sometimes find out the hard way that they don't have American rights yet, but what other countries see in the widespread U.S. media helps spread social ideas.

# THE ASSASSINATION OF JFK

President and Mrs. Kennedy were riding in a 1963 motorcade in Dallas when an assassin named Lee Harvey Oswald shot him in the head from an office building window.

Oswald was a 24-year-old mentally unbalanced former Marine who defected to the Soviet Union and later returned to the United States. He never stood trial for the assassination because he himself was shot by an enraged night club owner while in custody. President Kennedy was so respected and his death was so sudden that many people believed the shooting must have been a conspiracy to get rid of him.

After more than 40 years, during which hundreds of honest and intelligent people have devoted lifetimes' worth of research and scientific investigation to Kennedy's assassination, no credible proof of a conspiracy has ever surfaced. Although human nature impels people to look for a conspiracy to explain any major tragedy, sometimes the explanation is just that tragedy happens when scared or angry individuals think they can change history by killing a leader.

Although it's tempting to rely on conspiracy rumors to explain tragic events, it's up to people to make sad events meaningful by the work they do in memory of those who die. That's what Vice President Lyndon Johnson set out to do after he was sworn in as president. Johnson is discussed later in this chapter.

# THE HEIGHT OF THE CIVIL RIGHTS MOVEMENT

The fight for civil rights that started with Rosa Parks and the Montgomery bus boycott in the Eisenhower administration kept rolling with *sit-in demonstrations* (1960) (see Chapter 18). These efforts and more continued to challenge the segregation and discrimination that plagued America from the time of the Civil War.

Here are some key events of the Civil Rights struggle:

- ■ **Freedom Riders (1961):** Freedom Riders were civil rights activists who risked a trip on interstate buses into the segregated South to test the Supreme Court decision *Boynton v. Virginia* (1960), which made it illegal to discriminate on transportation that crossed state lines. Near the beginning of the Kennedy administration, buses of Freedom Riders were attacked in the South and riders beaten.

- **James Meredith's enrollment at the University of Mississippi:** Although Kennedy couldn't get the civil rights legislation he wanted through Congress, he used his personal clout to support black rights and voter registration. When Meredith, a 29-year-old African American air force veteran, faced violent mobs when he tried to register at the then-all-white University of Mississippi, Kennedy ordered the National Guard out to protect him.

- **MLK-led demonstrations n Birmingham:** Martin Luther King Jr. led a series of demonstrations in segregated Birmingham, Alabama, in the spring of 1963. After King and other peacefully demonstrating citizens were beaten and thrown in jail, thousands of students left school to join the protests. With the news full of pictures of children being blasted with high-pressure hoses and attacked by police dogs, the white leaders of Birmingham decided they'd better grant blacks some rights.

- **Desegregation at the University of Alabama:** A few weeks after King's Birmingham demonstrations, President Kennedy had to use troops again to move Alabama Governor George Wallace, who was personally blocking the door of the University of Alabama against two black students. That evening, Kennedy went on national television to talk about civil rights, a cause he said was "as old as the Scriptures" and "as clear as the American Constitution."

- **The murder of Medgar Evers:** The day following Kennedy's televised speech on civil rights, civil rights worker Medgar Evers was murdered in Mississippi.

- **The bombing of the Sixteenth Street Baptist Church:** A few months after Medgar Evers' murder, Ku Klux Klan members bombed the Sixteenth Street Baptist Church in Birmingham, Alabama, killing four young black girls.

- **Martin Luther King's "I Have a Dream" speech:** In August of 1963, Martin Luther King Jr. spoke to a peaceful demonstration of 200,000 black and white Americans in Washington, D.C.: "I have a dream that one day this nation will rise up and live out the true meaning of its creed: 'We hold these truths to be self-evident that all men are created equal.'"

## Separation versus integration

Both black and white people were beaten and killed in the South as they worked to register voters and integrate services. With the rise of the *Black Power* (1965) separatist movement in the mid-1960s and riots in black urban neighborhoods, whites became less interested in pushing for civil rights for blacks, who seemed to be pushing hard enough on their own. The fiery Black Muslim leader Malcolm X called for blacks to separate themselves from whites; he was assassinated by a black man from another faction of the Nation of Islam. Other separatist leaders included Black Panther Huey Newton and Student Nonviolent Coordinating Committee leader Stokely Carmichael.

Working for integration, not separation, was the National Association for the Advancement of Colored People (NAACP), chaired by Roy Wilkins. Latino farmworkers organized as well; Cesar Chavez founded the *United Farm Workers* (1972) in California.

**EXAMPLE**

**Question:** What was the Black Power movement?

**Answer:** The Black Power movement of the 1960s was some African Americans' rejection of integration in favor of black control over their own communities.

## Martin Luther King's legacy

In 1968, a white racist assassin, James Earl Ray, killed Martin Luther King Jr. King left a legacy of inspiration and solid progress that is now as much a part of American culture as freedom and independence.

In the time since King's death, black income, education, and community participation has risen steadily. In 2008, America elected Barack Obama as the first black president of the United States. After 200 years of slavery and another hundred years of racist discrimination, America still has miles to go, but Martin Luther King Jr. showed the way.

> **EXAMPLE**
>
> **Question:** What were the leading black organizations (and their leaders) of the civil rights movement?
>
> **Answer:** Important black civil rights organizations include the Southern Christian Leadership Conference (led by Martin Luther King Jr.), the Student Nonviolent Coordinating Committee (headed by Stokely Carmichael), the National Association for the Advancement of Colored People (chaired by Roy Wilkins), the Black Muslims (led by Malcolm X) and the Black Panthers (led by Huey Newton).

# LYNDON B. JOHNSON (LBJ)

Lyndon B. Johnson (LBJ) took the oath of office on a plane back to Washington while standing next to the wife of just-murdered President Kennedy. He had been only two cars behind in the motorcade when Kennedy was shot.

As soon as he could, President Johnson began to work to pass legislation. He told Congress that he knew no better way to "honor President Kennedy's memory than the earliest possible passage of the Civil Rights Bill for which he fought so long."

Over continuing Southern opposition, Congress passed the landmark *Civil Rights Act of 1964*. The act prohibited discrimination in public facilities, in government, and in employment, invalidating the Jim Crow laws in the South. Forced segregation of the races in schools, housing, or hiring became illegal. Opponents argued that the government couldn't legislate morality on the race issue; supporters countered that they didn't care what people thought in their minds as long as what they did was fair.

## Legislating for the Great Society

A year after Kennedy's assassination, Johnson ran for president against the conservative Republican Barry Goldwater. When Johnson pushed through the Civil Rights Act, he said (correctly) that it would cost the Democrats the votes of the South for a generation. Five states from the old South did vote for Goldwater, but except for his home state of Arizona, that was all Goldwater won; the rest of the country was for LBJ. Johnson's landslide helped sweep the Democrats to a two-to-one majority over the Republicans in both houses of Congress.

Johnson lacked Kennedy's charm, but he knew how to get things done; he may have been the most productive legislative president in U.S. history. When he was really rolling after his reelection, he got almost all the bills he wanted passed by Congress. These laws included the *Voting Rights Act of 1965*, which outlawed unfair qualifications tests that kept minorities from the polls, and the *Economic Opportunity Act of 1964*, which created programs to help poor people.

The road seemed open to creating what Johnson called the *Great Society* (1965). Great Society programs still in effect today include the *Job Corps* (1965), *Head Start* (1965), *Food Stamps* (1964), and the *Department of Housing and Urban Development (HUD)* (1965). These and other *War on Poverty* (1965) programs were designed to help lower the poverty rate in the United States. During the Great Depression, the poverty rate was 40 percent. When Johnson became president, it was 15 percent and dipped to 12 percent. Now with the Recession, it has risen again.

## Women's liberation

The 1960s saw a progressive tide that included a second wave of women's rights, often called *women's liberation*. Betty Friedan wrote *The Feminine Mystique* (1963) about unfulfilled women in households in the suburbs and helped found the *National Organization of Women* (NOW) in 1966.

An *Equal Rights Amendment* (1972) prohibiting discrimination on the basis of gender did not become law because it was ratified by only 35 of the minimum 38 states necessary to make it part of the Constitution.

 EXAMPLE

**Question:** What was the second wave of women's liberation?

**Answer:** The second wave focused on equal rights for women in the workplace and home and was supported by author Betty Friedan and the National Organization of Women (NOW).

## Medicare, Medicaid, and the 24th Amendment

The most extensive benefit program passed by President Johnson was the *Medicare Program* (1965), which pays for health care for older people, and the *Medicaid Program* (1965), which covers health care for poor people. These programs faced diehard opposition from both Republicans and the American Medical Association, but Johnson maneuvered around the foes of government-sponsored medical care to bring coverage to millions of people. This was also part of Johnson's Great Society plan.

 EXAMPLE

**Question:** What was LBJ's Great Society plan?

**Answer:** A set of training and social assistance programs designed to lower the poverty rate in the U.S.

Johnson appointed the first black Supreme Court justice and the first black Cabinet member. He guided the ratification of the *Twenty-fourth Amendment* (1964), which banned the use of a poll tax to limit voting in federal elections. The *Immigration and Nationality Act* (1965) abolished the national origins qualifications for immigrants and greatly increased the number of new Americans admitted to the country.

# THE VIETNAM WAR

As President Johnson was winning battles to control domestic legislation, he faced great difficulty in the battles to control Vietnam. Kennedy had limited U.S. involvement to a few thousand so-called advisers, but all the advice in the world couldn't get the corrupt South Vietnamese regime to defeat a dedicated group of South Vietnamese Communist rebels (called the Viet Cong by the U.S.) and their North Vietnamese allies.

Just before the 1964 election (which Johnson won in part by playing a peacemaker), the U.S. Navy had traded a few shots with North Vietnamese patrol boats when the U.S. ships pushed too close to the North Vietnamese shore. This *Gulf of Tonkin* (1964) incident led Congress to pass the *Gulf of Tonkin Resolution* (1964), authorizing the use of direct American force in Vietnam. When the Vietnamese rebels attacked an American adviser base after the elections, Johnson started a major bombing campaign and greatly increased U.S. forces in Vietnam.

By the end of 1965, almost 200,000 U.S. troops were in Vietnam, and Johnson was in a major fight with the Communist rebels. During Johnson's presidency, the troop levels grew: 200,000 became 300,000, which grew to 400,000 and finally 500,000 soldiers. It always seemed like just a few more troops ought to be enough to win, but it never was.

**EXAMPLE**

**Question:** What was the Gulf of Tonkin resolution?

**Answer:** In response to a minor naval confrontation, LBJ got Congress to authorize the use of direct U.S. force in Vietnam.

## Hard fighting in Vietnam

The battle in Vietnam was like a war between an elephant and a fly: The fly couldn't kill the elephant, but the elephant couldn't fly. American soldiers had a hard time fighting with no front line, in steaming jungles where the enemy could be anywhere. A young man in street clothes could shoot you in the back and then hide in a group of civilians.

Vietnamese farmers and their wives and kids were in the middle of the war — millions of them got killed, both by the rebels and by the U.S. Desperate to stop the Viet Cong, the U.S. dropped thousands of tons of bombs, some with chemicals to kill the trees the Vietnamese insurgents hid under.

## War protests

With the draft hanging over their heads, hundreds of thousands of students marched in protest demonstrations against the war. Demonstrators showed up wherever President Johnson tried to speak, chanting "Hey, hey, LBJ, how many kids did you kill today?" They ignored his attempts to change the subject to the War on Poverty and instead shouted against the real war in Vietnam that was killing the people of their generation at a rate of more than 20 deaths a day.

LBJ's Vietnam was eating up LBJ's Great Society. In violation of the law, Johnson used the CIA and the FBI to spy on antiwar protestors.

**EXAMPLE**

**Question:** How did the war in Vietnam affect LBJ's domestic Great Society program?

**Answer:** By taking money and political support, the war made Johnson's Great Society program less effective.

## The Tet offensive

Believers in the war kept saying that they could see the light at the end of the tunnel; they believed that the U.S. had almost won. The light at the end of the tunnel went out during the huge Vietnamese Tet offensive in early 1968.

Although the U.S. was hoping that the rebels were almost beaten, the Communists launched a simultaneous attack on most major South Vietnamese cities beginning during the Vietnamese New Year's holiday called Tet. The rebels penetrated the South Vietnamese capital of Saigon; a few of them even made it to the grounds of the U.S. embassy.

Although the rebels were pushed back and suffered heavy losses, the very fact that they could mount such a wide attack destroyed the confidence of both the American people and their politicians, including President Johnson. The long road to a negotiated peace began.

**EXAMPLE**

**Question:** What was the Tet offensive?

**Answer:** Widespread rebel attacks during the Vietnamese New Year that led to increased U.S. opposition to the war.

# RICHARD NIXON

With the U.S. population turning against the war, LBJ knew he stood little chance of reelection. Even though he had won by a huge landslide in 1964 and had passed the most legislation, he hardly beat an obscure challenger from his own party in an early primary.

What was worse, he was finally opposed by Robert Kennedy, the younger brother of the now-revered President Kennedy. In a surprise announcement, LBJ declared he wouldn't run again. Vietnam had ruined him. Robert Kennedy swept the primaries but was assassinated by an Arab immigrant only a month after Martin Luther King died. (As with the JFK assassination, no real evidence of a conspiracy in the second Kennedy killing has ever come to light.)

In the midst of demonstrations and police violence a few weeks later, the Democrats nominated Johnson's loyal vice president Hubert Humphrey. With a Southern segregationist running as a third-party candidate, Humphrey narrowly lost the presidential election to Republican former vice president Richard Nixon, who was elected on the promise that he was the experienced one who could bring an honorable peace both to Vietnam and to the demonstration-thronged streets of America.

## The established order versus the counterculture

The U.S. was deeply divided between the established order and a counterculture of mostly younger people who opposed the war and supported a civil rights revolution to liberate women, blacks, and other minorities. A social goal of the movement was to expand free personal behavior and expression. The counterculture also included a small violent fringe of Black Panthers, who advocated armed defense of African American interests, and mostly white radical Weathermen, who were willing to be violent because they thought the times demanded force. The Weathermen took their name from the words of a Bob Dylan song: "You don't need a weatherman to tell which way the wind blows . . ." Most of the counterculture, however, was a large peaceful tribe of flower-wearing and mind-expanding hippies.

>  **TIP**
>
> The U.S. actually has an unbroken and under-reported tradition of small group opposition to established power that limits any of the rights outlined in the Declaration of Independence. During the 1960s and '70s, the opposition got bigger; a lot of changes that had been in the works for hundreds of years came to the forefront. After much conflict, the social revolutionaries settled down to work for a new order that was freer than the old.

During the height of the demonstrations, Richard Nixon's vice president, Spiro Agnew, called the youthful protestors "nattering nabobs of negativism." Several of the young people cut off their easily identified long hair and sent it to Agnew in a pillow, neatly embroidered with the words "Now we could be anywhere."

## The expansion of the war into Cambodia

The rapid economic growth of the 1950s slowed in the late 1960s and throughout the 1970s. As the U.S. spent more money on military campaigns, it had less to invest in business growth and social programs. More research and development went into bombs, not cars and other consumer products. Unburdened with big military expenses, the World War II losers Japan and Germany became economic winners by producing products people wanted to buy. The U.S. economy slid into inflation and slow growth, called *stagflation*.

Richard Nixon said he would end the war in Vietnam, but he didn't. As the war dragged on and deaths mounted, antiwar demonstrations increased. Frustrated young soldiers in Vietnam became more disorderly, sometimes attacking their own officers. The *Pentagon Papers* (1971) leaked to the press showed 20 years of American secrets. Desperate to win, Nixon expanded the war to neighboring Cambodia.

In the United States, hard-pressed National Guard troops killed four student demonstrators at Kent State University in 1970; police got into shootouts with black nationalists. Young war protestors got some official reprieve as military draft calls were reduced, and the *Twenty-sixth Amendment* (1971) allowed young people to vote starting at age eighteen.

>  **EXAMPLE**
>
> **Question:** What happened at Kent State University?
>
> **Answer:** Protesting students were shot by the National Guard in 1970.

# China and the SALT talks

President Nixon's 20 years of experience in international affairs finally began to pay off with visits to China and the Soviet Union. Nixon normalized previously frozen U.S. relations with China and set the stage for further *détente,* or discussion. Nixon arranged the sale of much-needed American food to the U.S.S.R. and started U.S.-Soviet *SALT (Strategic Arms Limitation Talks)* (1972) that limited missile deployment.

EXAMPLE

**Question:** What are some examples of *détente* in Nixon's foreign relations policies?

**Answer:** Nixon reestablished relations with China, sold food to the Soviet Union, and initiated the SALT talks.

# Nixon's social programs

Conservative Nixon was surprisingly liberal on domestic social programs. He expanded welfare, Medicaid, and Food Stamps, and created a new *Supplemental Security Income (SSI)* program (1974) to help the disabled. In addition, he indexed Social Security payments to rise with inflation. As the U.S. moved toward being a modern welfare state, the portion of the national budget tied up in entitlement programs to pay for benefits rose to become larger than the money spent of the military.

Nixon supported affirmative action for the hiring of minorities but opposed busing to achieve racial balance in schools. He actively managed the economy by briefly imposing a wage and price freeze and by taking the U.S. off the gold exchange standard.

Perhaps most important in the long run, Nixon established the *Environmental Protection Agency* (1970) to attempt to clean up damage to the natural world. The need for urgent action was first made clear by author Rachel Carson in the book *Silent Spring* (1962), which warned that pesticides and pollution were poisoning song birds and other animals. The *Clean Air Act* (1970) and the *Endangered Species Act* (1973) began to set environmental standards for the country.

# Pulling out of Vietnam

Nixon, who had managed to get 95 percent of the troops out of Vietnam, won reelection in a landslide over the Democratic antiwar candidate George McGovern. He ended the war with a face-saving peace treaty in 1973; by 1975 the Communists had overrun the South Vietnamese government supported by the United States.

A murderous Communist tyrant called Pol Pot seized power during the postwar instability in nearby Cambodia and ended up killing a quarter of his own people. He was finally stopped by the very Communists the U.S. had been fighting.

EXAMPLE

**Question:** Who ended active U.S. participation in the war in Vietnam?

**Answer:** President Richard Nixon signed a treaty and withdrew U.S. troops.

The controversy over the war led to the *War Powers Act* (1973), which limited the president's ability to send troops into combat without Congressional approval. If the long war with its 56,000 American and millions of Vietnamese deaths proved anything, it showed Communists that the U.S. was willing to fight and die to oppose Communist beliefs. Twenty years later, militant Communism was all but gone from the world.

## Watergate

Richard Nixon got caught in political tricks that cost him his job only months after a landslide reelection when it was discovered that, back In 1972, burglars hired by the president's associates had broken into a local Democratic office in the *Watergate* apartment complex in Washington. A long investigation proved that Nixon had been involved in covering this up and in a number of other illegal actions against political opponents.

Meanwhile, Vice President Spiro Agnew was forced to resign in 1973 after being caught taking bribes. When Agnew went off to repay some of the money he stole, the *Twenty-fifth Amendment* (1967) handily provided for a replacement vice president. Congress gave the deeply-in-trouble Nixon only one choice: a well-liked Congressman named Gerald Ford. Ford would assume the presidency when Nixon, faced with impeachment, resigned it in 1974.

# GERALD FORD

Gerald Ford had been a congressman for 25 years without ticking people off or writing any legislation. Ford barely had time to warm up his vice president's chair before he became president upon Nixon's resignation.

Ford pardoned the departing Nixon, which made him almost as unpopular as Tricky Dick Nixon himself. He also signed the Helsinki Accords, marking a move toward *détente* in the Cold War, and supported women's rights and education for handicapped children. Despite President Ford's support, the proposed Equal Rights Amendment to the Constitution that would have legally prohibited discrimination against women fell three states short of passing.

Ford stood by without intervening as South Vietnam finally fell to the Communists; eventually half a million Vietnamese would escape to live in the U.S. Even though he was the sitting president, Ford barely won re-nomination in 1976.

During the Ford era, Congress passed *Title IX* (1972), making colleges give money to support women as well as men in sports. In *Milliken v. Bradley* (1974), the Supreme Court put a cap on the very school integration they had started 30 years before by holding that students couldn't be bused across school district lines to meet integration goals.

A few years later, in *University of California v. Bakke* (1978), the court found that universities can't have separate, easier admissions programs for minorities; race and underprivileged status can be a factor but not the only factor for getting into school.

# JIMMY CARTER

Jimmy Carter won the presidency in America's bicentennial year of 1976 by promising to be a good and honest leader. He may have been too good. Carter was a peanut farmer who had served a term as governor of Georgia. With no Washington political experience, he ruffled the feathers of congressmen in both parties used to feathering their own nests.

Carter tried to get America to cut down on its energy gulping habit by turning the thermostat down in federal buildings and even requesting a ban on Christmas lights. He signed the *SALT II* (1979) arms limitation treaty and patched up Social Security. Carter brokered a peace treaty between Israel and Egypt in the *Camp David Agreement* (1978). Putting human rights at the forefront of American policy, Carter began to withdraw support for brutal dictators, even if they were friendly to the U.S. The Soviet invasion of Afghanistan in late 1979 led to an American boycott of the 1980 Olympics in Moscow.

## The Iranian hostage crisis

One repressive guy Carter continued to support came back to haunt him. The U.S.-backed Shah of Iran was overthrown by Muslim fundamentalists, who seized the U.S. embassy and held its staff in the *Iranian Hostage Crisis* (1980) for over a year. Faced with an unhappy American public, Carter decided to tell the truth: "We've learned that piling up material goods cannot fill the emptiness of lives which have no confidence or purpose." That made Americans feel bad; they weren't willing to stop piling up the goods just yet.

## Mounting problems

The mood of the people wasn't improved when the *Three Mile Island* (1979) nuclear power plant experienced a near meltdown, and opposition to nuclear power increased. Carter's bad luck got worse when a swimming rabbit actually attacked him while he was out fishing. Americans were beginning to feel like maybe a tough-guy action hero would be a better choice than their good-guy President Carter.

> **EXAMPLE**
>
> **Question:** What was the result of trouble at Three Mile Island?
>
> **Answer:** Opposition increased to the development of nuclear power plants.

Carter lost the 1980 election to Ronald Reagan, a former actor who did a much better job looking the part of a president than Jimmy Carter (more on that in Chapter 20). Jimmy Carter went on to win the Nobel Peace Prize, working tirelessly for peace and human rights, often irritating politicians but impressing ordinary people. In the 1980s, America took a turn toward conservative politics and an uncertain future as world leader.

# 20

# Leading in the Modern World: 1980–The Present

The U.S. took a turn to the right under Ronald Reagan in the 1980s. Reagan saw the end of the Cold War with a lot of help from eastern European and Russian people who were tired of Communism. He also instituted a tax shift that let the rich get a lot richer and the middle class get a little poorer. Despite his talk against government, Reagan spent so much money on the military that, by the end of his term, he had tripled the debt of the country. But by energetically following the policy of containment of Communism started under Democratic President Truman after World War II and followed by every president, Republican or Democrat, since, Reagan got the honor of presiding over the end of the Cold War. The presidents who came after him got the dubious honor of facing a rising national debt.

As the U.S. sailed toward the 21st century, it seemed for a while that the entire world just wanted to live free and easy like the Americans they saw in movies. Republican presidents George Bush and George W. Bush bookended Democratic president Bill Clinton's two terms. Mostly the policy was stay-the-course moderation. Barack Obama brought active leadership as the country's first black president to a time of deep recession.

When the World Trade Center buildings came crashing to the ground on September 11, 2001 (9/11), Americans discovered that the America-is-cool sentiment wasn't exactly unanimous. Some people — including both home-grown bombers and foreign terrorists — hated the American lifestyle, attitude, and foreign policy so much they were ready to explode themselves and a bunch of innocent people to get even.

**TIP**

Although the AP U.S. History exam has few questions on modern times, an understanding of how themes and topics apply to recent issues helps show good analysis in essay writing.

# RONALD REAGAN AND REAGANOMICS

All the hippy-dippy demonstrating, impeachment, moralizing, and rabbit attacks of the 1970s had left Americans longing for a simpler life. But mostly they hated the stagflation and a struggling economy. They found their leader in Ronald Reagan, who handily defeated Jimmy Carter in the 1980 presidential election.

Reagan believed in small government and lower taxes. He was a champion of the *antis*: Reagan was anti-gay, anti-abortion, anti-feminism, and especially anti-special programs to help minorities. He was supported by right-wing religious people who called themselves the *Moral Majority* (1980) or the Religious Right and who believed that their Christianity was right and that anyone who believed differently was a tool of the devil.

In a strange way, Reagan's appeal was a reverse copy of FDR's crusade for the so-called forgotten man; Ronald Reagan defended hardworking regular people that modern society seemed to have forgotten. The only difference was that Reagan defended their feelings, and FDR defended their income. Reagan's tax breaks ended up helping the rich far more than the poor.

## New Conservative ideas

In addition to religious and free market conservatives, Ronald Reagan had the support of a small group of writers, pundits, and thinkers who called themselves new conservatives or *neo-conservatives* (*neocons*, for short) (1985).

## Trickle-down economics

The neocons believed in the counterintuitive proposition that, if Reagan cut taxes, tax income to the government would actually rise because people would have more money to spend and the economy would grow. This idea was called *trickle down economics*. It didn't work too well for Reagan; he managed to pass a large tax decrease, but the economy just sputtered along during much of his administration. When things did get better late in his administration, rising income for people with money went along with less money for the poor. The stock market was subject to more ups and downs. While inflation went down, the federal debt went up almost 300 percent under Reagan.

**TIP**

> Tax policy alone isn't the key to economic growth. High-tax Europe and Japan grew rapidly in the late 20th century. The low-tax United States slipped into the Great Depression in the 1920s and the Great Recession in 2008 under Republican presidents. How much money people have isn't the only issue — how people and the government choose to spend money controls the economy.

## Aggressive military intervention

Neocons also believed that aggressive military intervention would increase America's power in the world. They supported a large military buildup (difficult to do with lower tax revenues) and confrontation with Communists around the world.

Military power seemed to work best when it was restrained; America's potential for destruction helped force the U.S.S.R. to send Communism into a timely grave. When Reagan and Bush actually unleashed U.S. military might, the results were often not what was intended. The U.S. intervention in Lebanon under Reagan ended with Marines being bombed in their barracks (1983), and the large-scale invasions of Iraq and Afghanistan begun under the second President George Bush had mixed results.

# Reaganomics

As far as domestic government policy goes, Reagan was against it, saying that "Government is not the solution to our problem. Government is the problem." Although he didn't succeed in making the federal government much smaller, he did what he could to turn back the clock on government regulations.

Reagan's first Secretary of the Interior eased environmental regulations on polluting industries and favored opening wilderness areas and shorelines for oil and gas leases. When air-traffic controllers went on strike, Reagan fired them.

His economic policies were called *Reaganomics* (1982) or *supply-side economics*; less government was supposed to mean more growth in the economy and, almost magically, more tax revenue. Tax cuts under Reaganomics mostly succeeded in making more money for the wealthy. The economy actually grew at a slower rate during the Reagan administration than the post-World War II average. To the credit of Reagan's administration, the interest rate policy of the economists he appointed helped bring inflation, which had soared under Nixon and Carter, back under control. Reagan also won applause by appointing the first woman to the Supreme Court.

**EXAMPLE**

> **Question:** What was the most noticeable effect of Reaganomics?

> **Answer:** It got more money for rich people.

## A growing trade deficit

During the Reagan administration, the U.S. went heavily into debt and ran an international trade deficit of billions of dollars a year. Neither of these trends has stopped since the Reagan period; addiction to foreign oil and imported consumer products has made the U.S. spend far more overseas than it takes in from exports.

This discrepancy is called the *balance of payments* (1986) problem. The U.S., which in the first half of the 20th century was the master of international business, became the world's largest debtor nation beginning in the 1980s.

# COMMUNISM FADES

Reagan took an aggressive stance against Communism, which he called "the evil empire." He built up American military might and announced his intention to deploy a *Strategic Defense Initiative* (1983), better known as Star Wars, to shoot down Soviet missiles before they could get to the United States.

This plan apparently impressed the Soviets more than it did U.S. scientists; Star Wars was cited as one of the reasons the Soviet Union gave up the military race with the United States and began to dismantle their Communist economic system. The U.S. military was never actually able to deploy a large-scale missile defense system, but the bluff worked.

Before the fall of Communism in the U.S.S.R, tensions increased, sometimes dangerously. The Soviets clamped down on a freedom movement, sponsored by labor unions, called *Solidarity* (1981) in the government of Poland which they controlled. The U.S. responded with tough words and an economic embargo. When the U.S.S.R. shot down a South Korean passenger plane that had strayed into Soviet airspace in 1983, Reagan called it an act of barbarism. By the end of 1983, all arms-control negotiations had broken down. The Soviet Union almost launched nuclear weapons against the U.S. when they briefly mistook a Western military exercise for a nuclear attack. The Soviets also boycotted the 1984 Olympic Games held in Los Angeles. The Cold War was reaching the freezing point.

## The U.S. flexes its military muscles

In the 1980s, Iran and Iraq were fighting a war that the United States didn't mind watching; America had little love for the leaders of either country. The U.S. supplied arms to Iraq in the early 1980s as payback against Iran for holding American embassy people hostage up to the first hour of the Reagan administration. This arms deal was one reason that Iran may have been behind the 1983 Marine barracks bombing in Lebanon.

In 1983, Reagan sent troops into Lebanon to try to calm endless Middle East conflicts. More than 200 Marines died when an Arab extremist suicide bomber blew up their barracks. U.S. troops, who never had a clear mission to begin with, withdrew a few months later.

In the same month, Reagan sent a heavily armed invasion party to the tiny Caribbean island of Grenada to wipe out some Communist troublemakers. This military incursion succeeded in restoring democratic government in a move that would have made Teddy Roosevelt proud.

Reagan cruised to reelection against a Democratic ticket that included, for the first time in history, a woman as vice presidential nominee.

## Mikhail Gorbachev

The Soviet Union had a new leader in 1985: Mikhail Gorbachev promised *glasnost* and *perestroika* (1986), which mean openness and restructuring. Partly to be able to compete more effectively with the West, the Soviets began to shrink their military spending and concentrate on long-overdue civilian improvements.

In 1987, Ronald Reagan stood in front of the Berlin Wall, which divided East and West Berlin, and said, "General Secretary Gorbachev, if you seek peace . . . open this gate. Mr. Gorbachev, tear down this wall!" Later that year, the two leaders signed the *INF Treaty* (1987) banning all intermediate-range nuclear weapons from Europe. Two years later, the Berlin Wall came tumbling down.

## Iran-Contra and other problems

In an illegal and morally challenged international trick, Reagan administration officials later agreed (1985) to sell arms to the desperate Iranians in return for secret payments that these officials channeled to anti-Communist rebel forces in Nicaragua that Congress had officially rejected American aid to.

In making their secret deal, the Reagan administration officials weren't only helping a regime that had kidnapped Americans; they were also acting against the expressed direction of Congress. This kind of action is grounds on which Congress can impeach a president. Reagan pleaded ignorance of the plot; his Secretary of Defense and several other officials were charged with criminal behavior. An investigation found that Reagan knew or should have known about the bad deal.

Other holes appeared in the ethical shell of the administration elected with the support of the Moral Majority. Environmental Protection Agency officials resigned in disgrace after they misused staff and gave special deals to polluters. Three of Reagan's cabinet members, including the attorney general, were investigated for lying and stealing; Reagan's personal White House aide was convicted of perjury.

His last days in office were clouded by a stock market crash, but he remained sunny and optimistic. When he died in the early 21st century, his burial site was inscribed with his own words: "I know in my heart that man is good. That what is right will always eventually triumph. And there's purpose and worth to each and every life."

# GEORGE H.W. BUSH

George Herbert Walker Bush came as close as you can to inheriting the presidency. His grandpa was a presidential advisor to Hoover, and his dad was a U.S. Senator. He himself already had a White House office as vice president to Ronald Reagan.

Even though Bush had once called Reaganomics "voodoo economics," he was happy enough being Reagan's vice president and was easily elected president in 1988 against the hapless Democrat Michael Dukakis. Although Bush the elder was a former representative to China and head of the CIA, he stood by without even proposing economic sanctions in 1989 when Chinese tanks crushed democracy demonstrations in Beijing's Tiananmen Square. Democracy had more luck in Europe.

## The fall of the Soviet Union

In 1989, the former Soviet puppet governments in Eastern Europe fell, as did the Berlin Wall. Eastern European nations were now free to govern themselves. What had been the Soviet Union split into the Commonwealth of Independent States, the largest of which was Russia. A hero for helping the Communist empire open toward freedom, Mikhail Gorbachev fought off a coup attempt from party hardliners and then was dismissed, leaving behind a small world of independent nations struggling toward democracy.

Bush signed the *START II Treaty* (1993) with Russia, pledging both nations to reduce their long-range nuclear weapons by two-thirds. The U.S. military scaled back with the end of the Cold War.

In additional good news, Nelson Mandela gained freedom from prison and became president of a democratic interracial South Africa. Free elections in Nicaragua ousted the leftist government there without the necessity of the Iran-Contra plotting of the Reagan administration. The U.S. tossed a drug-lord dictator of Panama out by force.

## Operation Desert Storm

Saddam Hussein, the leader of Iraq, invaded the neighboring oil-rich country of Kuwait in 1990. Working through the United Nations, President Bush skillfully put together a coalition of the United States and 28 other nations to kick Saddam out. Although the U.S. contributed more than half a million troops, the other nations added 250,000 more on their own.

Operation Desert Storm tore through Iraqi forces like a hurricane; U.S. and coalition forces rolled over Hussein's army in four days. Kuwait was free; the only problem — and a big one — was that Saddam Hussein was left in power in his capital of Baghdad.

## Legislation under the elder Bush

On the domestic front, Bush signed the *Americans with Disabilities Act (ADA)* (1990), which prohibited discrimination against the one in seven people who have some form of physical or mental handicap. President Bush also appointed a conservative African American to the Supreme Court.

Bush grudgingly accepted some improvements in environmental water usage and civil rights, but the only controversial legislation he proposed was the tax increase that cost him the presidency.

Campaigning in 1988, Bush had dramatically said, "Read my lips: No new taxes." Faced with huge budget deficits, he was forced to go back on his word and raise taxes in 1990. The Democrats wouldn't let people forget that mistake.

# MODERN DEMOCRACY WITH BILL CLINTON

The Democrats hadn't elected a two-term president since World War II, but they had a charming centrist in William Jefferson Clinton. Bill Clinton defeated Bush's reelection bid by emphasizing the paycheck of the average American, which had actually grown smaller during the Bush administration. A sign in Clinton's headquarters said, "It's the economy, stupid."

Clinton ran a positive campaign based on pro-growth, strong defense, and anti-crime platforms that almost sounded like the Republicans. He promised to overhaul the creaky welfare and health care systems. He admitted (as indirectly as possible) to "causing pain" in his marriage and smoking marijuana. He was the perfect candidate for the baby boom generation, which by then made up most of the U.S. voting population.

## The new rainbow America

While Clinton won the presidency, the nation was undergoing a radical change in elected officials. The new House of Representatives in 1993 included 1 American Indian, 7 Asian Americans, 19 Hispanic Americans, and 39 African Americans; 48 of the representatives were women. That was more women and minorities than had ever been elected before, and their numbers continued to grow into the 21st century.

At the beginning of the Clinton administration, the nation wasn't willing to accept just how broad the rainbow was becoming; a bid by Clinton to allow homosexuals to serve openly in the armed forces was rejected for a don't-ask-don't-tell halfway measure.

Clinton appointed his wife Hillary to come up with a national health plan. Industries making big money off a piecemeal non-system that left one out of six Americans with no insurance managed to convince people that Hillary's reform proposals were scary. Health care reform took a back seat until the 21st century.

Although Republicans often accuse Democrats of being tax-and-spend crazies, Clinton managed to turn the huge budget deficits run up by 12 years of Republican administrations into modest budget surpluses. He passed anti-crime bills that also contained some gun control provisions.

## Battling extremism

Clinton was just in time to get tough on crime. In 1993, Muslim extremists took their first shot at the World Trade Center in New York with a bomb that killed 6 people. A couple of years later, home-grown American terrorist Timothy McVeigh blew up 168 people along with the federal building in Oklahoma City. Shootouts with extremists and in schools shocked the nation. Although the hundreds of deaths involved in these events were better than the thousands that happen in a war, domestic violence frightened Americans all the more for the very reason that overall violence has been declining in the world for at least 200 years.

People upset with the United States government were often members of the Moral Majority, who saw the country being swept by the devil's work of abortion, drugs, welfare, and religious apathy. They joined a Republican counterattack called the *Contract with America* (1994), which promised welfare and budget reform. The Republicans swept to victory, controlling both the House and the Senate for the first time in 40 years.

## Reforming welfare

When Republicans gained control of both the House and the Senate, Bill Clinton got to see what it had felt like to be a president with an opposing Congress, something that Republican presidents had put up with for years. Clinton survived by working with the Republicans; after all, he was a moderate Democrat. Clinton signed the *Welfare Reform Bill* (1996). Over the wails of old-school

Democrats, the bill forced welfare recipients to work when they could and restricted benefits for new immigrants. Despite angry opposition from social conservatives and Republicans, Clinton had most of the country with him when he breezed to reelection in 1996.

## Politics of the possible

Clinton was unable to expand health care coverage, but he added loans for college students and modest tax breaks for poor people and raised the minimum wage. His greatest political advantage was a robust U.S. economy that enjoyed the longest period of sustained growth in American history. Clinton supported international trade with the *North American Free Trade Agreement (NAFTA)* (1993) and the *World Trade Organization (WTO)* (1994); these agreements made exporting American manufacturing jobs easier but brought down the cost of goods in the United States to bargain levels. Clinton fought against tobacco and guns, both of which caused far more deaths in the U.S. than terrorism.

In international affairs, Clinton intervened without getting America stuck in any big wars. He failed to offer effective help when millions of people died in tribal violence in Africa, but he sent in troops to stabilize Haiti and to stop years of ethnic cleansing in the former Yugoslavia. Clinton took some missile shots at terrorists in Afghanistan and Sudan, but limited U.S. involvement in the Middle East to the ever-elusive goal of encouraging peace talks between Israel and its Palestinian neighbors.

## Personal politics

Like most presidents, Clinton's administration wasn't without controversy. He staunchly denied having an affair with a 20-something White House intern, but DNA evidence later forced him to backpedal. The Republican-controlled Congress brought Clinton up on impeachment charges for lying to a grand jury about his involvement, invoking that extreme Constitutional mechanism for only the second time in U.S. history.

The Republicans clearly took it more seriously than the American people; the Democrats actually gained seats in Congress during the run-up to the Congressional trial. Impeachment requires a two-thirds vote to pass; Clinton's charges couldn't even get a majority vote. Clinton's wife, Hillary, said that ongoing investigations of the Clintons during most of their time in the White House were a right-wing tactic to stall social legislation. After years of public investigation, the Clintons were never convicted of anything, and Clinton left office with the highest approval ratings of any post-World War II president.

Clinton held off Republican attacks on most social programs and modestly improved the lives of regular people by protecting wilderness land, hiring new teachers, and increasing opportunities for higher education through grants and loans. The economy offered nearly full employment, and real income for working people crept up after decades of inflation-adjusted doldrums. As he was leaving office, the issue of global warming was heating up, and Clinton's vice president, Al Gore, promised to do something about it if only he could get elected president.

# GEORGE W. BUSH

As the world faces the threats of climate change, it's tempting to think what would have happened if an environmentalist had won the most votes in the 2000 presidential election. But, wait a minute; Al Gore did win the most votes. He just didn't win the election because of a fluke in the way the Constitution structures the presidential election: indirect selection through an electoral college.

Due to the state-by-state, winner-takes-all *Electoral College,* a candidate who narrowly wins more states can win with a minority of the votes. You can't get any narrower than George W. Bush's election in Florida: He won by 500 votes out of 5 million. Voting along party lines, the Supreme Court stopped the Florida recounts, and Bush was declared the winner of the election.

Ironically enough, under the recount rules Gore initially requested, Bush would have won, and under the rules Bush requested, Gore would have won. The election was that close. In a further irony, Ralph Nader's environmentalist Green Party bid had siphoned off enough votes to deny environmentalist Gore a clear victory.

## Texas governor to U.S. President

George Bush grew up around the White House while his dad was Reagan's vice president and then a one-term president on his own. Young Bush had been a popular governor of Texas and cultivated a close relationship with Moral Majority Christians, based on his own story of being born again to true religion after a wild youth.

Without trying to turn the clock back on New Deal social reforms, Bush campaigned on social issues: he was against abortion and in favor of business growth. His faith-based social services distributed billions of dollars through Christian religious organizations that were supposed to provide social help, not religious preaching, to stay clear of the First Amendment's prohibition of the establishment of a government-supported religion.

## Increasing economic problems

If the key to being president is really, as Clinton felt, about "the economy, stupid," then the Bush administration could be judged on its economic numbers. The *gross domestic product (GDP,* the value of the output of goods and services produced within the nation's borders) grew at an average annual rate considerably slower than the average for the post-World War II period. Unemployment stayed low. Budget deficits rose rapidly, a change from the budget surplus in the last year of the Clinton administration.

The national debt went up by trillions of dollars during Bush's presidency, adding more than a third to the burden future generations would have to pay off. With the low cost of imported manufactured goods, living was easy for most Americans, but the bulk of income gains went to people earning more than $250,000 a year.

## Health care and children: Hot-button issues

President Bush signed the *No Child Left Behind Act* (2001), which improved educational standards but failed to provide much funding for schools. He vetoed the expansion of the *State Children's Health Insurance Program* (SCHIP), which would have expanded health care for poor children, because he said he was against socialized medicine.

He may not have supported children's health, but Bush took a turn toward government health care for older people when he signed the *Medicare Prescription Drug Improvement and Modernization Act* (2003), which added prescription drug coverage to Medicare (though people pay extra for it).

Bush also vetoed a bill that would have allowed for stem cell research to find cures for disease since some religious conservatives opposed the research.

# Climate change

Upon arriving in office in 2001, Bush withdrew United States support for the Kyoto Protocol, an amendment to the United Nations Convention on Climate Change trying to control global warming; as a major world polluter, the U.S. was the only leading country not to sign. Bush administration officials censored the reports of government officials on global warming, and Bush said he didn't take action on the problem because of "debate over whether it's man-made or naturally caused."

Bush did set aside the Northwestern Hawaiian Islands as a national monument, creating the largest marine reserve in the world. Reserve or not, due to climate change and pollution on which there had been no action, the beautiful coral reef and tropical fish were slowly dying all around the world.

# Hurricane Katrina

One of the worst natural disasters in U.S. history, Hurricane Katrina, struck early in Bush's second term. The storm destroyed much of the city of New Orleans and the surrounding north-central Gulf Coast of the United States. Many thought Bush was slow in getting aid to the region; his director of emergency management eventually resigned. To his credit, Bush took full responsibility for the problems.

# The terrorist attacks on 9/11

After his minority election, Bush wasn't very popular, but the country came together to back him after the 9/11 terrorist attacks on the World Trade Towers and the Pentagon in Washington. These attacks killed over 2,800 people, a higher death toll than at Pearl Harbor. As Bush stood in the smoking ruins of the twin towers, once the world's tallest buildings, promising justice and protection, over 90 percent of the American people said they approved of his actions.

After the 9/11 attacks by extremist Muslims in Al Qaeda, in which hijacked planes destroyed the twin 110-story World Trade Center buildings in New York and damaged the Pentagon in Washington, Bush condemned Osama bin Laden and his organization *Al Qaeda* (2001) (which means "the base"). Bush announced that the United States would attack other countries (even though they weren't directly threatening the U.S.) if those countries harbored terrorists.

President Bush gave the Taliban regime in Afghanistan, where bin Laden was operating, a warning to "hand over the terrorists, or . . . share in their fate." Bush announced a global War on Terrorism, and after the Afghan Taliban regime wasn't forthcoming with Osama bin Laden, he ordered an invasion of Afghanistan to overthrow the Taliban regime.

In 2003, he also invaded Iraq, whose connection to 9/11 was vague at best. Unlike his father's 1991 Iraq war, this time only a few thousand outside troops (mostly British and Australian) joined the largely American effort as the U.S. Army pushed into Iraq. The U.S. military was bogged down for years in both Iraq and Afghanistan in lengthy, often fruitless attempts at "nation-building." With chances for a clear victory dwindling, the American public got tired of the news of bombs and casualties.

Following the 9/11 attacks, Bush signed an executive order authorizing wiretaps without a court order. The American Bar Association said that move was illegal, and after years of wrangling, Bush agreed to abide by the law. Although President Bush felt he was standing tough in the cause of freedom, his popularity sunk to historic lows.

At the end of his administration — as conflicts in Iraq and Afghanistan dragged on with no end in sight — Bush's approval rating had sunk to just 24 percent, the lowest since Nixon resigned in disgrace 35 years earlier.

# THE 21ST CENTURY

As the 21st century rolled in, the old school world was clearly gone for good. Today, the United States is the senior modern democratic government in the world and the newest source of social innovation. In a sense, the U.S. is the U.N.; most of the nations of the world are represented in its population.

If the world can ever find a way to live together, the way to do so would have to start in the United States of America. During the early years of the 21st century, the U.S. has moved closer to fulfilling the democratic dream of its founders as minorities and women are increasingly freer to express themselves and leadership looks more like the pluralistic society it represents. In 2008, the United States elected Barack Obama, the first black president to ever run a majority white nation. He was reelected in 2012.

## Business changes with society

At the time of the Revolution in the 1700s, most people lived on farms and produced what they needed in isolation, except for a Sunday trip to church and maybe a little salt, sugar, and coffee from the country store. In the 1800s, canals and railroads stitched the states together. Buying or selling over distances as great as several hundred miles suddenly became possible. People got to know a wider world and formed associations that eventually changed women's rights, slavery, and government.

Large stores like Sears started out sending orders through the mail. With the growth of cities in the 1900s, stores built big buildings. As airplanes and telephones brought the world together, international trade made products cheaper, and world travel allowed people to appreciate both what was different and what was comfortably human about foreign lands.

In the early 2000s, the *Internet* (2000) brought general store sites like Amazon and the ability to trade pictures and text instantly anywhere in the world. Second-generation sites like Google, Wikipedia, YouTube, and Facebook allowed direct links to people, products, and ideas that the searcher may not have known even existed before. To the democracy of politics was added the democracy of culture and communication.

Today, because people can download any music for free (legally or otherwise), the economics of the recording industry has changed dramatically. Movies have to go to immediate release before they can be copied and passed around. People longing to communicate churn out even more writing, music, and videos. Computer games allow people to play with folks they've never met. Music players let everybody travel to her own soundtrack.

# A continuing trend: The rich get richer, the poor get poorer

The United States isn't a democracy with its economics; America has, in fact, one of the largest gaps between rich and poor in the developed world. In the second decade of the 21st century, the top 1 percent of people have 25 percent of all the wealth. They also pay a much smaller percentage of their income in taxes than middle class people do.

Part of this discrepancy is due to tax breaks passed by a Congress well funded by business contributions, and part of it is the natural rewards of educated workers in high tech industries. Previously, although the rich got richer, the middle class and most of the poor still had enough money to get by. This hasn't been the case since the Great Recession that started in 2008, at the end of George W. Bush's second term.

# Life in the USA

As family ties have broken down, people have established new families of friends. One out of two marriages end in divorce, and more and more people live alone or in single parent households. Chat sites have replaced front porches, and surfing the Internet has largely replaced reading newspapers.

More people exercise, and fewer people smoke. After waddling into the 21st century due to the yummy presence of cheap fast food everywhere, Americans are starting to get a grip on their waistlines. President Obama and Congress managed to pass the first national health care bill, the *Affordable Health Care Act* (2010).

Most elderly people now live comfortably into advanced age with Social Security and Medicare. Because Social Security is a pay-as-you-go system, the number of young workers available to pay taxes that support retirees is critical. In the early 21st century, there were seven young workers for every retiree; by the year 2050 there may be only four. Because people live longer, the need for new sources of funding threatens old-age benefits. Social Security already costs more than regular taxes for most working people.

**EXAMPLE**

**Question:** As more Americans became older, what system is threatened?

**Answer:** The Social Security system needs an overhaul to maintain benefits.

# Shifting demographics

Latinos have replaced African Americans as the second most populous minority group in the United States. More and more places, like the state of California, are *majority minority*: no single group makes up more than 50 percent of the population.

The U.S. currently takes in more immigrants than ever before — almost a million a year. These new legal residents keep the United States growing and full of new ideas. Illegal immigration is a real problem for social service providers; at least 12 million undocumented people from other countries are flooding the educational and health care systems. Illegal immigrants also pay taxes and seldom collect long-term benefits. Estimates indicate that one of every hundred dollars paid into the Social Security system comes from an illegal immigrant who will never be eligible to collect benefits.

In the early 21st century, Asian Americans families made 20 percent more money than the average white household. Many believe the three million American Indians and others who were part American Indian made up as big a population as was present when Columbus arrived. Some American Indian income went up as tribes operated gambling casinos in 29 states and took in billions of dollars a year in revenue.

In addition, Americans in the land of the free keep more of their citizens in prison than any other advanced society. The number of people in prison has gone up from less than 400,000 in 1980 to more than 2 million in the early 21st century. This increase was part of a great U.S. experiment to see whether locking up perpetrators actually held down crime. It seemed to work; major crime was down in the U.S. in the early 21st century.

## Into the future

Escaping urban problems, most Americans live in the suburbs. With air conditioning, more and more people live comfortably in the hot climates of the South and West. Both of these trends have increased energy demands and made coping with global climate change that much more challenging. Every year is hotter than the historic average, and the polar icecaps are melting.

Americans are used to being distrusted for their affluence and feared for their easygoing cultural influence around the world. They are often seen by those who don't like them as soft, yet Americans have stood up to frontier wars and civil wars; militarism, Nazism, Communism, discrimination, and terrorism. Americans are still working to break down the barriers of discrimination among races and ethnic groups. They still welcome the world. For better or for worse, the U.S. is more than just its past; the United States of America is the future.

# III

# Review of Key Trends, Events, and Supreme Court Cases

# 21

# Key Events in U.S. History

## KEY CONCEPTS

- Major events summary
- Social and economic factors behind important events
- Fitting events into their times

The AP Test wants you to know the grand picture of U.S. history, but every history picture consists of little pixels usually known as facts. Trends are important, but events are the proof that trends have arrived, the champagne-cork pop after years of social and economic ferment. Chapters 6 through 20 provide the details that may crop up on the test; this chapter offers a quick review of the *main events* that contain those details.

### TIP

Obviously you don't want to confuse Andrew Jackson with Michael Jackson. Make sure you have the big events in order, complete with a few facts to drop into essays and to help you avoid simple mistakes in multiple-choice questions.

# 1500–1675: SETTING UP THE COLONIES

Putting together the American colonies took time, effort, and some often-desperate action. As you can see from this timeline, the years from Columbus to the Revolution is almost 100 years longer than the time that has passed from the Revolution until now. Here's the sequence of events you need to remember from this period:

- American Indians were doing just fine without European culture for 15,000 or more years before Columbus. You get a pass on most of those 10,000 years because the New World Indians were too busy inventing the Aztec, Mayan, and Incan empires in Mesoamerica to write much down.

- The Spanish jaunted around Mexico and south looking for treasure and setting up colonies in the 1500s.

- By 1607, the British got around to founding Jamestown; the Pilgrims, blown off course, started New England a few years later. It was no party; half the colonists at both Jamestown and Plymouth died in the first six months.

- The colonists got early help from the American Indians:

  - The Pilgrims were greeted by Tisquantum, an American Indian they called Squanto, who, incredibly enough, had already been to Europe twice with passing explorers and spoke fluent English. *Tisquantum* (1621) taught the Pilgrims how to catch fish and build warmer houses.

  - In Jamestown, the settlers had the help of Pocahontas, who not only brought food but also actually married Englishman John Rolfe. The wives of Presidents Woodrow Wilson and Ronald Reagan were her descendants.

  - The American Indians shared gold, silver, potatoes, tomatoes, corn, squash, and tobacco — products that helped Europe become rich and powerful after their discovery of the New World.

- When the American Indians realized that the Europeans were more like hungry wolves than friendly dogs, they fought back in the mid-1600s. Too late; the colonists managed to hang on through *King Philip's War* (1675) in New England and similar battles in Virginia and New York.

# 1675–1775: BUILDING THE COLONIES

Because their land was being taken away, the American Indians fought when they could against increasingly overwhelming odds for another 200 years. With native attacks on the back burner during the late 1600s, colonies started popping up all along the Atlantic coast. You need to know details about the earliest (not all 13) colonies:

- Massachusetts was home to the Pilgrims and Puritans who came for religious freedom for themselves, but exiled spirit-filled freethinkers like Roger Williams and Anne Hutchinson.

- Roger Williams went on to found the tolerant, freethinking colony of Rhode Island.

- Maryland was a haven for Catholics, but Protestants were welcome, too. Maybe too welcome, because Protestants in some Maryland towns burned Catholic churches. It took years, but toleration made a comeback.

- William Penn founded Pennsylvania on freedom for everybody and fair treatment of the American Indians. Modest William was a little embarrassed that the king named the whole woodland or *silvania* for Penn, but that didn't stop him from founding the city of Philadelphia ("brotherly love") or proposing a uniting of the colonial states into a kind of united states. Outside of New England, more colonists came from places other than England, places like Scotland, Germany, and Wales.

- Virginia prospered with slaves and tobacco. Pocahontas's husband John Rolfe got the business rolling by growing tobacco at Jamestown, and despite a warning from King James himself that smoking was "dangerous to the Lungs," tobacco proved to be an addictive money-maker. Big tobacco bucks got the Southern colonies addicted to slavery, which was used after 1800 for growing cotton.

By 1700, the American colonies held about 300,000 people; 25,000 of them were slaves. The first Great Awakening of the 1730s and 1740s led to more religious devotion and communication between settlements. Talk turned toward freedom, covered in the next section.

# 1776: REVOLUTION

By the 1760s, the 13 colonies were almost 2 million people strong and feeling important. They'd helped the regular British army from back home beat the French and American Indians in the war by the same name that ended in 1763 and now wanted to take over land across the mountains. They were stopped, however, by a declaration of the British Parliament — the Proclamation of 1763 — that closed land west of the Appalachian mountains to settlement. Other restrictions and taxes followed, namely the Stamp Act of 1765, which taxed cards, documents, and even newspapers, and Parliament's taxing tea as a means to regulate prices in order to favor Britain's own investors.

Objecting to lawmaking without Colonial representation, colonists, thinly disguised as American Indians, staged the Boston Tea Party in which they boarded three British ships and dumped 45 tons of tea overboard. They didn't damage the ships, but tea washed up on shore for weeks.

Parliament then passed the Intolerable Acts in 1774 to punish the citizens of Boston by closing down their vital harbor. The British sent over a lot more troops, and the conflict finally erupted at Lexington and Concord, when colonial minutemen responded to what the British called an antiterrorist sweep by shooting up British regulars. Because the fighting had already started, the young and determined Congress had 33-year-old Thomas Jefferson write the Declaration of Independence in 1776. After the battle of Saratoga proved that the backwoods Americans could beat the British army, the French happily piled on to fight their traditional British foes.

George Washington rarely won a major battle, but he stayed in the field for six long years, usually without proper supplies or political support and with a desertion rate of 20 percent per year.

Finally the British decided to take a break from the conflict near the lovely seashore in Yorktown under the protective guns of their mighty navy. Unfortunately for the British, their navy wasn't there, and the French and Americans got the British cornered. Washington finally got the big win he deserved, and it was time for peace and independence.

# 1780–1800: THE CONSTITUTION

The United States knew what they didn't like about British rule, but what were they going to do about their own government? The first try was the Articles of Confederation in 1777 (not to be confused with Confederacy that came along 84 years later with the Civil War). The Articles called for more voluntary cooperation than was ever likely to happen in real life. The federal government had to politely ask the states for money because it had no power to tax on its own. Each state got one vote in Congress, and it took 9 of the 13 votes to pass any laws. With this weak government, the organization of the territory from Ohio north and west under the North-west Ordinance of 1787 is amazing.

In the same year, with much wrangling and a few drinks, Congress produced the U.S. Constitution, under which the nation is still governed. At that time, the average U.S. male had about 600 drinks a year — the first thing most of the Congressmen did after they passed the Constitution was to adjourn to the nearest tavern. A few years later, President Washington and Alexander Hamilton personally led a large army into Pennsylvania to put down the Whiskey Rebellion — not to get rid of whiskey, but to try to enforce a tax on this popular form of booze. Somehow, the nation sobered up enough to get organized.

The addition of the Bill of Rights (the first ten amendments to the Constitution) in 1791 strengthened the Constitution even further. Since then, the U.S. has made only 27 additional Amendment changes in more than 200 years. It took years of tough debate and friendly drinking to finish the original Constitution, but the results have lasted longer than any barroom promise in history.

# 1800–1840: DEMOCRACY AND MANIFEST DESTINY

Although plenty of drinking and tobacco-chewing went on in the early 1800s, politics was more of a gentlemen's game. The nation had been through an early attack on civil liberties in the Alien and Sedition Acts of 1798 and was settling down to enjoy its freedom.

European powers provided pesky challenges that resulted in the War of 1812, but for the most part the new United States was an increasingly prosperous one-party country. The time from 1815 to 1824 was even called the Era of Good Feelings.

Early 1800s U.S. democracy had one little catch: Only white males who owned a house or a farm could vote. Even people who could vote didn't always bother; many figured the system would take care of itself.

All that changed with the contested election of John Quincy Adams in 1824. This was the first election in which all white males in most states got to vote whether they owned property or not. In a four-way race, war hero Andrew Jackson got the most votes, but John Quincy Adams got to be president because he made a deal with the other losers. That ticked off Jackson and his many followers, and they came back in force for the next election.

Jackson was president for eight years, and several of the subsequent presidents — Martin Van Buren, John Tyler, and James Polk — were all Jackson followers.

Jacksonian democracy meant the end of rich guys controlling a central Bank of the United States. It also meant moving the American Indians out to make way for Manifest Destiny and westward expansion. Jackson invited ordinary people to be part of government, rewarding his friends with government jobs (through the spoils system) and pushing for full democracy for everyone (as long as they were white males). Jackson kept the government out of business because he thought that most of the time the government just ended up helping rich people.

# 1820–1860: THE LONG PREQUEL TO THE CIVIL WAR

The amazing thing wasn't that the United States eventually became temporarily disunited by the Civil War; it was that the slavery time bomb took so long to blow up. The U.S. abolished the importation of slaves in 1808, only a few months after Britain did the same thing. All northern U.S. states and a surprising number of southern plantation owners freed their slaves after the Revolution.

However, the invention of the cotton gin made slavery so profitable that it spread throughout the South in the first half of the 1800s, despite the intention of many of the Revolutionary Founding Fathers to bring it to an early end. Suddenly, Southern cotton made more money than anything else. North and South started a long stretch of legal wrangling over slavery:

- The first major bills passed under the early Confederation outlawed slavery in the new Northwest Ordinance of 1787.

- The Missouri Compromise, also known as the Compromise of 1820, assured a balance between free and slave state admissions and drew the Mason-Dixon line between slave and free states; the Compromise of 1850 later extended the Mason-Dixon line out west.

- The Kansas-Nebraska Act of 1854 weakened the earlier compromises, and the 1857 Dred Scott decision by the Southern-controlled Supreme Court blew all the compromises away.

While the South got rich from slavery, the years of compromise had given the North time to get industrialized and relatively united in opposition to slavery. With the election of Abe Lincoln in 1860, Southern politicians decided that it was showdown time.

If you'd been dropped into a random house in the United States in 1860, you'd have had about a 1 in 12 chance of being in a slave owning family. Of course, all the slave holding families were down South. If you had been dropped into a random life in the South, you'd have had a one in three chance of being a slave. Slaves never got paid, worked from dawn to dusk, and could be whipped, sexually exploited, or even killed at the whim of their owners.

Eventually, people who weren't making money off the work of slaves (and even a few people who were) couldn't stand to see the evil system continue. The United States fought through the most horrible war in its history to try to get honest with the proposition that "all men are created equal."

# 1860–1865: CIVIL WAR

When the compromises fell apart in the late 1850s, the South struck with the Dred Scott decision, essentially allowing slavery anywhere in the United States. The North had been reading *Uncle Tom's Cabin* and for the first time had a pretty good picture of just how barbaric Southern slavery could be.

Plus, the North was worried that the South might just march north with a factory's worth of slaves and take the North's paid jobs away. The South was worried that John Brown's botched raid on Harpers Ferry was the beginning of a North-sponsored slave rebellion. Neither of these situations would have happened, but a little paranoia about the other side is a traditional prelude to wars.

When Lincoln was elected, he had to sneak into Washington to become president. The train bringing him from his home in Illinois went through Maryland, a hotbed of Southern sympathy. The fear that someone would assassinate him before he ever took the oath of office was real.

The Southern states seceded and took over most of the federal forts in the South, but Lincoln wouldn't give up Fort Sumter, so the South started shooting. Lincoln was in a tight spot: Southern troops were nearing Washington, and all he had to defend the capital were a few ceremonial units including the Army band. Lincoln paced the top of Washington's hastily erected fortifications hoping to see reinforcements coming from the north. He even went to the Library of Congress and took out books on how to fight a war.

When the North got an army together, it didn't do them much good at first. The South won most of the early battles, fighting on its own territory with good generals. The North barely managed to turn back two Southern invasions, first at the Battle of Antietam and then at the Battle of Gettysburg. That was just enough.

Even though the North was fighting mostly for principle (one of the only times in history when an army has fought to free somebody else) while the South was fighting for its own land (usually worth three to one in fighting morale) and slave property, the North's determination through four long years of war won the day.

# 1865–1900: THE UNITED STATES GROWS UP

With the close of the Civil War in 1865, the U.S. was minus the free help of 4 million slaves but plus a determination to expand all across the continent and beyond. For the rest of the 1800s, mostly Republican presidents rode out economic downturns and political scandals while the U.S. economy steadily caught up with the world's only international superpower: Great Britain.

The U.S. got some technological breaks by inventing most of the useful gadgets in the late 1800s: the electric light, telephone, mechanical harvester, and mass production to name a few. Not held back by the need to support a large military or defend an empire, the U.S. poured all its capital into growth.

Because slavery was no longer an issue, new states got created as soon as they had the population to support a government. San Francisco was well established as the Queen of the Pacific, supported by both California gold and Nevada silver. Railroads spanned the continent, the longest creation of mankind since the Great Wall of China. Ironically, much of the western railroad starting in California was built by imported Chinese labor.

By the time the 1900s neared, the U.S. was starting to cast a hungry eye overseas for more territory. The country had bought Alaska from the Russians (1867), stolen the Southwest from Mexico (1848), and settled out the Northwest with the British (1846). The Hawaiian Islands fell like an unguarded flower into Yankee hands. In 1898, the U.S. fought the weak colonial power of Spain to take away Cuba and the far-off Philippines. President Teddy Roosevelt sent the fleet parading around the world. The United States had the glory; coming up next would be the burden of being a world power.

# 1900–1945: U.S. AS WORLD POWER

The U.S. entered the 1900s with an empire, sort of, and enough military power to scare away other nations from attacking the New World. Most of the United States wanted to mind its own business, but other nations were building up fleets and armies and trolling for more empire.

When World War I broke out in Europe in 1914, the United States stayed neutral. That was hard to do, because the British had been mother country to the U.S., and the French had helped the U.S. free itself. They were fighting together against Germany and clearly needed help. Even worse, ships carrying Americans kept getting sunk by German submarines, and the Germans even hatched a crazy plot to take over Mexico and the American Southwest. After three years of neutrality, the U.S. finally pitched in the war on the side of the Allies.

It didn't really take much fighting, but the U.S. tipped the balance, and the Allies defeated Germany in what turned out to be Round One of a two-round world war; Round Two (World War II) came later.

U.S. President Wilson had great plans for making a fair peace guaranteed by an international League of Nations that could keep future wars from developing. Congressional Republicans wouldn't go along with letting the United States help guard the peace. So, after what amounted to a 21-year truce to make more weapons, the major nations (including the United States) plunged into an even more destructive World War II.

This time the reluctant dragon U.S. sat behind its oceans for two years before being awakened by a punch in the nose from Japan. Although the U.S. lost only 2 percent of the people that Russia did fighting World War II, it was enough to convince the country to stay active in world affairs and try to preserve the peace in the future.

# 1930 TO NOW: GUARDIAN OF THE PEOPLE

Although the U.S. began to initiate social welfare programs after many European countries had already done so, the nation has been steadily developing services for its people for over 100 years. Public education grew rapidly after the Civil War to set an example for the whole world. At the end of that conflict, the U.S. had fewer than 100 high schools in the whole country, by 1920, basic education was available to almost everybody.

By the end of World War I, most towns in the U.S. had schools, and almost all children had at least some high-school education. College was for only a small minority of the elite (about 3 percent) before World War I. After that time, the GI Bill and the growth of state colleges and universities meant that by the 2000s, most U.S. citizens had the opportunity to get at least some college education.

The watershed for social programs was the Great Depression of the 1930s. As the Depression got worse and people stood in line for bread to feed their children, Republican President Hoover actually said that although the people helped the government, the government shouldn't help the people. The people soon voted him out of office, and Franklin Delano Roosevelt (FDR) took over for the longest presidency in U.S. history.

FDR started a lot of social programs that are still active today, including Social Security, the Federal Deposit Insurance Corporation, the Securities and Exchange Commission, and the Federal Housing Authority.

President Lyndon Johnson added Medicare and Medicaid in the 1960s, and President Nixon supported disability insurance in the 1970s. President Clinton expanded aid to education in the 1990s and President George W. Bush added a prescription drug benefit to Medicare in the 2000s. President Obama got a national health bill passed, something all other developed nations have had for years.

With its history of rugged individualism and free enterprise, the U.S. was slower to adopt social programs than many other countries, but eventually the nation began to recognize that services like police, education, and fire protection were more efficient if they were bought "in bulk" by the whole community.

# 22

# Key Issues in U.S. History

## KEY CONCEPTS

- Big trends in U.S. history
- Social and economic forces

The AP test pays special attention to social and economic trends. Knowing trends lets you tie events together for AP essays and pick out answers that don't fit on multiple-choice questions.

The United States is the largest, most diverse multiethnic and multiracial society in history, but all but one of the U.S. presidents have been a white male, and all but one have been male Protestants. Economic and social structures tend to keep society the same.

Despite established structures, change happens. In the 1800s, people usually worked 10, 12, or even 14 hours a day. Today, the 8-hour workday is the norm. In 1950, most Southern restaurants, hotels, and movie theaters didn't allow blacks to even come in the door. Today integration is the law of the land. In most of the United States in 1916, women couldn't even vote. Now women are in offices everywhere. Trends show how society changes.

## U.S. DIVERSITY

The United States is the most diverse country in the world today, but it was already that way at the time of the Revolution. Diversity helped to build understanding and a center of new ideas in 1776. Every major country in the world has contributed citizens to the United States. The Germans, Irish, Chinese, Polish, Italians, Japanese, and Africans have all taken turns being discriminated against and finally celebrated as part of the American experience.

Racial discrimination isn't quite over in the United States, but it raises its ugly head less in this country than in most other places on earth. The U.S. actually maintains a diversity visa, which provides a worldwide lottery for 50,000 people from countries that haven't sent many new citizens to the U.S. The people who win the drawing get to live in the United States. More than 9 million hopeful immigrants apply every year.

# THE AMERICAN IDENTITY

The meaning of American Identity has changed through the years. Right after the Revolution, the Naturalization Act increased the time an immigrant had to wait to become a citizen from 5 to 14 long years in an attempt to limit American citizenship to only those who were born in the country. This long wait ended soon after Jefferson became president when the *Alien and Sedition Acts* were largely repealed in 1802.

The *Know-Nothing Party* (1855) briefly elected mayors in Boston, Philadelphia, and San Francisco on a platform of allowing only native-born Protestants to hold office. The platform of the Know-Nothings quickly faded, and most of them joined the Republican Party and fought against slavery.

The 1950s saw an anti-Communist scare that tried to define *real Americans* as those who supported repression of certain political opinions. This behavior was so out of line with the beliefs on which the U.S. was founded that, after a few years without a Communist invasion, even rabid anti-Communists were ashamed of these tactics.

American identity has grown with the country and increasingly represents a bridge anyone can walk across if they believe in freedom and tolerance.

# AMERICAN CULTURE

Culture is the sum total of all the stories, songs, and ways of living that are important to people in any given time and place. Americans have made culture, and it has also made them. In the colonial period, religious notions of creating the perfect home (a "city on a hill") for a particular religion inspired some settlers to come to America. Movements like the *First Great Awakening* showed people from different denominations and settlements that they shared a common emotional response to God. Culture brings people together by helping them get a broader picture of their place in the world.

Reaction to pressure from the French and the American Indians as well as British authorities built up the idea in American culture of the rough-and-ready frontiersman shown in *The Last of the Mohicans* and in the image of the Minuteman with his rifle and plow. During the Revolution, patriots made it a point of honor to sing "Yankee Doodle Dandy," a song originally intended to mock their backwoods pretensions to civilization.

American culture may not have been fancy, but it was effective. *Uncle Tom's Cabin* helped ignite the Civil War. Books like *The Jungle,* written by *muckrakers* trying to prevent corruption from being swept under the rug, built support for progressive reform. Women's clubs helped get the vote for females and contributed to the freedom of blacks and the spread of public education. The image of *Uncle Sam* updated the backwoods *Yankee Doodle Dandy* to a kindly uncle — dressed in the American flag — who knew the right (patriotic) thing to do.

# DEMOGRAPHICS

The United States at the time of the Revolution was a country of young people. Without a hereditary aristocracy, the 2.5 million scattered settlers, mostly farmers, who made up the country at that time, relied on whoever had the energy to get the job done. Jefferson was only 33 when he wrote the Declaration of Independence, and Washington was 43 when he took command of the Continental Army. The 56 delegates to the Continental Congress weren't necessarily the richest men in America; the truly rich mostly stayed loyal to the King. The early Congressmen in 1775 showed how mobile people in America already were — more than a quarter of them had lived in two or more states.

At the time of the Revolution, about 60 percent of Americans were from England with the next biggest groups being African slaves at 15 percent, the Scotch-Irish at 8 percent, and Germans at 7 percent. The California Gold Rush of 1849 populated the West Coast almost overnight with the first 100,000 Americans settlers. Average Americans lived longer at the time of the Revolution than they did during early heavy industrialization a hundred years later in 1890.

As the U.S. developed, the percent of residents who had been born in other countries grew from 1 percent in 1810 to 14 percent after the Civil War. This jump had an unsettling effect, but it also provided manpower for the North in the conflict with the South and people to work in the new industries after the war. Bad harvests and revolutionary unrest drove people out of Europe, and family ties with earlier immigrants pulled them in to the U.S. Currently, 12 percent of the population of the United States is foreign born.

# ECONOMICS

The U.S. moved from being a prosperous-but-small farming nation at the time of the Revolution to the dominant international economic power with a quarter of the world's money in the early 2000s. Early colonies didn't work out as investments for absentee British investors, who subsequently turned them over to the people who lived here. Colonists learned to support themselves quite well; by the time of the Revolution, average American living standards were better than the ones in England. That gave them something to fight for.

Between 1920 and 1985, the U.S. lived through three depressions and six recessions lasting a total of 12 years during that 65-year period. With minor recessions, the U.S. economy was growing about 75 percent of the time and in decline about 25 percent of the time in the 1900s. The Great Depression of the 1930s was by far the worst, lasting almost six years and continuing until World War II. A recession starting in 2008 has lasted for four years.

Although the United States has experienced bad economic times, its general growth has been good through the end of slavery, the Industrial Revolution, and the postindustrial information society.

# WOMEN'S RIGHTS

Even though they made up more than half of the population of the colonies at the time of the Revolution, women exercised just about zero percent of the direct political power. They did have social and economic influence, which are evident in the letter in which Abigail Adams asks her Founding-Father husband, future second president John Adams, to "remember the ladies" when proposing rights for the new nation.

Women got their first higher education in the 1830s and began to get together in the gatherings of the *Second Great Awakening*. The *Seneca Falls Conference* of 1848 started the women's movement. Women put their own cause on hold to campaign for the abolition of slavery before the Civil War. In the late 1800s and early 1900s, feminist organization grew until the passage of the *Nineteenth Amendment* in 1920 gave women the right to vote. Women joined the work force temporarily during World War II and permanently starting in the 1960s. By the 1990s, they were a regular part of the armed forces, and by early 2012, 90 congresswomen were in the Capitol.

# RACIAL EQUALITY

Blacks, almost all of them slaves, made up 15 percent of the U.S. population at the time of the Revolution. The next largest minority from a non-English-speaking area was German; German Americans made up 7 percent of the population. As the United States grew other significant ethnic groups were the Irish, Hispanics, Polish, Jewish, Chinese, and Japanese. Each of these groups has been subject to discrimination that was in part proportional to their self-identification as a special group within America. As groups have mixed in American society, prejudice has declined.

Blacks gained freedom from slavery after the Civil War but were still subject to Jim Crow laws until the 1960s. The Chinese and Japanese were excluded from immigration in the late 1800s and early 1900s, but have since become an affluent part of the country. In 2010, 11 percent of the largest counties in the United States were *minority majority*, meaning that no one race or ethnic group formed a majority of their population. That number is expected to grow to 18 percent of U.S. counties by 2020. Currently, four whole states are minority majority: California, Hawaii, Texas, and New Mexico. Culture, population centers, group membership, and even families have begun to blend across ethnic groups since the 1970s.

# REFORM

The United States was the most democratic country in the world at the time of its founding. Britain had a parliament, but only 3 percent of the population could vote and parliament tended to represent the interests of rich landowners. The U.S. achieved universal white male voting without regard to property ownership in 1824, universal male voting in 1870, universal voting for men and women in 1920, and actual universal voting (including blacks) in 1964.

Major reforms included an end to the Alien and Sedition Acts (1802), more voter participation in elections (1824), the beginning of public education (1850), the abolition of slavery (1865), industrial regulation (1900), pure food (1908), the ten-hour workday (1910), election reform with direct election of the Senate (1914), no child labor (1920), the eight-hour workday and union rights (1935), Social Security (1936), the expansion of higher education (1950), civil rights (1964), Medicare and Medicaid (1966), the beginning of environmental protection (1970), and a national health plan (2010).

# U.S. RELATIONS WITH THE WORLD

The United States had an international population even during its colonial period, but the early colonies did not have that many resources to trade with the rest of the world. Tobacco proved a best seller, and merchants joined the international slave trade in the triangular exchange of slaves, sugar, rum, and guns.

After the Revolution, the new U.S. backpedaled hard to stay out of foreign wars until the nation fought the War of 1812 over expansion and trade rights. The country expanded west thanks to France's going-out-of-business sale of the Louisiana Purchase to the U.S. in 1803. The U.S. limited international involvement in central North America by taking half of Mexico's territory and getting Britain to agree to a compromise border with Canada. Real international involvement by the U.S. started with the Spanish-American War in 1898.

The U.S. tried to stay neutral but was drawn into World War I in Europe. Going back to splendid isolation behind the oceans, the U.S. paid for not helping keep the peace by having to fight World War II against both Germany and Japan. After World War II, the U.S. stepped up to the plate to be a world leader. In the early 2000s, the country began to accept responsibility to work with the rest of the world to limit damage to the earth's environment.

# SPIRITUALITY

*Spirituality* is defined as a relationship with the higher power believed to shape and bind the universe together. This relationship can be expressed as a deep personal love of justice, such as that of Thomas Jefferson and Abraham Lincoln. It can also come from active participation in a religious organization, such as those supported by Jimmy Carter and George W. Bush.

The U.S. has been a leader in both forms of the expression of spirituality. Early New England was a haven for the specific religious sects of Puritans and Pilgrims; they drove out and even killed people who disagreed with their religions. Freethinkers like William Penn, Jefferson, Henry David Thoreau, and Ralph Waldo Emerson kept the United States open to personal spirituality even though they themselves didn't go to church. The U.S. has always declined to declare any particular official religion; the very first Amendment to the Constitution separated church and state.

Spiritual revival has played a major role in American history. The *First Great Awakening* (1740) connected people who would later protect the colonies in the French and Indian War and led the new U.S. to freedom in the Revolution. The *Second Great Awakening* (1830) laid the groundwork for the women's movement and for opposition to slavery. Spirituality is a fountain that refreshes committed people.

# 23

# Key Supreme Court Decisions

## KEY CONCEPTS

- Decisions relating to privacy rights
- Decisions establishing the role of the Supreme Court and the primacy of federal law
- Decisions that changed the course of history

**N**o review of U.S. history (or the AP U.S. History test) would be complete without an assessment of important Supreme Court decisions. The U. S. Supreme Court is the sometimes overlooked third branch of national government that determines what is legal; it is the last word on the law of the land.

Being able to reference Supreme Court decisions is impressive evidence of your mastery of U.S. history on the AP exam. The Supreme Court is the sometimes overlooked third branch of national government that determines what is legal.

## MARBURY V. MADISON (1803)

In this early decision, the Supreme Court, under Chief Justice John Marshall, found that the court has the final word on whether any federal law is constitutional. The court refused to order that Marbury be awarded a federal legal job because the law under which he had been appointed was unconstitutional. Later this authority was extended to state and local laws.

# MCCULLOCH V. MARYLAND (1819)

This case established that federal law trumps state law. Maryland wanted to slap a state tax on the National Bank established by the federal government. John Marshall found that the feds had the power to set up a bank under the *Necessary and Proper Clause* of the Constitution and that states could no more tax the federal bank than they could tax the army.

# GIBBONS V. OGDEN (1824)

This decision states that only the feds can regulate business between the states ("interstate commerce"). New York tried to set steamboat guru Robert Fulton as the only guy who could run power boats between New York and New Jersey (or license others, like Ogden, to do so). Not fair, said the court; anything that runs between states is the business of the feds. When they got around to it 140 years later, this principle allowed Congress to require civil rights in planes, trains, hotels, and restaurants.

# DRED SCOTT V. SANDFORD (1857)

Dred Scott was a slave taken by his master to free territory in the North. When his master died, Scott sued for his freedom. The court decided that Scott was not a citizen and that in effect slaves could be taken to any state in the Union while remaining slaves. This decision was seen as upsetting 50 years of careful compromise and became a cause of the Civil War.

# PLESSY V. FERGUSON (1896)

The State of Louisiana required that railroads maintain separate but equal sleeping cars for white and black passengers. Plessy was one-eighth black but was refused a seat he had paid for in a whites only car. He sued, citing the post-Civil War Thirteenth and Fourteenth Amendments supporting equality for blacks. The Supreme Court turned him down, saying that separate but equal accommodations did not violate the law. This ruling held for almost 60 years until *Brown v. Board of Education* ruled that separate cannot be equal.

# WEST COAST HOTEL CO. V. PARRISH (1937)

This decision, rendered during the heart of the Great Depression, allowed the federal government to set minimum wages for work in private industry, something the court had previously prohibited. Parrish was a poor chambermaid whose hotel refused to pay her the minimum wage.

# BROWN V. BOARD OF EDUCATION (1954)

"Separate but equal" was the rule of the land before this decision came along. The *Brown* ruling set off the Civil Rights movement by declaring that segregated schools for different races were inherently unequal and had to go. Brown, an African American railroad worker, had a third-grade daughter who had been forced to travel miles to a segregated black school when a white-only public school was right in her neighborhood.

# MAPP V. OHIO (1962)

Police burst into Mapp's house without a search warrant and found some illegal material. Mapp protested that the evidence could not be used against her because it was obtained from an unauthorized raid that violated her Fourth Amendment protection against illegal search and seizure. The Supreme Court agreed, and police agencies can no longer use evidence obtained illegally as proof in trials.

# GIDEON V. WAINWRIGHT (1963)

Gideon was a poor prisoner who was barely literate. He had been denied a court appointed attorney because the crime for which he had been charged was not a capital offense and, therefore, had to act as his own council during the trial. In a touching, handwritten appeal, he asked the Supreme Court for help. The justices found that states have a duty to supply a lawyer for people who can't afford one. Gideon got a new trial and was found innocent.

# GRISWOLD V. CONNECTICUT (1965)

This case established the *right to privacy* that kept the states from regulating personal sexual behavior that hurts no one. Griswold had been fined by Connecticut for running a birth-control clinic.

# MIRANDA V. ARIZONA (1966)

Miranda was a Mexican American with little education who confessed under police questioning without having been informed that he had the right to remain silent and to have an attorney. The court ruled that statements made by a defendant during interrogation without benefit of an attorney present would be inadmissible in court unless the defendant was made aware of these right and voluntarily waived them before being questioned. The reading of Miranda rights by police officers is now routine. Even people arrested in totalitarian countries now sometimes demand that police read them their Miranda rights, based on what they see on TV. They don't know that because they're not from the U.S. they don't necessarily have these rights. But rights for the accused are increasing around the democratic world.

# ROE V. WADE (1973)

The Supreme Court held that abortion is a privacy issue and that, during the first trimester, it is the mother's and doctor's choice to control birth and states can't prohibit this procedure. Although many women favor the right to choose, conservative religious groups oppose abortion. The court has been a battleground ever since.

# UNITED STATES V. NIXON (1974)

In this case, the Supreme Court found that even the president has to follow the law; he can't hide behind executive privilege. During the Watergate scandal, the special prosecutor subpoenaed President Nixon to hand over audio tapes and documents related to his possible participation in the cover up. Nixon, supported by a few of his Republican allies, had tried to argue that he didn't have to turn over evidence of his own wrongdoing to Congress because as president he had special rights. The Supreme Court held that the president is not above the law. Shortly after this ruling, Nixon resigned to avoid impeachment.

# IV

# Practice Tests and Answer Sheets

# 24

# Practice Test 1

To help you spot time periods in which you may be weak, the practice test in this chapter covers the period from American Indian days to the Civil War. In addition, the multiple-choice questions here are arranged in chronological order, with the questions about the earliest time period at the beginning. The actual AP U.S. History exam, however, will have the time periods of the questions somewhat scrambled.

## GENERAL INSTRUCTIONS

Allow yourself 55 minutes to answer the 80 multiple-choice questions on the first part of this test. Keep track of the time: Set an alarm for 55 minutes and stick to it. The time limit breaks down to just 40 seconds per question, so mark and pass any question you're not sure of. (See Chapter 3 for more on timing strategies.) Don't even think about the rest of the test until you have the Section I multiple-choice challenge out of the way.

- **Multiple-Choice:** 80 questions, 55 minutes
- **Document-Based Question:** 1 essay, 60 minutes
- **Regular Essays:** 2 essays, 70 minutes

> **TIP**
>
> As you complete the multiple-choice section of the practice test, keep these suggestions in mind:
>
> - Practice tests are as much about figuring out timing as remembering answers. To gauge whether you're on track to complete the multiple-choice section in the allotted time, check how far along you are after 30 minutes. At 30 minutes, you should be passing about question 40; this pace ensures that you have enough time to go back and shore up any weak spots.
>
> - For best results, don't just *say* the answers to the questions you know. *Mark* the answer sheet just like you will when the big test goes live. That way, you get

in the rhythm of the real thing. Even if you are using a web-based app to review multiple-choice questions, use the paper and pencil method on this practice test; it will get you familiar with how the real test works.

- Do *not* flip ahead to the answers (Chapter 25) when you run into a tough question to see whether you're guessing right; you'll find out soon enough when the test is done. You're not going to be flipping around on test day, so make it real on the practice test.

After you complete the 80 multiple-choice questions, give yourself the mandatory 15-minute preparation period for the Document-Based Question (DBQ), followed by 45 minutes in which you write the best DBQ you can dredge up from your mind and associated imagination. When that is complete, pause, take a deep breath, and then go on to the regular essay questions. Pick the question that seems the least threatening from Part B. Take five big minutes to plan your response and 30 minutes to write the essay. Then do the same thing with Part C.

# SECTION I: MULTIPLE CHOICE

*Time: 55 minutes*

*80 Questions*

1. American natives were originally called *Indians* because

   (A) they came from India across a land bridge

   (B) Columbus thought he'd reached a land called Indiana

   (C) the Spanish Padres felt they were born *in Dios* or in God

   (D) Columbus believed he'd sailed all the way to the East Indies

   (E) that's what they called themselves

2. *Mesoamerica* in early American history means

   (A) people of the maize or corn

   (B) middle of the New World, around south Mexico and Central America

   (C) the mesas upon which many early people lived

   (D) the Midwest of the United States, where all the farms are

   (E) home of the Incas in the middle of the mountains

3. An early union of American Indian tribes in what is now New York and the surrounding area was

   (A) the Cherokee States

   (B) the land of the Sioux

   (C) the Iroquois Confederation

   (D) the Mesoamerican Empire

   (E) the Norseman Union

4. Place the major New World Indian empires in the same order as their homelands: 1) Mexico City, 2) north of Panama, and 3) from Colombia to Chile

   (A) Mayan, Aztec, Inca

   (B) Aztec, Meso, Inca

   (C) Inca, Mayan, Aztec

   (D) Meso, Inca, Mayan

   (E) Aztec, Mayan, Inca

5. What was an important food that Europeans learned to eat from the New World Indians?

   (A) corn

   (B) potatoes

   (C) tomatoes

   (D) chocolate

   (E) all of the above

6. The first explorer who sailed his boat all the way around the world was

   (A) Vasco Balboa

   (B) Ponce de Leon

   (C) Ferdinand Magellan

   (D) Francisco Coronado

   (E) Francisco Pizarro

7. The *encomienda* system

   (A) was a system of housing accommodations for Spanish padres

   (B) showed the Spanish how to cook Mexican food

   (C) governed relationships between the colonies

   (D) laid out royal land grants

   (E) assigned American Indians to colonists

8. The break that allowed England more power to colonize the New World came with the

   (A) defeat of the Spanish Armada

   (B) coronation of King George

   (C) wealth of King James

   (D) Henry Hudson's fur discovery

   (E) the War of the Roses

9. Popé's Rebellion (1680) was

   (A) an intrigue in which the pope divided up the New World

   (B) an American Indian rebellion against the Spanish

   (C) the revolt of Protestant settlers against Catholic rules

   (D) a brief fight for power in the Holy See

   (E) an insurrection over the right to make whiskey

10. The main goal for the founding of the British colony of Jamestown was
    (A) to establish religious freedom
    (B) to Christianize the American Indians
    (C) to raise crops and export tobacco
    (D) to find gold
    (E) to explore the natural world of North America

11. The first African slaves came to Virginia
    (A) just a few years before the Civil War
    (B) kidnapped in American Indian canoes years before the white men came
    (C) when America started growing cotton in the years just before the Revolution
    (D) almost 400 years ago, before the Pilgrims even landed
    (E) to fight in the French and Indian War

12. When the first wave of English settlers left for the New World in the mid 1600s, most of them headed for
    (A) Virginia
    (B) New England
    (C) New York
    (D) The West Indies
    (E) Cuba

13. Which English settlers in North America were the Separatists who wanted to split completely from the Church of England?
    (A) the Pilgrims
    (B) the Puritans
    (C) the Marylanders
    (D) the Jamestown farmers
    (E) the Carolina plantation workers

14. Anne Hutchinson (1638) was a
    (A) leader of the conservative family movement
    (B) the feminist wife of Captain John Smith
    (C) the English name for Pocahontas
    (D) a freethinking Puritan expelled for her beliefs
    (E) an early witch trial victim

15. Who founded the city that would become New York?

   (A) the Duke of York

   (B) Spanish conquistadores

   (C) the Dutch

   (D) Henry Hudson, exploring on behalf of King George

   (E) The Puritans

16. If you were an American Indian looking for fair treatment in early colonial America, in which colony would you have wanted to live?

   (A) Puritan New England

   (B) plantation Carolina

   (C) newly growing Georgia

   (D) Quaker Pennsylvania

   (E) booming New Jersey

17. King Philip's War caused

   (A) Philip to assume the crown of Portugal

   (B) American Indians to destroy 12 New England towns

   (C) the English and Spanish to fight a naval battle

   (D) raids on the Southern colonies of Georgia and South Carolina

   (E) the end of troubles for the American Indians

18. The Dominion of New England (1643) was

   (A) a local Puritan kingdom

   (B) a zone for controlling the American Indians

   (C) an area in which New England voters had complete control

   (D) an attempt by the king to control New England with a royal governor

   (E) an attempt by the New England colonies to get free from the direct control of the king

19. Which of these statements is true of slavery in the colonies before the Revolution?

   (A) the mainland British colonies got only a tiny minority of slaves taken from Africa to the New World

   (B) before 1700, most indentured servants were white

   (C) slave rebellions killed both blacks and whites

   (D) all of the above

   (E) none of the above

*The New York Public Library/Art Resource, NY*

20. This courtroom scene from late 1600s New England shows

    (A) the Case of the Stolen Bride

    (B) the community deciding who owns Magee's Farm

    (C) the Salem Witch Trails

    (D) girls reunited with their long-lost grandfather

    (E) the power of the church to save sinners

21. A high point of power for the American Indians in colonial America during the 1600s was

    (A) when they showed the Pilgrims how to have Thanksgiving

    (B) when Pocahontas got to marry a colonist

    (C) the founding of the first American Indian church school

    (D) when they besieged Plymouth and burned Jamestown

    (E) when settlers showed American Indians how to grow corn

22. The largest non-English speaking group in the British colonies before the Revolution was the

    (A) Germans

    (B) Spanish

    (C) French

    (D) Dutch

    (E) Irish

23. What was the approximate population of the American colonies in 1750, before the Revolution?

    (A) 10 million

    (B) 100,000

    (C) 100 million

    (D) 1 million

    (E) Nobody has any idea because there was no census.

24. The Scotch-Irish inhabitants in America before the Revolution

    (A) were peaceful, shy settlers

    (B) brought major investment money to the New World

    (C) settled on small farms on the frontier

    (D) made up much of the urban police force

    (E) were an important part of the Catholic church

25. Peaceful American Indians attacked by whites in Pennsylvania before the Revolution were defended by

    (A) the British Army

    (B) the Paxton Boys

    (C) Samuel Adams

    (D) Benjamin Franklin

    (E) the Indian Army

26. The colonies before the Revolution were made up of

    (A) 95 percent English settlers

    (B) a mixture of mostly English, Italian, and Spanish

    (C) almost no black people

    (D) a majority of non-English settlers in New England

    (E) the most multicultural population in the world at that time

27. The economic system in which colonies were supposed to send raw material to their mother country and buy manufactured products from only that country is

    (A) wage slavery

    (B) capitalism

    (C) mercantilism

    (D) syndication

    (E) distribution

28. The leading export crop for Virginia and Maryland before the Revolution was
    (A) tobacco
    (B) cotton
    (C) wheat
    (D) slaves
    (E) fish

29. The *Navigation Acts* passed beginning in 1650 were meant to
    (A) help ships avoid dangerous reefs
    (B) provide mapping assistance to explorers
    (C) increase New England ship production
    (D) block colonial trade with countries other than England
    (E) increase colonial trade with countries other than England

30. Economically, the colonies before the Revolution were
    (A) so equal in income that everybody had the same resources
    (B) one of the poorest places in the English-speaking world
    (C) one of the richest places in the English-speaking world
    (D) the home of large manufacturing plants
    (E) entirely self-sufficient

31. Early universities like Harvard, Yale, Princeton, and Brown originated to train
    (A) doctors
    (B) lawyers
    (C) ministers
    (D) scientific farmers
    (E) politicians

32. The *First Great Awakening* of the 1730s spread
    (A) a quiet, contemplative religious feeling
    (B) the idea that the colonies were getting the short end of the stick
    (C) feelings of sectionalism separating the colonies
    (D) *New light* emotional ministers
    (E) *Old light* rational believers

*Yale University Art Gallery/Art Resource, NY*

**33.** This portrait by Charles Willson Peale shows an American

(A) around the time of the Revolution

(B) just before the Civil War

(C) in the time of Wilson Democracy

(D) in the earliest colonial days

(E) living in the time of Greece

34. The *Three-Fifths Compromise* in the U.S. Constitution
    (A) allowed just over half of the states to block a new law
    (B) required three-fifths of Congress to approve any compromise
    (C) allowed three-fifths of the new states to forbid slavery
    (D) counted slaves as three-fifths of a person when deciding representation
    (E) mandated that three out of five voters must agree before any territory could become a state

35. The trial of *Peter Zenger* (1734) helped to further
    (A) the rights of the Dutch to equal treatment
    (B) freedom of the seas
    (C) freedom of the press
    (D) freedom of worship
    (E) access to law school

36. Which of the following conflicts was NOT a European war that included fighting in the colonies?
    (A) King William's War
    (B) Queen Anne's War
    (C) the War of Jenkins' Ear
    (D) the Opium War
    (E) the French and Indian War

37. The *Albany Congress* (1754) convened to
    (A) establish Albany as the capital of New York
    (B) win the support of the American Indians
    (C) begin a tax system for the colonies
    (D) negotiate an end to Queen Anne's War
    (E) begin planning for the Erie Canal

38. Put these British laws that angered the colonies in the right date order from earliest to latest:
    (A) Navigation Laws, Stamp Act, Intolerable Acts
    (B) Stamp Act, Navigation Laws, Intolerable Acts
    (C) Intolerable Acts, Stamp Act, Navigation Laws
    (D) Navigation Laws, Intolerable Acts, Stamp Act
    (E) Intolerable Acts, Navigation Laws, Stamp Act

39. During the American Revolution, the one-sixth of the colonists who sided with Britain were

    (A) Royalists

    (B) Loyalists

    (C) Patriots

    (D) Blue Coats

    (E) Monarchists

40. The Declaration of Independence and Tom Paine's *Common Sense* are examples of what kind of thinking?

    (A) Existential

    (B) Aristotelian

    (C) Epicurean

    (D) Machiavellian

    (E) Enlightenment

41. "I have a dream that one day this nation will rise up and live out the true meaning of its creed." These words are from a speech by

    (A) John F. Kennedy

    (B) Ronald Reagan

    (C) Martin Luther King Jr.

    (D) Harry S Truman

    (E) Abraham Lincoln

42. A major problem for the patriots in the Revolutionary War was

    (A) bad field position

    (B) lack of proper training

    (C) shortage of doctors

    (D) second rate generals

    (E) all of the above

43. The idea of *republican motherhood* (1780) elevated the role of women by

    (A) admitting women to the Republican Party

    (B) allowing anyone who was a mother to claim government support

    (C) viewing mothers as the most important source of democratic ideas for their children

    (D) giving women full voting rights

    (E) supporting the establishment of day-care facilities throughout the new republic

44. The Land Ordinance of 1785 and the Northwest Ordinance of 1787

    (A) established the new state of Tennessee in northwest Georgia

    (B) set up what would become the Midwestern states of Ohio, Indiana, Michigan, Illinois, and Wisconsin

    (C) gave free land beyond the Appalachian Mountains to veterans of the Revolutionary war

    (D) oversaw relationships with American Indian tribes on the frontier

    (E) worked on an alliance with Canada

45. The Articles of Confederation (1777)

    (A) left most of the power in the hands of the states

    (B) never took effect because of the Revolution

    (C) are still the basis of all government in the United States

    (D) helped to start the Confederacy in the Civil War

    (E) were passed after a vote by the people

46. One of the important pieces of legislation passed under the Articles of Confederation was the

    (A) Bill of Rights

    (B) Louisiana Purchase

    (C) Northwest Ordinance

    (D) Declaration of Independence

    (E) none of the above

47. When elder statesman Ben Franklin was leaving the Constitutional Convention, a woman asked him what form of government the United States was planning. Franklin said, "A republic, Madame, if you can keep it." What did he mean by that?

    (A) The U.S. was only going to be a republic if she could keep quiet about it.

    (B) The U.S. would be a loose confederation run by the states.

    (C) The new American government would have no judges or jails.

    (D) The U.S. was trying a real republican form of government that would require the active participation of all citizens.

    (E) The new U.S. government would choose Franklin as its leader.

48. An early government official who supported smaller government was

    (A) Thomas Jefferson

    (B) Alexander Hamilton

    (C) John Jay

    (D) John Adams

    (E) John Marshall

49. What does the First Amendment to the Constitution cover?

    (A) the right to bear arms

    (B) protection from unreasonable search and seizure

    (C) due process of law

    (D) freedom of religion, speech, and press

    (E) protection from quartering troops

50. What is the collective name for the first ten amendments to the Constitution?

    (A) the Charter of Freedom

    (B) the Bill of Liberty

    (C) the Bill of Rights

    (D) the Indomitable Agreement

    (E) the Founding Fathers

51. What was the most important belief of a Federalist at the time of the writing of the Constitution?

    (A) A strong central government was ideal.

    (B) The U.S. should federalize the frontier into three states.

    (C) The U.S. should have an express service for delivering mail.

    (D) Only people who had served in the federal army should be in Congress.

    (E) The government should be a confederation with most power reserved to the states.

52. Under the *Alien and Sedition Acts* of 1798, it was a crime to

    (A) criticize the president

    (B) house aliens without consent

    (C) cause sedition by failing to become a citizen

    (D) pay taxes to a foreign government

    (E) travel to Canada or Mexico without permission

53. John Marshall was

    (A) the third president

    (B) founder of the Marshall Plan

    (C) an influential Supreme Court chief justice

    (D) the famous inventor of the steam engine

    (E) the reason people often call sheriffs *marshals*

54. Jefferson's Louisiana Purchase

    (A) added 10 percent to the size of the United States

    (B) was in keeping with Jefferson's policy of a strong central government with broad policy-making power

    (C) was a good way of getting Texas into the Union

    (D) was actually contrary to Jefferson's policy of a weak central government with most power left to the states

    (E) wasn't explored for twenty years

55. The *Embargo Acts* (1807) were

    (A) designed to stop the Whiskey Rebellion

    (B) a way of putting a lid on smuggling whiskey from Canada

    (C) meant to limit trade and avoid war

    (D) the first legal attempt to stop the selling of guns to the American Indians

    (E) a way to encourage trade and growth

56. Sectionalism was an issue in the War of 1812 because

    (A) New England strongly supported the war

    (B) the South favored immediate negotiations

    (C) the Star-Spangled Banner wasn't yet the national flag

    (D) New England strongly opposed the war

    (E) the South wanted slaves to fight

57. Tecumseh was a great American Indian leader who

    (A) helped the Pilgrims survive

    (B) worked to save the life of Captain John Smith

    (C) put together an American Indian alliance and fought to save his land

    (D) signed a treaty turning over Louisiana

    (E) lead Lewis and Clark on their expedition

58. Free blacks fought for U.S. victories in

    (A) the Old Ironsides fight

    (B) the Battle of New Orleans

    (C) American Indian wars on the frontier

    (D) the Civil War

    (E) all of the above

59. The Era of Good Feelings was

   (A) a time of peace after the Civil War

   (B) another name for the hippie rock-and-roll era of the 1960s

   (C) several years of cooperation after the War of 1812

   (D) a time when the colonies had plenty of food before the Revolution

   (E) a time of peace between the U.S. and Canada declared in 1820

60. In the case of *Marbury v. Madison* (1803), the Supreme Court decided that

   (A) the court can review all laws for their constitutionality.

   (B) President Madison had to repay Marbury, thus establishing the role of executive privilege

   (C) only the federal government can collect tariffs

   (D) gun control is left to the states

   (E) Marbury could run steam boats on the Mississippi

© Bettman/Corbis

61. This picture represents

   (A) female soldiers drafted into the U.S. Army

   (B) target practice for the Women's Artillery

   (C) the Molly Pitcher spirit of women in the Revolutionary War

   (D) the fact that women often manned cannons

   (E) the role of women in the Civil War

62. Manifest Destiny means that the United States was

(A) bound to gain independence from England

(B) meant to rule the world

(C) certain to get Canada and Mexico some day

(D) fated to win World War I

(E) meant to spread west across the whole North American continent

63. American exceptionalism means that

(A) the U.S. has special rights and a mission in the world

(B) Manifest Destiny is wrong

(C) the U.S. is just like every other country

(D) Americans should be careful of foreign powers

(E) the U.S. may not be as sharp as other countries

64. The implied powers decision of the Supreme Court in *McCulloch v. Maryland* means that

(A) the president can do anything he wants in times of national emergency

(B) Congress can pass laws to carry out powers in the Constitution even though those acts aren't specifically mentioned

(C) the Army has the power to destroy as well as protect if it's in the national interest

(D) the Supreme Court can award titles to elected officials to carry out the Constitution

(E) states have the implied power to nullify federal laws

65. The appeals decision of the Supreme Court in *Cohens v. Virginia* means that

(A) defendants in a criminal case can appeal their conviction to the Supreme Court

(B) the Supreme Court automatically decides which side has the greater appeal

(C) the president has the right to appeal any law he doesn't agree with

(D) Congress can appeal directly to the people over a presidential veto

(E) an appeal signed by two thirds of the states is enough to get any law overturned

66. The Missouri Compromise

(A) made sure Missouri was divided equally between slave and free sections

(B) divided the power between the president and Congress in a historic meeting in old Missouri

(C) divided free and slave state territory

(D) allowed American Indians to remain in southern Missouri

(E) settled the tax issue along the lines proposed by Missouri

67. The Monroe Doctrine said that
    (A) President Monroe had the power to raise taxes
    (B) slavery would be confined to the South
    (C) new states could decide whether they were slave or free
    (D) foreign powers had to stay out of the United States
    (E) foreign powers had to stay out of the New World

68. Along the *Trail of Tears*,
    (A) civilized American Indians were forced to leave their Southern homes
    (B) blacks marched to slavery
    (C) Irish Americans fled their starving land
    (D) dust bowl settlers moved west looking for jobs
    (E) Revolutionary War widows looked for their husbands after battle

69. The biggest voting change in *Jacksonian Democracy* was that
    (A) women could vote
    (B) all men could vote
    (C) Congress no longer elected the president
    (D) all white men could vote
    (E) the voters directly elected the Senate

70. The *spoils system* meant that
    (A) the government disposed of spoiled food
    (B) political winners gave out government jobs
    (C) Army troops were entitled to keep any captured spoils on the campaigns
    (D) corruption in politics spoiled the election process
    (E) Congress established that laws had to be reconsidered every thirty years before they spoiled

71. When early presidents worried about *nullification*, they were concerned that
    (A) states would try to revoke federal laws
    (B) Congress would overturn the powers of the president
    (C) the Supreme Court would strike down sections of the Constitution
    (D) presidential rights to the spoils system would end
    (E) the British would declare American independence null and void

72. Railroads took over from canals as the main form of transportation in the United States
    (A) before the Revolution
    (B) before the Civil War
    (C) after the Civil War
    (D) during the Andrew Jackson administration
    (E) during the Thomas Jefferson administration

73. What is the most important aspect about the John Deere Company of Rock Island?
    (A) It produced the first steel plow, used to farm American land.
    (B) It's still in business.
    (C) Rock Island eventually became a railroad town.
    (D) It's the inventor of the tractor.
    (E) It proved that a manufacturer can sell both wholesale and retail.

74. In the *cult of domesticity* (1850),
    (A) men were supposed to help with the housework
    (B) women got the right to vote and demonstrate
    (C) everyone was urged to buy domestic products
    (D) women were thought to have weaker brains
    (E) the role of women as moral leader of the household was enshrined

75. The fact that Charles Finney, a Second Great Awakening preacher, was also president of Oberlin College most importantly shows
    (A) that ministers are smart enough to run colleges
    (B) the connection between religious revival and social action
    (C) the connection between Awakening and being president
    (D) that Oberlin was a conservative school
    (E) that Awakening preachers traveled the country

76. The Shakers, Brook Farm, New Harmony, and Oneida were all
    (A) early organic food brands
    (B) furniture manufacturers whose designs have lasted
    (C) farm leaders
    (D) utopian communities
    (E) Midwestern political movements

77. The Seneca Falls Convention (1848) was
    (A) the first important women's rights meeting in the U.S.
    (B) the first important environmental meeting in the U.S.
    (C) the labor meeting that passed the Seneca resolution
    (D) an American Indian rights convention
    (E) a religious service that was part of the Great Awakening

78. Ralph Waldo Emerson was a
    (A) Transcendentalist author
    (B) abolitionist leader
    (C) railroad organizer
    (D) textile manufacturer
    (E) leader of factory workers

79. The clauses on slavery in the Northwest Ordinance (1787) and on the future of the slave trade in the U.S. Constitution show

    (A) early opposition to slavery

    (B) early support for slavery

    (C) the value of slaves in the South

    (D) the spread of slaves to the North

    (E) the reason the U.S. was founded

80. The "peculiar institution" was

    (A) marriage

    (B) funerals

    (C) special schools

    (D) slavery

    (E) the Electoral College

# SECTION II: FREE-RESPONSE QUESTIONS

In this section, test takers confront first the Document-Based Question (DBQ) in Part A and then the two regular essays in Parts B and C.

## Part A: Document-Based Question

*Planning Time: 15 minutes*

*Suggested Writing Time: 45 minutes*

*Percent of Section II score: 45*

1. Discuss the changing nature of slavery and indentured servitude from the founding of the British North American colonies until the Civil War. What factors fostered the change from indentured servitude to slavery and influenced the evolution of slavery from the Revolution to the Civil War? Discuss the role of crops such as tobacco, cotton, and sugar. Use the documents and your knowledge of the time period in writing your response.

   ### Document A

   Source: Letter written by Christopher Columbus to his sponsors, the King and Queen of Spain, on his first voyage, 1493.

   . . . their Highnesses may see that I shall give them all the gold they require, if they will give me but a very little assistance, spices also, and cotton, as much as their Highnesses shall command to be shipped; and mastic, hitherto found only in Greece, [and]. . . slaves, as many of these idolaters as their Highnesses shall command to be shipped.

## Document B

Source: Grubb, Farley. "The Incidence of Servitude in Trans-Atlantic Migration, 1771–1804." *Explorations in Economic History* 22 (1985b): 316–39

English Emigration to the American Colonies, by Destination and Type, 1773–76

| Location | Number of Immigrants | Percent Indentured Servants |
| --- | --- | --- |
| New England | 54 | 1.85 |
| Middle Colonies | 1,162 | 61.27 |
| New York | 303 | 11.55 |
| Pennsylvania | 859 | 78.81 |
| Chesapeake | 2,984 | 96.28 |
| Maryland | 2,217 | 98.33 |
| Virginia | 767 | 90.35 |
| Lower South | 307 | 19.54 |
| Carolinas | 106 | 23.58 |
| Georgia | 196 | 17.86 |

## Document C

Source: Report on Indentured Servants, 1783

Those who can pay for their passage arrive in America free to take any engagement that suits them. Those who cannot pay are carried at the expense of the ship-owner, who in order to recoup his money, advertises on arrival that he has imported artisans, laborers and domestic servants and that he has agreed with them on his own account to hire their services for a period normally of three, four, or five years for men and women and 6 or 7 years for children.

## Document D

Source: Black appeal to the Governor of Massachusetts, 1773

We have no Property. We have no Wives. No Children. We have no City. No Country. But we have a Father in Heaven. . . .

## Document E

Source: Letter from Mississippi, 1836

. . .these were all merchants, who without much Capital went to speculating in Cotton. It is in truth the only country I ever read or heard of, where a poor man could in 2 or 3 years without any aid, become wealthy. . . . More than 6,000 Negroes and 10,000 horses and mules have been sold in Yazoo County alone.

## Document F

Source: A Northern merchant threatens an abolitionist, 1835

There are millions upon millions of dollars due from Southerners to the merchants and mechanics of this city alone, the payment of which would be jeopardized by any rupture between the North and the South. We cannot afford, sir, to let you and your associates succeed in your endeavor to overthrow slavery. It is not a matter of principle with us. It is a matter of business necessity.

## Document G

Source: Symbol of the Anti-Slavery Society

## Document H

Source: Report of a slave girl, 1813

If a slave resisted being whipped, the bloodhounds were unpacked, and set upon him, to tear his flesh from his bones. The master who did these things was highly educated, and styled a perfect gentleman. He also boasted the name and standing of a Christian, though Satan never had a truer follower.

### Document I

Source: Census data, Antebellum Economics

In 1860 the twelve wealthiest counties in the United States were all in the cotton growing South. Per capita income in the white South was higher by 1860 than in the North. With an economy based on slavery, the South was different from any other section of Europe or the United States.

Many Southerners initially opposed slavery; hundreds freed their slaves following the Revolution. With the invention of the cotton gin after the Revolution, cotton began to make huge amounts of money. As late as the 1830s, a bill in the Virginia legislature to abolish slavery came within a few votes of passing. After that, as the profits continued to rise from slavery based cotton, Southerners made the white fluffy fiber their "king" and became addicted to black slavery.

# Part B and Part C

*Total Suggested Planning and Writing Time: 70 minutes*

*Percent of Section II score: 55*

# Part B

*Choose ONE question from this part.*

2. In what ways did the cultural background of early settlers influence the development of the pre-Revolutionary colonies? Discuss the New England, Middle, and Southern colonies with regard for TWO of the following:

> National origins
>
> Religious beliefs
>
> Ethnic background
>
> Reasons for coming to America

3. Some historians say that Americans bought their freedom with slave labor. Explain how this charge relates to the development of the country before and after the Revolution in at least TWO of the following areas:

> Economic development
>
> Political power
>
> Social beliefs
>
> Behavioral changes

## Part C

*Choose ONE question from this part.*

4. How did the federal government change during the Jacksonian Era? Assess these changes in light of at least TWO of the following topics:

   Voting behavior

   Policy regarding American Indians

   States' rights

   Federal power

5. How did relationships between the North and the South change in the time between the Revolution and the Civil War with regard to at least TWO of the following developments:

   Missouri Compromise of 1820

   Compromise of 1850

   Kansas-Nebraska Act

   Dred Scott Decision

# 25

# Answers to Practice Test 1

**A**fter you complete your essays in the practice test (Chapter 24), check your answers in this chapter. For the essays, evaluate your response against the essay points offered in this chapter. Keep in mind, however, that the essay points noted here are only one way to handle the topic. The AP exam puts a premium on your own ability to do critical analysis. Your clear ideas and the political, economic, and social evidence you bring forward to support your ideas are what matter most. Consider having your teacher (or another student who's roughly as smart as your teacher) read your essay efforts to independently evaluate how you did.

> **TIP**
>
> For any question that really stumps you, go back and review the history in this book and in your school textbook. Taking sample tests gives you an early warning so you can tune up for success on the big AP exam. For general tips about scoring and how to handle questions, see the chapters in Part I.

# SECTION I: MULTIPLE CHOICE

1. **(D).** Columbus set sail for the East Indies, so the inhabitants at his destination would logically be "Indians."

2. **(B).** Remember, *meso* means middle.

3. **(C).** The Iroquois Confederation actually gave the early colonies ideas about the power of united action.

4. **(E).** *Meso* means middle, not an Indian tribe. Here's a mnemonic device: "I'm not forgetting the order of the Big Three tribes, **AM I**?" From north to south, the geographic order is **A**ztec, **M**aya, **I**nca.

5. **(E).** All four were important foods the settlers picked up from the American Indians. If you know for sure that at least two of the choices are correct, you know that (E) has to be the answer by default.

6. **(C).** Only Magellan has a GPS system named after him. The others were more local explorers.

7. **(E).** Even if you don't remember that the *encomienda* system gave Spanish colonists legal power over Indians, you can still throw out the smart-aleck answers about housing and cooking as being not worth an AP question. At worst, that gets you down to a three-choice guess, statistically worth the risk.

8. **(A).** With the Armada gone, Britain got set to rule the waves.

9. **(B).** Popé's Rebellion in the Spanish West and King Philip's War in New England were wars with the American Indians that happened at about the same time in the late 1600s. You can remember the difference if you think of the Indian leader who just happened to be called Popé as associated with the pope-following Catholic Spanish colonists.

10. **(D).** Settlers didn't find any gold, but not because they didn't try.

11. **(D).** Slavery happened early in the New World.

12. **(D).** The real money was in growing sugar in the West Indies.

13. **(A).** The Pil*grims* grimly wanted to get completely out of the Church of England; the Puritans simply wanted to *purify* it.

14. **(D).** The Puritans thought they were too *pure* to allow radical self expression, especially coming from a woman (like Anne Hutchinson).

15. **(C).** The Dutch founded New Amsterdam on the tip of Manhattan.

16. **(D).** The Quakers in Pennsylvania actually believed in treating the American Indians like human beings.

17. **(B).** Like Popé's Rebellion, King Philip's War was a battle with American Indians, so you can rule out any answer choice that doesn't include them.

18. **(D).** In the *Dominion* of New England, the king tried to *dominate*.

19. **(D).** Most slaves went to the West Indies and South America, white indentured servants did most of the hard work before 1700, and slaves rebelled when they could.

20. **(C).** The late-1600s clothes, stern judges, and multiple girls making accusations identify this picture as the Salem Witch Trials.

21. **(D).** At the height of their power and fury, the Indians came pretty close to wiping out the original colonial sites. And if you read the question carefully, you see that, although the other answer choices may be nice American Indian images, they're not about power. Regardless of the details, (D) is the only answer that satisfies the topic.

22. **(A).** The Germans were an important part of the population from the early days, complete with sausage and beer.

23. **(D).** The population of the colonies in 1750 was around 1 million; by the Revolution, it was over 2 million. The patriots fought the Revolution with fewer people than now live in the Sacramento area.

24. **(C).** The Scotch-Irish were poor-but-tough Protestant backwoods farmers.

25. **(D).** Ben Franklin called out the militia to defend peaceful American Indians *against* the bloodthirsty Paxton Boys.

26. **(D).** Outside the aptly named New England, a majority of the population wasn't technically English. Although they shared a government (often unwillingly), Scotland, Ireland, and Wales weren't part of England.

27. **(C).** *Mercantilism* means colonies send raw materials that get turned into *merchandise*. Colonies were expected to buy this merchandise at a nice profit to the mother country.

28. **(A).** Cotton was small-time before the cotton gin, but lots of people wanted to smoke.

29. **(D).** The Navigation Acts were mercantilism under sail: They were meant to block trade with anybody but England.

30. **(C).** The colonies were doing very well financially, thank you. See Chapter 8.

31. **(C).** Early universities were all about religion.

32. **(D).** *New light* ministers put emotion into the First Great Awakening.

33. **(A).** By the clothes and classical pose, this is the picture of a Revolutionary Enlightenment man. The other answers are wrong by generations.

34. **(D).** The *Three-Fifths Compromise* gave slaveholding states three-fifths voting credit for every slave, even though they didn't give the slaves much credit as human beings.

35. **(C).** The Peter Zenger trial helped establish freedom of the press. Notice the repeat of the word *freedom* in three of the five choices for this question. The correct answer is usually one that's part of the pattern.

36. **(D).** With sugar, tobacco, and slaves, America had its share of bad habits, but opium wasn't one of them.

37. **(B).** The Albany Congress was an American-Indian-and-settlers meeting.

38. **(A).** Remember the order of the laws goes from general to worst: first Navigation, then Stamp, and finally Intolerable.

39. **(B).** Loyalists viewed themselves as the real patriots — to England.

40. **(E).** The Revolution and its writings were pure Enlightenment. See Chapter 9.

41. **(C).** This excerpt is from Martin Luther King's famous "I have a dream" speech. Be ready for out-of-chronological-order questions: The real AP test will be full of them.

42. **(E).** Marching is difficult if you don't have shoes.

43. **(C).** This is the only answer that even fits the time period; you can throw out all the other answer choices as being too late.

44. **(B).** The ordinances set up what was then the Northwest of the new United States. In this case, you can get a clue by going with the most important answer: The AP isn't going to bother you with questions about small happenings.

45. **(A).** State power goes with the idea of a loose confederation.

46. **(C).** The Confederation's biggest legislation was the Northwest law.

47. **(D).** Look closely at the longest answers. Because test writers don't want arguments, they usually phrase the right answer carefully. In this case, (D) is the most specific, precisely worded choice (and one of only two that deal with the concept of a republic at all).

48. **(A).** Thomas Jefferson was one of the most prominent supporters of small government (although he did add a lot of territory to be governed with the Louisiana Purchase).

49. **(D).** Freedom starts in your mind with religion, speech, and press.

50. **(C).** Notice that a couple of answers contain the word *bill;* after you pick that pattern out, the Bill of Rights is hopefully ringing some bells. You can definitely get rid of (E), the Founding Fathers, as a smart-aleck answer.

51. **(A).** *Federalists* wanted a strong *federal* government. You can chuck (C) as a smart-aleck choice.

52. **(A).** The first thing a repressive government moves to protect is itself. The other answers aren't sedition.

53. **(B).** John Marshall made the Supreme Court into a powerful third branch of the federal government.

54. **(D).** Of the choices, (B) and (D) present the most important concepts. If you remember that Jefferson was for small government, you can eliminate answer (B) right away and recognize (D) as the most likely possibility.

55. **(C).** Because *embargo* means to stop trade, (E) doesn't make sense. (C) is the most important remaining choice and the correct answer.

56. **(D).** You can eliminate (C), about the Star-Spangled Banner, as a smart-aleck throwaway. Even if you don't know history, if you can eliminate one choice it's statistically best to guess.

57. **(C).** With the AP's emphasis on social struggle, people in questions will tend to be those who fought back, not just folks who went along with powerful interests. In this case, that points to (C) as the most likely answer.

58. **(E).** If you know blacks fought in more than one of these battles, you know it has to be all of them, choice (E).

59. **(C).** The Era of Good Feelings was a victory lap for the new United States, which hasn't experienced an oversupply of political good feelings since.

60. **(A).** "Review all laws for constitutionality" is the most important answer choice and the right one for this question.

61. **(C).** This picture represents the real, in spirit at least, Molly Pitcher. The other choices aren't even in the right time period; the three-cornered hats give away the time.

62. **(E).** Manifest Destiny was the idea that God intended for the U.S. to push westward to the Pacific.

63. **(A).** If you remember that American exceptionalism is the philosophy behind Manifest Destiny, you can eliminate (B) right away and zero in on (A), the choice that best corresponds to the idea of Manifest Destiny (which you've already associated with American exceptionalism).

64. **(B).** (B) is the most precise answer, which is a pretty decent indicator.

65. **(A).** Unless you're going to be a lawyer, your mind can go blank when you see *Cohens v. Virginia*. Carefully checking out the choices can turn the light back on.

66. **(C).** The U.S. wasn't in the business of compromising with the American Indians, so you can rule out (D). (B) and (E) don't make much sense, either; of the two choices remaining, the dividing land between slave and free is the most significant. In this case, it's not the longest answer, but it's the best one.

67. **(E).** Europe wasn't welcome to grab any more New World land.

68. **(A).** The Trail of Tears was ethnic cleansing for American Indians.

69. **(D).** The big voting news in Jacksonian democracy was that non-property-owning white men finally got to vote, so (D) is your answer.

70. **(B).** The spoils system was campaign financing before big money. In return for a little pre-election back-scratching, winning politicians gave their friends and influential supporters cushy government jobs. Answer (B) is your best choice.

71. **(A).** *Nullification* was when a state would try to make a federal law *null* and void (not applicable) within the nullifying state.

72. **(B).** Railroads started to be practical before the Civil War. In Andrew Jackson's time, canals were still the happening thing.

73. **(A).** The humble steel plow changed American prairie grassland into one of the richest agricultural areas in the world.

74. **(E).** Women began to get power just by running their own households. You can eliminate (B) as being too early for women's suffrage.

75. **(B).** Pay attention to the wording of the question: It asks for the most important answer, which is that religion and social action were connected.

76. **(D).** (B) and (C) don't seem terribly important. Of the choices left, "utopian communities" seems to better describe groups with names like Brook Farm and New Harmony, and (D) is the correct answer.

77. **(A).** Women begin to stand up as a group at the Seneca Falls Convention in 1848. The date helps supply the clue.

78. **(A).** Ralph Waldo Emerson was Mr. Transcendentalism, the pivot point for separating personal spirituality from religious dogma.

79. **(A).** The United States had intended to get rid of slavery much sooner than it did. The documents in question provide for the phasing out of slavery, so you can rule out (B) and home in on (A).

80. **(D).** Even slavery's supporters called it peculiar; guilty conscience, anyone?

# SECTION II: FREE-RESPONSE QUESTIONS

The following essay points show sample information that you can organize for your practice essays. Chapter 4 contains detailed guidance on how to write the DBQ response, and Chapter 5 gives you the lowdown on tackling the regular essays.

## Part A: Document-Based Question

The DBQ asks you to discuss the changing nature of slavery and indentured servitude in relation to their evolution, economics, and crops. Here are some general PES (political, economic, and social) facts on the subject of servitude you may want to pull in to your essay:

- Before 1700, white indentured servants outnumbered black slaves.

- In the Chesapeake Bay area, indentured servants grew enough tobacco to increase highly profitable exports of the smoking leaf from 1 million pounds in the 1630s to 40 million pounds in 1700.

- Three out of four English immigrants to this region in the 1700s were servants indentured for around five years of service to pay for their passage.

- The *headright* system allowed anyone bringing in a laborer to get 50 acres of land per imported worker — instant wealth.

- Almost half of the white indentured servants died before they finished their term of service.

- After 1700, more jobs in England made for fewer indentured servants.

- Plantation owners without indentured servants substituted black African slaves who lived longer and worked until they died.

- At the time of the American Revolution, the U.S. was home to fewer than 1 million slaves, mostly in the South.

- After the Revolution, Southern owners freed thousands of slaves, and all Northern states ended slavery. The U.S. banned the importation of slaves in 1808.

- The cotton gin, invented in the late 1790s, made slavery hugely profitable. One slave with a gin could do the work of 50 without; American cotton brought high prices from newly mechanized cotton mills in the U.S. and Britain.

- Slaves cleared new land, and cotton land spread over much of the South, as did sugar in Louisiana.

- By the time of the Civil War in 1860, the South was prosperous, with more than 4 million slaves.

Material from at least some of the provided documents (like the points in the following list) should appear with document letters in brackets in your DBQ essay.

- A: Shows slavery from the very first voyage of Columbus

- B: Shows that a majority of immigrants to the Middle South in the years just before the Revolution were indentured English servants

- C: Demonstrates indentured arrangements

- D: Shows the agony of slavery for Africans at the time of the Revolution

- E: Relates wealth from cotton and reporting Negro sales alongside horses and mules

- F: Reveals the complicity of Northern merchants in Southern slavery

- G: The often-reproduced symbol of the antislavery societies

- H: First-person report of slave driver cruelty

- I: Details the economics of slavery

- J: Emancipation of slaves, as imagined during the Civil War, with horrors of slavery behind and benefits of freedom ahead

# Part B and Part C

In this section is an overview of some points you may want to include on each of the essay choices in Parts B and C. You don't have to have all of these points, but you should have reasonable political, economic, and social (PES) proof to support your thesis and analysis. See Chapter 5 for more on regular essays.

2. Cultural background of colonies

National origins: The concentration of the English in New England, the majority non-English (but still mostly English-speaking) population in central and Southern colonies, and national origin differences can be overplayed. Both rock-ribbed New England farmers and Southern planters were English. German farmers did well in the central states, and Dutch planters added farming experience to central New York.

Religious beliefs: Protestants settled in New England, Catholics in Maryland and Rhode Island, and Church of England in the South. Quakers in Pennsylvania created a safe haven for American Indians and other religions. German Lutherans and Scotch-Irish Presbyterians added religious diversity.

Ethnic background: Most early colonists were of northern European stock with African slaves (and free Africans) accounting for almost 18 percent of the U.S. population by the time of the Revolution. Within the European background of settlers, the Scotch-Irish folks tended to be independent small farmers in mountainous regions, and German Americans often owned productive farms in the central states.

Reasons for coming to America: New England reflected the reform and separatist beliefs of the Puritans and Pilgrims who came to the colonies to found a pure society. Indentured servants in the Middle South came from desperate economic necessity and, when they survived, often demanded better treatment from colonial rulers. Scotch-Irish settlers had faced oppression in Northern Ireland; they didn't put up with being pushed around in the New World. Together, the colonists, with visions of freedom and chips on their shoulders, made a formidable constituency for independence.

3. Charge that America bought freedom with slave labor before and after the Revolution

Economic development: The wealth of the South and some business profits of the North depended on slavery by the time of the Civil War. However, the growth of the colonies up to 1700 centered mostly on individual and indentured English labor. The South managed to recover and grow without slavery after the Civil War. At the time of the Revolution, 82 percent of the population wasn't in slavery. That free percentage actually increased as the Civil War approached, and the growth of the country outstripped the growth of slavery. Initial Revolutionary activity occurred in New England, which had few, if any, slaves. The U.S. would have achieved freedom even without slaves.

Political power: Slavery both retarded and advanced the political power of the United States. The rich Southern slave-owning economy added to the wealth of the nation. On the other hand, the escalating fight over slavery drained political resources. The South managed to control much of the political life of the country due to the three-fifths rule that gave Southern states partial representation for all their nonvoting slaves.

Social beliefs: The unity of national purpose that began in the Second Great Awakening of the 1830s quickly dissipated as religious congregations split over slavery. Southerners had little interest in labor issues or women's rights and a complete hostility to the abolitionist movement. Due to the fragmented, almost-feudal nature of Southern society, public education failed to develop there before the Civil War.

Behavioral changes: Although the North moved West, the South moved no further than the Mississippi River bottom land where it could grow cotton and sugar cane with slave labor. The Northern population soon greatly exceeded that of the South, and almost all industrial development took place in the North. Even with the wealth from cotton, the South and slavery were quickly losing ground to the free states. The U.S. got a financial boost from slavery, but it became free despite slavery's moral burden, not because of slave work's extra profits.

4. How the federal government changed in the Jacksonian Era

Voting behavior: With the beginning of universal white male suffrage, voting and electioneering became national preoccupations. This shift attracted more involvement in government policy and in polarizing issues like the Bank of the U.S. It also made American democracy more real and less of the Enlightenment experiment that had frozen in the polite-but-sterile confines of the Era of Good Feelings.

Policy regarding American Indians: Democracy is often less than idealistic when the economic interests of the voters conflict with the rights of a minority. That's what happened to the American Indians under old fighter Andrew Jackson. Jackson refused to follow a Supreme Court decision favoring American Indian landowners, and he eventually set up their deportation to the West, opening up rich land for Southern settlers and slave owners.

States' rights: Although Jackson's American Indian policy helped the South, his insistence on federal rule stopped an early attempt at nullification by South Carolina (see Chapter 10). Greater male voting led to polarization in states' rights issues.

Federal power: Jackson increased federal power by fighting nullification and opposing the independent economic clout of the Bank of the U.S. His was the first *imperial presidency,* and although voting democracy increased, so did the power of the federal government.

5. North and South relationship changes

Missouri Compromise: Also known as the Compromise of 1820, the agreement admitted Missouri as a slave state, balanced by Maine's entrance as a free state. More importantly, the compromise drew the Mason-Dixon line between slave and free states at the 36th parallel. The agreement bought 30 years of peace between the states, but an aging Thomas Jefferson wrote that the line would eventually tear the Union apart. He was right; attempts to extend and modify the line between slave and free states led to disagreements and bloodshed that led in turn to the Civil War.

Compromise of 1850: This compromise divided land taken from Mexico; admitted California as a free state; allowed New Mexico, Utah, and Arizona to choose to be slave or free; and established the Fugitive Slave law, which made all Americans legally obligated to help catch runaway slaves even if the slaves escaped to free states. The Fugitive Slave law upset the free states, and the uneconomical prospect of slaves on dry western land did nothing to help the South. This compromise lasted only four years; its replacement (the Kansas-Nebraska Act) was an even worse deal for the North.

Kansas-Nebraska Act: The 1854 legislation allowed both Kansas and Nebraska to decide whether they wanted to be slave or free. Because Kansas and Nebraska were north of the Mason-Dixon line, the Kansas-Nebraska Act effectively repealed the Missouri Compromise, which would've designated the two new states as free. Throwing Kansas up in the air led to armed competition between slave and free forces for control of the new state constitution. Now the sides were killing each other on the field of attempted compromise. The Union's relationship was coming apart.

Dred Scott decision: The South had lost control of the Congress, but it still controlled the Supreme Court. In this decision, the court sent freed slave Dred Scott back to slavery and declared that no ruling body could make slavery illegal anywhere in the United States. The Dred Scott decision invalidated all previous, carefully crafted compromises. The North had gone beyond having a simple moral objection to slavery; with the Fugitive Slave law, the battle over Kansas, and now the Dred Scott decision, many in the North felt that the South was out to extend slavery all over the United States. The North suspected that what it called the *slave power* would send slaves to compete for their jobs. What had started as a gentlemanly compromise in 1820 was degenerating into a street fight.

# 26

# Practice Test 2

Practice Test 2 gives you experience with questions from the Civil War until the day before right now. Although the AP exam will be light on questions about very recent events, at least half the test will cover events from the Civil War on. While the actual AP will present questions from all of U.S. history on one exam, this book divides the practice tests at the Civil War to give you a better idea of time periods you may need more work on. The multiple-choice section is first, followed by the essay questions.

- **Multiple Choice:** 80 questions, 55 minutes
- **Document-Based Question:** 1 essay, 60 minutes
- **Regular Essays:** 2 essays, 70 minutes

> **TIP**
>
> As you take this practice test, re-create as best as you can the actual exam conditions: Sit up at a desk, pencil in hand, where the loudest sound is the clock. Turn off your phone and computer. Although wanting to use a computer to type out your essays on this practice test is perfectly normal, handwrite instead to give yourself a better idea of how the exam will feel. You won't get to use computers, phones, or other electronic devices on AP U.S. History game day.

# SECTION I: MULTIPLE CHOICE

*Time: 55 minutes*

*80 Questions*

1. Southerners thought England would have to support them in the Civil War because England needed

   (A) slaves

   (B) Southern cotton

   (C) Southern steel

   (D) a friend in America

   (E) Southern mint juleps

2. Most families in the pre-Civil War South

   (A) owned about ten slaves

   (B) owned no slaves

   (C) secretly supported abolition

   (D) worked for a Republican victory

   (E) were opposed to slavery

3. Northern businessmen before the Civil War

   (A) often profited from slavery

   (B) always opposed slavery

   (C) never lent money to the South

   (D) often secretly held slaves

   (E) thought the South was sure to win

4. Which statement is true of American slavery?

   (A) Slaves were generally happy.

   (B) Slaves staged several revolts.

   (C) All blacks in the U.S. were slaves.

   (D) Importation of new African slaves continued right up to the Civil War.

   (E) The value of slavery declined until it ended.

5. *Uncle Tom's Cabin* was

   (A) the first stop on the Underground Railroad

   (B) a play about a jolly frontiersman

   (C) the most important novel of the 1800s

   (D) a favorite song of the South

   (E) the name of the first national maple syrup brand

6. Gold was discovered in California

   (A) by early Spanish missionaries

   (B) on unclaimed land days before California joined the U.S.

   (C) after years of prospecting

   (D) on land that belonged to the president

   (E) on land that belonged to rich investors

7. The policy of *popular sovereignty* meant that

   (A) whoever was most popular got to be president

   (B) the people elected whomever they wanted

   (C) new states could choose whether to be slave or free

   (D) new states could decide their own capital cities

   (E) people were responsible for their own budgets

8. The big Southern win in the Compromise of 1850 was

   (A) Arizona's slave-state status

   (B) the railroad through Atlanta

   (C) the Force Act

   (D) the Fugitive Slave Act

   (E) the Kansas-Nebraska Act

9. John Brown acted before the Civil War as a

   (A) militant abolitionist

   (B) Southern compromiser

   (C) Northern factory leader

   (D) Southern slaveholder

   (E) Northern diplomat

10. In the Dred Scott case

    (A) the North won a victory for freedom

    (B) the South won a legal battle but stirred up Northern opposition

    (C) the North won a legal battle but stirred up Southern opposition

    (D) slavery became illegal

    (E) John Brown saved Kansas

11. James Buchanan was

    (A) the last president before the Civil War

    (B) the leader of the abolitionists

    (C) one of the founders of the Underground Railroad

    (D) opposed to the Dred Scott decision

    (E) a tough leader with lots of children

12. In his first election, Lincoln got

    (A) 60 percent of the vote

    (B) support from only two Southern states

    (C) less than 40 percent of the vote

    (D) respect even from those who opposed him

    (E) the majority vote in a two-party election

13. The *Monitor* and the *Merrimack* were

    (A) musicals that helped start the Civil War

    (B) two trains that raced between the North and the South

    (C) two early forms of television

    (D) the ships in the first battle between ironclads

    (E) the planes in the first battle between airplanes

14. Lincoln's Emancipation Proclamation

    (A) freed all the slaves

    (B) was in planning before Lincoln's election

    (C) followed the Battle of Gettysburg

    (D) freed only slaves in Confederate states

    (E) was politically unpopular in Europe

15. The Battle of Gettysburg

    (A) stopped the South in the Civil War

    (B) saved George Washington in the Revolution

    (C) began the American advance in the Mexican War

    (D) stopped the British in the War of 1812

    (E) was the only U.S. defeat in World War I

16. The U.S. Civil War saw

    (A) over 600,000 men die

    (B) slaves made free and economically equal

    (C) cotton die out as a crop

    (D) massive killing by angry slaves

    (E) a completely white Northern army free the slaves

17. One leader in the 1880s said that his opponents were "laying the foundation for their colossal fortunes on the bodies and souls of living men." He was probably a

    (A) labor leader

    (B) religious leader

    (C) conservative Republican

    (D) business leader

    (E) inventor

18. The main goal of Reconstruction was
    (A) building new governments and social help for the South
    (B) obtaining war reparations to repay Northern losses
    (C) rebuilding New Orleans following a hurricane
    (D) curing economic ills following the Great Depression
    (E) promoting home ownership through low-interest construction mortgages

19. The first states to give women the right to vote were predominately in the
    (A) North
    (B) South
    (C) East
    (D) Midwest
    (E) West

20. The Ulysses S. Grant administration was marked by
    (A) great economic progress by freed slaves
    (B) opposition from war veterans
    (C) landslide victories by the Republicans
    (D) honest government by all parties
    (E) corruption by Grant appointees but not Grant

21. The Republicans won the Hayes election of 1876 by agreeing to
    (A) help the ex-slaves in the South
    (B) keep the tariffs low
    (C) expand the Homestead Act to the whole West
    (D) withdraw federal troops from the South
    (E) let the Democrats control the Senate

22. Frederick Douglass said, "Peace with the old master class has been war to the Negro. As one has risen, the other has fallen. The reaction has been sudden, marked, and violent." He was talking about
    (A) slavery before the Civil War
    (B) federal troops right after the Civil War
    (C) Sherman's march to the sea during the Civil War
    (D) the end of Reconstruction after the Civil War
    (E) the Spanish-American War

23. Unions in the late 1800s almost all fought for this change in the workplace, which didn't become standard until the 1900s.
    (A) equal rights for women
    (B) fair treatment of minorities
    (C) one-hour lunch breaks
    (D) the eight-hour workday
    (E) equal pay for blacks

24. Charles Darwin's theory of evolution was
    (A) immediately opposed by all major Christian churches
    (B) a challenge to everything most Americans believed
    (C) opposed by the government
    (D) endorsed by the old Confederacy
    (E) accepted by most scientists and many religious leaders

25. Most settlers in the West
    (A) got land for free from the government
    (B) bought their land from private companies or states
    (C) made plenty of money ranching
    (D) opposed the introduction of barbed wire
    (E) had enough water to grow almost anything

26. The national program that helped stop the bank panic during the Great Depression was the
    (A) Civilian Conservation Corps
    (B) Emergency Relief Administration
    (C) Twenty-first Amendment
    (D) Federal Deposit Insurance Corporation
    (E) Federal Housing Administration

27. The purpose of Jim Crow laws was to
    (A) help blacks get ahead
    (B) keep blacks in their place
    (C) allow the South to expand industry
    (D) force Crows opposed to the railroad to cooperate
    (E) honor the memory of a great American

28. The Pendleton Act of 1883
    (A) fought government corruption
    (B) allowed hiring of more government employees
    (C) regulated wool production
    (D) ended big money involvement in politics
    (E) helped farmers recover from the recession

29. The Populist Party

    (A) supported Grover Cleveland

    (B) elected only two presidents

    (C) saw many of its proposals enacted eventually

    (D) was against the eight-hour workday

    (E) campaigned in only one election

30. The 30 years following the Civil War saw the U.S.

    (A) suffering from the Great Recession

    (B) going from destruction to being the manufacturing leader of the world

    (C) banning most people from immigrating

    (D) steadily helping blacks to prosper

    (E) fighting constant wars

31. Booker T. Washington, George Washington Carver, and W.E.B. Du Bois were

    (A) political leaders

    (B) union leaders

    (C) Civil War generals

    (D) black leaders

    (E) early recording artists

32. Which one of the following was an important leader in the women's movement?

    (A) Judith Ben-Hur

    (B) Emily Dickinson

    (C) Daisy Miller

    (D) Susan B. Anthony

    (E) Belle Starr

33. A leader said, "[T]he antelope have gone; the buffalo wallows are empty. . .We are like birds with a broken wing." He was probably

    (A) an American Indian leader in 1700

    (B) an American Indian leader in 1800

    (C) a trapper in the 1820s

    (D) a frontiersman in the 1850s

    (E) an American Indian in the 1890s

34. When did historian Frederick Turner say that the American Western frontier was closed?

    (A) in 1790

    (B) in 1820

    (C) by 1850

    (D) after 1920

    (E) around 1890

35. *The Washington Post* editorialized that "The taste of Empire is in the mouth of the people even as the taste of blood is in the jungle." What period in American history was the *Post* describing?

    (A) the U.S. after World War II

    (B) the national mood during the Revolution

    (C) the North after the Civil War

    (D) the country before the Spanish American War

    (E) American opinion during World War I

36. The U.S. got Hawaii because

    (A) the Hawaiians didn't want it

    (B) sugar cane business interests grabbed the government

    (C) Hawaiian Queen Liliuokalani loved America

    (D) the British ceded it to the U.S. in return for Cuba

    (E) the U.S. defeated Hawaii in the Pacific War

37. The expansion of the United States to overseas territories like Puerto Rico and the Philippines was

    (A) supported by all Americans

    (B) opposed by radicals in the labor unions

    (C) supported by only a few conservatives

    (D) opposed by leaders like Mark Twain, Andrew Carnegie, and the presidents of Harvard and Stanford

    (E) so controversial that it led to a new government

38. Hippies, civil rights, Vietnam, and student demonstrations all became national movements in the

    (A) Roaring '20s

    (B) 1950s

    (C) 1960s

    (D) 1970s

    (E) 1980s

39. Teddy Roosevelt was

    (A) the father of Franklin Roosevelt

    (B) a champion of conservation and business reform

    (C) a conservative Republican

    (D) a liberal Democrat

    (E) a hero of World War I

40. The Roosevelt Corollary to the Monroe Doctrine meant that

    (A) the U.S. would partner with any European intervention

    (B) the U.S. would intervene to fix South American problems instead of letting European powers in

    (C) the U.S. also protected Canada and Asia

    (D) the American Navy patrol would no longer exist

    (E) South American countries could do what they wanted

41. When women and working people didn't win their crusades for rights in the 1880s, they

    (A) mostly turned to violence

    (B) gave up for a while in the face of opposition

    (C) kept working so they would win someday

    (D) made a deal with big business and sold out

    (E) depended on politicians to get them some help

42. Early investigative reporters who publicized needed reforms were

    (A) spy-tellers

    (B) national enquirers

    (C) scandalrakers

    (D) muckrakers

    (E) troublemongers

43. The only president ever to resign from office was

    (A) Richard Nixon

    (B) Lyndon Johnson

    (C) Andrew Jackson

    (D) James Monroe

    (E) Jimmy Carter

44. Progressives who changed American politics in the early 1900s were

    (A) radical reformers

    (B) liberal Democrats

    (C) labor union leaders

    (D) middle class reformers

    (E) Republican conservatives

45. The first president to set aside large areas of land for national parks was

    (A) William Howard Taft

    (B) Abraham Lincoln

    (C) Franklin Roosevelt

    (D) Teddy Roosevelt

    (E) Ulysses S. Grant

46. In the 1800s, high tariffs were usually supported by
    (A) Republican businessmen
    (B) Democrats
    (C) Labor unions
    (D) British manufacturers
    (E) Farmers and ranchers

47. The Federal Reserve Act
    (A) created a national banking system without a national bank for the United States
    (B) gave the U.S. one government-owned bank to run everything with central control of loans
    (C) reserved federal land for parks
    (D) saved valuable oil for time of war
    (E) reserved financial deposits to buy U.S. Bonds

48. President Wilson's early policy toward World War I was to
    (A) try to get the U.S. involved early to help Britain
    (B) wait until Japan attacked the U.S. at Pearl Harbor
    (C) sell supplies to the Allies but not to Germany
    (D) help Germany until they caused a problem
    (E) try to stay out of the fight

49. During World War I, the goal of open treaties, freedom of the seas, national self-determination, and an international peacekeeping organization were all part of
    (A) Wilson's 14 Points
    (B) Britain's Royal War Aims
    (C) Germany's Imperial Policy
    (D) the Peace Proposals of France
    (E) the Republican legislative program

50. Which of these gave women the right to vote all over the United States?
    (A) the Nineteenth Amendment of 1920
    (B) the Twentieth Amendment of 1910
    (C) the Thirteenth Amendment of 1900
    (D) the Women's Suffrage Act of 1931
    (E) the Equal Rights Act of 1940

51. Who most strongly supported the Treaty of Versailles?

    (A) Germany

    (B) Russia

    (C) U.S. Republicans

    (D) isolationists

    (E) Woodrow Wilson

52. The movie *The Birth of a Nation* helped to popularize

    (A) the Ku Klux Klan

    (B) the Boy Scouts

    (C) fair treatment of blacks

    (D) immigration reform

    (E) the American Revolution

53. America's Roaring '20s were a time of

    (A) limited drinking

    (B) liberal government

    (C) fair treatment of immigrants

    (D) conservative presidents

    (E) prosperity for everybody

54. Who said that "the only thing we have to fear is fear itself — nameless, unreasoning, unjustified terror which paralyzes needed efforts to convert retreat into advance"?

    (A) Teddy Roosevelt

    (B) Woodrow Wilson

    (C) Franklin Roosevelt

    (D) Ronald Reagan

    (E) John F. Kennedy

55. The Scopes Monkey Trial concerned

    (A) the treatment of zoo animals

    (B) jungle exploration rights

    (C) the establishment of rights in hunting

    (D) the teaching of evolution

    (E) the teaching of radical politics

56. Republican President Hoover's response to the Great Depression was

    (A) a massive public relief program

    (B) to increase the size of the Army in an attempt to create jobs

    (C) to give money to businesses so that it would trickle down to the poor

    (D) to lower tariffs to make more jobs

    (E) to support veterans who marched on Washington

57. Franklin Roosevelt's program of relief, recovery, and reform was

    (A) the New Deal

    (B) the New Society

    (C) the Monroe Doctrine

    (D) the War on Poverty

    (E) America First

58. The Federal Housing Administration (FHA) started under President

    (A) Lyndon Johnson

    (B) Andrew Johnson

    (C) Franklin Roosevelt

    (D) Herbert Hoover

    (E) George H.W. Bush

59. John Steinbeck's most famous book was

    (A) *Gone with the Wind*

    (B) *Little Women*

    (C) *The Grapes of Wrath*

    (D) *Uncle Tom's Cabin*

    (E) *Moby-Dick*

60. The New Deal program that guaranteed small pensions for the elderly and the handicapped was the

    (A) Tennessee Valley Authority

    (B) National Recovery Administration

    (C) Emergency Relief Administration

    (D) Public Works Administration

    (E) Social Security Act

61. The Congress of Industrial Organizations (CIO) was a union dedicated to organizing

    (A) Congress

    (B) skilled workers

    (C) industry office workers

    (D) the part of an organization that had assembly line workers

    (E) whole industries including unskilled workers

62. What was the purpose of the Lend-Lease Bill?

    (A) to lend the leases on foreclosed houses to banks

    (B) to help the Allies in World War I

    (C) to make as much money as possible during war

    (D) to get supplies to the Allies in World War II

    (E) to ensure American neutrality

63. The Allies of the United States in World War II were
    (A) Britain and Russia
    (B) Britain and Japan
    (C) Japan and Germany
    (D) France and Italy
    (E) Russia and Italy

64. The last war the U.S. Army fought in which white troops were segregated from black troops was
    (A) World War I
    (B) the Civil War
    (C) World War II
    (D) the Korean War
    (E) the Spanish-American War

65. Up until 1944, almost all of the ground fighting against the Germans in Europe was done by the
    (A) British
    (B) Italians
    (C) Americans
    (D) Russians
    (E) French

66. The form of government in shortest supply in the world before World War II was
    (A) democracy
    (B) dictatorship
    (C) monarchy
    (D) colonialism
    (E) military control

67. The popular name for the legislation passed during World War II to help returning servicemen was the
    (A) Adjustment Act
    (B) Soldier's Pension
    (C) GI Bill
    (D) Bonus March
    (E) Victory Bond

68. The name that Russia and its associated countries went by during their Communist period was
    (A) Mother Russia
    (B) the Union of Soviet Socialist Republics (U.S.S.R.)
    (C) the People's Republic of Soviet Eurasia
    (D) Bolshevik Workers Republic
    (E) Russian Confederation of States

69. The United Nations and the International Monetary Fund started at the end of
    (A) the Korean War
    (B) the War between the States
    (C) World War I
    (D) World War II
    (E) the Cold War

70. The financial assistance that helped Europe recover after World War II was the
    (A) Truman Doctrine
    (B) Marshall Plan
    (C) Lend-Lease Bill
    (D) Ford Foundation
    (E) Nuremberg Federation

71. The Supreme Court decision in *Brown v. Board of Education* helped
    (A) fund women's athletics
    (B) provide college loans to poor people
    (C) end segregation in education
    (D) soldiers get a college education
    (E) expand schools in the West

72. The United States fought Communist troops in
    (A) Korea and Vietnam
    (B) Vietnam and Japan
    (C) Korea and Europe
    (D) Vietnam and the Middle East
    (E) the first Gulf War

73. The president who said he was against government but spent enough money to triple the national debt was
    (A) John F. Kennedy
    (B) Woodrow Wilson
    (C) Ronald Reagan
    (D) Bill Clinton
    (E) Dwight Eisenhower

74. The president who tried to start the Great Society and sent hundreds of thousands of troops into Vietnam was
    (A) Andrew Johnson
    (B) Lyndon Johnson
    (C) John F. Kennedy
    (D) Jimmy Carter
    (E) Dwight Eisenhower

75. "Ask not what your country can do for you; ask what you can do for your country." These words are from a speech by
    (A) John F. Kennedy
    (B) George W. Bush
    (C) Bill Clinton
    (D) Grover Cleveland
    (E) Lyndon Johnson

76. A standoff between the Soviet Union and the United States in 1962 that could have led to nuclear war was
    (A) the Panama Canal Showdown
    (B) the Congo War
    (C) the Berlin Airlift
    (D) the Italian Bomber Crisis
    (E) the Cuban Missile Crisis

77. What were the Southern Christian Leadership Conference and the Student Nonviolent Coordinating Committee?
    (A) Great Awakening congregations
    (B) peace movements in the 1970s
    (C) teaching commissions for ministers
    (D) civil rights organizations
    (E) women's rights organizations

78. Gerald Ford became president after
    (A) Richard Nixon resigned over the Watergate scandal
    (B) John F. Kennedy was shot
    (C) William Van Buren died in office
    (D) William Howard Taft chose him as vice president
    (E) a hard-fought election with Jimmy Carter

79. The Supreme Court case of *Engel v. Vitale* said that
    (A) abortion is legal in the U.S.
    (B) officials can't require prayers in school
    (C) officers must read arrested suspects their rights
    (D) federal law supersedes state law
    (E) women must be granted Title IX rights

80. The World Trade Organization has worked to
    (A) lower tariffs
    (B) promote products
    (C) raise tariffs to protect developing nations
    (D) trade the United Nations for another world organization
    (E) restrict trade to healthy products

# SECTION II: FREE-RESPONSE QUESTIONS

In this section, take the DBQ in Part A and then complete the two regular essays in Parts B and C.

## Part A: Document-Based Question

*Planning Time: 15 minutes*

*Suggested Writing Time: 45 minutes*

*Percent of Section II score: 45*

---

1. How did World War II change the lives of men and women in the United States? Discuss the role of social and economic trends as well as the changing nature of the U.S. political situation. Use the documents and your knowledge of the time period in writing your response.

### Document A

Source: Jerome B. Cohen, *Japan's Economy in War and Reconstruction* (1949) p 354

### Real Value Consumer Spending

|         | 1937 | 1939 | 1940 | 1941 | 1942 | 1943 | 1944 | 1945 |
|---------|------|------|------|------|------|------|------|------|
| Japan   | 100  | 107  | 109  | 111  | 108  | 99   | 93   | 78   |
| Germany | 100  | 108  | 117  | 108  | 105  | 95   | 94   | 85   |
| USA     | 100  | 96   | 103  | 108  | 116  | 115  | 118  | 122  |

## Document B

Source: Letter home from a U.S. soldier, 1945

I think I'm well qualified to report that the Yank, 1943 version, is doing a good job in upholding the traditions of his father and his grandfather and all who came before him. His few weaknesses are a source of pride rather than otherwise. He occasionally gets drunk, but that's because he loves his home and family and is terrifically lonely for both. He's slow to anger, but when he does get mad, he fights like hell. He's quick to forgive — the picture of him giving his candy ration to Italian kids is not a publicity gag. Sometimes he gets cheated, but it's because he has a deep faith in human nature. I think he's the best there is.

We could have done very nicely without this war, but I do think it has given us a new sense of values which will go a long way in canceling any future wars.

## Document C

Source: Letter from the front

First is the absolute futility of war. Seen at close range, it becomes so brutal and stupid that we have to rub our eyes to believe the world is capable of it.

A second impression is the fundamental similarity of the peoples of the United Nations. I've lived and worked with British, French, Australian, South African, New Zealand, Polish, and Belgian soldiers to name a few. I'm convinced that we all seek the same general sort of life. We criticize one another for our little individual eccentricities; each of us thinks his is the best nation; but fundamentally we differ little. When this war is won, we must remember only the fundamentals and get together in a big way.

A third impression is that of America's own capabilities. London, Algiers, Paris, Rome, Florence, Marseilles, and every other city and town in every liberated country teeming with American traffic. Huge depots of American supplies, throngs of American men everywhere. If we can put forth one half the effort for peace that we've extended in this war, because it was necessary, there should never be need for another war. We must realize that peace, now, is just as necessary as the war has been.

I'm now living in a half-wrecked miner's house. There's snow and there's cold....

## Document D

Source: War Bonds, U.S. Treasury Department, 1942

*Courtesy of Northwestern University Library*

## Document E

Source: Map of Japanese Internment Camps

*Map by Wiley, Composition Services Graphics*

## Document F

Source: World War II Experiences of a Child

I wrote letters to servicemen on tissue-thin V-mail paper that folded into a self envelope. My friends and I saved tinfoil from packages and crimped it around growing balls of foil to turn in to help the war effort. Every week at school we purchased a ten-cent War Savings Stamp and glued it into our war stamp book until we had enough to purchase an $18 War Bond which matured years later for $25. Meat and gasoline were rationed and eggs were difficult to obtain. No matter how much money you had you could only purchase the amounts for which you had unused ration stamps. People walked, took public transportation, and car-pooled. During air raid drills at elementary school we sat on the floor in the halls and sang patriotic songs

## Document G

Source: U.S. Office of War Information, 1943

*Courtesy of Northwestern University Library*

## Document H

Source: World War II News

Food worst problem; costs up, but pay up more

There may not be the abundance of food at home today that there was a year ago, but there is plenty to go around and although prices have risen wages have gone ahead of them. Machinery already is in motion, both governmental and private, to see that men get jobs as soon as they take off their uniforms.

People are eating differently, that's all: less meat and more of other items. Restaurants have introduced meatless days; the Waldorf in New York, for instance, has three a week. Except for shoes — which are limited to three pairs a year for each person — clothes rationing is not in sight. Candy is still plentiful, and the guy with a thirst still can slake it with all the beer he wants.

Whatever complaints are heard are directed mostly at the lack of gasoline. With one car to every four and a half people, Americans had all but forgotten how to walk. Now they're obliged to learn all over again. The Government is strict about the ban on pleasure driving. Agents check the race tracks and baseball stadiums for cars, and even the vicinity of movie houses. The only large-scale chiseling evident has been the black market in food, which the Government is taking drastic steps to wipe out.

### Document I

Source: GI Bill Statistics

To be eligible for GI Bill education benefits, a World War II veteran had to serve 90 days or more after September 16, 1940.

In the peak year of 1947, veterans accounted for 49 percent of college enrollment. Mortgages for GI's could cover all costs. Out of a veteran population of 15,440,000, some 7.8 million were trained, including:

- 2,230,000 in college (1/3 of all returning veterans entered college)
- 3,480,000 in other schools
- 1,400,000 in on-job training
- 690,000 in farm training
- College enrollment in millions: 1939 = 1.5, 1949 = 2.6, 1969 = 8.0, 1989 = 13.5, 2005 = 18.5 million
- Number of Americans who owned their own homes: pre-War = 1 in 3, post-War = 2 in 3.

# Part B and Part C

*Total Planning and Writing Time: 70 minutes*

*Percent of Section II score: 55*

# Part B

*Choose ONE question from this part.*

2. In what manner did the political climate of the U.S. change from the 1890s to the 1910s? Discuss these changes with regard to TWO of the following:

   Public opinion

   Business

   Environment

   International policy

3. Explain the participation of the United States in World War I and its consequences. In your explanation, include TWO of the following topics:

   Military outcomes

   Impact on the United States

   Impact on other countries

   International trade

## Part C

*Choose ONE question from this part.*

4. Outline the causes and effects of the Great Depression in TWO of the following periods:

   1924–1929

   1930–1934

   1935–1939

   1940–1945

5. Conservative presidents sometimes take progressive steps. Discuss the contributions of TWO of the following presidents to the modern United States:

   Dwight D. Eisenhower (1952–1960)

   Richard M. Nixon (1969–1974)

   Ronald Reagan (1980–1988)

   George H. W. Bush (1988–1992)

# 27

# Answers to Practice Test 2

**U**se the information in this chapter to score Practice Test 2. For the essays, evaluate your response against the essay points offered here, keeping in mind that these points are only one way to handle the topic.

> **TIP**
>
> Consider having your teacher read your essay efforts and evaluate how you did. For questions that stump you, review the relevant time period in this book and in your school textbook.

For general information about scoring and how to handle questions, see the chapters in Part I.

## SECTION I: MULTIPLE CHOICE

1. **(B).** It's the cotton. But, as it turned out, Britain was willing to go without a few shirts to avoid helping slavery.

2. **(B).** They were fighting for their Southern white pride against the Yankees.

3. **(A).** Hatred and fear of the slave power overcame the profit motive.

4. **(B).** Slaves sometimes fought against an overwhelmingly brutal system.

5. **(C).** If you don't know about *Uncle Tom's Cabin,* maybe you haven't been paying close enough attention. The other answers are smart-aleck choices.

6. **(B).** The Spanish were all about finding gold, but they never found it along the American River in their former possession of California.

7. **(C).** *Popular sovereignty* actually means that the people rule, but the most important issue folks were arguing about before the Civil War was to keep or free slaves.

8. **(D).** With the Fugitive Slave Act, the North had to help the South recapture slaves, something most in the North hated.

9. **(A).** John Brown was an extremely militant abolitionist, certainly no compromiser or diplomat.

10. **(B).** This is an example of a *wrong trend* question. In wrong trend questions, all of the answers except the correct one follow one pattern. Because only one answer can be right, if you can find one choice that shows a different trend, it's often correct. Of course, you have to know something about history to spot a wrong trend.

11. **(A).** Buchanan may have done better not to show up at all.

12. **(C).** Lincoln barely slipped into office.

13. **(D).** This is an example of a question you can *logic out*. Toss out the unimportant choices: musicals, train races, TV. That leaves airplanes and ships, which gives you a pretty good shot at guessing correctly even if you don't remember the *Monitor* and the *Merrimack*.

14. **(D).** Sometimes it's important to stand for principle, at least against your enemy.

15. **(A).** Gettysburg is one of the most famous battles in the Civil War, largely because the North's victory was a huge turning point in the conflict.

16. **(A).** It took a lot of deaths to free the slaves.

17. **(A).** A labor leader opposes fortunes that rob workers.

18. **(A).** Answers (C), (D), and (E) are from the wrong time period, and the North never asked that the South pay it back. That leaves (A).

19. **(E).** Tough cowboys were nice to women.

20. **(E).** Borderline-smart-aleck wrong answers: The freed slaves never made great economic progress, no one had landslide victories in the late 1800s, and completely honest government was rare.

21. **(D).** Withdrawing the federal troops that were protecting the blacks was the deal the Republicans made to hang on to power.

22. **(D).** When occupying troops withdraw, the people they've been protecting suffer.

23. **(D).** If you like the eight-hour workday, thank the unions.

24. **(E).** Most scientists, religious organizations, and Christians accepted Darwin's theory as just another way God may work in the world. A minority became upset and believed Darwin's theory threatened their faith.

25. **(B).** Land in the West wasn't cheap or easy to work.

26. **(D).** The Federal Deposit Insurance Corporation (FDIC) insured individual deposits and gave people the confidence to leave their money in the bank.

27. **(B).** Jim Crow was the name of a popular minstrel character. The Jim Crow laws restricted the rights of black people.

28. **(A).** The Pendleton Act cleaned up most corruption in government hiring, leaving only fundraising as a form of shady influence.

29. **(C).** The Populists never won a battle, but they eventually won the war.

30. **(B).** The industrial states were doing very well financially, thank you.

31. **(D).** You need to know basic background information about minorities.

32. **(D).** You need to know the high points of the women's rights movement.

33. **(E).** It took 400 years from the landing of Columbus until the last American Indians lost their right to roam a natural world.

34. **(E).** Americans settlers finished occupying the West around 1890.

35. **(D).** The U.S. saw how much fun England was having and wanted some of the world for itself. The Spanish-American War was America's attempt to build a small empire and "save" Spanish colonies by taking them over.

36. **(B).** It was a business agreement that the Hawaiians didn't fight.

37. **(D).** Like lots of people, these leaders thought loving freedom and building empires didn't work together.

38. **(C).** These struggles and a lot more started in the 1960s. Note that this question is out of chronological order; the real AP will have the multiple-choice time periods completely scrambled.

39. **(B).** Theodore Roosevelt was a Progressive Republican.

40. **(B).** Theodore Roosevelt said that the U.S. would keep Latin America tidy — no Europeans allowed.

41. **(C).** Women and working people never gave up.

42. **(D).** They raked up the muck of scandal so everyone could live in a cleaner barnyard.

43. **(A).** It was "Tricky Dick" Nixon. This is another out-of-time-order question to keep your mind flexible.

44. **(D).** The Progressives were as middle class as a mortgage payment.

45. **(D).** Teddy Roosevelt started the magnificent legacy of national parks.

46. **(A).** Republicans were in favor of the kind of government that helped them make money.

47. **(A).** The Fed doesn't have cute checks or credit cards, but it moves the money behind them. The last three answer choices are *red herrings* designed to draw you off the path.

48. **(E).** Wilson was more evenhanded before World War I than Roosevelt was before World War II. Wilson really thought the U.S. could stay neutral; Roosevelt in his time didn't believe that.

49. **(A).** Wilson had a dream of peace called the 14 Points.

50. **(A).** Women got the right to vote nationally after World War I.

51. **(E).** Wilson got what he could in the treaty, but the world wasn't ready to police international peace.

52. **(A).** This good entertainment brought back a bad nightmare.

53. **(D).** The Republican presidents of the 1920s did as little as possible.

54. **(C).** FDR's big line couldn't have come at a better time.

55. **(D).** You have to know about evolution. All the other answer choices are red herrings.

56. **(C).** Hoover never met a business he didn't like.

57. **(A).** FDR was the real deal, and that meant a New Deal.

58. **(C).** If an agency has as an acronym, chances are fair it started with FDR.

59. **(C).** You don't need to be a culture vulture, but you should know the literary milestones.

60. **(E).** Despite early Republican efforts to kill it, Social Security is still very much part of the plans of most elderly people.

61. **(E).** The CIO formed to represent whole industries, including often-overlooked unskilled and minority workers.

62. **(D).** Beware the red herrings. If you know the historical background, you know the answer is supplies in World War II.

63. **(A).** Every other answer choice contains at least one enemy.

64. **(C).** After World War II, the U.S. woke up to the fact that freedom means integration.

65. **(D).** Russia did the vast majority of the European ground fighting in World War II.

66. **(A).** Before World War II, you could count the real democracies of the world on one hand.

67. **(C).** The bill helped change life in America.

68. **(B).** Maybe you've heard the shortened version of that name — the Soviet Union. Or maybe you've heard the Beatles' song "Back in the U.S.S.R."

69. **(D).** After World War II, the world started to go international with organizations like the United Nations and the International Monetary Fund (IMF). Nobody wanted to see World War III.

70. **(B).** The Marshall Plan *marshaled* the forces of good to help battered Europe.

71. **(C).** *Brown v. Board* said separate isn't equal.

72. **(A).** The U.S. jumped into the middle of two civil wars because one side was Communist.

73. **(C).** Reagan's the one.

74. **(B).** LBJ all the way.

75. **(A).** Idealism from John F. Kennedy.

76. **(E).** Some of the other answer choices are fake; the ones that did happen weren't close to 1962.

77. **(D).** Know your social movements.

78. **(A).** Ford had a bad act to follow.

79. **(B).** The First Amendment means officials can't require prayer in schools.

80. **(A).** The World Trade Organization (WTO) is all about getting the world to trade, trade, trade, which is what lower tariffs promote.

# SECTION II: FREE-RESPONSE QUESTIONS

The following sections provide sample information that you can utilize for your practice essays. Chapter 4 contains detailed guidance on how to write the DBQ response, and Chapter 5 gives you the lowdown on tackling the regular essays.

## Part A: Document-Based Question

The DBQ asks you to discuss how WWII changed American life socially, economically, and politically. The following list gives you some sample PES facts you may want to include in your essay:

- When World War II started, civilian industry changed to wartime production.
- Standardization of wartime production led to more job opportunities for less-skilled workers.

- With more work available, consumer spending went up 20 percent even though production was down.

- People had to have ration coupons *and* money to buy most commodities. Gas limits were three gallons per week.

- War production was half of the economy. The U.S. outproduced all of its enemies put together.

- By the end of the war, most people were paying federal income tax. Before the war, only 10 percent of the people paid the tax.

- Mexican workers replaced farmers off to war. Women replaced men on the assembly lines.

- Pay went up; unions organized but mostly didn't strike. The CIO fought racism and sexism in union ranks.

- World War II ended the Depression, and almost everybody had a job.

- Women worked as Rosie the Riveter in wartime industry and as *government girls* in federal agencies.

- A baby boom started right after the war; births went up by 30 percent.

- The federal Fair Employment Practices Committee was the most important aid up to that time for fair treatment of blacks and women on the job.

- Over 120,000 Japanese Americans were interned in camps.

- Celebrities from Humphrey Bogart to Donald Duck supported the war effort.

- The United States was really united to fight the good war.

Material (such as the following points) from at least some of the provided documents should show up in your DBQ essay, with the document letters in brackets.

- A: Starting at an equalized norm, the chart shows how the war benefited un-bombed U.S. consumers but hurt their enemies.

- B: This document shows new internationalism.

- C: Internationalism and the U.S. were in the world to stay.

- D: This poster shows the threat to U.S. families from the Nazis. The solution to this threat was to buy war bonds to help finance the war effort.

- E: Japanese internment camps were all over the West, showing lingering suspicion of foreigners.

- F: Careful living on the home front meant the whole country was working together to support the armed forces in the field.

- G: This poster shows the Allies working together as a powerful cannon blasting the enemy.

- H: This document shows home front sacrifices but also optimism that problems are solvable.

- I: Wounds would slowly heal, and opportunities grew with victory.

- J: The GI Bill and changes in the economy in general were a tremendous boost for getting ahead in the new postwar United States.

# Part B and Part C

This section outlines some points you may want to include in your essays over the prompts in Parts B and C. You don't have to use all of these specific points, but make sure you have reasonable political, economic, and social (PES) proof to support your thesis and analysis.

2. Changes from the 1890s to the 1910s

Public opinion: Literacy improved, and for the first time the public started to have informed opinions based on widespread reading. Newspapers and magazines in the 1900s started to feature muckraker exposés of scandals in housing, government, and food manufacturing.

Business: Teddy Roosevelt and the presidents who followed him broke up big businesses that used their corporate power to cheat consumers. Businesses continued to expand on the strength of product innovation rather than pure power. Some big businessmen like Andrew Carnegie and John D. Rockefeller gave money for the public good.

Environment: With the frontier closed, Teddy Roosevelt began the creation of a national system of public parks that became the model for the U.S. and the world.

International policy: The U.S. asserted itself more in world affairs as the 1890s drew to a close, with the Spanish-American War and increased U.S. interests in Asia.

3. U.S. participation in World War I

Military outcomes: The U.S. got to France just in time to keep the Germans from winning. Although only relatively small numbers of U.S. troops got into the fighting, they encouraged the Allies and discouraged the Germans into surrendering. Because no international policing organization existed, the Germans rearmed for World War II.

Impact on the United States: Despite President Wilson's idealistic 14 Points program for world peace, the U.S. withdrew into its isolationist shell after the war. Politicians refused to support Wilson's plan for the League of Nations. The U.S. had been a hero, but came away more determined than ever to stick to its own business.

Impact on other countries: Britain and France were so worn out that they were willing to sell out most of Europe to Germany to avoid another war. Russia's defeat in World War I paved the way for a Communist government. Hitler rose to save an impoverished Germany, which thought it had been stabbed in the back by giving up in World War I just when it had almost won. World War II was really an extension of World War I with a recess.

International trade: The U.S. was never fully repaid for supplies sent to the Allies in World War I. When the U.S. economy collapsed at the end of the 1920s, the country slapped a record-high tariff on trade, which shut off any chance of working together with other nations to solve world economic problems.

4. Causes and effects of the Great Depression

1924 through 1929: Conservative Republican presidents let business do what it wanted. The stock market boomed; no one could see an end in sight for the new U.S. economy, which was based on consumer debt and high consumer spending. Republicans raised the tariff, making products more expensive. When the stock market crashed on Black Tuesday in 1929, it was the end of a long, profitable ride.

1930 through 1934: Republican President Hoover's response to the crash was the Smoot-Hawley Tariff, the highest peacetime import taxes in U.S. history. Unemployment went from 9 percent in 1930 to 16 percent in 1931 and 25 percent in 1933. Following Republican trickle-down theory, Hoover started the Reconstruction Finance Corporation, which opponents called the *millionaires' dole*. Democratic President Franklin Roosevelt took over in 1933 and started passing New Deal programs to help ordinary people.

1935 through 1939: New Deal programs like the Federal Deposit Insurance Corporation, the Civilian Conservation Corps, the Federal Emergency Relief Administration, and the Works Administrations started to create jobs and restore hope. Other federal initiatives included the Tennessee Valley Authority (TVA), Federal Housing Administration (FHA), Securities and Exchange Commission (SEC), National Recovery Administration (NRA), and Agricultural Adjustment Act (AAA). The greatest benefit for elderly people was the passage of Social Security in 1935.

1940 through 1945: New Deal programs cut unemployment in half from 25 percent to 12 percent. World War II took care of the rest of the Great Depression. By 1943, unemployment was almost nonexistent. Due in part to the economic safety net built by the Roosevelt administration, the U.S. came out of the war ready for further growth.

5. Conservative presidents take Progressive steps

Dwight Eisenhower: Eisenhower reluctantly used federal troops to enforce the school integration called for by *Brown v. Board of Education*. He set up a Civil Rights Commission to investigate discrimination. Eisenhower started the nationwide interstate highway system. Upon leaving office, he warned against the growing power of the military-industrial complex.

Richard Nixon: Nixon expanded welfare, Medicaid for the poor, and food stamps for the hungry. He created a new Supplemental Security Income program (SSI) for the disabled. Nixon started the Environmental Protection Agency, the Clean Air Act, and the Endangered Species Act.

Ronald Reagan: Reagan helped end the Cold War by continuing the long-established policies of opposition to Communist expansion that had been popular with both Democratic and Republican presidents before him. Reagan's tax cuts benefited the rich and didn't help the economy enough. He appointed the first woman to the Supreme Court and remained sunny and optimistic in troubled times.

George H. W. Bush: The elder Bush was president when the Berlin Wall fell, signaling the end of Communism as a major movement. He signed the START II treaty to limit nuclear weapons. Bush successfully kicked the invading Iraqis out of neighboring Kuwait but left Saddam Hussein in power. He also signed the Americans with Disabilities Act, which prohibited discrimination against the disabled.

# ANSWER SHEET FOR PRACTICE TEST 1

Use this bubble sheet to mark your answers for Section I of the exam.

| | | |
|---|---|---|
| 1 Ⓐ Ⓑ Ⓒ Ⓓ Ⓔ | 31 Ⓐ Ⓑ Ⓒ Ⓓ Ⓔ | 61 Ⓐ Ⓑ Ⓒ Ⓓ Ⓔ |
| 2 Ⓐ Ⓑ Ⓒ Ⓓ Ⓔ | 32 Ⓐ Ⓑ Ⓒ Ⓓ Ⓔ | 62 Ⓐ Ⓑ Ⓒ Ⓓ Ⓔ |
| 3 Ⓐ Ⓑ Ⓒ Ⓓ Ⓔ | 33 Ⓐ Ⓑ Ⓒ Ⓓ Ⓔ | 63 Ⓐ Ⓑ Ⓒ Ⓓ Ⓔ |
| 4 Ⓐ Ⓑ Ⓒ Ⓓ Ⓔ | 34 Ⓐ Ⓑ Ⓒ Ⓓ Ⓔ | 64 Ⓐ Ⓑ Ⓒ Ⓓ Ⓔ |
| 5 Ⓐ Ⓑ Ⓒ Ⓓ Ⓔ | 35 Ⓐ Ⓑ Ⓒ Ⓓ Ⓔ | 65 Ⓐ Ⓑ Ⓒ Ⓓ Ⓔ |
| 6 Ⓐ Ⓑ Ⓒ Ⓓ Ⓔ | 36 Ⓐ Ⓑ Ⓒ Ⓓ Ⓔ | 66 Ⓐ Ⓑ Ⓒ Ⓓ Ⓔ |
| 7 Ⓐ Ⓑ Ⓒ Ⓓ Ⓔ | 37 Ⓐ Ⓑ Ⓒ Ⓓ Ⓔ | 67 Ⓐ Ⓑ Ⓒ Ⓓ Ⓔ |
| 8 Ⓐ Ⓑ Ⓒ Ⓓ Ⓔ | 38 Ⓐ Ⓑ Ⓒ Ⓓ Ⓔ | 68 Ⓐ Ⓑ Ⓒ Ⓓ Ⓔ |
| 9 Ⓐ Ⓑ Ⓒ Ⓓ Ⓔ | 39 Ⓐ Ⓑ Ⓒ Ⓓ Ⓔ | 69 Ⓐ Ⓑ Ⓒ Ⓓ Ⓔ |
| 10 Ⓐ Ⓑ Ⓒ Ⓓ Ⓔ | 40 Ⓐ Ⓑ Ⓒ Ⓓ Ⓔ | 70 Ⓐ Ⓑ Ⓒ Ⓓ Ⓔ |
| 11 Ⓐ Ⓑ Ⓒ Ⓓ Ⓔ | 41 Ⓐ Ⓑ Ⓒ Ⓓ Ⓔ | 71 Ⓐ Ⓑ Ⓒ Ⓓ Ⓔ |
| 12 Ⓐ Ⓑ Ⓒ Ⓓ Ⓔ | 42 Ⓐ Ⓑ Ⓒ Ⓓ Ⓔ | 72 Ⓐ Ⓑ Ⓒ Ⓓ Ⓔ |
| 13 Ⓐ Ⓑ Ⓒ Ⓓ Ⓔ | 43 Ⓐ Ⓑ Ⓒ Ⓓ Ⓔ | 73 Ⓐ Ⓑ Ⓒ Ⓓ Ⓔ |
| 14 Ⓐ Ⓑ Ⓒ Ⓓ Ⓔ | 44 Ⓐ Ⓑ Ⓒ Ⓓ Ⓔ | 74 Ⓐ Ⓑ Ⓒ Ⓓ Ⓔ |
| 15 Ⓐ Ⓑ Ⓒ Ⓓ Ⓔ | 45 Ⓐ Ⓑ Ⓒ Ⓓ Ⓔ | 75 Ⓐ Ⓑ Ⓒ Ⓓ Ⓔ |
| 16 Ⓐ Ⓑ Ⓒ Ⓓ Ⓔ | 46 Ⓐ Ⓑ Ⓒ Ⓓ Ⓔ | 76 Ⓐ Ⓑ Ⓒ Ⓓ Ⓔ |
| 17 Ⓐ Ⓑ Ⓒ Ⓓ Ⓔ | 47 Ⓐ Ⓑ Ⓒ Ⓓ Ⓔ | 77 Ⓐ Ⓑ Ⓒ Ⓓ Ⓔ |
| 18 Ⓐ Ⓑ Ⓒ Ⓓ Ⓔ | 48 Ⓐ Ⓑ Ⓒ Ⓓ Ⓔ | 78 Ⓐ Ⓑ Ⓒ Ⓓ Ⓔ |
| 19 Ⓐ Ⓑ Ⓒ Ⓓ Ⓔ | 49 Ⓐ Ⓑ Ⓒ Ⓓ Ⓔ | 79 Ⓐ Ⓑ Ⓒ Ⓓ Ⓔ |
| 20 Ⓐ Ⓑ Ⓒ Ⓓ Ⓔ | 50 Ⓐ Ⓑ Ⓒ Ⓓ Ⓔ | 80 Ⓐ Ⓑ Ⓒ Ⓓ Ⓔ |
| 21 Ⓐ Ⓑ Ⓒ Ⓓ Ⓔ | 51 Ⓐ Ⓑ Ⓒ Ⓓ Ⓔ | |
| 22 Ⓐ Ⓑ Ⓒ Ⓓ Ⓔ | 52 Ⓐ Ⓑ Ⓒ Ⓓ Ⓔ | |
| 23 Ⓐ Ⓑ Ⓒ Ⓓ Ⓔ | 53 Ⓐ Ⓑ Ⓒ Ⓓ Ⓔ | |
| 24 Ⓐ Ⓑ Ⓒ Ⓓ Ⓔ | 54 Ⓐ Ⓑ Ⓒ Ⓓ Ⓔ | |
| 25 Ⓐ Ⓑ Ⓒ Ⓓ Ⓔ | 55 Ⓐ Ⓑ Ⓒ Ⓓ Ⓔ | |
| 26 Ⓐ Ⓑ Ⓒ Ⓓ Ⓔ | 56 Ⓐ Ⓑ Ⓒ Ⓓ Ⓔ | |
| 27 Ⓐ Ⓑ Ⓒ Ⓓ Ⓔ | 57 Ⓐ Ⓑ Ⓒ Ⓓ Ⓔ | |
| 28 Ⓐ Ⓑ Ⓒ Ⓓ Ⓔ | 58 Ⓐ Ⓑ Ⓒ Ⓓ Ⓔ | |
| 29 Ⓐ Ⓑ Ⓒ Ⓓ Ⓔ | 59 Ⓐ Ⓑ Ⓒ Ⓓ Ⓔ | |
| 30 Ⓐ Ⓑ Ⓒ Ⓓ Ⓔ | 60 Ⓐ Ⓑ Ⓒ Ⓓ Ⓔ | |

# ANSWER SHEET FOR PRACTICE TEST 2

Use this bubble sheet to mark your answers for Section I of the exam.

| | | |
|---|---|---|
| 1 Ⓐ Ⓑ Ⓒ Ⓓ Ⓔ | 31 Ⓐ Ⓑ Ⓒ Ⓓ Ⓔ | 61 Ⓐ Ⓑ Ⓒ Ⓓ Ⓔ |
| 2 Ⓐ Ⓑ Ⓒ Ⓓ Ⓔ | 32 Ⓐ Ⓑ Ⓒ Ⓓ Ⓔ | 62 Ⓐ Ⓑ Ⓒ Ⓓ Ⓔ |
| 3 Ⓐ Ⓑ Ⓒ Ⓓ Ⓔ | 33 Ⓐ Ⓑ Ⓒ Ⓓ Ⓔ | 63 Ⓐ Ⓑ Ⓒ Ⓓ Ⓔ |
| 4 Ⓐ Ⓑ Ⓒ Ⓓ Ⓔ | 34 Ⓐ Ⓑ Ⓒ Ⓓ Ⓔ | 64 Ⓐ Ⓑ Ⓒ Ⓓ Ⓔ |
| 5 Ⓐ Ⓑ Ⓒ Ⓓ Ⓔ | 35 Ⓐ Ⓑ Ⓒ Ⓓ Ⓔ | 65 Ⓐ Ⓑ Ⓒ Ⓓ Ⓔ |
| 6 Ⓐ Ⓑ Ⓒ Ⓓ Ⓔ | 36 Ⓐ Ⓑ Ⓒ Ⓓ Ⓔ | 66 Ⓐ Ⓑ Ⓒ Ⓓ Ⓔ |
| 7 Ⓐ Ⓑ Ⓒ Ⓓ Ⓔ | 37 Ⓐ Ⓑ Ⓒ Ⓓ Ⓔ | 67 Ⓐ Ⓑ Ⓒ Ⓓ Ⓔ |
| 8 Ⓐ Ⓑ Ⓒ Ⓓ Ⓔ | 38 Ⓐ Ⓑ Ⓒ Ⓓ Ⓔ | 68 Ⓐ Ⓑ Ⓒ Ⓓ Ⓔ |
| 9 Ⓐ Ⓑ Ⓒ Ⓓ Ⓔ | 39 Ⓐ Ⓑ Ⓒ Ⓓ Ⓔ | 69 Ⓐ Ⓑ Ⓒ Ⓓ Ⓔ |
| 10 Ⓐ Ⓑ Ⓒ Ⓓ Ⓔ | 40 Ⓐ Ⓑ Ⓒ Ⓓ Ⓔ | 70 Ⓐ Ⓑ Ⓒ Ⓓ Ⓔ |
| 11 Ⓐ Ⓑ Ⓒ Ⓓ Ⓔ | 41 Ⓐ Ⓑ Ⓒ Ⓓ Ⓔ | 71 Ⓐ Ⓑ Ⓒ Ⓓ Ⓔ |
| 12 Ⓐ Ⓑ Ⓒ Ⓓ Ⓔ | 42 Ⓐ Ⓑ Ⓒ Ⓓ Ⓔ | 72 Ⓐ Ⓑ Ⓒ Ⓓ Ⓔ |
| 13 Ⓐ Ⓑ Ⓒ Ⓓ Ⓔ | 43 Ⓐ Ⓑ Ⓒ Ⓓ Ⓔ | 73 Ⓐ Ⓑ Ⓒ Ⓓ Ⓔ |
| 14 Ⓐ Ⓑ Ⓒ Ⓓ Ⓔ | 44 Ⓐ Ⓑ Ⓒ Ⓓ Ⓔ | 74 Ⓐ Ⓑ Ⓒ Ⓓ Ⓔ |
| 15 Ⓐ Ⓑ Ⓒ Ⓓ Ⓔ | 45 Ⓐ Ⓑ Ⓒ Ⓓ Ⓔ | 75 Ⓐ Ⓑ Ⓒ Ⓓ Ⓔ |
| 16 Ⓐ Ⓑ Ⓒ Ⓓ Ⓔ | 46 Ⓐ Ⓑ Ⓒ Ⓓ Ⓔ | 76 Ⓐ Ⓑ Ⓒ Ⓓ Ⓔ |
| 17 Ⓐ Ⓑ Ⓒ Ⓓ Ⓔ | 47 Ⓐ Ⓑ Ⓒ Ⓓ Ⓔ | 77 Ⓐ Ⓑ Ⓒ Ⓓ Ⓔ |
| 18 Ⓐ Ⓑ Ⓒ Ⓓ Ⓔ | 48 Ⓐ Ⓑ Ⓒ Ⓓ Ⓔ | 78 Ⓐ Ⓑ Ⓒ Ⓓ Ⓔ |
| 19 Ⓐ Ⓑ Ⓒ Ⓓ Ⓔ | 49 Ⓐ Ⓑ Ⓒ Ⓓ Ⓔ | 79 Ⓐ Ⓑ Ⓒ Ⓓ Ⓔ |
| 20 Ⓐ Ⓑ Ⓒ Ⓓ Ⓔ | 50 Ⓐ Ⓑ Ⓒ Ⓓ Ⓔ | 80 Ⓐ Ⓑ Ⓒ Ⓓ Ⓔ |
| 21 Ⓐ Ⓑ Ⓒ Ⓓ Ⓔ | 51 Ⓐ Ⓑ Ⓒ Ⓓ Ⓔ | |
| 22 Ⓐ Ⓑ Ⓒ Ⓓ Ⓔ | 52 Ⓐ Ⓑ Ⓒ Ⓓ Ⓔ | |
| 23 Ⓐ Ⓑ Ⓒ Ⓓ Ⓔ | 53 Ⓐ Ⓑ Ⓒ Ⓓ Ⓔ | |
| 24 Ⓐ Ⓑ Ⓒ Ⓓ Ⓔ | 54 Ⓐ Ⓑ Ⓒ Ⓓ Ⓔ | |
| 25 Ⓐ Ⓑ Ⓒ Ⓓ Ⓔ | 55 Ⓐ Ⓑ Ⓒ Ⓓ Ⓔ | |
| 26 Ⓐ Ⓑ Ⓒ Ⓓ Ⓔ | 56 Ⓐ Ⓑ Ⓒ Ⓓ Ⓔ | |
| 27 Ⓐ Ⓑ Ⓒ Ⓓ Ⓔ | 57 Ⓐ Ⓑ Ⓒ Ⓓ Ⓔ | |
| 28 Ⓐ Ⓑ Ⓒ Ⓓ Ⓔ | 58 Ⓐ Ⓑ Ⓒ Ⓓ Ⓔ | |
| 29 Ⓐ Ⓑ Ⓒ Ⓓ Ⓔ | 59 Ⓐ Ⓑ Ⓒ Ⓓ Ⓔ | |
| 30 Ⓐ Ⓑ Ⓒ Ⓓ Ⓔ | 60 Ⓐ Ⓑ Ⓒ Ⓓ Ⓔ | |

# Index

# Prepare for your AP Exam
## with these titles from Wiley

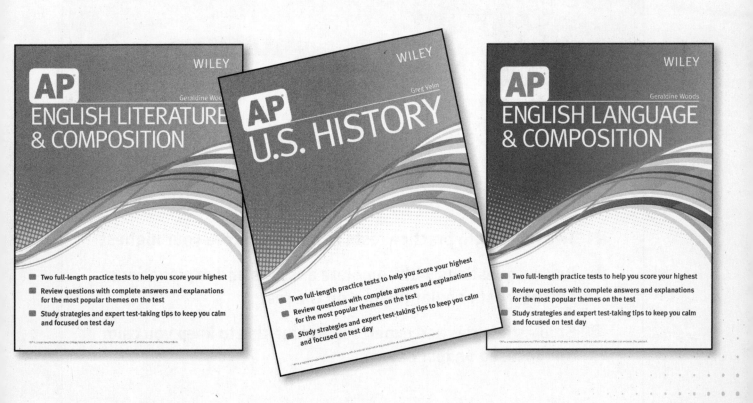
Visit Wiley.com for more information

WILEY

# AP*

Geraldine Woods

# ENGLISH LANGUAGE & COMPOSITION

- Two full-length practice tests to help you score your **highest**

- **Review questions with complete answers and explanations for the most popular themes on the test**

- **Study strategies and expert test-taking tips to keep you calm and focused on test day**

978-1-118-49017-4

WILEY

# AP*
Greg Velm

# U.S. HISTORY

- Two full-length practice tests to help you score your highest

- Review questions with complete answers and explanations for the most popular themes on the test

- Study strategies and expert test-taking tips to keep you calm and focused on test day

978-1-118-49026-6